Counter-Terrorism Law and Returnees

Counter-Terrorism Law and Returnees

The Belgian Legal Framework Applicable to Returnees from War Zones in Syria and Iraq

Ward Yperman
Jogchum Vrielink

Boomjuridisch
Antwerpen

eleven

Published, sold and distributed by Eleven
P.O. Box 85576
2508 CG The Hague
The Netherlands
Tel.: +31 70 33 070 33
Fax: +31 70 33 070 30
e-mail: sales@elevenpub.nl
www.elevenpub.com

Sold and distributed in USA and Canada
Independent Publishers Group
814 N. Franklin Street
Chicago, IL 60610, USA
Order Placement: +1 800 888 4741
Fax: +1 312 337 5985
orders@ipgbook.com
www.ipgbook.com

Boom juridisch Antwerpen
ISBN 978-94-6451-111-6
ISBN 978-94-6451-211-3 (e-book)
NUR 824
D/2023/15251/08

Eleven is an imprint of Boom uitgevers Den Haag.
ISBN 978-94-6236-718-0
ISBN 978-94-0011-278-0 (e-book)

Table of Contents

Introduction

Counter-terrorism has permeated the entire Belgian legal system, with rules being introduced out of counter-terrorism considerations throughout many branches of law.[1] This book came into existence in the context of the Reguide project, which is financed by Belspo. The Reguide project aims to develop a holistic, restorative and gendered approach towards the reintegration of returnees and their families into the Belgian society, and by doing so, directly addresses two interrelated societal challenges: security and returnee reintegration.[2] The issue of reintegration of returnees and their families is an important one for many countries and especially for Belgium as it has one the highest ratios of returnees per capita in Europe. In alignment with the scope of the rest of the Reguide project, this book focusses on the legal framework relevant to people returning from jihadist war zones, such as Syria. The aim of this book is twofold. Firstly, the goal is to describe the relevant legislation so as to set out the legal framework currently in force. Secondly, we point out some inconsistencies and issues within the legislation and make suggestions for how the legal approach could be improved.

The first Chapter of the book discusses the different terrorism offences in Belgian criminal law. Following on from this discussion, a few particularly relevant rules of criminal procedure are highlighted, being the competence of different courts, the rules on trials in absentia (*verstekprocedure; procédure par défaut*) and on immediate arrest warrants (*onmiddellijke aanhouding; arrestation immediate*). After this, the discussion is shifted to sentencing, with a focus on prison sentences, the additional sentence of being at the disposal of the sentence enforcement court (*terbeschikkingstelling van de strafuitvoeringsrechtbank; mise à la disposition du tribunal de l'application des peines*), alternative sentences and the possibility of suspension of sentence (*opschorting; suspension*) and postponement of the enforcement of sentences (*uitstel van tenuitvoerlegging; sursis*). The fourth Chapter focusses specifically on the execution of the most frequently imposed sentence, that of imprisonment. This Chapter discusses the rules specific to terrorist detainees within prison and also rules relevant to move beyond prison, the so called external legal position (*externe rechtspositie; statut juridique externe*). The fifth Chapter describes other relevant measures related to people returning from jihadist war zones such as asset freezing, revoking ID cards and passports and revoking nationality and finally the possibility of repatriation of those still present in the jihadist war zones.

---

1 For an overview, see: Ana Laura Claes and Ward Yperman, 'Overzicht(elijk) – Recente Ontwikkelingen in de Contraterrorismewetgeving' [2022] Politie & Recht 69.

2 For more information, see: https://reguide.be/.

At the end of Chapters one through to three, we will briefly refer to a case law analysis. The analysis refered to is that of the large majority of Correctional Court and Court of Appeal trial cases[3] concerning terrorism offences from their introduction in 2003 until the end of 2018.[4] Since there is no central database for case law, it is very likely that not all cases which fit these perametres were included. In total 192 cases were analysed. Within these cases a selection was made based on where the facts took place. If the list of charges did not include facts outside of the EU, then the case was disregarded. This way a total of 94 Correctional Court and 22 Court of Appeal cases were identified as relevant. In those cases, a total of 336 people were prosecuted for terrorist offences.[5] In addition to this, there were seven people whose case was retried (see Section 2.2 below), bringing the total to 343 individual judgments.

Alongside this case law analysis, reference will be made throughout the book to an expert seminar. This seminar was organised at the Faculty of Law of KU Leuven in mid-October 2022. A group of 13 experts attended this seminar, consisting of both practitioners and academics. All participants were selected because of their expertise on the counter-terrorism legislation.

With a view to the rehabilitation of people returning from a jihadist war zone, it is important to mention that since 2018 there is an instruction letter from the college of Prosecutors-General which gives guidance on the conditions which can be imposed upon people who are being prosecuted or have been convicted for terrorism offences or who are linked to violent extremism.[6] These instructions are mentioned here since they span the entire criminal process. They are applicable, for example, in cases of conditional release during the execution of a prison sentence, as well as in situations where the judge imposes a postponement of sentence enforcement subject to probation or in case of provisional releases in the pre-trial phase.

3 Meaning that the youth courts were excluded, as well as the investigation supervision courts, Court of Cassation and Constitutional Court.

4 Cases from 2019 onwards were not available to us.

5 Note that one judgment was a retrial for a judgment *in absentia* which we could not find.

6 COL10/2018 – Voorwaarden die opgelegd kunnen worden aan personen die vervolgd of veroordeeld worden voor feiten van terrorisme of die gelinkt worden aan gewelddadig extremisme, 28 June 2018.

1 Terrorist offences

Introduction to Chapter 1

Before 2003, there were no specific terrorist offences in Belgian criminal law and terrorism suspects were prosecuted under other 'ordinary' offences.[7] The introduction of terrorist offences into the criminal code (hereafter CC) was prompted by a host of international and European legal instruments.[8] For Belgium, the EU instruments are the most important and relevant ones. The EU has three major instruments regarding terrorist offences. In 2002 the EU issued a Framework Decision on Combatting Terrorism.[9] This Framework Decision was amended by another Framework Decision in 2008[10] and finally replaced by the EU Directive on Combatting Terrorism (hereinafter referred to as the Directive) in

7 I De La Serna, 'Des Infractions Terroristes', *Les Infractions* (Larcier 2013) 170 and 173; Adrien Masset, 'Terrorisme' [2013] Postal Memorialis – Lexicon strafrecht, strafvordering en bijzondere wetten 411, T60/8-T60/11; Martin Moucheron, 'Délit politique et terrorisme en Belgique : du noble au vil' [2006] Cultures & conflits 77, paras 1 and 15; Anne Weyembergh and Laurent Kennes, 'Domestic Provisions and Case Law: The Belgian Case' in Francesca Galli and Anne Weyembergh (eds), *EU counter-terrorism offences: What impact on national elgislation and case-law?* (Editions de l'Université de Bruxelles 2012) 150; Anne Weyembergh and Laurent Kennes, 'Le Titre Iter Du Livre II Du Code Pénal: Des Infractions Terroristes', *Droit pénal spécial: tome 1* (Anthémis 2011) 103-104; Alain Winants, 'De invloed van terrorisme op de strafwetgeving: actualia materieel strafrecht' (2019) 14 Nullum Crimen 343, 345.

8 See for example: UNSC Resolution 2178 of 24 September 2014; Council of Europe Treaty on the Prevention of Terrorism, Warsaw 16 May 2005, *Pb. EU* 2018, 159/3; Council Framework Decision 2002/475/JHA of 13 June 2002 on combating terrorism, *OJ* 22 June 2002, L 164/3; Council Framework Decision 2008/919/JHA of 28 November 2008 amending Framework Decision 2002/475/JHA on combating terrorism, *OJ* 9 December 2008, L 330/21; Directive (EU) 2017/541 of the European Parliament and of the Council of 15 March 2017 on combating terrorism and replacing Council Framework Decision 2002/475/JHA and amending Council Decision 2005/671/JHA, *OJ* 31 March 2017, L 88/6.

9 Council Framework Decision 2002/475/JHA of 13 June 2002 on combating terrorism, *OJ* 22 June 2002, L 164/3. For an analysis, see: De La Serna (n 7) 170-174; Elise Delhaise, *Infractions terroristes* (Larcier 2019) 15-17; Daniel Flore, 'La Loi Du 19 Décembre 2003 Relative Aux Infractions Terroristes: Genèse, Principes et Conséquences', *Questions d'actualité de droit pénal et de procédure pénale* (Bruylant 2005) 209; An Fransen and Jan Kerkhofs, 'Het Materieel Terrorismestrafrecht' in Jan Kerkhofs, Antoon Schotsaert and Philippe Van Linthout (eds), *Contra-terrorisme: De gerechtelijke aanpak van terrorisme in België* (Larcier 2018) 6-8; Sabine Gless, 'Fighting Terrorism in a "Rechtsstaat"' in Toine Sapens, Marc Groenhuijsen and Tijs Kooijmans (eds), *Universalis: Liber amicorum Cyrille Fijnaut* (Intersentia 2011) 931-939; Weyembergh and Kennes, 'Le Titre Iter Du Livre II Du Code Pénal: Des Infractions Terroristes' (n 7) 105-107; Anne Weyembergh, 'L'impact Du 11 Septembre Sur l'équilibre Sécurité/Liberté Dans l'espace Pénal Européen' in Emmanuelle Bribosia and Anne Weyembergh (eds), *La convention Européenne des droits de l'homme à l'épreuve de la lutte contre le terrorisme* (Bruylant-Nemesis 2002) 161-173. See also: Jean-Christophe Martin, *Les Règles Internationales Relatives à La Lutte Contre Le Terrorisme* (Bruylant 2006) 109-110.

10 Council Framework Decision 2008/919/JHA of 28 November 2008 amending Framework Decision 2002/475/JHA on combating terrorism, *OJ* 9 December 2008, L 330/21-23. De La Serna (n 7) 174; Delhaise (n 9) 18; Fransen and Kerkhofs (n 9) 9-10; Gless (n 9) 934.

2017.[11] Since the Belgian legislation was influenced by these (and a few other) instruments, the offences were introduced in waves, in step with the international and European evolutions. The first wave of terrorist offences came in 2003, adding a new title to the criminal code: Title I*ter*: Terrorist offences.[12] This new title contained articles 137 to 140 and 141 to 141*ter* CC.[13] Roughly a decade later, the offences of article 140*bis* to 140*quinquies* CC were added in what can be called a second wave. Subsequently, article 140*sexies* CC was introduced in 2015 and 140*septies* CC in the following year. That same piece of legislation in 2016 also rephrased the offence of article 141 CC. A, for the time being, last wave of changes was made in 2019, when the legislature introduced aggravating circumstances into many of the existing offences and added a new offence both to article 140 and article 140*quinquies* CC.

Art. 137 and 138 CC

Actus Reus

The first terrorist offence in Title I*ter* is terrorism *sensu stricto*: the actual terrorist attack. This offence was introduced in the first wave of 2003, following the 2002 EU Framework Decision on Combating Terrorism.[14] The Belgian legislature adhered closely to the wording of the European instruments when transposing this offence into Belgian law. It is the core of the terrorism offences, since the *mens* rea (the mental element of a criminal act: *moreel element; élément moral du délit*) of all of the terrorism offences *sensu lato* refers (sometimes in combination with other terrorist offences *sensu lato*) to terrorism *sensu stricto*.

---

11 Directive (EU) 2017/541 of the European Parliament and of the Council of 15 March 2017 on combating terrorism and replacing Council Framework Decision 2002/475/JHA and amending Council Decision 2005/671/JHA, *OJ* 31 March 2017, L 88/6. See also: Delhaise (n 9) 19; Fransen and Kerkhofs (n 9) 12-15.

12 Weyembergh and Kennes, 'Le Titre Iter Du Livre II Du Code Pénal: Des Infractions Terroristes' (n 7) 102.

13 Masset (n 7) T60/1; Weyembergh and Kennes, 'Domestic Provisions and Case Law: The Belgian Case' (n 7) 151.

14 Art 1 Council Framework Decision 2002/475/JHA of 13 June 2002 on combating terrorism, *OJ* 22 June 2002, L 164/5; art 3 wet van 19 december 2003 betreffende terroristische misdrijven, *BS* 29 december 2003, 61689. See also: Marie-Aude Beernaert, 'La Loi Du 19 Décembre 2003 Relative Aux Infractions Terroristes : Quand Le Droit Pénal Belge Évolue Sous La Dictée de l'Union Européenne' (2004) 24 Journal des tribunaux 585, 586; Bjorn Ketels, 'Titel Iter Terroristische Misdrijven' in Martine De Busscher and others (eds), *Strafrecht: Duiding* (Larcier 2018) 236. For a short analysis of this offence in the Framework Decision, see: Maria Luisa Cesoni, 'Terrorisme et Involutions Démocratiques' [2002] Rev Dr Pén Crim 141, 143-145; Stéphanie Bosly and Mathieu Van Ravenstein, 'L'harmonisation Des Incriminations' in Daniel Flore (ed), *Actualités de droit pénal Européen* (La Charte 2003) 47-48; Daniel Flore, *Droit Pénal Européen: Les Enjeux d'une Justice Pénale Européenne* (Larcier 2008) 140-143.

The *actus reus* (criminal act: *materieel element; élément matériel du délit*) of terrorism *sensu stricto* consists of two lists. Article 137, §2 CC contains the first list, which consists of criminal offences that are also punishable under Belgian law outside of the context of terrorism, for example murder or hostage taking.[15] Article 137, §3 CC contains the second list, which consists of acts that do not constitute criminal offences outside of a terrorism context, for example hijacking a vehicle other than an aircraft or a ship (the hijacking of these vehicles is a pre-existing offence featured in §2), or threatening to commit terrorism *sensu stricto*.[16] After its introduction in 2003, article 137 CC was amended three times. All three amendments added items to the aforementioned lists. Firstly, in 2009 piracy was added to the list of §2 of potential terrorist offences.[17] Secondly, in 2013 the legislature changed the reference to the arms legislation (which had been replaced in 2006)[18] and added a §2, 11°, which adds to the list attempts (*strafbare poging; tentative punissable*) of the standard offences (*wanbedrijven; délits*) on that list.[19] This mattered because attempted standard offences are only punishable in Belgium when the law explicitly states this

15 Beernaert, 'La Loi Du 19 Décembre 2003 Relative Aux Infractions Terroristes : Quand Le Droit Pénal Belge Évolue Sous La Dictée de l'Union Européenne' (n 14) 587; Ignacio De La Serna, 'Des infractions terroristes' in Christian De Valkeneer and Ignacio De La Serna, *À la découverte de la justice pénale : Paroles de juriste* (Larcier 2015) 207; Flore (n 9) 214-215; Johan Delmulle and Stefaan Guenter, 'Gerechtelijke Aanpak Inzake Terrorisme', *Strafrecht en Strafprocesrecht* (Wolters Kluwer 2006) 4; Véronique Hameeuw, 'Strafbaarstelling van terroristische misdrijven: van Europees Kaderbesluit tot het Belgische Strafwetboek' [2005] Tijdschrift voor Strafrecht 2, 5; Ketels (n 14) 237; Philip Traest, 'Ontwikkeling van nieuwe deelnemingsvormen' [2007] Nullum Crimen 241, 257; Weyembergh and Kennes, 'Domestic Provisions and Case Law: The Belgian Case' (n 7) 152; Weyembergh and Kennes, 'Le Titre Iter Du Livre II Du Code Pénal: Des Infractions Terroristes' (n 7) 108; Winants (n 7) 347.

16 Beernaert, 'La Loi Du 19 Décembre 2003 Relative Aux Infractions Terroristes : Quand Le Droit Pénal Belge Évolue Sous La Dictée de l'Union Européenne' (n 14) 587; Delhaise (n 9) 30; De La Serna (n 7) 167 and 180; De La Serna (n 15) 207; Delmulle and Guenter (n 15) 4; Alain De Nauw, 'Titel Iter: Terroristische misdrijven', *Inleiding tot het bijzonder Strafrecht* (sixth edition, Kluwer 2010) 7; Alain De Nauw and Franklin Kuty, *Manuel de Droit Pénal Spécial* (Wolters Kluwer 2014) 17; Filiep Deruyck and Alain De Nauw, *Inleiding Tot Het Bijzonder Strafrecht* (Kluwer 2020) 8; Flore (n 9) 216; Fransen and Kerkhofs (n 9) 19-20; Hameeuw (n 15) 5-6; Ketels (n 14) 237; Masset (n 7) T60/18; Traest (n 15) 257; Weyembergh and Kennes, 'Domestic Provisions and Case Law: The Belgian Case' (n 7) 152; Weyembergh and Kennes, 'Le Titre Iter Du Livre II Du Code Pénal: Des Infractions Terroristes' (n 7) 108; Winants (n 7) 347.

17 Art 7 wet van 30 december 2009 betreffende de strijd tegen piraterij op zee, *BS* 14 januari 2010, 1485. See also: Ketels (n 14) 236.

18 The 'wet van 8 juni 2006 houdende regeling van economische en individuele activiteiten met wapens (*BS* 9 juni 2006, 29840)' replaced the 'wet van 3 januari 1933 op de vervaardiging van, de handel in en het dragen van wapens en op de handel in munitie, gewijzigd bij de wetten van 30 januari en 5 augustus 1991, 9 maart 1995, 24 juni 1996, 18 juli 1997, 10 januari 1999 en 30 maart 2000'. See also: Caroline Van Deuren, 'Nieuwe Straffen Bij Terroristische Misdrijven' [2013] 2013 Rechtspraak Antwerpen Brussel Gent 508, 508.

19 Art 2 wet van 18 februari 2013 tot wijziging van boek II, titel Iter van het Strafwetboek, *BS* 4 maart 2013, 13233. Article 3 of this statute amended article 138 CC to set the sentence for these attempted standard offences. See also: Delhaise (n 9) 81; Fransen and Kerkhofs (n 9) 19; Ketels (n 14) 236; Van Deuren (n 18) 508-509.

(contrary to attempted felonies (*misdaden; crimes*), which are always punishable).[20] Because of this standard rule certain attempted terrorist standard offences were not punishable, despite this being one of the obligations of the Framework Decision.[21] Thirdly, the statute of 5 May 2019 added a new §2, 4°/1, which adds the unlawful disturbance of (data in) an IT-system[22] to the list of possible terrorist offences. The same statute also expanded §3, 3° to radiological weapons.[23]

Almost all the listed acts require that human lives are put in danger. However, for offences of large-scale destruction or damage, causing significant economic damage is sufficient.[24] Where to draw the line between terrorism and other offences is often a difficult question to answer. Some academics have stated that offences which do not constitute violence against people or at least the threat thereof, should not be labelled terrorism.[25] This is because the label 'terrorist' can have far-reaching consequences, both within

---

20 Art 53 CC; Henri Berkmoes, 'De Niet-Strafbare Poging' in M De Busscher and others (eds), *Strafrecht: duiding* (Larcier 2018) 88; De La Serna (n 7) 207; Delhaise (n 9) 81; A De Nauw and F Deruyck, *Overzicht van het Belgisch algemeen strafrecht* (Die Keure / la Charte 2017) 51 and 72-73; Françoise Tulkens and others, *Introduction Au Droit Pénal* (10th edn, Wolters Kluwer 2014) 418-419; Chris Van den Wyngaert and Steven Vandromme, *Strafrecht en strafprocesrecht in hoofdlijnen* (Maklu 2014) 356; Chris Van den Wyngaert, Steven Vandromme and Philip Traest, *Strafrecht en strafprocesrecht in hoofdlijnen* (11th edn, Gompel&Svacina 2019) 197 and 367-368; Van Deuren (n 18) 509; Steven Vandromme and Chris De Roy, 'De Strafbaarheid van Voorbereidingshandelingen En Uitvoeringshandelingen: De Nieuwste Ontwikkelingen in Het Leerstuk van de Strafbare Poging En de Gevolgen Ervan Voor Het Strafprocesrecht', *Strafrecht en Strafprocesrecht* (Wolters Kluwer 2006) 512.

21 Art 4.2 Council Framework Decision 2002/475/JHA of 13 June 2002 on combating terrorism, *OJ* 22 June 2002, L 164/5. Now art 14.3 Directive (EU) 2017/541 of the European Parliament and of the Council of 15 March 2017 on combating terrorism and replacing Council Framework Decision 2002/475/JHA and amending Council Decision 2005/671/JHA, *OJ* 31 March 2017, L 88/6. See also: Memorie van Toelichting bij wetsontwerp van 13 november 2012 tot wijziging van Titel 1ter van het Strafwetboek, *Parl. St.* Kamer 2012-2013, nr. 53-2502/001, (4) 10; Bosly and Van Ravenstein (n 14) 49-50; Ketels (n 14) 238-239; Weyembergh and Kennes, 'Domestic Provisions and Case Law: The Belgian Case' (n 7) 156; Winants (n 7) 350.

22 Art 550*ter*, §1-3 CC.

23 Art 74 wet van 5 mei 2019 houdende diverse bepalingen in strafzaken en inzake erediensten, en tot wijziging van de wet van 28 mei 2002 betreffende de euthanasie en van het Sociaal Strafwetboek, *BS* 24 mei 2019, 50023; Stéphanie De Coensel, 'De Wet Diverse Bepalingen in Strafzaken II: Terroristische misdrijven in lijn met de Europese verplichtingen?' (2019) 40 Panopticon 211, 212; Winants (n 7) 357.

24 Art 137, §2, 4° CC; Fransen and Kerkhofs (n 9) 19.

25 B Ganor, 'Defining Terrorism: Is One Man's Terrorist Another Man's Freedom Fighter?' [2002] Police Practice and Research 287, 294; B Hoffman, *Inside Terrorism, Revised and Expanded Edition* (Columbia University Press 2006) 40-41; R Jackson, 'In Defence of "Terrorism": Finding a Way through a Forest of Misconceptions' [2011] Behavioral Sciences of Terrorism and Political Aggression 116, 123; J Lutz and B Lutz, *Global Terrorism* (Routledge 2013) 8-9; Anthony Richards, 'Conceptualizing Terrorism' (2014) 37 Studies in Conflict & Terrorism 213, 230.

criminal law and criminal procedure[26] and outside of it[27]. However, the requirement that significant economic damage is caused, seems to us to suffice. Significant economic damage can have a large effect on the stability of a nation, and can indirectly endanger human lives. In this sense the wording of the article could have been clearer if it reflected that idea. The Constitutional Court (*Grondwettelijk Hof; Cour constitutionnelle*) did not find the current wording in violation of the principle of legality (see below), nonetheless in our opinion a better alternative to 'significant damage' would have been 'damage that could endanger the stability of the country and the security of its citizens'. Delhaise in turn points out that many sexual offences are not on the list, despite the fact that these offences, especially when committed in a systematic manner and on a large scale, are used as a weapon by terrorist organisations.[28]

Article 137 CC also requires that the offence may, given its nature or context, seriously damage a country or an international organisation. Legal doctrine calls this the 'contextual element' of the offence.[29] This requirement was copied from the 2002 EU Framework Decision on combating terrorism.[30] The damage does not need to have happened already,

---

26 Aggravated sentences, but also procedural exceptions. For an overview and analysis of some of these procedural consequence, see (in French and Dutch): Noémie Blaise and Elise Delhaise, 'La répression des voyages à visée terroriste à l'aune des droits fondamentaux' [2019] Journal Tribunaux 173; Masset (n 7) T60/20-T60/22; Jan Roelandt, 'De strijd tegen het terrorisme: een overzicht van de recente wetgevende ingrepen in het straf(proces)recht' [2017] Nullum Crimen 10; Ward Yperman, 'De bestrijding van terrorisme en strafprocesrecht: vele kleintjes maken een grote' [2019] Tijdschrift voor Strafrecht 8.

27 In other branches of law, by for example the revocation of passports or asset freezing as an administrative measure (see below), but also outside of the law, for example through stigmatisation (W Mucha, 'Polarization, Stigmatization, Radicalization. Counterterrorism and Homeland Security in France and Germany' [2017] Journal for deradicalization 230; G Mythen, S Walklate and F Khan, '"Why Should We Have to Prove We're Alright?": Counter-Terrorism, Risk and Partial Securities' [2012] Sociology 383; S Samuel Justin and A Daniel, *The Psychology of Terrorism Fears* (Oxford University Press 2012) 14; Victor Tadros, 'Justice and Terrorism' [2007] New Criminal Law Review 658, 685).

28 Delhaise (n 9) 30. Note that this is mainly the case in quasi-war situations outside of Europe (for example in the Middle East or Africa). It seems that the definition is mainly shaped by the type of terrorism experienced in Europe so far.

29 De La Serna (n 7) 177; De La Serna (n 15) 204-205; Delhaise (n 9) 28-29; Elise Delhaise and Coline Fievet, 'Frontières Intelligentes et Nouvelles Incriminations Pénales : L'Union Européenne Face à La Problématique Des « Foreign Terrorist Fighters »' (2017) 2017 Journal des tribunaux 113, 118; Flore (n 9) 213; Flore (n 14) 142; Fransen and Kerkhofs (n 9) 21; Traest (n 15) 257; Winants (n 7) 347. Ketels does not do so and discusses it as part of the *actus reus*, see: Ketels (n 14) 237-238. Hameeuw states that the wording of what others call the contextual element is so broad that it cannot constitute a part of an offence. However, she seems to be the only one in the literature taking this stance. See: Hameeuw (n 15) 6. When briefly discussing the offence, Moucheron mentions what is usually called the contextual element as part of the *mens rea*. However, he seems to be the only one to do so. See: Moucheron (n 7) para 20.

30 Art 1.1 Council Framework Decision 2002/475/JHA of 13 June 2002 on combating terrorism, *OJ* 22 June 2002, L 164/4. Now art 3.1 Directive (EU) 2017/541 of the European Parliament and of the Council of 15 March 2017 on combating terrorism and replacing Council Framework Decision 2002/475/JHA and amending Council Decision 2005/671/JHA, *OJ* 31 March 2017, L 88/6. See also: Masset (n 7) 18. Borgers, however, argues that it is not clear at all that the Framework Decision actually requires this. See: Matthias

the possibility for damage is sufficient.[31] This 'contextual element' takes into account not only the nature of the offence, but also its wider consequences for the organisation and government of a country.[32] However, viewing contextual information as a separate element is unnecessary. Taking into account contextual information (legal facts) when defining an offence is something that happens regularly, and terrorism is in this respect not so special in comparison to other criminal offences. Contextual information is also part of the *actus reus* of other offences or serves as an aggravating circumstance. For example, for the offences of larceny, the fact that it is committed by night[33] is an aggravating circumstance[34]; for the offence of raping a person who is less than fourteen years old[35], the age of the victim used to be part of the *actus reus* of the offence[36]; and for bankruptcy offences[37], the fact that the company is bankrupt is part of the *actus reus* as well. Legal facts such as these are part of the *actus reus* and there is no need to create a new and special 'contextual element'.[38] The Parliamentary preparatory works themselves call it an additional 'objective element'.[39]

Mens Rea

The required *mens rea* is a form of special intent.[40] The offence needs to be committed 'with the aim of seriously intimidating a population, or unduly compelling a government

---

Borgers, 'Een Gevaarzettingsvereiste Voor Terroristische Misdrijven?' in Toine Sapens, Marc Groenhuijsen and Tijs Kooijmans (eds), *Universalis: Liber amicorum Cyrille Fijnaut* (Intersentia 2011).

31 Delhaise (n 9) 33; Ann Fransen and Jan Kerkhofs, 'Het Materieel Terrorismestrafrecht in België: De Misdrijven' (2018) 3 Tijdschrift voor Strafrecht 150, 21; Hameeuw (n 15) 6; Ketels (n 14) 238; Traest (n 15) 257.

32 Verslag namens de commissie van justitie bij wetsontwerp van 6 oktober 2003 betreffende terroristische misdrijven, *Parl.St.* Kamer 2003, nr. 51-0258/004, 14; P De Hert and J Millen, 'Terrorisme' (2013) VIII.2013 Qualifications et Jurisprudence Penales 1, 3; De La Serna (n 15) 204-205; Delmulle and Guenter (n 15) 3; Fransen and Kerkhofs (n 31) 21; Ketels (n 14) 237.

33 Art 471 CC.

34 Patrick Arnou, 'Nacht', *Strafrecht en strafvordering. Artikelsgewijze commentaar met overzicht van rechtspraak en rechtsleer* (Wolters Kluwer 2010) 71-73; De Nauw and Kuty (n 16) 707-708.

35 Previously art 375, section 6 CC. Now this would fall under article 417/16 CC.

36 Cass. 10 maart 1930, *Pas.* 1930, I, 156; De Nauw and Kuty (n 16) 229; Gaëlle Marlier, *Familie in het straf- en strafprocesrecht: afbrokkelende hoeksteen van de samenleving?* (Wolters Kluwer 2018) 299.

37 Art 489-489*sexies* CC.

38 A difference is that the age of the victim and the time of the offence are relatively easy to establish after the fact, while this may not be the case for the context. However, this difference does not change the finding that the context is a legal fact which can be part of the *actus reus*.

39 Memorie van Toelichting bij wetsontwerp van 6 oktober 2003 betreffende terroristische misdrijven, *Parl.St.* Kamer 2003, nr. 51-0258/001, (4) 10.

40 Beernaert, 'La Loi Du 19 Décembre 2003 Relative Aux Infractions Terroristes : Quand Le Droit Pénal Belge Évolue Sous La Dictée de l'Union Européenne' (n 14) 586; De La Serna (n 7) 179; De La Serna (n 15) 207; Delhaise and Fievet (n 29) 118; De Hert and Millen (n 32) 3; Fransen and Kerkhofs (n 9) 20; Hameeuw (n 15) 5; Ketels (n 14) 238; Weyembergh and Kennes, 'Le Titre Iter Du Livre II Du Code Pénal: Des Infractions Terroristes' (n 7) 109; Winants (n 7) 347.

or international organisation to perform or abstain from performing any act, or seriously destabilising or destroying the fundamental political, constitutional, economic or social structures of a country or an international organisation'.[41] This phrasing is also taken directly from the 2002 EU Framework Decision on Combating Terrorism.[42] The three options are not cumulative and a political, religious or philosophical motive is not required.[43] The words 'international organisation' only refer to international organisations under public international law and not to NGOs for example.[44] However, Belgium does not necessarily have to be a member of this organisation.[45] Legal doctrine states that the words 'a population' can refer to a nation's whole population, but also to the populations of smaller areas such as a specific region or city.[46] It does imply that the aim of intimidating a single person or small group of people does not suffice.[47] 'Government', refers not only to the Belgian government, but to any government, regardless of its democratic character.[48] For the offence of threatening a terrorist attack, it is irrelevant whether or not the

41 Own translation, original in Dutch and French: "*met het oogmerk om een bevolking ernstige vrees aan te jagen of om de overheid of een internationale organisatie op onrechtmatige wijze te dwingen tot het verrichten of het zich onthouden van een handeling, of om de politieke, constitutionele, economische of sociale basisstructuren van een land of een internationale organisatie ernstig te ontwrichten of te vernietigen; dans le but d'intimider gravement une population ou de contraindre indûment des pouvoirs publics ou une organisation internationale à accomplir ou à s'abstenir d'accomplir un acte, ou de gravement déstabiliser ou détruire les structures fondamentales politiques, constitutionnelles, économiques ou sociales d'un pays ou d'une organisation internationale*" (Art 137, §1 CC). Delhaise (n 9) 31-33; Masset (n 7) 18; Traest (n 15) 256; Weyembergh and Kennes, 'Le Titre Iter Du Livre II Du Code Pénal: Des Infractions Terroristes' (n 7) 109; Winants (n 7) 347.

42 Art 1.1 Council Framework Decision 2002/475/JHA of 13 June 2002 on combating terrorism, *OJ* 22 June 2002, L 164/4. Now art 3.2 Directive (EU) 2017/541 of the European Parliament and of the Council of 15 March 2017 on combating terrorism and replacing Council Framework Decision 2002/475/JHA and amending Council Decision 2005/671/JHA, *OJ* 31 March 2017, L 88/6. See also: Flore (n 14) 140; Hameeuw (n 15) 5; Weyembergh and Kennes, 'Domestic Provisions and Case Law: The Belgian Case' (n 7) 153.

43 Delhaise (n 9) 31; Flore (n 9) 211; Fransen and Kerkhofs (n 9) 20; Hameeuw (n 15) 6; Ketels (n 14) 238; Traest (n 15) 256.

44 Verslag namens de commissie van justitie bij wetsontwerp van 6 oktober 2003 betreffende terroristische misdrijven, *Parl.St.* Kamer 2003, nr. 51-0258/004, 14; Beernaert, 'La Loi Du 19 Décembre 2003 Relative Aux Infractions Terroristes : Quand Le Droit Pénal Belge Évolue Sous La Dictée de l'Union Européenne' (n 14) 587; De La Serna (n 7) 178; De La Serna (n 15) 206; Flore (n 9) 212; Flore (n 14) 141; Fransen and Kerkhofs (n 9) 21; Ketels (n 14) 237; Masset (n 7) T60/18.

45 Ketels (n 14) 237.

46 De La Serna (n 7) 178; De La Serna (n 15) 206; Delhaise (n 9) 32; Flore (n 9) 212; Flore (n 14) 141; Fransen and Kerkhofs (n 9) 20. Hameeuw wonders where to draw the line though. When is a group of people too small to be a population? See: Hameeuw (n 15) 6.

47 De La Serna (n 7) 178; Flore (n 9) 212; Flore (n 14) 140.

48 See the GICM case: Corr. Brussel 16 Februari 2006, *onuitg.*; Brussel 19 januari 2007, *T.Strafr.* 2008, 281, noot F Schuermans. See as well: De La Serna (n 7) 198-199; Fransen and Kerkhofs (n 9) 39; Ketels (n 14) 237; Christophe Marchand, 'Impact Des Nouvelles Infractions Terroristes Quant à La Qualification de Participation à Un Groupe Terroriste et à l'usage d'une Preuve Secrète Devant Le Tribunal: Commentaires d'un Avocat' in Francesca Galli and Anne Weyembergh (eds), *EU counter-terrorism offences: What impact on national elgislation and case-law?* (Editions de l'Université de Bruxelles 2012) 281; Traest (n 15) 257.

perpetrator was planning to actually execute the attack.[49] What matters is whether the victims could reasonably feel threatened.[50]

Constitutional Court

An appeal for nullification of part of the statute of 19 December 2003 was filed to the Constitutional Court, at the time still called Arbitration Court, by the *Ligue des droits de l'homme* and others. The appeal focussed on the introduction of articles 137 and 138 CC and the expansion of Belgium's territorial jurisdiction. The introduction of article 140 and 141 CC was not challenged before the Constitutional Court. The appeal, which was based on the legality principle and the prohibition of discrimination, led to the judgment of 13 July 2005. The appeal came as no surprise since the introduction of the offence was criticised by the doctrine, defence lawyers and NGOs.[51]

The introduction of article 137 CC was challenged on the basis of the principle of legality. The applicants considered that terrorism *sensu stricto* was defined too broadly and inaccurately, in particular because the 'contextual element' and parts of the *mens rea* were not sufficiently clear.[52] The Arbitration Court, referring to the case law of the European Court of Human Rights (ECtHR)[53], stated that the legality principle does not prohibit the judge from having a margin of appreciation. Laws have a general character and the situations to which they are applied are diverse and changeable.[54] The Arbitration Court reiterated that the definition of terrorism *sensu stricto* resulted from the 2002 EU Framework Decision on Combating Terrorism. It admitted that the wording of the *mens*

49 Corr. West-Vlaanderen (afd. Brugge) (vakantiekamer) 14 juli 2016, TGR-TWVR 2016, afl. 5, 386; Ketels (n 14) 238.

50 Corr. West-Vlaanderen (afd. Brugge) (vakantiekamer) 14 juli 2016, TGR-TWVR 2016, afl. 5, 386; Ketels (n 14) 238.

51 Hameeuw (n 15) 6; Traest (n 15) 256-257; Weyembergh and Kennes, 'Domestic Provisions and Case Law: The Belgian Case' (n 7) 156. Flore, on the other hand, was of the opinion the offence did not violate the legality principle. See: Flore (n 9) 213-214.

52 Arbitragehof 13 juli 2005, 125/2005, B.4. See also: De Hert and Millen (n 32) 3; Benoit Dejemeppe and Marie-Françoise Rigaux, 'Lutte contre le terrorisme moderne : le contrôle des droits fondamentaux entre le marteau et l'enclume' in R Leysen and others (eds), *Semper perseverans – Liber amicorum André Alen* (Intersentia 2020) 758; Jean Spreutels and Sylviane Velu, 'La Lutte Contre Le Terrorisme Dans La Jurisprudence de La Cour Consitutionnelle de Belgique' in Koen Lemmens, Stephan Parmentier and Louise Reyntjens (eds), *Human rights with a human touch: Liber amicorum Paul Lemmens* (Intersentia 2019) 132-133; Traest (n 15) 257; Weyembergh and Kennes, 'Le Titre Iter Du Livre II Du Code Pénal: Des Infractions Terroristes' (n 7) 127.

53 *Müller v Switzerland* App no 10737/84 (ECHR, 24 May 1988) 29; *Kokkinakis v Greece* App no 14307/88 (ECHR, 25 May 1993) 40; *SW v UK* App no 20166/92 (ECHR, 22 November 1995) 36; *Cantoni v France* App no 17862/91 (ECHR, 11 November 1996) 31 and 35.

54 Arbitragehof 13 juli 2005, 125/2005, B.6.2 -B.6.3. See for example as wel: Arbitragehof 30 juni 2005, 116/2005 B.3.2-B.3.3 and GwH 19 maart 2019, 44/2019, B.19.1-B.19.2.

rea could, in certain cases, give rise to difficulties of interpretation.[55] However, words such as 'serious', 'unlawful', and 'destroy', alongside the obligation of a strict interpretation of criminal offences, mean that a certain seriousness is required and therefore the definition is sufficiently clear.[56] The applicants had also claimed some of the *actus reus* in §3 was not sufficiently clear, but the Arbitration Court similarly reasoned that terminology such as 'large-scale' or 'significant' ensures that it is impossible for judges to qualify acts of which the consequences are insignificant as terrorism. Finally, the Arbitration Court referred to articles 139, section 2 and 141*ter* CC, which are intended to keep the balance between efficiency and fundamental rights, before ruling that although the legislation leaves a wide margin of appreciation for the judge, it does not grant him an autonomous competence and therefore there is no legality issue.[57] This is in line with the opinion of the Council of State (*Raad van State; Conseil d'Etat*), which emphasised the importance of a restrictive interpretation.[58]

The applicants also argued that terrorism *sensu stricto* violated the principle of equality and non-discrimination. This argument was based on the difference in treatment between terrorism and other offences. The difference is apparent throughout a criminal trial, starting in the investigation phase, where more investigatory measures are possible for terrorism, and continuing throughout the trial phase, where anonymous witness testimony can be a full-fledged piece of evidence, until sentencing.[59] These differences are predominantly related to the aggravated sentences. Examples include, but are not limited to, pre-trial detention (*voorlopige hechtenis; détention preventive*), investigative measures and the impossibility of out-of-court settlement with the prosecution, which all have thresholds of sentences that have to be met. By raising the sentences in cases of terrorism, these requirements are met in cases where they would not be in general criminal law. The Arbitration Court stated that, taking into account Belgium's international obligations, it is

55 Arbitragehof 13 juli 2005, 125/2005, B.7.2.

56 Arbitragehof 13 juli 2005, 125/2005, B.7.2; Delhaise (n 9) 34-35; De La Serna (n 7) 175-176; Fransen and Kerkhofs (n 9) 21; Traest (n 15) 257.

57 Arbitragehof 13 juli 2005, 125/2005; De La Serna (n 7) 175-176; Delmulle and Guenter (n 15) 5; Ketels (n 14) 236; Masset (n 7) 18; Jos Silvis, 'Terrorism and Human Rights' in Koen Lemmens, Stephan Parmentier and Louise Reyntjens (eds), *Human Rights with a human touch: Liber amicorum Paul Lemmens* (Intersentia 2019) 132-133; Weyembergh and Kennes, 'Domestic Provisions and Case Law: The Belgian Case' (n 7) 157; Weyembergh and Kennes, 'Le Titre Iter Du Livre II Du Code Pénal: Des Infractions Terroristes' (n 7) 128-129; Winants (n 7) 347 en 349. Despite this ruling, Comité T argues that article 137 CC does in fact violate the legality principle. See: Comité T, 'Rapport 2019: Le respect des droits humains dans le cadre de la lutte contre le terrorisme: Un chantier en cours', 15.

58 Advies Raad van State bij wetsontwerp van 6 oktober 2003 betreffende terroristische misdrijven, *Parl.St.* Kamer 2003, nr. 51-0258/001, 30-31. See also: Flore (n 9) 214; Weyembergh and Kennes, 'Domestic Provisions and Case Law: The Belgian Case' (n 7) 156; Weyembergh and Kennes, 'Le Titre Iter Du Livre II Du Code Pénal: Des Infractions Terroristes' (n 7) 126.

59 Arbitragehof 13 juli 2005, 125/2005, B.9. See also: Weyembergh and Kennes, 'Le Titre Iter Du Livre II Du Code Pénal: Des Infractions Terroristes' (n 7) 127-128.

not up to the Court to decide whether it is opportune to increase the sentences.[60] Furthermore, enabling certain investigatory measures to be used, is justified by the need to effectively fight terrorism. Finally, the Arbitration Court refers to the constant care the legislature took not to detract from fundamental rights, as shown by article 139, section 2 and 141*ter* CC (see below) and the fact that the legislature decided not to introduce a system of sentence reduction in return for information on co-perpetrators, which was suggested by the 2002 EU Framework Decision on Combating Terrorism.[61] The introduction of extraterritorial jurisdiction for terrorism based on passive personality[62] was also deemed non-problematic by the Arbitration Court.[63] In conclusion, the Court did not see any problems in terms of equal treatment and discrimination.[64]

In subsequent cases in front of the lower courts, the defence has tried to argue that the legality principle was violated. However, lower courts have explicitly referred to this judgment of the Arbitration Court to support their conclusion that article 137 CC does not violate the legality principle.[65]

ART. 139 AND 140 CC

Terrorist groups

Article 140 CC contains three offences, all three of which criminalise conduct related to terrorist groups. Therefore, an important question for these three offences is under which circumstances a group of people is considered to be a terrorist group. Article 139 CC defines a terrorist group as 'any structured group of more than two persons, established over a period of time and acting in concert to commit terrorist offences, as meant in article 137'.[66] The preparatory works add that a structured group is a group that 'is not

60 Arbitragehof 13 juli 2005, 125/2005 B.11.1. See also: De La Serna (n 7) 176.

61 Arbitragehof 13 juli 2005, 125/2005, B.11.2. Note that years later the legislature did in fact introduce such a system. See: Wet 22 juli 2018 tot wijziging van het Wetboek van strafvordering betreffende toezeggingen in het kader van de strafvordering, de strafuitvoering of de hechtenis wegens het afleggen van een verklaring in het kader van de strijd tegen de georganiseerde criminaliteit en het terrorisme, *BS* 7 augustus 2018, 62054.

62 Meaning the jurisidiction is based on the nationality or resident status of the victim.

63 Arbitragehof 13 juli 2005, 125/2005, B.11.3.

64 Spreutels and Velu (n 52) 148-149; Winants (n 7) 349.

65 Corr. Mechelen 5 december 2012, *onuitg.*, 37-40; Antwerpen 8 januari 2014, *onuitg.*, 26-28, annulled by Cass. 16 december 2014, P.14.1048.N for violating article 40 Taalwet Gerechtszaken; Gent 26 januari 2016, *onuitg.*, 31, annulled by Cass. 13 september 2016, *RW* 2017-2018, 421 for violating the right to contradiction. See also: Fransen and Kerkhofs (n 9) 21-22; Winants (n 7) 347.

66 Own translation, original in Dutch and French: "*iedere gestructureerde vereniging van meer dan twee personen die sinds enige tijd bestaat en die in onderling overleg optreedt om terroristische misdrijven te plegen, als bedoeld in artikel 137; l'association structurée de plus de deux personnes, établie dans le temps, et qui agit*

randomly formed and that does not need to have formally defined roles for its members, continuity of its membership or a developed structure'.[67] Both the definition of a terrorist group in article 139 CC and the definition of a structured group in the preparatory works, are almost literal copies of an article of the 2002 EU Framework Decision on Combating Terrorism.[68] While 'acting in concert' suggests a form of mutual deliberation and coherence of actions,[69] the extent of the collaboration required is uncertain. For example, all members do not have to be informed about each other's actions or even know each other, as long as they all contribute to the existence of the group.[70] Nor does contact between members have to be in person, but can also be over the internet[71] or by other means of correspondence.[72] The legislature treats a terrorist group as a separate entity with its own intent, that being the perpetration of terroristm *sensu stricto*. In the context of criminal organisations, Verbruggen has called this form of group with its own intent an 'illegal entity'.[73] In order to correctly judge the goal of a certain group, a high level of geopolitical knowledge is often required.[74] The situation on the ground can be chaotic and allegiances are not always clear, nor are the aims and origins of every group which is active in such areas. Furthermore, the fact that a group is part of a European or international list of

---

de façon concertée en vue de commettre des infractions terroristes visées à l'article 137" (art 139, section 1 CC). See also: Delmulle and Guenter (n 15) 4.

67 Own translation, original in Dutch and French: "*Zulks onderstelt dat de vereniging niet toevallig tot stand is gekomen, zonder dat evenwel sprake moet zijn van formeel afgebakende taken voor de leden van de vereniging, noch van continuïteit in de samenstelling van de leden van een uitgewerkte structuur; Cela signifie que l'association ne s'est pas constituée fortuitement, sans pour autant que l'on doive parler de tâches formellement délimitées dans le chef des membres de l'association, ni de continuité dans la composition des membres d'une structure élaborée.*" (Memorie van Toelichting bij wetsontwerp van 6 oktober 2003 betreffende terroristische misdrijven, *Parl.St.* Kamer 2003, nr. 51-0258/001, (4) 12). See also: De Hert and Millen (n 32) 4; Delhaise (n 9) 36-37; Deruyck and De Nauw (n 16) 8; Hameeuw (n 15) 8; Ketels (n 14) 241; Vandromme and De Roy (n 16) 536; Winants (n 7) 347-348.

68 Art 2 Council Framework Decision 2002/475/JHA of 13 June 2002 on combating terrorism, *OJ* 22 June 2002, L 164/4. Now art 2.3 Directive (EU) 2017/541 of the European Parliament and of the Council of 15 March 2017 on combating terrorism and replacing Council Framework Decision 2002/475/JHA and amending Council Decision 2005/671/JHA, *OJ* 31 March 2017, L 88/6. See also: Beernaert, 'La Loi Du 19 Décembre 2003 Relative Aux Infractions Terroristes : Quand Le Droit Pénal Belge Évolue Sous La Dictée de l'Union Européenne' (n 14) 587; Bosly and Van Ravenstein (n 14) 49; De La Serna (n 7) 181-182; Delhaise (n 9) 35; Delhaise and Fievet (n 29) 118; Flore (n 9) 216-217; Flore (n 14) 144; Weyembergh and Kennes, 'Domestic Provisions and Case Law: The Belgian Case' (n 7) 153; Weyembergh and Kennes, 'Le Titre Iter Du Livre II Du Code Pénal: Des Infractions Terroristes' (n 7) 106.

69 De La Serna (n 15) 211; Fransen and Kerkhofs (n 9) 28; Winants (n 7) 348.

70 De La Serna (n 7) 183; De La Serna (n 15) 209-211.

71 Which is used extensively. See: Sophie Lavaux, 'Terrorisme: La Stratégie de l'union Européenne En Matière de Radicalisation et de Recrutement (Troisième Partie)' [2015] Vigiles 114, 117-118.

72 De La Serna (n 7) 183.

73 In Dutch: "strafrechtspersoon". See: Frank Verbruggen, *Schaduwboksen in het donker: de dogmatische onderbouw van het strafrechtelijk overheidsoptreden tegen georganiseerde criminaliteit* (PhD at the Faculty of Law of KU Leuven 2001) 195.

74 De La Serna (n 7) 184 and 201; De La Serna (n 15) 211.

terrorist organisations, does not automatically result in it qualifying as a terrorist group under article 139 CC or vice versa.[75] While the goal of a terrorist group has to be the perpetration of terrorist offences *sensu stricto*, it is not required that these offences have actually been committed[76], or even prepared already.[77] The mere act of conspiracy or collusion, or of making plans, is said to be sufficient. However, how does one prove that the intent of the illegal entity is the perpetration of a terrorist attack if the preparations for the attack have not even started? The danger of a broad interpretation arises where groups are labelled as 'terrorist' based on vague notions that they might intend to perpetrate a terrorist attack. Given that different types of involvement in the group constitute terrorist offences, this vague definition of a terrorist group can raise legal certainty issues.

The tenth consideration of the 2002 EU Framework Decision on Combating Terrorism states that 'nothing in this Framework Decision may be interpreted as being intended to reduce or restrict fundamental rights or freedoms such as the right to strike, freedom of assembly, of association or of expression, including the right of everyone to form and to join trade unions with others for the protection of his or her interests and the related right to demonstrate'.[78] The legislature decided to include this consideration in the legislation. First, the consideration was copied into article 139, section 2 CC but after some discussion, the commission for justice decided to move the consideration to a new article 141*ter* CC. This was done in order to clarify that the consideration is applicable to the entire title of the code.[79] In section two of article 139 CC, parliament then copied the second section of article 324*bis* CC about the criminal organisation, since this was considered the 'least bad

75 De La Serna (n 7) 186-187; De La Serna (n 15) 214; Fransen and Kerkhofs (n 9) 29. The council chamber and indictment chamber in Brussels for example ruled that the PKK was not a terrorist organisation, even though it is on the EU list of terrorist organisation. See: KI Brussel 14 september 2017, *RW* 2017-18, 1611, noot J Wouters and T Van Poecke; KI Brussel 8 maart 2019, *onuitg.*, 44; RK Brussel 3 november 2016, *onuitg.*, 11; Ketels (n 14) 242; Jan Wouters and Thomas Van Poecke, 'Van Strijdkrachten, Terroristen En Het Belgisch Strafrecht (Noot Onder KI Brussel 14 September 2017)' [2017-2018] Rechtskundig Weekblad 1616.

76 Delmulle and Guenter (n 15) 4.

77 Brussel 19 januari 2007, *T.Strafr.* 2008, 281, noot F Schuermans; Corr. Brugge 28 februari 2006, *T.Strafr.* 2006, 159, noot P De Hert; Emma Dekrem, 'Naar Een Veralgemeende Strafbaarheid van Voorbereidende Handelingen?' [2020] Nullum Crimen 133, 140; De La Serna (n 7) 186; De La Serna (n 15) 212-213; Delhaise (n 9) 38; Deruyck and De Nauw (n 16) 8-9; Fransen and Kerkhofs (n 9) 29; Hameeuw (n 15) 8; Ketels (n 14) 241; Traest (n 15) 257; Weyembergh and Kennes, 'Domestic Provisions and Case Law: The Belgian Case' (n 7) 159; Winants (n 7) 348.

78 Consideration 10 Council Framework Decision 2002/475/JHA of 13 June 2002 on combating terrorism, *OJ* 22 June 2002, L 164/3. Now Consideration 35 Directive (EU) 2017/541 of the European Parliament and of the Council of 15 March 2017 on combating terrorism and replacing Council Framework Decision 2002/475/JHA and amending Council Decision 2005/671/JHA, *OJ* 31 March 2017, L 88/6.

79 Amendement nr. 15 bij het wetsontwerp betreffende terroristische misdrijven van 21 oktober 2003, *Parl.St.* Kamer 2003, nr. 51-0258/003, 5; verslag namens de commissie van justitie bij wetsontwerp betreffende terroristische misdrijven van 6 oktober 2003, *Parl.St.* Kamer 2003, nr. 51-0258/004, 16-20; Beernaert, 'La Loi Du 19 Décembre 2003 Relative Aux Infractions Terroristes : Quand Le Droit Pénal Belge Évolue Sous La Dictée de l'Union Européenne' (n 14) 588; De La Serna (n 7) 197.

solution'.[80] So, the second section of article 139 CC now contains an exclusion clause for organisations whose factual goal is exclusively political, professional organisational, humanitarian, philosophical, or religious or that exclusively pursue any other lawful purpose.[81]

The purpose article 139, section 2 CC serves is unclear. According to the preparatory works 'this section aims to provide clarification and protection against the misuse of the statute'.[82] Whether it succeeds in doing so remains doubtful. The Council of State noted both for article 324*bis*, section 2 CC[83] and article 139, section 2 CC[84] that two interpretations were possible. Either this exclusion clause means that an organisation which pursues a legitimate aim has not been established for the purpose of committing offences in concert, or that investigating or prosecuting an organisation (also) pursuing a legitimate aim is not allowed. The latter interpretation would render the offences moot. The former interpretation therefore is the correct one[85], but it is in turn merely stating the obvious, and therefore does not belong in a criminal code.[86] Although some members of parliament were of the same mind, the majority ignored this criticism, claiming that it was better to be needlessly expressive than dangerously mute.[87] In our opinion, this claim was unjustified. Because of the lack of added value, and the possibility for confusion, the legislature would do better to delete article 139, section 2 CC.[88] The same goes for article 141*ter* CC, which similarly has no added value.[89] It is worth noting that one participant of the expert seminar considered these clauses good for peace of mind.

80 Amendement nr. 14 bij het wetsontwerp betreffende terroristische misdrijven van 21 oktober 2003, *Parl.St.* Kamer 2003, nr. 51-0258/003, 4; verslag namens de commissie van justitie bij wetsontwerp betreffende terroristische misdrijven van 6 oktober 2003, *Parl.St.* Kamer 2003, nr. 51-0258/004, 20; Delhaise (n 9) 23.

81 Art 139, section 2 CC; Weyembergh and Kennes, 'Le Titre Iter Du Livre II Du Code Pénal: Des Infractions Terroristes' (n 7) 110.

82 Own translation, original in Dutch and French: "*is dit lid erop gericht een verduidelijking en een bescherming tegen verkeerd gebruik van de wet te bieden; cet alinéa a pour objet de fournir des précisions et d'offrir une protection contre une utilisation abusive de la loi.*" (Memorie van Toelichting bij wetsontwerp van 6 oktober 2003 betreffende terroristische misdrijven, *Parl.St.* Kamer 2003, nr. 51-0258/001, (4) 12).

83 Advies 28.026/2, van de Raad van State bij wetsontwerp van 12 maart 1997 betreffende criminele organisaties, 96/97 nr. 49-954/24, 2; Verbruggen (n 73) 307.

84 Advies 34.362/4 van de Raad van State bij wetsontwerp van 6 oktober 2003 betreffende terroristische misdrijven, *Parl.St.* Kamer 2003, nr. 51-0258/001, (22) 33; De La Serna (n 7) 197.

85 De La Serna (n 7) 186; De La Serna (n 15) 213-214; Flore (n 9) 217-218; Fransen and Kerkhofs (n 9) 29-30; Winants (n 7) 348.

86 Hameeuw (n 15) 8; Vandromme and De Roy (n 16) 531 and 536.

87 Verslag namens de commissie van justitie bij wetsontwerp van 6 oktober 2003 betreffende terroristische misdrijven, *Parl.St.* Kamer 2003, nr. 51-0258/004, 11; Beernaert, 'La Loi Du 19 Décembre 2003 Relative Aux Infractions Terroristes : Quand Le Droit Pénal Belge Évolue Sous La Dictée de l'Union Européenne' (n 14) 588; De La Serna (n 7) 197.

88 See also: Inneke Onsea, 'Wet Betreffende de Criminele Organisaties: Een Eerste Effectieve Stap in de Strijd Tegen Georganiseerde Criminaliteit?' [1999] Panopticon 278, 284.

89 See also: De La Serna (n 7) 198; De La Serna (n 15) 228-230; Delhaise (n 9) 142; Hameeuw (n 15) 10; Traest (n 15) 258; Vandromme and De Roy (n 16) 538.

Actus Reus: art. 140, §1 CC

The terrorist offence for which by far the most prosecutions are brought before the courts is that of participating in the activities of a terrorist group.[90] As was the case for article 137 CC, article 140 CC was also introduced in 2003[91] in response to the 2002 EU Framework Decision on Combating Terrorism[92]. Article 140, §1 CC targets any person who participates in the activities of a terrorist group while they knew or should have known that their participation could contribute to the committal of a felony or standard offence by the terrorist group. The *actus reus* is the participation in any activity of a terrorist group. The Criminal Code, echoing the Directive, explicitly adds to this definition: 'be it by providing data or material resources to a terrorist group or any form of financing of any activity of a terrorist group'.[93] However, this enumeration of actions is not exhaustive.[94] Furthermore, the contribution to the activities of the group does not need to be systematic, an occasional contribution suffices.[95] The action does not have to have a direct connection to the committal of the offence by the group either.[96]

The case law has given a broad interpretation to participating in any activity of a terrorist group, made possible by the broad wording of the legislation[97]. Article 140, §1 CC requires a concrete act of participation of a person, but the case law considers almost anything a possible act of participation. This includes following military training with a

90 Art 140, §1 CC; Fransen and Kerkhofs (n 9) 16; Winants (n 7) 349.

91 Art 6 wet van 19 december 2003 betreffende terroristische misdrijven, *BS* 29 december 2003, 61689.

92 Art 2 Council Framework Decision 2002/475/JHA of 13 June 2002 on combating terrorism, *OJ* 22 June 2002, L 164/3. Now art 4 Directive (EU) 2017/541 of the European Parliament and of the Council of 15 March 2017 on combating terrorism and replacing Council Framework Decision 2002/475/JHA and amending Council Decision 2005/671/JHA, *OJ* 31 March 2017, L 88/6.

93 Own translation, original in Dutch and French: "*zij het ook door het verstrekken van gegevens of materiële middelen aan een terroristische groep of door het in enigerlei vorm financieren van enige activiteit van een terroristische groep; y compris par la fourniture d'informations ou de moyens matériels au groupe terroriste, ou par toute forme de financement d'une activité du groupe terroriste*" (art 140, §1 CC).

94 Memorie van Toelichting bij wetsontwerp van 6 oktober 2003 betreffende terroristische misdrijven, *Parl.St.* Kamer 2003, nr. 51-0258/001, (4) 13; Corr. Brussel 3 mei 2016, 35, *onuitg.*; De La Serna (n 7) 191; De La Serna (n 15) 219.

95 Memorie van Toelichting bij wetsontwerp van 6 oktober 2003 betreffende terroristische misdrijven, *Parl.St.* Kamer 2003, nr. 51-0258/001, (4) 13; Corr. Brussel 10 mei 2019, *NjW* 2019, 663, noot W Yperman; De La Serna (n 7) 191; De La Serna (n 15) 219; Delhaise (n 9) 40; Fransen and Kerkhofs (n 9) 30; Hameeuw (n 15) 9; Ketels (n 14) 243; Weyembergh and Kennes, 'Le Titre Iter Du Livre II Du Code Pénal: Des Infractions Terroristes' (n 7) 111.

96 Memorie van Toelichting bij wetsontwerp van 6 oktober 2003 betreffende terroristische misdrijven, *Parl.St.* Kamer 2003, nr. 51-0258/001, (4) 13; Corr. Brussel 10 mei 2019, *NjW* 2019, 663, noot W Yperman; Delhaise (n 9) 40-41; Delmulle and Guenter (n 15) 4; Deruyck and De Nauw (n 16) 9; Fransen and Kerkhofs (n 9) 30.

97 Traest (n 15) 258; Weyembergh and Kennes, 'Le Titre Iter Du Livre II Du Code Pénal: Des Infractions Terroristes' (n 7) 129.

terrorist group[98]; fighting for a terrorist group in a war zone[99]; sending a package of civilian clothes to a family member who is a member of a terrorist group[100]; cooking or being a driver for the group[101]; mentally encouraging fighters of the group by sending them messages from their families or promising them to join them[102]; providing moral support[103] and marrying and having a sexual relationship with a fighter of the group[104]. If a suspect has travelled to Syria to join a terrorist group, it is not required that the exact assignments of the suspect for that group in Syria can be identified.[105] Because of this very wide interpretation of the *actus reus*, article 140, §1 CC has a very wide potential scope of application.[106]

An interesting note to make in this context concerns the offences regarding criminal organisations. In the context of a criminal organisation, mere involvement with the organisation is an offence, without it being required that the person participates in the activities of the organisation.[107] Involvement equals membership of the organisation (knowingly and willingly being part of it[108])[109] while participation in the activities requires an action. Consequently, for terrorist organisations an act of participation to the activities of the group is required and mere membership is not sufficient.[110] The Constitutional

98 Brussel 28 mei 2015, *onuitg.*, 29.

99 Corr. Brussel 3 mei 2016, *onuitg.*, 52.

100 Corr. Brussel 14 mei 2014, *onuitg.*

101 Corr. Antwerpen (afd. Antwerpen) 11 februari 2015, *onuitg.*, 50; Corr. Antwerpen 30 maart 2015, *onuitg.*, 4; Corr. Antwerpen (afd. Antwerpen) 25 januari 2016, *onuitg.*, 3.

102 Corr. Brussel 3 mei 2016, *onuitg.*, 38-39.

103 Brussel 2 juni 2017, *onuitg.*, 22; Corr. Brussel 3 mei 2016, *onuitg.*, 36; Corr. Brussel 8 mei 2017, *onuitg.*, 5; Fransen and Kerkhofs (n 9) 32; Fransen and Kerkhofs (n 31) 159; Deruyck and De Nauw (n 16) 9; Ward Yperman and Sofie Royer, 'Veroordeling Jihadibruid' [2017] Nieuw Juridisch Weekblad 813.

104 Corr. Oost-Vlaanderen (afd. Gent) 16 oktober 2017, *NjW* 2017, 805, noot W Yperman en S Royer. The right to marry and the right to respect for private and family life are both human rights enshrined in the ECHR (respectively articles 12 and 8 ECHR). These rights, however, are not absolute and can be limited. E.g. the offence of bigamy (art 391 CC) which is not in violation of either article of the ECHR. See: *X v UK* App no 3898 (ECHR, 22 July 1970); *RB v UK* App no 19628/92 (ECHR, 29 June 1992); Marlier (n 36) 409-410.

105 Corr. Brussel 10 mei 2019, *NjW* 2019, 663, noot W Yperman.

106 Ketels also notes this, see: Ketels (n 14) 243.

107 Art 324*ter*, §1 CC. See also: De La Serna (n 7) 191.

108 This was the original phrasing of the statute. This phrasing was adapted in 2005 (art 5 wet van 10 augustus 2005 tot wijziging van diverse bepalingen met het oog op de versterking van de strijd tegen mensenhandel en mensensmokkel en tegen praktijken van huisjesmelkers, *BS* 2 september 2005, 38454), but with the explicit intention to keep the content of the offence unaltered (Amendementen bij wetsontwerp van 9 maart 2005 tot wijziging van diverse bepalingen met het oog op de versterking van de strijd tegen mensenhandel en mensensmokkel, *Parl.St.* Kamer 2004-2005, nr. 51-1560/004, 7-8).

109 Memorie van Toelichting bij wetsontwerp van 12 maart 1997 betreffende criminele organisaties, *Parl.St.* Kamer 1996-1997, nr. 49-954/1, 1-2; amendementen bij wetsontwerp van 9 maart 2005 tot wijziging van diverse bepalingen met het oog op de versterking van de strijd tegen mensenhandel en mensensmokkel, *Parl.St.* Kamer 2004-2005, nr. 51-1560/004, 7-8; GwH 19 september 2014, 122/2014, *NjW* 2014, 840, B.4.2-B.4.3.

110 Corr. Antwerpen (afd. Antwerpen) 11 februari 2015, *onuitg.*, 50; Corr. Antwerpen 30 maart 2015, *onuitg.*, 4; De La Serna (n 7) 191; De La Serna (n 15) 219; Delhaise (n 9) 40; Fransen and Kerkhofs (n 9) 30;

Court stated that this difference between criminal organisations and terrorist groups was justified because there is an objective difference in the nature of the offences the organisation or group aims to commit.[111] The aim of terrorist groups is to commit terrorist offences *sensu stricto* while that of criminal organisations is to commit crimes punishable by three years' imprisonment or more, in order to, directly or indirectly, obtain financial benefits. The offence of article 140, §1 CC, however, is interpreted so expansively that the distinction between participating in the activities and mere membership is illusory. When discussing the offence of membership in article 324*ter*, §1 CC, the representative of the secretary of justice gave the following examples when replying to the question what knowingly and willingly being part of an organisation is: the driver, house staff, and security personnel of the leader of the organisation and 'the people who in are any form reimbursed by the criminal organisation to build a social network for the organisation, with the goal of apparent legitimate embedding and social implantation of the organisation in society'.[112] Furthermore it is clarified that membership of a criminal organisation can be deduced from, for example, 'frequently being present at meetings of the criminal organisation' or 'being a shareholder in the corporate law structure the organisation uses as a cover'.[113] It is striking that the abovementioned examples of membership, when transposed to the context of a terrorist group, would, in all probability, fall under article 140, §1 CC. It is safe to say that the alleged difference between the two does not actually exist in practice. The Council of State had in 1997 already stated that there is no difference between 'knowingly and willingly being a part of' and 'participating in'. As it explains 'only when a suspect has participated in an activity of the organisation, can it be

---

Hameeuw (n 15) 9; Ketels (n 14) 243; Traest (n 15) 258; Weyembergh and Kennes, 'Le Titre Iter Du Livre II Du Code Pénal: Des Infractions Terroristes' (n 7) 111-112; Winants (n 7) 348.

111 GwH 19 september 2014, 122/2014, *NjW* 2014, 840, B.7.1-B.7.2. See also: Ketels (n 14) 246-247; Eef Vandebroek, 'Eenvoudig lidmaatschap van criminele vereniging' [2014] Nieuw Juridisch Weekblad 846, 847.

112 Own translation, original in French: "*personnes qui sont rémunérées sous une forme ou une autre par l'organisation pour constituer un cercle de relations sociales d'apparence licite*" (Advies van de Raad van State bij wetsontwerp van 12 maart 1997 betreffende criminele organisaties, 96/97 nr. 49-954/1, (13) 15-16). See as well: Arbitragehof 30 juni 2005, 116/2005, B.4.2; GwH 19 september 2014, 122/2014, *NjW* 2014, 840, B.4.3; Onsea (n 88) 282; Inneke Onsea, *De Bestrijding van Georganiseerde Misdaad: De Grens Tussen Waarheidsvinding En Grondrechten* (Intersentia 2003) 39.

113 Own translation, original in Dutch and French: "*De minister is van oordeel dat in een concreet geval het geregeld aanwezig zijn op vergaderingen een feit is waaruit de aansluiting bij de organisatie zou kunnen worden afgeleid; Le ministre estime que, dans un cas concret, l'affiliation à une organisation pourrait être déduite de la présence régulière aux réunions.*" and "*Hetzelfde kan onder bepaalde omstandigheden het geval zijn voor een aandeelhouder van een vennootschapsrechtelijke structuur die door een criminele organisatie als dekmantel wordt gebruikt; Il pourrait en être de même, dans certaines circonstances, pour l'actionnaire d'une structure relevant du droit des sociétés, utilisée comme écran par une organisation criminelle.*" (Verslag namens de commissie voor Justitie bij wetsontwerp van 12 maart 1997 betreffende criminele organisaties, 96/97 nr. 49-954/6, 18). See also: Arbitragehof 30 juni 2005, 116/2005, B.4.2; GwH 19 september 2014, 122/2014, *NjW* 2014, 840, B.4.3.

assumed and proved that he knows the organisation and knows that it is a criminal organisation'.[114] Once again, the Council of State seems to have been right. In order to be able to meaningfully apply the concept of membership, an act of participation will almost always be required, however minimal it may be. The fact that the Constitutional Court found the distinction justified, does not mean it is a meaningful distinction.

This distinction between the concepts of membership and participation has also led to a peculiar analogy made in some case law.[115] In several cases, the Brussels Correctional Court first refers to the preparatory works of the legislation on criminal organisation 'by analogy'. After quoting the abovementioned examples of membership (being the driver, etc.) from these preparatory works, it then refers to the preparatory works that compare a different offence, being participation in any permitted activity of a criminal organisation, with participation in a terrorist group. The court states that article 324*ter* CC envisions participation closely linked to the organisation's activities while article 140 CC targets all forms of participation, as long as the participant knows they will contribute to the commission of a standard offence or crime by the group. It is confusing that the court uses an analogy with an offence that is not comparable. The courts themselves state that mere membership of a terrorist organisation is not sufficient. This analogy, which is a recurring theme in the case law of the Brussels Correctional Court, demonstrates the difficulty the courts have in clearly and consistently applying such concepts.

In 2019, the Brussels Correctional Court also ruled that the offence of participation in the activities of a terrorist offence was a continuous offence (*voortdurend misdrijf; infraction continue*).[116] The court decided so in order to solve an issue of the effect of legislative change over time (see below). However, since an act of participation is required, the offence in article 140, §1 CC seems to be an immediate offence, which takes place the moment the act of participation is performed (in combination with the required *mens rea*). Therefore, other courts, including the Brussels Court of Appeal, have not held that

114 Own translation, original in Dutch and French: "*Pas wanneer een verdachte aan een handeling van de organisatie heeft deelgenomen, kan ervan uit worden gegaan en worden bewezen dat hij de organisatie kent en weet dat het om een misdaadorganisatie gaat; La connaissance de l'organisation et de son caractère criminel ne peut se concevoir, dans le chef de l'inculpé, et ne peut être prouvée contre lui, que par la participation de celui-ci à un acte de l'organisation.*" (Advies van de Raad van State bij wetsontwerp van 12 maart 1997 betreffende criminele organisaties, 96/97 nr. 49-954/1, (13) 16).

115 Corr. Brussel 25 november 2015, *onuitg.*, 8; Corr. Brussel 3 mei 2016, *onuitg.*, 35-36; Corr. Brussel 8 mei 2017, *onuitg.*, 5; Corr. Brussel 29 maart 2018, *onuitg.*, 21. The court states: "*Il faut néanmoins considérer que la participation au groupe terroriste est conçue plus largement que la participation à l'organisation criminelle dans la mesure où l'article 324ter du Code pénal envisage une participation étroitement liée aux activités de l'organisation criminelle tandis que l'article 140 vise toute forme de participation, pour autant que le participant soit conscient qu'il contribue à la commission d'un crime ou délit du groupe terroriste.*"

116 Corr. Brussel 10 mei 2019, *NjW* 2019, 663, noot W Yperman.

participation in the activities of a terrorist offence is a continuous offence.[117] If several acts of participation succeed each other and/or other offences, they can constitute a continued offence (*voortgezet misdrijf; infraction continuée*) or collective offence (*collectief misdrijf; infraction collective)*[118], but that does not make the participation a continuous one.

Actus Reus: art. 140, §1/1 CC

With the statute of 5 May 2019, the legislature added a new paragraph to article 140 CC. This paragraph was placed in between §1 and §2 and its sentence also fits neatly in between the sentences for those offences (see below).[119] The legislature even explicitly stated that he wanted to create an intermediate sentencing level.[120] Article 140, §1/1 punishes the participation in the taking of any decision in the context of the activities of the terrorist group.[121] Once more, the legislature was inspired by the pre-existing offences concerning the criminal organisation.[122]

However, this means that any criticism applicable to this offence in the context of a criminal organisation can also be applied to the terrorist offence. In the context of the offence of participating in the making of any decision in the framework of the activities of a criminal organisation, Verbruggen states that 'making any decision' is not a suitable *actus reus* for an offence.[123] The same criticism can be levelled against article 140, §1/1 CC. People make a plethora of decisions every single day, making this criterion void. Deciding what to drink during a meeting, whether or not to open the window, where to sit, etc. Those are all decisions, which will lead a person to commit this offence when they are made in the context of the activities of a terrorist group. Since making a decision is almost inevitable, anyone who came within the ambit of the offence of participating in the activities of the group, will now come within the ambit of this new offence. As we have

117 See for example: Brussel 21 december 2018, *onuitg.*; Corr. Oost-Vlaanderen (afd. Dendermonde) 14 december 2018, *onuitg.*; Corr. Antwerpen 17 december 2018, *onuitg.*; Corr. Luik 18 januari 2019, *onuitg.*

118 This means there were several separate offences, but they were seen as intrinsically linked because they were part of a single criminal project.

119 Maria Luisa Cesoni, 'Les "Infractions Terroristes": De La Répression Des Actes à La Police de La Pensée' in Christian De Valkeneer and Henri D Bosly (eds), *Actualités en droit pénal 2019* (Larcier 2019) 239; De Coensel (n 23) 214; Winants (n 7) 357.

120 Wetsvoorstel van 6 februari 2019 houdende diverse bepalingen in strafzaken en inzake erediensten, *Parl.St.* Kamer 2018-2019, nr. 54-3515/001, 102-103.

121 Art 75 wet van 5 mei 2019 houdende diverse bepalingen in strafzaken en inzake erediensten, en tot wijziging van de wet van 28 mei 2002 betreffende de euthanasie en van het Sociaal Strafwetboek, *BS* 24 mei 2019, 50023.

122 Art 324*ter*, §3 CC; wetsvoorstel van 6 februari 2019 houdende diverse bepalingen in strafzaken en inzake erediensten, *Parl.St.* Kamer 2018-2019, nr. 54-3515/001, 102-103; De Coensel (n 23) 214; Winants (n 7) 357.

123 Verbruggen (n 73) 347-348.

seen, this is a very broad category of people. The man who sent clothes to his brother who is a terrorist fighter decided to send those clothes, the woman who married the terrorist fighter decided to marry him, etc. Furthermore, not only making decisions is punishable, but also participating in the making of a decision. This means that a member of the group who voted against committing a terrorist attack participated in the making of this decision, and would therefore be liable for the higher sentence. Even an outsider, non-member, who tries to convince his friend who is a member of such a group not to do something stupid, is participating in the making of this decision. Therefore, it is clear that the offence is too broad. While the legislature attempted to create an offence which targets members of terrorist organisations higher up the ladder, he created one with an *actus reus* which is almost as broad as the offence of participating in the activities of the group. This offence with its exceedingly broad *actus reus*, which is not part of the EU Directive, runs afoul of the legality principle and the legislature would do well to remove it. The federal prosecution service has stated in the media that in future situations of foreign terrorist fighters, they will prosecute for the offence of article 140, §1/1 CC.[124] Statements such as these clearly show that this offence fails to target people higher up the ladder of the group.

Actus Reus: art. 140, §2 CC

The second paragraph of article 140 CC criminalises leadership of a terrorist group. This offence was also introduced in 2003, in the wake of the Framework Decision, and is still part of the Directive. While the Directive imposes on member states the obligation to criminalise directing a terrorist group, the definition of leadership and directing is ambiguous. The preparatory works define leaders as 'the people who take upon themselves the more important responsibilities within the group'.[125] On top of that, they are 'because of their central role within the terrorist group, better informed than anyone about the offences and take the final decisions'.[126] The Council of State thought that the legislature

124 G.V.V., 'België gaat terroristen dubbel zo zwaar proberen te straffen: dit zijn de plannen' (2021) *De Morgen* 16 November 2021, www.demorgen.be/nieuws/belgie-gaat-terroristen-dubbel-zo-zwaar-proberen-te-straffen-dit-zijn-de-plannen~b4c41f42/; Guy Van Vlierden, 'België gaat terroristen dubbel zo zwaar proberen te straffen: van 5 naar 10 jaar voor "welke beslissing dan ook"' (2021) *Het Laatste Nieuws* 16 November 2021, www.hln.be/binnenland/belgie-gaat-terroristen-dubbel-zo-zwaar-proberen-te-straffen-van-5-naar-10-jaar-voor-welke-beslissing-dan-ook~a4c41f42/.

125 Own translation, original in Dutch and French: "*de personen die binnen de groep de belangrijkste verantwoordelijkheden op zich nemen; des personnes qui assument les principales responsabilités au sein du groupe*" (Memorie van Toelichting bij wetsontwerp van 6 oktober 2003 betreffende terroristische misdrijven, *Parl.St.* Kamer 2003, nr. 51-0258/001, (4) 14). See also: Ketels (n 14) 244.

126 Own translation, original in Dutch and French: "*zij wegens hun centrale rol in de terroristische groep beter dan wie ook op de hoogte van de misdrijven en nemen ze de eindbeslissingen; du fait de leur rôle central dans le groupe terroriste, elles sont plus que quiconque au courant des infractions et parce qu'elles prennent les décisions finales*" (Memorie van Toelichting bij wetsontwerp van 6 oktober 2003 betreffende terroristische

should clarify the article so that it reflected this intention more clearly.[127] Despite this advice, the legislature decided not the change the article. With the introduction of the offence in §1/1, the question now also arises as to what the difference is between a final decision (taken by a leader) and any other decision. The offence of leadership does not require that the person himself had the intention of committing a terrorist offence or that he was involved in committing it.[128] Nor does it require that the person is the one, absolute leader of the entire group.[129] Actions such as having a central role, being able to speak for the group, coordinating actions or raising funds suffice.[130] The size and importance of the group are irrelevant as well, as long as it is a terrorist group.[131]

In practice, the jurisprudence interprets 'leadership' quite broad. For the Court of Appeal in Antwerp for example, close involvement in several meetings, and not excluding that one would commit an attack themself, was enough to be a leader.[132] The fact that two other people were designated as respectively leader of the cell and spiritual leader, did not change this. The Court of Appeal in Brussels, in turn, convicted a person for leadership who provided material support to terrorist fighters in Syria (who were departing or already on-site), who was an intermediary and facilitated communication between jihadists, jihadist candidates and their families, and who was an advisor when it came to indoctrination and exfiltration to Syria.[133] In our opinion, these actions make them active members of the group, but not necessarily leaders. The ambiguity of this definition is also evidenced by the Court of Appeal's jurisprudence which frequently overturns convictions for participation and converts them into leadership and vice versa.[134] All of this is caused by the lack of definition of leadership in article 140, §2 CC. The legislature should have probably thought twice before ignoring the advice of the Council of State.

---

misdrijven, *Parl.St.* Kamer 2003, nr. 51-0258/001, (4) 14). See also: De Hert and Millen (n 32) 6; De La Serna (n 15) 215; Fransen and Kerkhofs (n 9) 35-36; Weyembergh and Kennes, 'Le Titre Iter Du Livre II Du Code Pénal: Des Infractions Terroristes' (n 7) 112; Winants (n 7) 348.

127 Advies 34.362/4 van de Raad van State bij wetsontwerp van 6 oktober 2003 betreffende terroristische misdrijven, *Parl.St.* Kamer 2003, nr. 51-0258/001, (22) 40-41.

128 Cass. 24 juni 2008, *Arr.Cass.* 2008, 1654; De Hert and Millen (n 32) 6; De La Serna (n 7) 188; De La Serna (n 15) 215-216; Delhaise (n 9) 44; De Nauw (n 12) 8; De Nauw and Kuty (n 16) 18; Deruyck and De Nauw (n 16) 9; Ketels (n 14) 244-245.

129 Ketels (n 14) 244.

130 De La Serna (n 7) 187-188; De La Serna (n 15) 215; Delhaise (n 9) 41; Fransen and Kerkhofs (n 9) 37; Winants (n 7) 348.

131 Winants (n 7) 348.

132 Antwerpen 8 januari 2014, *onuitg.*, 42.

133 Brussel 2 juni 2017, *onuitg.*, 26-30.

134 Brussel 19 januari 2007, *T.Strafr.* 2008, 281; Antwerpen 8 januari 2014, *onuitg.*; Brussel 18 november 2016, *onuitg.*; Brussel 31 maart 2017, *onuitg.*

Mens Rea

The *mens rea* of article 140 CC is: 'while he knew or should have known that his participation could contribute to the committal of a felony or standard offence by the terrorist group'.[135] This felony or standard offence does not necessarily have to be a terrorist offence, any felony or standard offence suffices, and the participant does not need to know to which specific and concrete offence he is contributing.[136] Nor does the offence actually have to be committed.[137] The person also does not have to have the intention of committing this offence himself.[138] Committing offences is the intention of the 'illegal entity' but not necessarily of the individual people participating in its activities. Their connection to the committal of the offence by the group does not have to be a direct one.[139] When article 140, §1 was introduced in 2003, the *mens rea* was 'while he knows that his participation contributes to the committal of a felony or standard offence by the terrorist group'.[140] This was copied from the Framework Decision and the Directive is still worded similarly.[141] In December 2016 the Belgian legislature changed this to 'knew or should have known' and 'could contribute'.[142] He did this to make the article more repressive.[143] This is remarkable

135 Own translation, original in Dutch and French: "*terwijl hij wist of moest weten dat zijn deelname zou kunnen bijdragen tot het plegen van een misdaad of wanbedrijf door de terroristische groep; en ayant eu ou en ayant dû avoir connaissance que cette participation pourrait contribuer à commettre un crime ou un délit du groupe terroriste*" (art 140, §1 CC).

136 Memorie van Toelichting bij wetsontwerp van 6 oktober 2003 betreffende terroristische misdrijven, *Parl.St.* Kamer 2003, nr. 51-0258/001, (4) 13; Luik (6e kamer) 18 oktober 2017, *JLMB* 2017, 1878; De Hert and Millen (n 32) 5; De La Serna (n 7) 189; De La Serna (n 15) 216; De Nauw (n 12) 8; Deruyck and De Nauw (n 16) 8; Flore (n 9) 218; Flore (n 14) 144-145; Fransen and Kerkhofs (n 9) 30; Hameeuw (n 15) 9; Traest (n 15) 258; Vandromme and De Roy (n 16) 537; Weyembergh and Kennes, 'Le Titre Iter Du Livre II Du Code Pénal: Des Infractions Terroristes' (n 7) 111; Winants (n 7) 348.

137 Flore (n 9) 218.

138 De La Serna (n 7) 189; De La Serna (n 15) 213; Delhaise (n 9) 42-43; Flore (n 9) 218; Ketels (n 14) 243; Vandromme and De Roy (n 16) 537; Weyembergh and Kennes, 'Le Titre Iter Du Livre II Du Code Pénal: Des Infractions Terroristes' (n 7) 114.

139 Memorie van Toelichting bij wetsontwerp van 6 oktober 2003 betreffende terroristische misdrijven, *Parl.St.* Kamer 2003, nr. 51-0258/001, (4) 13; Delhaise (n 9) 40-41; Delmulle and Guenter (n 15) 4; Fransen and Kerkhofs (n 9) 30.

140 Own translation, original in Dutch and French: "*terwijl hij weet dat zijn deelname bijdraagt tot het plegen van een misdaad of wanbedrijf door de terroristische groep; en ayant connaissance que cette participation contribue à commettre un crime ou un délit du groupe terroriste*" (Memorie van Toelichting bij wetsontwerp van 6 oktober 2003 betreffende terroristische misdrijven, *Parl.St.* Kamer 2003, nr. 51-0258/001, (4) 13). See also: Fransen and Kerkhofs (n 9) 28; Weyembergh and Kennes, 'Le Titre Iter Du Livre II Du Code Pénal: Des Infractions Terroristes' (n 7) 110-111; Winants (n 7) 348.

141 Art 4 (b) Directive (EU) 2017/541 of the European Parliament and of the Council of 15 March 2017 on combating terrorism and replacing Council Framework Decision 2002/475/JHA and amending Council Decision 2005/671/JHA, *OJ* 31 March 2017, L 88/6.

142 Art 2 wet van 14 december 2016 tot wijziging van het Strafwetboek wat betreft de bestraffing van terrorisme, *BS* 22 december 2016, 88017. See also: Deruyck and De Nauw (n 16) 8.

143 As was acknowledged by the Correctional Court Limburg, see: Corr. Limburg (afd. Hasselt) 23 juni 2017, *Limburgs Rechtsleven* 2018, 51.

because at the introduction of the article in 2003, the explanatory memorandum still stated that knowing that a person contributes to the committal of felonies and standard offences by the terrorist group was the decisive criterion.[144] The change was made with the Dutch concept of '*mogelijkheidsbewustzijn*'[145] in mind.[146] This *mogelijkheidsbewustzijn* is present when 'somebody intentionally acts or refrains from acting, and in doing so has imagined a consequence of that behaviour (which is not in itself intended) as [possible], but does not allow himself to be deterred by it. This possibility is accepted by the perpetrator'.[147] This closely resembles the Belgian concept of potential intent.[148] Potential intent is a more flexible version of general intent ('knowingly and willingly') in two ways. First, the knowledge element ('knowingly') is relaxed to knowledge of the possibility of consequences instead of certainty. Second, the will element ('willingly') is relaxed to accepting the consequences instead of actually wanting them.[149] Despite it being more flexible, legal doctrine considers potential intent as a form of general intent.[150] Regarding

144 Memorie van Toelichting bij wetsontwerp van 6 oktober 2003 betreffende terroristische misdrijven, *Parl.St.* Kamer 2003, nr. 51-0258/001, (4) 7. See also: Cesoni (n 119) 240; De Hert and Millen (n 32) 5; Weyembergh and Kennes, 'Domestic Provisions and Case Law: The Belgian Case' (n 7) 154; Winants (n 7) 348.

145 Which literally translates to opportunity awareness. Another term for it can be translated as 'conditional intent'.

146 Toelichting bij wetsvoorstel van 13 januari 2016 tot wijziging van het Strafwetboek wat betreft de bestraffing van terrorisme, *Parl.St.* Kamer 2015-2016, nr. 54-1579/001, 3; Fransen and Kerkhofs (n 9) 35; Winants (n 7) 355.

147 Own translation, original in Dutch: "*iemand opzettelijk iets doet of nalaat en zich daarbij een (op zichzelf niet beoogd) gevolg van die gedraging heeft voorgesteld als [mogelijk], maar zich daardoor niet laat weerhouden. [...] Deze mogelijkheid neemt de dader op de koop toe*" (Conclusie A-G Berger bij Hoge Raad 30 May 1975, ECLI:NL:PHR:1975:AC5594 (bierglasarrest)). See also: Gerechtshof Den Haag 27 October 2016, ECLI:NL:GHDHA:2016:3699; Gerechtshof Amsterdam 24 July 2018, ECLI:NL:GHAMS:2018:2580; JLM Boek, 'Een pleidooi voor het afschaffen van voorwaardelijk opzet' 2016 Strafblad 64, 439-444; AC 'T Hart, Noot Onder Hoge Raad 15 oktober 1996, ECLI:NL:HR:1996:ZD0139; Nico Jörg, Constantijn Kelk and André Klip, *Strafrecht met mate* (14th edition, Wolters Kluwer 2019) 101-103; MJ Kronenberg and B de Wilde, *Grondtrekken van het Nederlandse strafrecht* (8th edition, Kluwer 2020) 60-62; AJ Machielsen, 'Materiële verweren', in MF Attinger et al (eds), *Handboek Strafzaken* (Wolters Kluwer 2018) 36.1.1.1; J Verboon and KAWM Schuurmans, 'Grenzen aan exonereren voor aansprakelijkheid' 2019 ORP 8, 15.

148 Stéphanie De Coensel, *Counter-Terrorism & Criminal Law: A Normative Legitimacy Test of Terrorism-Related Offences on Expression, Information and Movement* (Maklu 2020) 105; J De Groote, 'De Bovengrens Der Fout En de Ondergrens van Het Opzet Met Bijzondere Aandacht Voor Het Eventueel Opzet: Een Doctrinale En Rechtsvergelijkende Analyse' (2017) special number April 2017 Nullum Crimen (NC) 66, 75-79; De Nauw and Deruyck (n 20) 42; Lieven Dupont, *Beginselen van Strafrecht, Deel I* (Acco 1983) 184; Bjorn Ketels, 'De Strafrechtelijke Context van Risicovol Seksueel Gedrag' [2008] Tijdschrift voor Strafrecht 354, 361; Van den Wyngaert, Vandromme and Traest (n 16) 331-332; V Vereecke, 'Het eventueel opzet bij de beoordeling van het oogmerk om te doden' (2019) 2019 Rechtspraak Antwerpen Brussel Gent (RABG) 25, 26-27; J Verhaegen, 'Le Dol Éventuel et Sa Place En Droit Pénal Belge', *Liber Amicorum Hermann Bekaert* (Snoeck-Ducaju & Zoon 1977) 441-442.

149 Dupont states that potential intent is a weakening of the knowledge element and Vereecke states that it is a weakening of the will element. In my opinion both are correct and both elements are weakened.

150 Dirk Dewandeleer, 'Opzettelijk Doden En Opzettelijk Toebrengen van Lichamelijk Letsel (Art. 392 t/m 417 Sw.), Algemeen', *Postal Memorialis – Lexicon strafrecht, strafvordering en bijzondere wetten* (2001) 8-10; Ketels (n 14) 366 and 368; Marlier (n 36) 732; Verhaegen (n 148) 445-446.

article 140, §1 CC, commentators and the case law state that this is a form of special intent.[151] The original *mens rea* seems to indeed be a special intent.[152] Special intent is a specialisation of the will element (a specific goal or evil intention).[153] Knowing you are contributing to an offence by a terrorist group with your participation, and still going ahead with it, implies the will to contribute to an offence by the group, which is more specific than just the will to participate in its activities. However, the changes made in 2016 still need to be factored in. Looking at both changes to the *mens rea* separately, it becomes evident that the second change ('could contribute') is a part of *mogelijkheidsbewustzijn*/ potential intent: the knowledge element is being relaxed to knowledge of the possibility. The first change ('should have known'), by contrast, is not a relaxation of the knowledge element, nor of the will element. The Council of State described it as a 'potential knowing' instead of a 'real knowing'.[154] This 'potential knowing' can only be concluded based on concrete elements of the file and not from abstract criteria.[155] It is a way to prove intent rather than a form of intent[156], a type of 'he should have known so he knew'-reasoning.[157] The combination of both changes results in a relaxation of the knowledge element and a rule of evidence.

The 2016 legislature made the *mens rea* broader and thereby moved it further away from a special intent and toward negligence. Indeed, a phrase such as 'should have known' is reminiscent of negligence. This issue has already been discussed in the context of other

151 This is the case post-2016: Corr. Brussel 8 mei 2017, *onuitg.*, 5; Delhaise (n 9) 42; Fransen and Kerkhofs (n 9) 30; Fransen and Kerkhofs (n 31) 158; An Fransen, Jan Kerkhofs and Pieter Verrest, *Terrorisme: Een analyse van het Belgische en Nederlandse Materieel Strafrecht* (Wolf Legal Publishers 2017) 46, as well as pre-2016: Ketels (n 14) 244; Weyembergh and Kennes, 'Le Titre Iter Du Livre II Du Code Pénal: Des Infractions Terroristes' (n 7) 111.

152 Note that in the past one of the current authors has stated this was a general intent. They now believe this to be wrong. See: Ward Yperman, 'De terroristische misdrijven in de artikelen 137 en 140 Sw.: geen legistieke voltreffer' [2020] Tijdschrift voor Strafrecht 323; Ward Yperman, 'Terrorism Offences in Belgian Criminal Law: Is Less More?' [2021] Queen Mary Law Journal 150.

153 De Nauw and Deruyck (n 20) 42; Dupont (n 148) 182; R Legros, *Opzet* (Larcier 1959) 13; Van den Wyngaert and Vandromme (n 16) 316-317.

154 Advies 59.789/3 van de Raad van State van 19 juli 2016 bij wetsvoorstel van 13 januari 2016 tot wijziging van het Strafwetboek wat betreft de bestraffing van terrorisme, *Parl.St.* Kamer 2015-2016, nr. 54-1579/006, 8.

155 Advies 59.789/3 van de Raad van State van 19 juli 2016 bij wetsvoorstel van 13 januari 2016 tot wijziging van het Strafwetboek wat betreft de bestraffing van terrorisme, *Parl.St.* Kamer 2015-2016, nr. 54-1579/006, 9; Fransen and Kerkhofs (n 9) 35; Winants (n 7) 355.

156 For money laundering and the trade of animals in violation of the hormone regulation (both discussed below) see: De Nauw and Deruyck (n 20) 43.

157 De Groote (n 148) 96-97; W Devroe and A Rombouts, 'Wissel Als Witsel. De Beteugeling van Het Witwassen van Gelden via Geldwissel in Het Belgisch Financieel En Strafrecht (Noot Onder Corr. Antwerpen 23 Februari 1993)' [1994] TRV 199, 204. Van den Wyngaert et al. wonder whether this actually does make difference in terms of proof, see: Van den Wyngaert, Vandromme and Traest (n 16) 336.

offences. The legislation on money laundering contains similar[158] phrasing.[159] This phrasing has its origins in a judgement of the Court of Cassation.[160] Although the wording led to some confusion at first, it is by now generally accepted when it comes to the legislation on money laundering that general intent is required.[161] In the preparatory works, members of parliament even explicitly refer to the concept of potential intent.[162] In the legislation on the trade of animals in violation of the hormone regulation, a similar wording is used to convey a heightened duty of care, which resembles negligence.[163] However, it is clear from the preparatory works of the terrorism legislation that the legislature had the objective of using the same form of intent as in the money laundering legislation, which is general intent.[164]

So, what kind of intent does the post-2016 article 140 CC require? The reasoning above, which infers the specialisation of the will element from a more specific knowledge

158 In Dutch the wording is different, but the meaning is the same. Both Dutch phrases translate to the same thing in English: knew or should have known.

159 Art 505, section 1, 2° and 4°CC; De Groote (n 148) 77. Van Den Wyngaert and Vandromme call it a potential knowing or a 'should have known test', just as the Council of State did for the terrorism legislation (Van den Wyngaert and Vandromme (n 16) 323).

160 Cass. 13 november 1983, *Arr.Cass.* 1984-85, 363.

161 Corr. Antwerpen 23 februari 1993, *T.R.V.* 1994, 195, noot W Devroe and A Rombouts; corr. Antwerpen 14 april 1994, *T.R.V.* 1994, 285, noot F Hellemans; Cesoni (n 119) 256-257; Filiep Deruyck, 'Witwassen', *Strafrecht en strafvordering. Artikelsgewijze commentaar met overzicht van rechtspraak en rechtsleer* (Wolters Kluwer) 245-247; Devroe and Rombouts (n 157) 204; N Hustin-Denies, 'La Législation Belge Sur Le Blachiment de Capiteaux d'origine Criminelle: Un Instrument d'indemnisation Des Victimes et de Lutte Contre La Criminalité Organisée?' [1995] Ann dr Louv 53, 62-63; Bart Spriet and Kristel De Schepper, 'De Nieuwe Witwas(Straf)Wet – Een Schematisch Overzicht' [2009-2010] T Fin R 21; Van den Wyngaert and Vandromme (n 16) 324; Van den Wyngaert, Vandromme and Traest (n 16) 335-336; Raf Verstraeten and Dirk Dewandeleer, 'Witwassen Na de Wet van 7 April 1995: Kan Het Nog Witter?' [1995] Rechtskundig Weekblad 689, 692-693 and 701. *Contra*: L Cornelis and R Verstraeten, 'Mag Er Nog Witgewassen Worden?' [1992] TBH 176, 203-204; D Devos, 'Le Blanchiment Des Capitaux d'origine Criminelle' [1992] Bank Fin 201, 202; F Hellemans, 'Witwassen: Een Strafbaar Maar Lonend Misdrijf? (Noot Onder Corr. Antwerpen 14 April 1994)' [1994] TRV 287, 290.

162 Verslag namens de commissie voor de justitie van 20 juni 1990 bij het ontwerp van wet tot wijziging van de artikelen 42, 43 en 505 van het Strafwetboek en tot invoeging van een artikel 43*bis* in hetzelfde Wetboek, *Gedr.St.* Senaat 1989-90, nr. 890/2, 28; Cornelis and Verstraeten (n 161) 193-205; Verstraeten and Dewandeleer (n 161) 692-693.

163 Antwerpen 18 oktober 1990, *RW* 1990-91, 856, noot B Spriet; Bart Spriet, 'Het Verhandelen van Dieren Waaraan Stoffen Met Hormonale of Antihormonale Werking Zijn Toegediend (Noot Onder Antwerpen 18 Oktober 1990)' [1990] Rechtskundig Weekblad 857, 858; M Sterkens, 'Hormonen: De Misdrijven', *Postal Memorialis – Lexicon strafrecht, strafvordering en bijzondere wetten* (2015) 8. The statute reads: 'of whom it is reasonable to assume that he knows or should know' (own translation, original in Dutch and French: "*van wie men redelijkerwijze kan aannemen dat hij weet of moet weten; celui dont on peut raisonnablement admettre qu'il sait ou devrait savoir*" (art 10, §1, 2°, b wet van 15 juli 1985 betreffende het gebruik bij dieren van stoffen met hormonale, anti-hormonale, beta-adrenergische of produktie-stimulerende werking, *BS* 4 september 1985, 12669)).

164 Verslag van de eerste lezing van 20 oktober 2016 namens de tijdelijke commissie "terrorismebestrijding" bij wetsvoorstel tot wijziging van het Strafwetboek wat betreft de bestraffing van terrorisme, *Parl.St.* Kamer 2015-16, nr. 54-1579/008, 9.

requirement, does not apply anymore. Acting while you know you could contribute to an offence does not seem to necessarily imply the will to contribute, since contribution is only a possibility and not a certainty anymore. Therefore, article 140, §1 CC in its current version has a general intent rather than a special one.[165] Although potential intent, as already discussed, is seen as a form of general intent, the relaxation of the knowledge element it entails is not without danger in this context. The concept 'contributing to the commission of a felony or standard offence by the group' is an abstract one in any case, and further relaxing the knowledge element to 'could contribute' makes it even more abstract and thus more vague.[166]

In 2016 another amendment to the *mens rea* was proposed, but it was not passed: 'while he knew or should have known that the group is a terrorist group'.[167] The Council of State was rather critical for this amendment because it would significantly broaden the offence and give a very wide margin of appreciation to the judge.[168] This addition of a very broad *mens rea* to an already broad *actus reus*, which is mainly defined by the case law, could lead to legality issues, according to the Council of State.[169] It thought that at the very least that the legislation should clarify that involvement in the criminal activities of the terrorist group is required.[170] The wording as it was eventually implemented, was less problematic in the eyes of the Council of State.[171] However, it is striking that a recurring sentence in judgments of French speaking courts is that participation in the activities of a group is punishable 'provided that the participant is aware of the vocation of the movement'.[172] With these words, the courts seem to refer to a more lenient *mens rea* which was not passed by the legislature.

165 See also: Cesoni (n 119) 256.

166 For similar criticism, see: Cesoni (n 119) 240-241; Comité T, 'Raport 2022: Évaluation des mesures visant à lutter contre le terrorisme à la lumière des droits humains', 51.

167 Own translation, original in Dutch and French: "*terwijl hij wist of moest weten dat de groep een terroristische groep is; alors qu'elle savait ou devait savoir que le groupe est un groupe terroriste*".

168 Advies 59.789/3 van de Raad van State van 19 juli 2016 bij wetsvoorstel van 13 januari 2016 tot wijziging van het Strafwetboek wat betreft de bestraffing van terrorisme, *Parl.St.* Kamer 2015-2016, nr. 54-1579/006, 5-7; Fransen and Kerkhofs (n 9) 35; Winants (n 7) 355.

169 Advies 59.789/3 van de Raad van State van 19 juli 2016 bij wetsvoorstel van 13 januari 2016 tot wijziging van het Strafwetboek wat betreft de bestraffing van terrorisme, *Parl.St.* Kamer 2015-2016, nr. 54-1579/006, 7; Winants (n 7) 355.

170 Advies 59.789/3 van de Raad van State van 19 juli 2016 bij wetsvoorstel van 13 januari 2016 tot wijziging van het Strafwetboek wat betreft de bestraffing van terrorisme, *Parl.St.* Kamer 2015-2016, nr. 54-1579/006, 7. See also: Cesoni (n 119) 241.

171 Advies 59.789/3 van de Raad van State van 19 juli 2016 bij wetsvoorstel van 13 januari 2016 tot wijziging van het Strafwetboek wat betreft de bestraffing van terrorisme, *Parl.St.* Kamer 2015-2016, nr. 54-1579/006, 8-9.

172 Own translation, original in French: "*pourvue que celui qui les apporte ait connaisance de la vocation du mouvement*". See for example: Corr. Brussel 9 maart 2016, *onuitg.*, 14; Corr. Brussel 3 mei 2016, *onuitg.*; Corr. Brussel 8 mei 2017, *onuitg.*; Corr. Brussel 29 maart 2018, *onuitg.*; Corr. Mons 14 mei 2018, *onuitg.*; Corr. Brussel 11 juni 2018, *onuitg.*

It is clear that even without the further expansion of the *mens rea* by the legislature, the Council of State's fear of extensive application has become reality. The *actus reus* of the offence is so broad that it can encompass pretty much any action and the *mens rea* is very open and vague as well. As a result, people who in any way support a member of a terrorist group, without supporting the group itself and without wanting their actions to contribute to the committal of a felony or standard offence by the group, are being convicted anyway.[173] Support to a member of the group is being equated to support to the group itself.[174] This is regrettable because many of those people may not be supporters of a terrorist group. They could simply be people who want to help their brother, son or lover, even though the latter have made very questionable and illegal choices. Employing the criminal justice system against a person whose only action is sending clothes to their brother is not the best solution to say the least. As the Council of State feared in 2016, this all leads to a legality issue: it grants very wide discretion to the judge and creates uncertainty in the minds of the person committing these actions about whether or not they are committing an offence.[175] A few participants at the expert seminar were of the opinion that while the legislation is broad, prosecutors and judges are capable of limiting its application. They argued that those practitioners are best placed to make decisions on respectively who to prosecute and convict based on the legislation. We do not agree. The case law shows quite a broad application of the offences, and it is the task of the legislature to abide by the legality principle and write clear legislation. The legislature should be clearer on what the offences entail, and should not have to rely on the common sense of practitioners to limit the application of the legislation. We therefore believe it to be a good idea for the legislature to limit the *mens rea* again to its original wording, which is also what is required by the Directive. This will hopefully be a signal for the courts to require an actual link between the act of participation and the committal of a felony or standard offence by the group. These changes would bring the Belgian legislation back in line with the Directive and

173 See also, dating as far back as 2012: Marchand (n 48) 281-282; Coline Moreau, 'Droit Pénal de l'ennemi versus Droit Pénal Du Citoyen: Réflexions Sur La Fonction Sécuritaire Du Système de Droit Criminel Mise En Avant Par Les Infractions Terroristes Incriminées Par Les Articles 140sexies et 140septies Du Code Pénal' [2021] Revue de Droit Pénal et de Criminologie (Rev. dr. pén.) 101, 113-114.

174 This reduces a person to one aspect of their identity: that of member of the group. However, it could be sensible to emphasise other aspects of their identity (father, brother, etc.) which are not shared with the group, in order to make them break away from the group. If all 'healthy contacts' of a member of a terrorist group are being forced to keep a distance under threat of criminal action, the group member only has the group and its sympathisers to fall back on. This just strengthens their bond with the group and their break with the rest of society.

175 Advies 59.789/3 van de Raad van State van 19 juli 2016 bij wetsvoorstel van 13 januari 2016 tot wijziging van het Strafwetboek wat betreft de bestraffing van terrorisme, *Parl.St.* Kamer 2015-2016, nr. 54-1579/006, 7. This was also stated by Comité T in 2019, see: Comité T, 'Rapport 2019: Le respect des droits humains dans le cadre de la lutte contre le terrorisme: Un chantier en cours', 18-20. See also: Cesoni (n 119) 242.

reduce the scope of the offence. During the expert seminar, however, the view was expressed that this change would not noticeably alter the situation on the ground.

Art. 140bis CC

Actus Reus

Article 140*bis* CC was introduced in 2013 in response to the Council of Europe Convention on the Prevention of Terrorism[176] and the Council Framework Decision 2008/919/JHA[177]. At the moment of its introduction the *actus reus* of the offence was the following: disseminating or otherwise making available to the public a message when such conduct, whether or not directly aimed at the commission of terrorist offences, carries a risk that one or more of these offences may be committed.[178] With this offence the legislature wanted to criminalise both direct and indirect incitement to commit a terrorist offence.[179] The general prohibition of public incitement, which is applicable to all felonies and standard offences, only criminalises direct incitement (to the relevant felonies and offences).[180] Several factors are important for the analysis of whether or not there is a risk that terrorist offences may be committed. These factors are: the perpetrator (e.g. whether he is a person of influence and charisma), the receiver (e.g. the amount of people who receive the message and how easy they are to influence), the nature of the message (e.g. whether the words themselves call for violence or hatred) and the context (e.g. political tension).[181] In the original bill, the risk that one or more terrorist offences is committed was not required.[182] However, the Council of State pointed out that this risk requirement

176 See fn 8. Article 5 of this convention states that parties should criminalise public provocation to commit a terrorist offence.

177 Council Framework Decision 2008/919/JHA of 28 November 2008 amending Framework Decision 2002/475/JHA on combating terrorism *OJ* 9 December 2008, L 330/21-23. For an analysis of this offence in the Framework Decision and Directive, see: De Coensel (n 148) 197-206; Flore (n 14) 147-149. Currently it is article 5 of the Directive.

178 Olivier Bonfond, 'Incitation au terrorisme: qui trop embrasse, mal étreint' (2018) 26 Jurisprudence de Liege, Mons et Bruxelles 1237, 1237-1238.

179 Memorie van Toelichting bij wetsontwerp van 13 november 2012 tot wijziging van Titel 1ter van het Strafwetboek, *Parl.St.* Kamer 2012-2013, nr. 53-2502/001, (4) 11; Delhaise (n 9) 48; Ketels (n 14) 250-251; Winants (n 7) 350.

180 Art 66 CC; Memorie van Toelichting bij wetsontwerp van 13 november 2012 tot wijziging van Titel 1ter van het Strafwetboek, *Parl.St.* Kamer 2012-2013, nr. 53-2502/001, (4) 11; Weyembergh and Kennes, 'Domestic Provisions and Case Law: The Belgian Case' (n 7) 151-152.

181 Memorie van Toelichting bij wetsontwerp van 13 november 2012 tot wijziging van Titel 1ter van het Strafwetboek, *Parl.St.* Kamer 2012-2013, nr. 53-2502/001, (4) 12-13. Delhaise (n 9) 51; Fransen and Kerkhofs (n 9) 52-53; Ketels (n 14) 251; Van Deuren (n 18) 509; Winants (n 7) 350.

182 Memorie van Toelichting bij wetsontwerp van 13 november 2012 tot wijziging van Titel 1ter van het Strafwetboek, *Parl.St.* Kamer 2012-2013, nr. 53-2502/001, (19) 19-20; Winants (n 7) 354.

was part of the Convention and Framework Decision, and that omitting it might lead the offence to violate the freedom of speech.[183] The legislature amended the bill to remedy this issue, stating that 'it is imperative to specify that the criminalisation of public incitement to commit terrorist acts must not lead to the punishment of acts which have no connection whatsoever with terrorism and would thus create the danger of restricting the freedom of speech. Therefore, it is important to stress that these offences may only be aimed at those situations in which there are serious indications that a danger exists that a terrorist offence would be committed.'[184]

Three years later, however, the legislature changed his mind again. In 2016, vaguely referring to the altered security situation, the foreign terrorist fighter problem and the role of social media in radicalisation, he decided to remove the risk requirement because it made it too difficult to provide the evidence required.[185] The Council of State suggested that because the new wording also included less serious cases, the legislature should verify whether the minimum sentence should not be lowered.[186] The legislature refused this because he thought it necessary to decisively tackle the problem of public incitement to terrorism, especially in light of the development of social media.[187]

When article 140*bis* CC was introduced into the Criminal Code, an appeal for annulment was filed with the Constitutional Court (see also below). One of the arguments

183 Advies nr. 51 806/3 van de Raad van State van 18 september 2012 bij wetsontwerp van 13 november 2012 tot wijziging van Titel 1ter van het Strafwetboek, *Parl.St.* Kamer 2012-2013, nr. 53-2502/001, (22) 25-27. See also: Cesoni (n 119) 246; Jan Velaers, 'La Lutte Contre Le Terrorisme et Les Droits de l'homme: Dévelopements Récents En Belgique' in P D'Argent, D Renders and M Verdussen (eds), *Les Visages de L'Etat: Liber Amicorum Yves Lejeune* (Bruylant 2017) 778-779; Winants (n 7) 354.

184 Own translation, original in Dutch and French: "*Er moet absoluut nader worden bepaald dat de strafbaarstelling van de publieke aanzetting tot het plegen van terroristische handelingen niet mag leiden tot de bestraffing van handelingen die geen enkel verband hebben met het terrorisme en waardoor de vrijheid van meningsuiting gevaar loopt aangetast te worden. Daarom is het belangrijk te beklemtonen dat deze strafbaarstelling slechts die situatie mag beogen waarin er ernstige aanwijzingen zijn dat een gevaar bestaat dat een terroristisch misdrijf gepleegd zou worden; Il est indispensable de préciser que l'incrimination de la provocation publique à commettre des actes de terrorisme ne peut pas aboutir à la répression d'actes n'ayant aucun rapport avec le terrorisme et risquant de porter atteinte à la liberté d'expression. C'est pourquoi, il est important de souligner que cette incrimination ne doit viser que la situation dans laquelle des indices sérieux indiquent qu'il existe un risque qu'une infraction terroriste soit commise.*" (Memorie van Toelichting bij wetsontwerp van 13 november 2012 tot wijziging van Titel 1ter van het Strafwetboek, *Parl.St.* Kamer 2012-2013, nr. 53-2502/001, (4) 12).

185 Memorie van Toelichting bij wetsontwerp van 6 juli 2016 houdende diverse bepalingen ter bestrijding van terrorisme (III), *Parl.St.* Kamer 2015-2016, nr. 54-1951/001, (4) 8; Bonfond (n 178) 1238-1239; Cesoni (n 119) 245; Delhaise (n 9) 49; Deruyck and De Nauw (n 16) 12; Fransen and Kerkhofs (n 9) 51; Winants (n 7) 353-354.

186 Advies nr. 59 147/3 van de Raad van State van 22 april 2016 bij wetsontwerp van 6 juli 2016 houdende diverse bepalingen ter bestrijding van terrorisme (III), *Parl.St.* Kamer 2015-2016, nr. 54-1951/001, (19) 24-25; Bonfond (n 178) 1240; Fransen and Kerkhofs (n 9) 52.

187 Memorie van Toelichting bij wetsontwerp van 6 juli 2016 houdende diverse bepalingen ter bestrijding van terrorisme (III), *Parl.St.* Kamer 2015-2016, nr. 54-1951/001, (4) 8; Deruyck and De Nauw (n 16) 11; Fransen and Kerkhofs (n 9) 52.

made for annulment was based on freedom of expression. The Constitutional Court stated that freedom of expression is one of the pillars of a democratic society and therefore exceptions need to be interpreted strictly.[188] Article 140*bis* CC is one of those exceptions and must comply with article 10.2 ECHR.[189] It must therefore be demonstrated that the restrictions are necessary in a democratic society, that they correspond to an overriding societal need, and that they remain proportionate to the legitimate objectives they pursue.[190] The Court stated that it is necessary to protect society against those who would undercut it through violence and terrorism. The government may limit freedom of expression to attain that goal. The legislature had stated it did not aim to punish actions that are not connected to terrorism. This, in combination with the special intent required and the fact that the judge needs to take into account the person who spreads the message, the person who receives it, and the nature and the context of the message, meant that although the judge had a wide margin of appreciation, article 140*bis* CC did not violate the freedom of expression.[191] After the removal of the risk requirement, the article was brought before the Constitutional Court again. The Court made the same analysis of limitations to the freedom of expression. However, this time around the Court's conclusion was that article 140*bis* CC did violate the freedom of expression and the article removing the risk requirement was annulled.[192] The need to facilitate the proof of the offence does not justify the imposition of an imprisonment and fine when there are no serious indications that there is a risk of a terrorist offence. Therefore, article 140*bis* CC, without the risk requirement, is not necessary in a democratic society and limits the freedom of expression unduly.[193] In closing, the Court remarked that both the Framework Decision and the new Directive include such a risk requirement.[194] Because of the annulment of the part of the

188 GwH 28 januari 2015, 9/2015, *TVW* 2015, 179, B.24.

189 GwH 28 januari 2015, 9/2015, *TVW* 2015, 179, B.25.3.

190 GwH 28 januari 2015, 9/2015, *TVW* 2015, 179, B.24 and B.25.3.

191 GwH 28 januari 2015, 9/2015, *TVW* 2015, 179, B.25.4-B.25.5. See also: Comité T, 'Rapport 2019: Le respect des droits humains dans le cadre de la lutte contre le terrorisme: Un chantier en cours', 16; Bonfond (n 178) 1238; Dejemeppe and Rigaux (n 52) 765-766; Ketels (n 14) 252-253; Spreutels and Velu (n 52) 141-142; Velaers (n 183) 779.

192 GwH 15 maart 2018, 31/2018, *NjW* 2018, 477, B.8. See also: Comité T, 'Rapport 2019: Le respect des droits humains dans le cadre de la lutte contre le terrorisme: Un chantier en cours', 16; De Coensel (n 148) 207; Dejemeppe and Rigaux (n 52) 765-766; Deruyck and De Nauw (n 16) 12; Fransen and Kerkhofs (n 9) 53-54; Ketels (n 14) 248-250; Winants (n 7) 354.

193 GwH 15 maart 2018, 31/2018, *NjW* 2018, 477, B.7.6. See also: Bonfond (n 178) 1239-1240; Cesoni (n 119) 246; Delhaise (n 9) 49; Spreutels and Velu (n 52) 143; Winants (n 7) 354; Ward Yperman, 'Terro III dan toch een stap te ver' [2018] Nieuw Juridisch Weekblad 480.

194 GwH 15 maart 2018, 31/2018, *NjW* 2018, 477, B.7.7. See also: Bonfond (n 178) 1240; Cesoni (n 119) 246; Delhaise (n 9) 50; Winants (n 7) 354.

article that deleted the risk requirement, the risk requirement was revived and is part of article 140*bis* CC again.[195]

This raises questions under the principle of non-retroactivity, which is enshrined within the legality principle.[196] The principle entails that new legislation which elevates sentences, creates new offences or expands the scope of an existing offence, cannot be applied to facts that took place before this legislation was in force, even if it is in force when those facts are tried.[197] For article 140*bis* CC this means that the deletion of the risk requirement should not work retroactively. Annulment, on the other hand, works retroactively. Once annulled, a piece of legislation disappears from the legal order *ex tunc* (meaning that the provision ought legally to be considered to never having existed). Anybody who was convicted under this legislation, can start a procedure of repeal.[198]

The Criminal Code criminalises the dissemination or making available in any other way of a message to the public. This implies a positive action, and refraining from undertaking a certain action does therefore not suffice.[199] In order to be punishable, the incitement does not have to be aimed at a specific person or group of people (*intuitu personae*).[200] Therefore, incitement can also happen over the internet, as long as it is public.[201] Any mode of dissemination can be punishable.[202] The message has to be made available to the public, which means that a conversation between two people is probably not covered.[203] According to the case law, however, individual messages to people can be public because the internet allows them to spread and multiply quickly.[204] In addition, the incitement does not have to be aimed at the committal of a concrete offence.[205] Nor does the incited offence actually have to take place.[206] The term 'message' is not defined, so it

195 Ketels (n 14) 250; J Petersen, 'Naar nieuwe verbale uitingsmisdrijven in de strijd tegen terreur?' (2019) 14 Nullum Crimen (NC) 50, 56.

196 De Nauw and Deruyck (n 20) 22; Franklin Kuty, *Principes Généraux Du Droit Pénal Belge. Tome 1: La Loi Pénale* (3rd edn, Larcier 2018) 69; Tulkens and others (n 16) 274.

197 De Nauw and Deruyck (n 20) 22-23; N De Nil, F Deruyck and J Meese, 'Misdrijven', *Strafrecht geannoteerd* (die Keure 2020) 273-274; Kuty (n 195) 297-301; Tulkens and others (n 16) 274-280; Van den Wyngaert, Vandromme and Traest (n 16) 110-118.

198 Raoul Declercq, *Beginselen van Strafrechtspleging* (6de herwerkte ed., Kluwer 2014) 1839-1845; Yperman, 'Terro III dan toch een stap te ver' (n 193) 481.

199 Delhaise (n 9) 50.

200 Fransen and Kerkhofs (n 9) 55; Ketels (n 14) 253; Winants (n 7) 350.

201 Memorie van Toelichting bij wetsontwerp van 13 november 2012 tot wijziging van Titel 1ter van het Strafwetboek, *Parl.St.* Kamer 2012-2013, nr. 53-2502/001, (4) 13; Deruyck and De Nauw (n 16) 11; Fransen and Kerkhofs (n 9) 55; Winants (n 7) 350.

202 Delhaise (n 9) 50.

203 Delhaise (n 9) 50-51.

204 Corr. West-Vlaanderen (afd. Brugge) 26 juli 2018, *onuitg.*, 10; Fransen and Kerkhofs (n 9) 60-61.

205 Delhaise (n 9) 52; Fransen and Kerkhofs (n 9) 55-56; Ketels (n 14) 253; Winants (n 7) 350.

206 Amendement nr. 1 van 7 juli 2016 bij wetsvoorstel van 13 januari 2016 tot wijziging van het Strafwetboek wat betreft de bestraffing van terrorisme, *Parl.St.* Kamer 2015-2016, nr. 54-1579/005, 6; Deruyck and De Nauw (n 16) 11; Van Deuren (n 18) 508; Winants (n 7) 350.

must be interpreted in its general sense: as a form of communication that is transmitted, be that orally or written.[207]

Mens Rea

A special intent is required, that being 'the intention of inciting the commission of one of the offences referred to in article 137 or 140*sexies*, with the exception of the offence referred to in article 137, § 3, 6°'.[208] The article thus refers to terrorism *sensu stricto*, with the exception of threatening a terrorist offence, and the offence of traveling for terrorist purposes (see below). This corresponds to the Directive, except for traveling, which is not part of the *mens rea* in the Directive. Traveling for terrorist purposes was not part of the original *mens rea* in the Belgian legislation either, since the offence did not exist yet in 2013. It was added when the offence was amended in 2016.[209] In doing so, the Belgian legislature took a more repressive approach than the Directive. Since the traveling offence has a very broad *mens rea* itself, the *mens rea* of article 140*bis* CC is similarly broad, and significantly broader than that of the Directive. In 2016, the legislature also added the words 'directly or indirectly' after the word intention. This was because, when removing the risk requirement, the legislature also removed the reference to indirect incitement. To clarify this was still covered by the offence, they explicitly inserted it into the *mens rea*.[210] However, after the Constitutional Court judgment which reinstated the risk requirement, this idea of 'direct or indirect incitement' was part of the offence twice.[211] Therefore, the

207 According to Van Dale, the official Dutch dictionary (*boodschap: mondeling of schriftelijk bericht; bericht: overgebrachte mededeling, inlichting*). According to Delhaise, the French definition is: "*une information, une nouvelle transmise à une persone*" (Delhaise (n 9) 51.). These two definitions match and are translated in the text above.

208 Own translation, original in Dutch and French: "*met het oogmerk aan te zetten tot het plegen van één van de in de artikelen 137 of 140sexies bedoelde misdrijven, met uitzondering van het in artikel 137, § 3, 6°, bedoelde misdrijf; avec l'intention d'inciter à la commission d'une des infractions visées aux articles 137 ou 140sexies, à l'exception de celle visée à l'article 137, § 3, 6°*" (art 140bis CC). See also: Memorie van Toelichting bij wetsontwerp van 13 november 2012 tot wijziging van Titel 1ter van het Strafwetboek, *Parl.St.* Kamer 2012-2013, nr. 53-2502/001, (4) 13; Delhaise (n 9) 52; Fransen and Kerkhofs (n 9) 56; Ketels (n 14) 251; Winants (n 7) 350.

209 Memorie van Toelichting bij wetsontwerp van 6 juli 2016 houdende diverse bepalingen ter bestrijding van terrorisme (III), *Parl.St.* Kamer 2015-2016, nr. 54-1951/001, (4) 7; Delhaise (n 9) 49; Deruyck and De Nauw (n 16) 12; Fransen and Kerkhofs (n 9) 51; Petersen (n 195) 56.

210 Memorie van Toelichting bij wetsontwerp van 6 juli 2016 houdende diverse bepalingen ter bestrijding van terrorisme (III), *Parl.St.* Kamer 2015-2016, nr. 54-1951/001, (4) 8; Delhaise (n 9) 49; Fransen and Kerkhofs (n 9) 57.

211 Fransen and Kerkhofs (n 9) 54-55; Winants (n 7) 354; Yperman, 'Terro III dan toch een stap te ver' (n 193).

legislature removed it from the *mens rea* again in 2019, returning to the original text of 2013.[212]

Constitutional Court

As explained above, the introduction of article 140*bis* CC was challenged in front of the Constitutional Court based on the freedom of expression and freedom of association. In its judgment of 28 January 2015, the Court dismissed this claim.

In that same judgment, the Court also had to rule on the application of the legality principle on article 140*bis* CC. The applicants thought that words such as 'indirectly incite', 'indirectly provoke' and 'risk' were insufficiently clear.[213] The Constitutional Court explains the legality principle and reiterates that it does allow for the judge to have a margin of appreciation.[214] The Court then notes that the wording of article 140*bis* CC is identical to that of the Framework Decision on which the article is based.[215] It is true that the legislature did not define the aforementioned terms. The Court of Cassation has already stated that if that is the case, terms need to be interpreted according to their usual meaning.[216] The Constitutional Court explains that the usual meanings of 'incite', 'aim' and 'risk' are clear.[217] Finally, once more referring to articles 139, section 2 and 141*ter* CC as proof of the constant care the legislature takes to protect fundamental freedoms when fighting terrorism, the Court states that article 140*bis* CC grants judge a large margin of appreciation, but no autonomous competence.[218] Therefore, the legality principle has not been violated.[219]

As mentioned above, the Constitutional Court had to rule on article 140*bis* CC again approximately three years later. The disputed piece of legislation[220] had made three changes to article 140*bis* CC. Its second article introduced the words 'directly or indirectly' in the

212 Art 76 wet van 5 mei 2019 houdende diverse bepalingen in strafzaken en inzake erediensten, en tot wijziging van de wet van 28 mei 2002 betreffende de euthanasie en van het Sociaal Strafwetboek, *BS* 24 mei 2019, 50023; Toelichting bij wetsvoorstel van 6 februari 2019 houdende diverse bepalingen in strafzaken en inzake erediensten, *Parl.St.* Kamer 2018-2019, nr. 54-3515/001, (3) 103; Deruyck and De Nauw (n 16) 13; Winants (n 7) 357.

213 GwH 28 januari 2015, 9/2015, *TVW* 2015, 179, B.9.

214 GwH 28 januari 2015, 9/2015, *TVW* 2015, 179, B.13.

215 GwH 28 januari 2015, 9/2015, *TVW* 2015, 179, B.15-B.16.

216 Cass. 27 april 1999, *Arr.Cass.* 1999, 568; Cass. 8 oktober 2014, P.14.0955.F.

217 GwH 28 januari 2015, 9/2015, *TVW* 2015, 179, B.17.1-B.17.3.

218 GwH 28 januari 2015, 9/2015, *TVW* 2015, 179, B.18-B.19.

219 GwH 28 januari 2015, 9/2015, *TVW* 2015, 179, B.20. See also: Dejemeppe and Rigaux (n 52) 762-763; Ketels (n 14) 252; Spreutels and Velu (n 52) 133-135; Winants (n 7) 351. For criticism on this conclusion, see: Cesoni (n 119) 234-235.

220 Wet van 3 augustus 2016 houdende diverse bepalingen ter bestrijding van terrorisme (III), *BS* 11 augustus 2016, 50973.

mens rea (1°), added the offence of article 140*sexies* CC to the *mens rea* (2°) and deleted the risk requirement (3°). The introduction of article 140*sexies* CC into the *mens rea* (2°) was not challenged by the appellants and therefore, the Court did not rule on this part of the article. The other two sections (1° and 3°) were challenged. The deletion of the risk requirement was found in violation of the freedom of expression and therefore annulled (see above). The appellant also alleged a violation of the freedom of association. However, since the section (3°) of the article was already annulled based on the freedom of expression, the Court did not analyse the freedom of association.[221] Breaches of the legality principle and proportionality principle were also put forward, but the Court likewise ruled that they required no analysis since the section (3°) had already been annulled.[222] The applicants also claimed that the section of the article that introduced 'directly or indirectly' into the *mens rea* (1°) violated the legality principle. The Court, however, stated that it was only a formal adjustment which did not change the interpretation of the article. Therefore, the legality principle had not been violated.[223]

ART. 140*TER* CC

Actus Reus

Article 140*ter* CC criminalises recruitment for terrorist purposes. It was also introduced in 2013, in the wake of the Council of Europe Convention and the update of the Framework Decision.[224] The article criminalises anybody who recruits another person to commit, or contribute to the commission, of one of the offences in article 137, 140 or 140*sexies* CC, with the exception of article 137, §3, 6° CC. This is, therefore, terrorism *sensu stricto*, with the exception of threatening terrorism, the offences relating to terrorist groups, and traveling for terrorist purposes (see below).[225] The preparatory works mention recruitment to become a member of a terrorist group.[226] However, membership in itself is not

221 GwH 15 maart 2018, 31/2018, *NjW* 2018, 477, B.9.

222 GwH 15 maart 2018, 31/2018, *NjW* 2018, 477, B.12 and B.15.

223 GwH 15 maart 2018, 31/2018, *NjW* 2018, 477, B.13.2-B.14.

224 Art 6 Council of Europe Convention on the Prevention of Terrorism. Article 5 of which states that parties should criminalise public provocation to commit a terrorist offence. Council Framework Decision 2008/919/JHA of 28 November 2008 amending Framework Decision 2002/475/JHA on combating terrorism, *OJ* 9 December 2008, L 330/21-23; Memorie van Toelichting bij wetsontwerp van 13 november 2012 tot wijziging van Titel 1ter van het Strafwetboek, *Parl.St.* Kamer 2012-2013, nr. 53-2502/001, (4) 14; Ketels (n 14) 254. For a short analysis of this offence in the Framework Decision, see: Flore (n 14) 149-150.

225 Delhaise (n 9) 55; Fransen and Kerkhofs (n 9) 61; Winants (n 7) 351. It is now article 6 of the Directive.

226 Memorie van Toelichting bij wetsontwerp van 13 november 2012 tot wijziging van Titel 1ter van het Strafwetboek, *Parl.St.* Kamer 2012-2013, nr. 53-2502/001, (4) 14. See also: De La Serna (n 15) 223.

punishable under article 140 CC (see above). The reference to article 140*sexies* CC was added in 2016, after this offence was created.[227] As was the case for article *140bis* CC, the Belgian legislature expanded upon the Directive by this addition. The section reading 'or contribution to the commission', was added in 2019.[228] This wording is part of the Directive on combatting terrorism, but was not part of the Belgian legislation yet.[229] If necessary, these actions could be prosecuted under article 140 CC or as aiding and abetting (*strafbare deelneming; participation punissable*).[230] However, since 2016 it was part of the offence in article 141 CC (see below) and to maintain uniformity, the legislature decided to also introduce it in article 140*ter* CC.[231] This addition, while maintaining uniformity, did so at the cost of increased overlap between offences.[232] There will be very few situations of recruiting a person to contribute to the commission of a terrorist offence, which are not covered by article 140 CC. This situation will always involve three people (the recruiter, the contributor to the ultimately intended offence and its perpetrator), and three people is the threshold for a terrorist group. Even if there is no terrorist group, the rules on aiding and abetting apply both to the recruitment offence and to the ultimately intended terrorist offence. Instead of criminalising new situations, the addition of this phrase predominantly brought situations within the ambit of this offence which were already covered by other terrorist offences. An exact definition of recruitment has not been provided by the legislature. In the context of human trafficking, the Court of Cassation has stated that recruitment is enlisting recruits or getting someone to join a group.[233] For the offence of recruitment to take place, it is not required that the recruited person actually commits one

227 Art 3 wet van 3 augustus 2016 houdende diverse bepalingen ter bestrijding van terrorisme (III), *BS* 11 augustus 2016, 50973; Deruyck and De Nauw (n 16) 12; Fransen and Kerkhofs (n 9) 62; Ketels (n 14) 256; Winants (n 7) 353.

228 Art 77, 1° wet 5 mei 2019 houdende diverse bepalingen in strafzaken en inzake erediensten, en tot wijziging van de wet van 28 mei 2002 betreffende de euthanasie en van het Sociaal Strafwetboek, *BS* 24 mei 2019, 50023; De Coensel (n 23) 212.

229 Art 6 Directive (EU) 2017/541 of the European Parliament and of the Council of 15 March 2017 on combating terrorism and replacing Council Framework Decision 2002/475/JHA and amending Council Decision 2005/671/JHA, *OJ* 31 March 2017, L 88/6-L 88/21; Winants (n 7) 357.

230 Toelichting bij wetsvoorstel van 6 februari 2019 houdende diverse bepalingen in strafzaken en inzake erediensten, *Parl.St.* Kamer 2018-2019, nr. 54-3515/001, (3) 104; Comité T, 'Rapport 2020: Evaluation des mesures visant à lutter contre le terrorisme à la lumière des droits humains', 15.

231 Toelichting bij wetsvoorstel van 6 februari 2019 houdende diverse bepalingen in strafzaken en inzake erediensten, *Parl.St.* Kamer 2018-2019, nr. 54-3515/001, (3) 104-105; Comité T, 'Rapport 2020: Evaluation des mesures visant à lutter contre le terrorisme à la lumière des droits humains', 15.

232 See also: Cesoni (n 119) 246-247.

233 Cass. 8 oktober 2014, P.14.0955.F; Delhaise (n 9) 55.

of the offences they were recruited for.[234] What is required, is that the recruiter successfully approaches the other person, meaning they convinced them to perpetrate the offence.[235]

The usefulness of including article 140 CC in the list of punishable offences for recruitment can be questioned. Will recruiting somebody to participate in the activities of a terrorist group not always also be a participation in the activities of that group? This inclusion therefore seems a bit futile. The Court of Appeal of Liège, for example, had a case of recruitment to join a terrorist group (taking place after 2013), which was only prosecuted under article 140 CC.[236]

Mens Rea

Article 140*ter* CC does not explicitly include a *mens rea*. However, this does not mean that one is not required. Under Belgian criminal law, offences always require both *actus reus* and *mens rea*.[237] The Directive states that the offence must be committed intentionally. However, as the Belgian legislation requires special intent for the majority of terrorist offences, it would only be logical to also require it here. It is therefore generally accepted that 'recruitment to commit', one of the offences mentioned above, actually means 'recruitment with the aim of seeing one of these offences being committed'.[238] This is a type of special intent.[239] As was explained previously, the traveling offence was added to the *mens rea* in 2016, expanding it beyond the scope of offence in the Directive. The Belgian offence is therefore broader than the one in the Directive.

---

234 Memorie van Toelichting bij wetsontwerp van 13 november 2012 tot wijziging van Titel 1ter van het Strafwetboek, *Parl.St.* Kamer 2012-2013, nr. 53-2502/001, (4) 14; amendement nr. 1 van 7 juli 2016 bij wetsvoorstel van 13 januari 2016 tot wijziging van het Strafwetboek wat betreft de bestraffing van terrorisme, *Parl.St.* Kamer 2015-2016, nr. 54-1579/005, 6; De La Serna (n 15) 223; Delhaise (n 9) 55; Deruyck and De Nauw (n 16) 11; Fransen and Kerkhofs (n 9) 61; Van Deuren (n 18) 508; Winants (n 7) 351.

235 Memorie van Toelichting bij wetsontwerp van 13 november 2012 tot wijziging van Titel 1ter van het Strafwetboek, *Parl.St.* Kamer 2012-2013, nr. 53-2502/001, (4) 14; De La Serna (n 15) 223-224; Fransen and Kerkhofs (n 9) 61; Deruyck and De Nauw (n 16) 11; Ketels (n 14) 254; Winants (n 7) 351. Delhaise talks about the proposal being received (*"la proposition du recruteur est accueillie par la personne approchée"* (Delhaise (n 9) 55.)).

236 Luik (6e kamer) 18 oktober 2017, *JLMB* 2017, 1878.

237 Cass. 12 mei 1987, *Arr.Cass.* 1986-87, 1194, concl. Du Jardin; Cass. 13 december 1994, *RW* 1995-96, 533, noot B Spriet; De Nil, Deruyck and Meese (n 197) 269; Bart Spriet, 'Elk Misdrijf - Ook Dat Uit Het Bijzonder Strafrecht - Vereist Een Moreel of Schuldbestanddeel (Noot Onder Cass. 13 December 1994)' (1995) 1995-96 Rechtskundig Weekblad 533; Tulkens and others (n 16) 474-475; Van den Wyngaert, Vandromme and Traest (n 16) 192; Winants (n 7) 359. In special criminal statues, it is possible, however, that indications of the existence of the *mens rea* are derived from the proven existence of the *actus reus*. See: Cass. 24 februari 2014, S.13.0031.N; Cass. 8 april 2008, P.08.0006.N; Cass. 12 mei 1987, *Arr.Cass.* 1986-87, 1194, concl. Du Jardin; Spriet, 'Elk Misdrijf - Ook Dat Uit Het Bijzonder Strafrecht - Vereist Een Moreel of Schuldbestanddeel (Noot Onder Cass. 13 December 1994)' 536-537.

238 Delhaise (n 9) 56; Fransen and Kerkhofs (n 9) 62-63; Winants (n 7) 351.

239 Ketels (n 14) 256.

Constitutional Court

In the same judgement of 28 January 2018 in which the Constitutional Court ruled on article 140*bis*, it also ruled on article 140*ter* CC. With regard to article 140*ter* CC, the applicants claimed it violated the legality principle for two reasons. Firstly, the wording of the article was not clear enough. Secondly, sentencing was unforeseeable because an offence of recruiting people for foreign armies already existed with a sentence of three months to two years imprisonment.[240] The Constitutional Court first refers to the Council of Europe Treaty and the Framework Decision on which the article is based. It then reiterates that article 140*ter* CC requires that the proposal was accepted by the person being recruited. Therefore, the article does not make it possible to convict every person who approaches another person with a discourse that is considered unlawful, radical or extreme by the prosecuting authority.[241] Article 140*ter* CC is sufficiently accurate and clear, ensuring that anyone can know which conduct is punishable and which sentence is provided for. The fact that it can be difficult for the prosecuting authorities to furnish the evidence does not change this, nor does the fact that the same conduct can be punished under a different article of the Criminal Code.[242] Hence, there is no violation of the legality principle.[243] The second argument does not change this. The circumstances of the two offences are different and, even then, concurrence (*samenloop; concours*) is possible.[244] A person who recruits another person for a foreign army in circumstances that fall within the scope of article 140*ter* CC, can therefore know he can be sentenced to the higher sentence.

The applicants also alleged that article 140*ter* CC violated both the freedom of expression and the freedom of association. The Court stated that the article did not even restrict the freedom of expression and therefore did not need to be analysed in this regard.[245] As to the freedom of association, while it is restricted by the article, this restriction is necessary in a democratic society in order to protect national security, public safety and public order, to prevent criminal offences, or to protect the rights and freedoms of others.[246] The Court is thus of the opinion that the restriction of the right to association is justified.[247]

---

240 Art 1 wet 1 augustus 1979 betreffende diensten bij een vreemde leger- of troepenmacht die zich op het grondgebied van een vreemde Staat bevindt, *BS* 24 augustus 1979, 9272.

241 GwH 28 januari 2015, 9/2015, *TVW* 2015, 179, B.30.1.

242 GwH 28 januari 2015, 9/2015, *TVW* 2015, 179, B.30.2.

243 GwH 28 januari 2015, 9/2015, *TVW* 2015, 179, B.33. See also: Ketels (n 14) 254-255; Spreutels and Velu (n 52) 136; Winants (n 7) 351.

244 GwH 28 januari 2015, 9/2015, *TVW* 2015, 179, B.31.2-B.31.3.

245 GwH 28 januari 2015, 9/2015, *TVW* 2015, 179, B.36.

246 GwH 28 januari 2015, 9/2015, *TVW* 2015, 179, B.37. See also: Ketels (n 14) 255-256.

247 Spreutels and Velu (n 52) 144; Winants (n 7) 351-352.

ART. 140QUATER CC

Actus Reus

Article 140*quater* CC was also introduced in 2013, in the wake of the Council of Europe Convention and the update of the Framework Decision.[248] For both the *actus reus* and *mens rea* of this offence, the Belgian legislature passed wording very similar to the European instruments.[249] The *actus reus* of article 140*quater* CC is to instruct or provide training in the manufacturing or use of explosives, firearms or other weapons or harmful or dangerous substances or in other specific methods and techniques.[250] This is a non-exhaustive list, so any training or instruction that is provided with the required *mens rea* can fall within the scope of this article. The preparatory works provide as extra examples of training in the sense of article 140*quater* CC flying or driving lessons, or lessons on how to hack a website.[251] The training provided can be theoretic or practical.[252] Both 'instruct' and 'provide' imply an action on behalf of the perpetrator.[253]

Mens Rea

The *mens rea* is a special intent, that being: with a view to commit, or contribute to the commission of, one of the offences referred to in article 137, with the exception of the offence referred to in article 137, §3, 6° CC.[254] Therefore, the training has to be provided with the view to commit or contribute to the commission of terrorism *sensu stricto*, once more with the exception of threatening a terrorist attack. This is the same as in the Framework Decision.[255] Here too, the phrase 'or contribute to the commission of' was

248 Art 1 Council Framework Decision 2008/919/JHA of 28 November 2008 amending Framework Decision 2002/475/JHA on combating terrorism, *OJ* 9 December 2008, L 330/21-23; art 7 Council of Europe Convention on the Prevention of Terrorism; Ketels (n 14) 256.

249 Art 7 Directive (EU) 2017/541 Directive (EU) 2017/541 of the European Parliament and of the Council of 15 March 2017 on combating terrorism and replacing Council Framework Decision 2002/475/JHA and amending Council Decision 2005/671/JHA, *OJ* 31 March 2017, L 88/6. See also: Fransen and Kerkhofs (n 9) 63.

250 Art 140*quater* CC. See also: Flore (n 14) 150.

251 Memorie van Toelichting bij wetsontwerp van 13 november 2012 tot wijziging van Titel 1ter van het Strafwetboek, *Parl.St.* Kamer 2012-2013, nr. 53-2502/001, (4) 15; De La Serna (n 15) 224; Deruyck and De Nauw (n 16) 11; Fransen and Kerkhofs (n 9) 64; Ketels (n 14) 257; Winants (n 7) 351.

252 Delhaise (n 9) 58.

253 Delhaise (n 9) 57.

254 Art 140*quater* CC; Memorie van Toelichting bij wetsontwerp van 13 november 2012 tot wijziging van Titel 1ter van het Strafwetboek, *Parl.St.* Kamer 2012-2013, nr. 53-2502/001, (4) 15; De La Serna (n 15) 224; Delhaise (n 9) 58; Fransen and Kerkhofs (n 9) 65; Ketels (n 14) 257.

255 Fransen and Kerkhofs (n 9) 64.

added in 2019[256], as it is part of the wording of the Directive and the legislature wanted to increase coherence.[257] Concreteness is not required, meaning that the person providing the training does not need to know the exact terrorist offence for which the training is provided.[258] He does need to know, however, that the aim is to perpetrate one of the aforementioned offences.[259] Then again, it is not required that the offence for which the training was provided actually takes place.[260]

Constitutional Court

The case which led to the aforementioned Constitutional Court judgment of 28 January 2015 also concerned article 140*quater* CC. The applicants deemed the wording of article 140*quater* CC unclear. The Court again started by referring to the Council of Europe Treaty and the Framework Decision.[261] The Court notes that the preparatory works stated that the article does not only cover providing training for methods specific for terrorist purposes, such as weapons training, but also other methods such as flying or driving lessons or hacking websites. The Framework Decision, however, only targets training for specific methods and techniques, meaning, according to the Court, methods and techniques specific to committing terrorist offences. The Court took into consideration the wording of the article: 'training in the manufacturing or use of explosives, firearms or other weapons or harmful or dangerous substances or in other specific methods and techniques, with a view to commit or contribute to the commission of one of the offences referred to in article 137, with the exception of the offence referred to in article 137, §3, 6° CC'. It found the *actus reus* sufficiently accurate and clear, since the potential ambiguity of the preparatory works cannot have precedence over the clear wording of the statute.[262] The *mens rea* is also sufficiently accurate and clear. The offence only exists when the person providing the training knows that this is done with the intention to commit one of the

256 Art 78, 1° wet 5 mei 2019 houdende diverse bepalingen in strafzaken en inzake erediensten, en tot wijziging van de wet van 28 mei 2002 betreffende de euthanasie en van het Sociaal Strafwetboek, *BS* 24 mei 2019, 50023; De Coensel (n 23) 212.

257 Art 7 Directive (EU) 2017/541 of the European Parliament and of the Council of 15 March 2017 on combating terrorism and replacing Council Framework Decision 2002/475/JHA and amending Council Decision 2005/671/JHA, *OJ* 31 March 2017, L 88/6-21; Toelichting bij Wetsvoorstel van 6 februari 2019 houdende diverse bepalingen in strafzaken en inzake erediensten, *Parl.St.* Kamer 2018-2019, nr. 54-3515/001, (3) 104-105; Winants (n 7) 357.

258 Delhaise (n 9) 58 and 78; Fransen and Kerkhofs (n 9) 65; Winants (n 7) 351.

259 GwH 28 januari 2015, 9/2015, B.41.3; Ketels (n 14) 257.

260 Deruyck and De Nauw (n 16) 11; Van Deuren (n 18) 508.

261 GwH 28 januari 2015, 9/2015, *TVW* 2015, 179, B.40.1-B.40.3.

262 GwH 28 januari 2015, 9/2015, *TVW* 2015, 179, B.41.2.

aforementioned offences.[263] The Court concludes that as long as this last interpretation is adhered to, there is no violation of the legality principle.[264]

Regarding the alleged violation of the freedom of expression and freedom of association, the Court followed the same reasoning as for article 140*ter* CC. It states that article 140*quater* CC does not make it possible to convict every person who approaches another person with a discourse that is considered unlawful, radical or extreme by the prosecuting authority.[265] Therefore article 140*quater* CC does not restrict the freedom of expression.[266] It does restrict the freedom of association, but this restriction is necessary in a democratic society in order to protect national security, public safety and public order, to prevent criminal offences, or to protect the rights and freedoms of others.[267] Therefore, there is no violation of the freedom of association.[268]

ART. 140*QUINQUIES* CC

Actus Reus

Together with the offence of providing instruction or training, the legislature introduced the offence of receiving training for terrorism.[269] He stated that it made operational and logical sense to also criminalise the person who receives the training.[270] The wording of this offence also closely resembles that of the Directive.[271] Article 140*quinquies* CC criminalises anybody who, in Belgium or abroad, receives instruction or training as described in article 140*quater* CC. The article explicitly refers to article 140*quater* CC with regard to the type of instruction or training, so anything mentioned there is also applicable here.[272] The training can be in person or, for example, via the internet.[273]

263 GwH 28 januari 2015, 9/2015, *TVW* 2015, 179, B.42.3.

264 GwH 28 januari 2015, 9/2015, *TVW* 2015, 179, B.42. See also: Ketels (n 14) 257; Spreutels and Velu (n 52) 137-138; Winants (n 7) 351.

265 GwH 28 januari 2015, 9/2015, *TVW* 2015, 179, B.44.

266 GwH 28 januari 2015, 9/2015, *TVW* 2015, 179, B.45. See also: Ketels (n 14) 257-258.

267 GwH 28 januari 2015, 9/2015, *TVW* 2015, 179, B.46.

268 Ketels (n 14) 257-258; Spreutels and Velu (n 52) 144-145; Winants (n 7) 351-352.

269 Art 7 wet van 18 februari 2013 tot wijziging van boek II, titel Iter van het Strafwetboek, *BS* 4 maart 2013, 13233. See also: De La Serna (n 15) 225.

270 Memorie van Toelichting bij wetsontwerp van 13 november 2012 tot wijziging van Titel 1ter van het Strafwetboek, *Parl.St.* Kamer 2012-2013, nr. 53-2502/001, (4) 16; Fransen and Kerkhofs (n 9) 67.

271 Art 8 Directive (EU) 2017/541 of the European Parliament and of the Council of 15 March 2017 on combating terrorism and replacing Council Framework Decision 2002/475/JHA and amending Council Decision 2005/671/JHA, *OJ* 31 March 2017, L 88/6-21.

272 Delhaise (n 9) 60; Winants (n 7) 351.

273 Delhaise and Fievet (n 29) 118.

The legislature added a new section to article 140*quinquies* CC in 2019 containing a second offence.[274] The *actus reus* of this offence is: in Belgium or abroad, acquiring knowledge yourself or educating yourself in the matters referred to in article 140*quater* CC. Due to the wording of the first section, it is generally accepted that its scope only covers people receiving training from somebody else.[275] Because the considerations to the Directive state that training should also include self-study[276], the legislature decided to introduce this second section, focusing on just that.[277] In the preparatory works, he emphasises that occasionally visiting a website, or visiting it for academic purposes does not suffice in order to be punishable. There needs to be an active and conscious action of the perpetrator.[278] Cesoni argues that this is insufficient, and warns for a reversal of the burden of proof, violations of the presumption of innocence and the possibility of thought police.[279]

Both sections explicitly state that the training is received or undertaken in Belgium or abroad.[280] This is not specified in the offence of providing training, nor in many of the other terrorist offences. It is unclear as to why the legislature decided to specify this in article 140*quinquies* CC.[281] It is highly unlikely that the Belgian legislature wanted to imply that the other offences, such as providing training, are not punishable if they did not take place on Belgian soil. As imposed by the Framework Decision[282] and the Directive[283],

274 Art 79, 2° wet 5 mei 2019 houdende diverse bepalingen in strafzaken en inzake erediensten, en tot wijziging van de wet van 28 mei 2002 betreffende de euthanasie en van het Sociaal Strafwetboek, *BS* 24 mei 2019, 50023. A similar proposal was already tabled once before, in 2018. See: Wetsvoorstel van 18 januari 2018 tot wijziging van het Strafwetboek teneinde zelfinstructie in het kader van terrorisme strafbaar te stellen, *Parl.St.* Kamer 2017-2018, nr. 54-2900/001.

275 Toelichting bij wetsvoorstel van 6 februari 2019 houdende diverse bepalingen in strafzaken en inzake erediensten, *Parl.St.* Kamer 2018-2019, nr. 54-3515/001, (3) 106; Delhaise (n 9) 60-61; Winants (n 7) 357.

276 Consideration 11 Directive (EU) 2017/541 of the European Parliament and of the Council of 15 March 2017 on combating terrorism and replacing Council Framework Decision 2002/475/JHA and amending Council Decision 2005/671/JHA, *OJ* 31 March 2017, L 88/6-21; Toelichting bij wetsvoorstel van 6 februari 2019 houdende diverse bepalingen in strafzaken en inzake erediensten, *Parl.St.* Kamer 2018-2019, nr. 54-3515/001, (3) 106. Cesoni argues that this is not binding upon member states, however. See: Cesoni (n 119) 238.

277 Cesoni (n 119) 237-238; De Coensel (n 23) 213-214.

278 Toelichting bij wetsvoorstel van 6 februari 2019 houdende diverse bepalingen in strafzaken en inzake erediensten, *Parl.St.* Kamer 2018-2019, nr. 54-3515/001, (3) 106. See also: Comité T, 'Rapport 2019: Le respect des droits humains dans le cadre de la lutte contre le terrorisme: Un chantier en cours', 17; Deruyck and De Nauw (n 16) 13; Winants (n 7) 357.

279 Cesoni (n 119) 238-239.

280 Ketels (n 14) 258; Winants (n 7) 351.

281 Fransen and Kerkhofs (n 9) 67.

282 Art 9 Council Framework Decision 2002/475/JHA of 13 June 2002 on combating terrorism, *OJ* 22 June 2002, L 164/3. See also: Beernaert, 'La Loi Du 19 Décembre 2003 Relative Aux Infractions Terroristes : Quand Le Droit Pénal Belge Évolue Sous La Dictée de l'Union Européenne' (n 14) 588; Gless (n 9) 938.

283 Art 19 Directive (EU) 2017/541 of the European Parliament and of the Council of 15 March 2017 on combating terrorism and replacing Council Framework Decision 2002/475/JHA and amending Council Decision 2005/671/JHA, *OJ* 31 March 2017, L 88/6-21.

Belgian legislation includes grounds of extraterritorial jurisdiction for terrorism.[284] The Preceding Title to the Code of Criminal Procedure states that any Belgian, or person who has his main residence in Belgium, can be prosecuted in Belgium when he commits a terrorist offence (*sensu lato* or *sensu stricto*) outside of Belgium (active personality principle).[285] Furthermore, it also states that anybody who commits a terrorist offence (*sensu stricto* or *sensu lato*) outside of Belgium can be prosecuted in Belgium if this offence was aimed at a Belgian subject or institution or against an institution of the European Union or of a body established in accordance with the Treaty establishing the European Community or the Treaty on the European Union, which is located in Belgium.[286] Furthermore, as a general rule, to prosecute a person who commits an extraterritorial offence for which the statute allows prosecution in Belgium, it is required that the suspect can be found in Belgium.[287] However, in case of prosecutions for terrorism *sensu stricto*,[288] this rule does not apply.[289] In this case, if the suspect is not Belgian and cannot be found

284 See: De La Serna (n 7) 209; De Nauw (n 12) 8-9; Hameeuw (n 15) 10-11; R Malagnini, 'La poursuite en Belgique des infractions terroristes commises à l'étranger' [2018] Revue de Jurisprudence de Liège, Mons et Bruxelles (JLMB) 1423; Weyembergh and Kennes, 'Domestic Provisions and Case Law: The Belgian Case' (n 7) 155; Weyembergh and Kennes, 'Le Titre Iter Du Livre II Du Code Pénal: Des Infractions Terroristes' (n 7) 122-123. In addition, an offence is a territorial offence as soon as one constituent element of the offence took place in Belgium (see among other cases: Cass. 4 februari 1986, *Pas.*, 1986, I, 671; Cass. 4 oktober 2017, *NC* 2018, 303). So for example a Frenchman residing in France recruiting a Frenchman residing in Belgium over the internet for a terrorist attack in France, would be a Belgian territorial offence. In a recent case, the Court of Cassation went even further and stated that a material act which prepares one of the constituent elements of the offence taking place in Belgium is sufficient for the offence to be a Belgian territorial offence. (Cass. 10 maart 2021, *JLMB* 2021, 1122, noot F Kuty).

285 Art 6, 1°*ter* PTCCP. See also: Beernaert, 'La Loi Du 19 Décembre 2003 Relative Aux Infractions Terroristes : Quand Le Droit Pénal Belge Évolue Sous La Dictée de l'Union Européenne' (n 14) 588; De Hert and Millen (n 32) 11-12; De La Serna (n 7) 209; Deruyck and De Nauw (n 16) 16; Flore (n 9) 222; Hameeuw (n 15) 10; Kuty (n 195) 455; Malagnini (n 283) 1425-1426; Tulkens and others (n 16) 302-303; Van den Wyngaert, Vandromme and Traest (n 16) 170; Winants (n 7) 349.

286 Art 10*ter*, section 1, 4° PTCCP. See also: Beernaert, 'La Loi Du 19 Décembre 2003 Relative Aux Infractions Terroristes : Quand Le Droit Pénal Belge Évolue Sous La Dictée de l'Union Européenne' (n 14) 588; De Hert and Millen (n 32) 12; De La Serna (n 7) 209; Deruyck and De Nauw (n 16) 16; Flore (n 9) 222; Hameeuw (n 15) 10; Kuty (n 195) 457-458; Malagnini (n 283) 1425; Tulkens and others (n 16) 303-304; Van den Wyngaert, Vandromme and Traest (n 16) 170; Winants (n 7) 349.

287 Art 12, section 1 PTCPP BE. See also: Beernaert, 'La Loi Du 19 Décembre 2003 Relative Aux Infractions Terroristes : Quand Le Droit Pénal Belge Évolue Sous La Dictée de l'Union Européenne' (n 14) 588; Kuty (n 195) 447; Tulkens and others (n 16) 301.

288 Some commentators suggest that this is the case for all terrorist offences. See: Deruyck and De Nauw (n 16) 16; Malagnini (n 283) 1426-1428. However, other commentators do not agree.

289 Art 12, 1° and 4° PTCCP. See also: Deruyck and De Nauw (n 16) 16; Kuty (n 195) 449; Van den Wyngaert, Vandromme and Traest (n 16) 170. Before this statute was adapted in 2012, there was discussion about whether or not this general rule applied to terrorism offences. See: Weyembergh and Kennes, 'Le Titre Iter Du Livre II Du Code Pénal: Des Infractions Terroristes' (n 7) 123. The majority of commentators seemed to be of the opinion that the rule did apply. For example: Beernaert, 'La Loi Du 19 Décembre 2003 Relative Aux Infractions Terroristes : Quand Le Droit Pénal Belge Évolue Sous La Dictée de l'Union Européenne' (n 14) 588; De La Serna (n 7) 210; Delmulle and Guenter (n 15) 5; Flore (n 9) 222-223; Hameeuw (n 15) 11.

on Belgian soil, the prosecution can only take place after the complaint has been evaluated by the public prosecution service.[290] In addition to the grounds of extraterritorial jurisdiction, it is noteworthy that one of the examples in the preparatory works of article 140*quater* explicitly refers to training provided abroad.[291]

Mens Rea

The *mens rea* for both offences in article 140*quinquies* CC is again a form of special intent: with a view to commit or contribute to the commission of one of the offences referred to in article 137, with the exception of the offence referred to in article 137, § 3, 6°.[292] So here too the training has to be received or undertaken with the view to commit or contribute to the commission of terrorism *sensu stricto*, with the exception of threatening a terrorist attack. In the first section of the article, the part 'or contribute to the commission of' was added in 2019[293], because this is part of the wording of the Directive and the legislature wanted to increase coherence.[294] The second section of the article was only introduced in 2019, with this phrase already included. Concreteness is not required, so the person receiving or undertaking the training does not need to know the exact terrorist offence for which he is training, nor does this offence actually have to be committed.[295]

Constitutional Court

The final terrorist offence discussed in the Constitutional Court judgment of 28 January 2015 was article 140*quinquies* CC. Regarding this article, a violation of the principle of legality and the freedoms of expression and association was alleged as well. However, the Court refers to the inextricable link between articles 140*quinquies* and 140*quater* CC, and to its reasoning for the latter article, in order to conclude that the

290 Art 10*ter*, section 2 PTCCP. See also: Van den Wyngaert, Vandromme and Traest (n 16) 170.

291 Memorie van Toelichting bij wetsontwerp van 13 november 2012 tot wijziging van Titel 1ter van het Strafwetboek, *Parl.St.* Kamer 2012-2013, nr. 53-2502/001, (4) 16; Fransen and Kerkhofs (n 9) 67-68.

292 Art 140*quinquies* CC; Delhaise (n 9) 62; Delhaise and Fievet (n 29) 118; Fransen and Kerkhofs (n 9) 68; Ketels (n 14) 258-259.

293 Art 79, 1° wet 5 mei 2019 houdende diverse bepalingen in strafzaken en inzake erediensten, en tot wijziging van de wet van 28 mei 2002 betreffende de euthanasie en van het Sociaal Strafwetboek, *BS* 24 mei 2019, 50023; De Coensel (n 23) 212; Winants (n 7) 357.

294 Art 8 Directive (EU) 2017/541 of the European Parliament and of the Council of 15 March 2017 on combating terrorism and replacing Council Framework Decision 2002/475/JHA and amending Council Decision 2005/671/JHA, *OJ* 31 March 2017, L 88/6-21; Toelichting bij wetsvoorstel van 6 februari 2019 houdende diverse bepalingen in strafzaken en inzake erediensten, *Parl.St.* Kamer 2018-2019, nr. 54-3515/001, (3) 106.

295 Delhaise (n 9) 62; Fransen and Kerkhofs (n 9) 68; Ketels (n 14) 259; Van Deuren (n 18) 508; Winants (n 7) 351.

former also does not violate the legality principle.[296] The same reasoning is applied in relation to the freedom of expression and freedom of association.[297]

ART. 140SEXIES CC

Actus Reus

When the issue of foreign terrorist fighters took the foreground, the UN Security Council stated in a resolution 'that all States shall ensure that their domestic laws and regulations establish serious criminal offences sufficient to provide the ability to prosecute and to penalize in a manner duly reflecting the seriousness of the offence: (a) their nationals who travel or attempt to travel to a State other than their States of residence or nationality, and other individuals who travel or attempt to travel from their territories to a State other than their States of residence or nationality, for the purpose of the perpetration, planning, or preparation of, or participation in, terrorist acts, or the providing or receiving of terrorist training'.[298] After this resolution, the Council of Europe included a similar provision in an additional protocol to the Convention on the Prevention of Terrorism.[299] The EU also included a comparable provision in its Directive on combating terrorism.[300] However, on top of outbound travel, the Directive also covers inbound travel. With regard to inbound travel the member states have two options: criminalise inbound travel as the mirror image of outbound travel, or criminalise preparatory acts undertaken by a person entering the member state with the intention to commit or contribute to the commission of terrorism *sensu stricto*.[301] The second option thus requires a stronger link between the inbound travel

---

296 GwH 28 januari 2015, 9/2015, *TVW* 2015, 179, B.49. See also: Ketels (n 14) 259; Spreutels and Velu (n 52) 138; Winants (n 7) 351.

297 GwH 28 januari 2015, 9/2015, *TVW* 2015, 179, B.53. See also: Ketels (n 14) 259; Winants (n 7) 351-352.

298 UNSC Resolution 2178 of 24 September 2014, 6(a). See also: Memorie van Toelichting bij wetsontwerp van 22 juni 2015 tot versterking van de strijd tegen terrorisme, *Parl.St.* Kamer 2014-15, nr. 54-1198/001, 5; Blaise and Delhaise (n 26) 173-174; Lavaux (n 71) 124.

299 Art 4 Additional Protocol to the Council of Europe Convention on the Prevention of Terrorism, 2015, CETS 217; Alejandro Sánchez Frías, 'Public Security Derogations to the Free Movement of EU Citizens and Preventive Criminal Law: A Collision between Ever-Expanding Concepts?' [2019] European Journal of Crime, Criminal Law and Criminal Justice 293, 298-303; Guy Stessens, 'Terroristen Op Reis: Over de Strafbaarstelling van Reizen Met Terroristisch Oogmerk En Andere Maatregelen Ter Beperking van de Reisvrijheid van (Vermeende) Terroristen' in Steven Dewulf (ed), *La [CVDW] Liber Amicorum Chris Van den Wyngaert* (Maklu 2017) 443-445.

300 Art 9 Directive (EU) 2017/541 of the European Parliament and of the Council of 15 March 2017 on combating terrorism and replacing Council Framework Decision 2002/475/JHA and amending Council Decision 2005/671/JHA, *OJ* 31 March 2017, L 88/6-21.

301 Art 9.2 Directive (EU) 2017/541 of the European Parliament and of the Council of 15 March 2017 on combating terrorism and replacing Council Framework Decision 2002/475/JHA and amending Council Decision 2005/671/JHA, *OJ* 31 March 2017, L 88/6-21; De Coensel (n 148) 245; Stessens (n 299) 446-448.

and the intended terrorist offence (*sensu stricto*). The Belgian legislature decided on the first option, and fulfilled his international obligations by introducing article 140*sexies* into the Criminal Code.[302] The *actus reus* of this offence is leaving[303] or entering[304] the national territory. This is an everyday action, which makes the *mens rea* the core of this offence.[305] The wording of the article implies the *actus reus* is present once the person crosses the Belgian border, not when he starts or ends his journey.[306]

Mens Rea

The *mens rea* is the aim to commit, or contribute to the commission, in Belgium or abroad, of one of the offences in article 137, 140 to 140*quinquies* and 141 CC, with the exception of the offence in article 137, §3, 6°. This covers all terrorist offences under Belgian law, except for those of threatening a terrorist offence (*sensu stricto*)[307] and preparing a terrorist offence (*sensu stricto*)[308] (see below). This is broader than the Directive, which does not include incitement and recruitment, however, at the same time it is also slightly more restrictive, as the Directive does not exclude threatening. This aim, which is a special intent, needs to be present simultaneously with the *actus reus*, meaning at the time of leaving or entering the national territory.[309] Concreteness is not required, therefore the traveller does not need to know exactly which terrorist offence he will commit.[310] *A fortiori* it is not required that the intended offence is actually committed.[311] In the case of an offence that revolves almost exclusively around the *mens rea* the danger is that mere

302 Art 2 wet van 20 juli 2015 tot versterking van de strijd tegen het terrorisme, *BS* 5 augustus 2015, 49326; Memorie van Toelichting bij wetsontwerp van 22 juni 2015 tot versterking van de strijd tegen terrorisme, *Parl.St.* Kamer 2014-15, nr. 54-1198/001, 5; Marie-Aude Beernaert, 'Renforcement de l'arsenal législatif anti-terroriste: entre symboles et prévention' [2015] Journal des tribunaux 833, 834; Deruyck and De Nauw (n 16) 13; Velaers (n 183) 786-787. De Coensel points out that when applied to a Belgian national, this offence violates the right to enter that person's own country. See: De Coensel (n 148) 264.

303 Art 140*sexies*, 1° CC.

304 Art 140*sexies*, 2° CC.

305 Advies 57.127/AV van de Raad van State van 24 maart 2015, *Parl.St.* Kamer 2014-15, nr. 54-1198/001, 17; Beernaert, 'Renforcement de l'arsenal législatif anti-terroriste: entre symboles et prévention' (n 302) 834; Delhaise (n 9) 65; Ward Yperman, 'Heiligt het doel de middelen?' [2018] Nieuw Juridisch Weekblad 304.

306 Delhaise (n 9) 63-64.

307 Art 137, §3, 6° CC. See also: Ketels (n 14) 259.

308 Art 140*septies* CC.

309 Advies 57.127/AV van de Raad van State van 24 maart 2015, *Parl.St.* Kamer 2014-15, nr. 54-1198/001, 18; Delhaise (n 9) 65; Deruyck and De Nauw (n 16) 13; Fransen and Kerkhofs (n 31) 179-180; Fransen and Kerkhofs (n 9) 70-71; Ketels (n 14) 260; Winants (n 7) 352.

310 Fransen and Kerkhofs (n 31) 180; Fransen and Kerkhofs (n 9) 72; Ketels (n 14) 260; Winants (n 7) 352.

311 Memorie van Toelichting bij wetsontwerp van 22 juni 2015 tot versterking van de strijd tegen terrorisme, *Parl.St.* Kamer 2014-15, nr. 54-1198/001, 6; Blaise and Delhaise (n 26) 174; Beernaert, 'Renforcement de l'arsenal législatif anti-terroriste: entre symboles et prévention' (n 302) 834; Delhaise (n 9) 65; Deruyck and De Nauw (n 16) 13; Fransen and Kerkhofs (n 9) 70; Moreau (n 173) 107; Winants (n 7) 352.

thoughts become punishable, whereas in Belgium the principle is that only acts are punishable.[312] The Council of State noted in this respect that the offence is situated on the border between the material and the intentional by criminalising an everyday action.[313] The Council pointed towards the need for sufficient concrete, objective and material indications for the intention of the perpetrator.[314] The use of stereotypes and presumptions has to be avoided.[315] The explanatory memorandum explicitly states that the evidence and the facts of the case will be of crucial importance for the assessment of the *mens rea*.[316]

In 2019 the scope of article 140*sexies* CC was further extended. As with the other terrorist offences, the Directive requires member states to criminalise not only travel to commit a terrorist offence, but also travel to contribute to the commission of such an offence.[317] As a result, the legislature inserted the words 'or contributing to the commission' twice (both for leaving and for entering the national territory) in article 140*sexies* CC.[318] Many, if not all, of these actions are already punishable under (attempted) article 140 CC or (participation in) one of the other terrorist offences *sensu lato*. Nevertheless, the legislature wanted to increase coherence and legal certainty and therefore thought the addition necessary.[319]

Constitutional Court

The introduction of article 140*sexies* CC was appealed as well. This appeal was based on the principle of legality and the free movement of persons, but was rejected by the Constitutional Court.[320] The argumentation resembles the discussion that had already

312 Fransen and Kerkhofs (n 31) 179; Fransen and Kerkhofs (n 9) 71.

313 Advies 57.127/AV van de Raad van State van 24 maart 2015, *Parl.St.* Kamer 2014-15, nr. 54-1198/001, 17; Blaise and Delhaise (n 26) 174; Velaers (n 183) 787-788; Winants (n 7) 352.

314 Advies 57.127/AV van de Raad van State van 24 maart 2015, *Parl.St.* Kamer 2014-15, nr. 54-1198/001, 17; Fransen and Kerkhofs (n 31) 179; Moreau (n 173) 107-108; Velaers (n 183) 787-788.

315 Beernaert, 'Renforcement de l'arsenal législatif anti-terroriste: entre symboles et prévention' (n 302) 834; Delhaise (n 9) 65-66; Moreau (n 173) 107-108; Velaers (n 183) 787-788.

316 Memorie van Toelichting bij wetsontwerp van 22 juni 2015 tot versterking van de strijd tegen terrorisme, *Parl.St.* Kamer 2014-15, nr. 54-1198/001, 5.

317 Art 9 Directive (EU) 2017/541 of the European Parliament and of the Council of 15 March 2017 on combating terrorism and replacing Council Framework Decision 2002/475/JHA and amending Council Decision 2005/671/JHA, *OJ* 31 March 2017, L 88/6-21.

318 Art 80 wet van 5 mei 2019 houdende diverse bepalingen in strafzaken en inzake erediensten, en tot wijziging van de wet van 28 mei 2002 betreffende de euthanasie en van het Sociaal Strafwetboek, *BS* 24 mei 2019, 50023; Memorie van Toelichting bij wetsvoorstel van 6 februari 2019 houdende diverse bepalingen in strafzaken en inzake erediensten, *Parl.St.* Kamer 2018-2019, nr. 54-3515/001, (3) 106-107; De Coensel (n 23) 212; Winants (n 7) 357.

319 Memorie van Toelichting bij wetsvoorstel van 6 februari 2019 houdende diverse bepalingen in strafzaken en inzake erediensten, *Parl.St.* Kamer 2018-2019, nr. 54-3515/001, (3) 104-105.

320 GwH 18 januari 2018, 8/2018, *NjW* 2018, 299-304, noot W Yperman. See also: Spreutels and Velu (n 52) 138-139; Winants (n 7) 352-353.

taken place before the Council of State. Firstly, the question was raised as to whether article 140*sexies* CC complies with the principle of legality. The Constitutional Court replied that the provision was drafted in a sufficiently precise and clear manner and thus provided sufficient legal certainty.[321] With regard to the *mens rea*, the Court stressed that a person can reasonably determine whether he intends to commit one of the listed offences and that the court must consider objective elements, taking into account the specific circumstances of each case.[322] The fact that the *mens rea* refers to another offence, with its own particular special intent, does not prevent a person from assessing what the criminal consequence of his conduct will be.[323] All this is in line with what the Council of State had said.

Subsequently, it was argued that article 140*sexies* CC did not criminalise anything that was not already punishable. On this point, the explanatory memorandum had already clarified that not all terrorists travel to follow a training course before committing an attack (article 140*quinquies* CC) or to join a terrorist group (article 140CC).[324] Either way, concurrence is possible[325], so any potential overlap would not be problematic.[326] The Council of State also inquired about this overlap, stating that the government had not given a concrete example of a situation that does not fall under other terrorist offences (and specifically article 140 CC).[327] However, the Council of State agreed that from a legal perspective, this was not a problem. Wanting absolute certainty that all the targeted situations would be punishable is a sufficient reason to introduce a new offence.[328] In line with its aforementioned judgment of 28 January 2015, the Constitutional Court ruled that the principle of legality has not been violated if two provisions criminalise the same conduct.[329]

Secondly, the applicant stated that article 140*sexies* CC is contrary to the free movement of persons. The Constitutional Court similarly did not agree with this argument. Without further explanation, the Court referred to the fact that the provision was introduced in

321 GwH 18 januari 2018, 8/2018, *NjW* 2018, 300-301, B.7; Dejemeppe and Rigaux (n 52) 763-764; Delhaise (n 9) 67.

322 GwH 18 januari 2018, 8/2018, *NjW* 2018, 301-302, B.9.1; Blaise and Delhaise (n 26) 174; Delhaise (n 9) 67.

323 GwH 18 januari 2018, 8/2018, *NjW* 2018, 302-303, B.9.3.

324 Memorie van Toelichting bij wetsontwerp tot versterking van de strijd tegen terrorisme, *Parl.St.* Kamer 2014-15, nr. 54-1198/001, 6-7; See also: Blaise and Delhaise (n 26) 175; Delhaise (n 9) 66; Ketels (n 14) 261.

325 There is ideal concurrence when several qualifications are applicable to the same set of facts. In such cases, only the most severe penalty is applied (art 65, section 1 CC).

326 Memorie van Toelichting bij wetsontwerp tot versterking van de strijd tegen terrorisme, *Parl.St.* Kamer 2014-15, nr. 54-1198/001, 7; Blaise and Delhaise (n 26) 175.

327 Advies 57.137/AV van de Raad van State bij wetsontwerp houdende diverse bepalingen ter bestrijding van terrorisme, *Parl.St.* Kamer 2014-2015, nr. 54-1198/001, (13) 18-19; Fransen and Kerkhofs (n 9) 70-71.

328 Advies 57.137/AV van de Raad van State van 24 maart 2015 bij wetsontwerp houdende diverse bepalingen ter bestrijding van terrorisme, *Parl.St.* Kamer 2014-15, nr. 54-1198/001, (13) 19.

329 GwH 18 januari 2018, 8/2018, *NjW* 2018, 302-303, B.9.3; Blaise and Delhaise (n 26) 175; Delhaise (n 9) 66-67. Moreover, both the sentences and the procedural regime are the same.

order to combat terrorism within the framework of UN Security Council Resolution no. 2178, and therefore does not violate the free movement of persons.[330] The Council of State, however, explicitly stated that, on the basis of European case law[331], this does not exempt states from their obligations to protect fundamental rights.[332] Article 2 of the Fourth Protocol to the ECHR, which protects the free movement of persons, states that restrictions on free movement must be provided for by law, be necessary in a democratic society and be proportionate to the objective pursued.[333] For the assessment of whether the restriction is provided for by law, the Council of State referred to the discussion of the principle of legality.[334] The Council furthermore stated that the restriction is necessary for national security, public safety, the maintenance of public order and the protection of the rights and freedoms of others, therefore making it necessary in a democratic society.[335] The proportionality analysis is less straightforward. The sentence in article 140*sexies* CC is the same as for many other terrorist offences. The Council of State noted that the compatibility with the principle of proportionality 'must be assessed and justified in a comprehensive manner, in the light of the possible coherence of that article with other draft legislative provisions aimed at restricting, in a similar manner but by other means, the free movement of persons in the context of the fight against terrorism'.[336] The Council

330 GwH 18 januari 2018, 8/2018, *NjW* 2018, 304, B.13.4. See also: Spreutels and Velu (n 52) 145; Winants (n 7) 353. On this point the comparison with the UN Human Rights Committee case Sayadi can prove interesting. In this case the Committee did analyse Belgium's compliance with human rights and found it lacking, depite the fact that the measures were based on a UN Security Council resolution. See: *Sayadi v. Belgium* UN Doc CCPR/C/94/D/1472/2006 (Official Case No) IHRL 3216 (UNHRC 2008). See also: F Krenc, 'La Belgique "Condamnée" Pour La Première Fois Par Le Comité Des Droits de l'homme Sur Fond de Lutte Contre Le Terrorisme – Cap Sur Genève!' [2009] Journal des tribunaux 621, 622-624.

331 *Al-Dulimi and Montana Management Inc v Switzerland* App no 5809/08 (ECHR Grand Chamber, 21 June 2016) §95-96; *Nada v Switzerland* App no 10593/08 (ECHR Grand Chamber, 12 September 2012) §168-171; *Al-Jedda v UK* App no 27021/08 (ECHR Grand Chamber, 7 July 2011) §101-102; Case C-584/10, C-593/10 and C-595/10 *European Commission et al v Yassin Abdullah Kadi* [2013] CJEU ECLI:EU:C:2013:518; Case C-402/05 and C-415/05 *Yassin Abdullah Kadi and Al Barakaat International Foundation v Council of the European Union and Commission of the European Communities* [2008] CJEU ECLI:EU:C:2008:461.

332 Advies 57.127/AV van de Raad van State van 24 maart 2015, *Parl.St.* Kamer 2014-15, nr. 54-1198/001, 14-15.

333 Art 2 ECHR Fourth Protocol; advies 57.127/AV van de Raad van State van 24 maart 2015, *Parl.St.* Kamer 2014-15, nr. 54-1198/001, 20.

334 Advies 57.127/AV van de Raad van State van 24 maart 2015, *Parl.St.* Kamer 2014-15, nr. 54-1198/001, 20.

335 Advies 57.127/AV van de Raad van State van 24 maart 2015, *Parl.St.* Kamer 2014-15, nr. 54-1198/001, 20; Blaise and Delhaise (n 26) 175; Velaers (n 183) 787.

336 Own translation, original in Dutch and French: "*op een alomvattende manier beoordeeld en gerechtvaardigd [moet] worden, in het licht van de mogelijke samenhang van dat artikel met andere ontworpen wetgevende bepalingen die op een soortgelijke wijze maar met andere middelen het vrij verkeer van personen in het kader van de strijd tegen het terrorisme beogen te beperken; doit être appréciée et justifiée de manière globale, à la lumière de sa combinaison possible avec d'autres dispositifs législatifs en projet qui semblablement visent à restreindre par d'autres biais la liberté de circulation des personnes dans le cadre de la lutte contre le terrorisme.*" See: Advies 57.127/AV van de Raad van State van 24 maart 2015, *Parl.St.* Kamer 2014-15, nr. 54-1198/001, 21.

of State referred to the legislation governing the refusal, withdrawal or invalidation of passports, travel documents and identity cards (see below). However, by doing so, the Council of State does not address the specific situation of article 140*sexies* CC, and therefore does not actually give its opinion on the issue of proportionality.

This is disappointing since the question of proportionality is essential. Article 140*sexies* CC is a felony, meaning the attempt thereof is also punishable.[337] Article 140*sexies* CC furthermore criminalises not only travelling to commit an attack, but also, for example, travelling to follow a training course (article 140*quinquies* CC). Therefore, a start of execution (attempt) of an act of preparation (travelling) for an act of preparation (attending training) for an actual attack can be punished.[338] Referring to a statement by the secretary of justice in the House of Representatives, the Constitutional Court stated that, for example, buying an airplane ticket after having openly announced the intention to kill people is sufficient.[339] It can be questioned whether this should indeed be punishable.

ART. 140*SEPTIES* CC

Actus Reus

In 2016, the legislature wanted to crack down further on terrorism.[340] In this context, he decided to criminalise preparatory actions, because a terrorist offence is often impossible without these actions.[341] The Directive does not contain a similar offence. Indeed, it simply states that criminalising preparatory acts undertaken by a person entering a member state with the intention to commit or contribute to the commission of terrorism *stricto sensu* is a way to respond to terrorist travel.[342] Article 140*septies* CC criminalises anybody who prepares a terrorist offence meant in article 137 CC, with the exception of article 137, §3, 6°. This means every terrorist offence *sensu stricto* except for threatening terrorism. The second paragraph of the article includes a list of actions that can be preparation:

337 Art 52CC; GwH 18 januari 2018, 8/2018, *NjW* 2018, 302, B.9.2.

338 Yperman, 'Heiligt het doel de middelen?' (n 305).

339 GwH 18 januari 2018, 8/2018, *NjW* 2018, 302, B.9.2.

340 Samenvatting van wetsvoorstel van 13 januari 2016 tot wijziging van het Strafwetboek wat betreft de bestraffing van terrorisme, *Parl.St.* Kamer 2015-2016, nr. 54-1579/001, 1. See also: Cesoni (n 119) 251-252.

341 Toelichting bij wetsvoorstel van 13 januari 2016 tot wijziging van het Strafwetboek wat betreft de bestraffing van terrorisme, *Parl.St.* Kamer 2015-2016, nr. 54-1579/001, (3) 4.

342 Art 9.2 (b) Directive (EU) 2017/541 Directive (EU) 2017/541 of the European Parliament and of the Council of 15 March 2017 on combating terrorism and replacing Council Framework Decision 2002/475/JHA and amending Council Decision 2005/671/JHA, *OJ* 31 March 2017, L 88/6-21.

1° Gathering information on locations, occurrences, events or people which makes it possible to carry out an action on those locations or during those occurrences or events or to cause damage to those people, and observe those locations, occurrences, events or people;
2° The possession, purchase, transport or manufacture of or search for objects or substances which are of such a nature that they can be dangerous to other people or cause substantial economic damage;
3° The possession, purchase, transport or manufacture of or search for financial or material resources, false or illegally obtained documents, information carriers, means of communication, means of transport;
4° The possession or acquisition of or search for premises that acts as a hideout, meeting place, place for gathers or shelter;
5° The prior claiming of a terrorist offence, with the exception of the offence of article 137, §3, 6° CC, regardless of the form or means of the claim.

The Criminal Code states that preparation can mean these five things 'among others'. In other words, this list is non-exhaustive.[343] Anything can be preparation, including an omission[344]. The Council of State found that a non-exhaustive list does not necessarily violate the legality principle, on the condition that the general description of the offence is sufficiently detailed, clear and predictable.[345] On the one hand the list needed to be non-exhaustive because terrorism is a changeable form of criminality.[346] On the other hand, a kind of list was needed in order to delimit the offence and to indicate the type of conduct particularly intended.[347] The preparatory works state that it is not the intention to target people who provide limited and non-decisive help.[348] However, that help can be considered as aiding and abetting the preparation of a terrorist offence or financing terrorism (art. 141

343 Advies van de Raad van State (II) nr. 59 147/3 van 22 april 2016 bij wetsontwerp houdende diverse bepalingen ter bestrijding van terrorisme (III), *Parl.St.* Kamer 2015-2016, nr. 54-1951/001, 26; Delhaise (n 9) 69; Deruyck and De Nauw (n 16) 14-15; Fransen and Kerkhofs (n 9) 75; Winants (n 7) 356.

344 Amendement nr. 1 van 7 juli 2016 bij wetsvoorstel van 13 januari 2016 tot wijziging van het Strafwetboek wat betreft de bestraffing van terrorisme, *Parl.St.* Kamer 2015-2016, nr. 54-1579/005, 10; Deruyck and De Nauw (n 16) 15; Fransen and Kerkhofs (n 9) 76; Winants (n 7) 356.

345 Advies 59.789/3 van de Raad van State van 19 juli 2016 bij wetsvoorstel van 13 januari 2016 tot wijziging van het Strafwetboek wat betreft de bestraffing van terrorisme, *Parl.St.* Kamer 2015-2016, nr. 54-1579/006, 13; advies van de Raad van State (II) nr. 59 147/3 van 22 april 2016 bij wetsontwerp houdende diverse bepalingen ter bestrijding van terrorisme (III), *Parl.St.* Kamer 2015-2016, nr. 54-1951/001, 28; Fransen and Kerkhofs (n 9) 75; Delhaise (n 9) 69.

346 Fransen and Kerkhofs (n 9) 75.

347 Amendement nr. 1 van 7 juli 2016 bij wetsvoorstel van 13 januari 2016 tot wijziging van het Strafwetboek wat betreft de bestraffing van terrorisme, *Parl.St.* Kamer 2015-2016, nr. 54-1579/005, 10.

348 Amendement nr. 1 van 7 juli 2016 bij wetsvoorstel van 13 januari 2016 tot wijziging van het Strafwetboek wat betreft de bestraffing van terrorisme, *Parl.St.* Kamer 2015-2016, nr. 54-1579/005, 3; Fransen and Kerkhofs (n 9) 75.

CC, see below).[349] In the preparatory works, it is also explained that point 1° on the list is mainly aimed at observing people or locations, including via the internet.[350] As an example for point 2°, purchasing explosives, or materials to create explosives is cited.[351] The words 'means of communication' in point 3° cover new technologies and their evolutions and an example of point 5° can be a video claiming an attack yet to be committed.[352]

Preparation is not to be confused with an attempted offence. Under Belgian criminal law, there is an attempted offence, if the intention to commit the offence has been manifested by external acts which constitute the beginning of the commission of that offence and which have ceased or have missed their effect solely as a result of circumstances beyond the control of the perpetrator.[353] In general criminal law, preparatory actions that are not the beginning of the commission of the offence are not punishable.[354] To ascertain the difference between a mere act of preparation and the beginning of the commission of the offence, one must ask whether the action is susceptible to multiple interpretations. If there can be no doubt about the intention of the perpetrator and the act will necessarily lead to the commission of the offence, the action is the beginning of the commission of the

349 Amendement nr. 1 van 7 juli 2016 bij wetsvoorstel van 13 januari 2016 tot wijziging van het Strafwetboek wat betreft de bestraffing van terrorisme, *Parl.St.* Kamer 2015-2016, nr. 54-1579/005, 3.

350 Amendement nr. 1 van 7 juli 2016 bij wetsvoorstel van 13 januari 2016 tot wijziging van het Strafwetboek wat betreft de bestraffing van terrorisme, *Parl.St.* Kamer 2015-2016, nr. 54-1579/005, 9; Fransen and Kerkhofs (n 9) 76.

351 Amendement nr. 1 van 7 juli 2016 bij wetsvoorstel van 13 januari 2016 tot wijziging van het Strafwetboek wat betreft de bestraffing van terrorisme, *Parl.St.* Kamer 2015-2016, nr. 54-1579/005, 9; Fransen and Kerkhofs (n 9) 76.

352 Amendement nr. 1 van 7 juli 2016 bij wetsvoorstel van 13 januari 2016 tot wijziging van het Strafwetboek wat betreft de bestraffing van terrorisme, *Parl.St.* Kamer 2015-2016, nr. 54-1579/005, 9; Fransen and Kerkhofs (n 9) 76.

353 Art 51 CC; Cass. 3 november 2004, *RW* 2005-06, 1583, noot C De Roy; Henri Berkmoes, 'Bestanddelen van de Strafbare Poging' in M De Busscher and others (eds), *Strafrecht: duiding* (Larcier 2018) 85-88; Delhaise (n 9) 81; De Nauw and Deruyck (n 20) 69-71; C De Roy, 'De strafbare poging als klassiek leerstuk in het raam van de hedendaagse strijd tegen het terrorisme (Noot Onder Cass. 3 november 2004)' (2005-2006) 69 Rechtskundig Weekblad 1584, 1585; Onsea (n 112) 41; Bart Spriet, 'Poging Tot Misdaad of Tot Wanbedrijf', *Strafrecht geannoteerd* (die Keure 2020) 336-338; Tulkens and others (n 16) 420-424; Van den Wyngaert, Vandromme and Traest (n 16) 362-367; Vandromme and De Roy (n 16) 511.

354 Berkmoes (n 353) 86; De Nauw and Deruyck (n 20) 67 and 70; Onsea (n 112) 41; Spriet, 'Poging Tot Misdaad of Tot Wanbedrijf' (n 348) 337; Tulkens and others (n 16) 421; Van den Wyngaert, Vandromme and Traest (n 16) 363; Winants (n 7) 355. Other statutes that criminalise preparatory actions are the statute on combating piracy at sea and the statute on the trade of narcotics. See: art 3, § 1, c), wet van 30 december 2009 betreffende de strijd tegen piraterij op zee, *BS* 14 januari 2010, 1485; art 2*bis*, §6 and 2*quater*, 6° wet van 7 februari 2014 tot wijziging van de wet van 24 februari 1921 betreffende het verhandelen van gifstoffen, slaapmiddelen en verdovende middelen, psychotrope stoffen, ontsmettingsstoffen en antiseptica en van de stoffen die kunnen gebruikt worden voor de illegale vervaardiging van verdovende middelen en psychotrope stoffen, *BS* 6 maart 1921, 1834; amendement nr. 1 van 7 juli 2016 bij wetsvoorstel van 13 januari 2016 tot wijziging van het Strafwetboek wat betreft de bestraffing van terrorisme, *Parl.St.* Kamer 2015-2016, nr. 54-1579/005, 6.

offence.[355] The fact that actions are required that constitute the beginning of the commission of the offence, is an expression of the traditional objective doctrine within Belgian criminal law.[356] The idea behind criminalising preparatory acts, is to not wait for the beginning of the commission of the offence but intervene sooner.[357] However, the preparatory works explain that sometimes actions listed as preparation can be a beginning of the commission of the offence as well, depending on the circumstances of the case.[358] An excellent example of this is the Verviers case, which took place before article 140*septies* CC existed.[359] In this case, acts such as forging documents, searching a safe house, renting vehicles to transport jihadists, weapons and parts of explosives, buying phones, buying ingredients for bombs, and buying weapons and police uniforms were ruled to be attempted terrorism *sensu stricto*, although they are all listed as possible acts of preparation in article 140*septies* CC as well.

Mens Rea

Once more, the *mens rea* is not explicit in the text of the article. The preparatory works explain that next to the *actus reus* the intention to commit a terrorist offence as described in article 137 CC is necessary.[360] The action in itself never suffices. This intention is a form of special intent[361] and for this offence there is a requirement of concreteness: the prosecution has to prove which offence was intended.[362] The Council of State emphasised

---

355 Cass. 3 november 2004, *RW* 2005-06, 1583, noot C De Roy; Berkmoes (n 353) 86; Dekrem (n 77) 138; De Nauw and Deruyck (n 20) 70; De Roy (n 353) 1585; Tulkens and others (n 16) 421-422; Van den Wyngaert, Vandromme and Traest (n 16) 364; Vandromme and De Roy (n 16) 514.

356 Van den Wyngaert, Vandromme and Traest (n 16) 364; Vandromme and De Roy (n 16) 513.

357 Amendement nr. 1 van 7 juli 2016 bij wetsvoorstel van 13 januari 2016 tot wijziging van het Strafwetboek wat betreft de bestraffing van terrorisme, *Parl.St.* Kamer 2015-2016, nr. 54-1579/005, 5; advies van de Raad van State (II) nr. 59 147/3 van 22 april 2016 bij wetsontwerp houdende diverse bepalingen ter bestrijding van terrorisme (III), *Parl.St.* Kamer 2015-2016, nr. 54-1951/001, 25; Comité T, 'Rapport 2019: Le respect des droits humains dans le cadre de la lutte contre le terrorisme: Un chantier en cours', 18; Fransen and Kerkhofs (n 9) 76; Ketels (n 14) 262; Moreau (n 173) 109-110; Onsea (n 112) 41-42.

358 Amendement nr. 1 van 7 juli 2016 bij wetsvoorstel van 13 januari 2016 tot wijziging van het Strafwetboek wat betreft de bestraffing van terrorisme, *Parl.St.* Kamer 2015-2016, nr. 54-1579/005, 5; Fransen and Kerkhofs (n 9) 76; Ketels (n 14) 262.

359 Corr. Brussel 5 juli 2016, *onuitg.* This was confirmed by the Court of Appeal for one of them after he appealed (Brussel 31 maart 2017, *onuitg.*, 34-36). See also: Fransen and Kerkhofs (n 9) 24-25; Moreau (n 173) 114-115.

360 Amendement nr. 1 van 7 juli 2016 bij wetsvoorstel van 13 januari 2016 tot wijziging van het Strafwetboek wat betreft de bestraffing van terrorisme, *Parl.St.* Kamer 2015-2016, nr. 54-1579/005, 8; Fransen and Kerkhofs (n 9) 77.

361 Ketels (n 14) 262.

362 Advies 59.789/3 van de Raad van State van 19 juli 2016 bij wetsvoorstel van 13 januari 2016 tot wijziging van het Strafwetboek wat betreft de bestraffing van terrorisme, *Parl.St.* Kamer 2015-2016, 54-1579/006, 14; advies van de Raad van State (II) nr. 59 147/3 van 22 april 2016 bij wetsontwerp houdende diverse

the importance of concrete and consistent factual elements that provide proof of the intention to commit a terrorist offence.[363] However, this intent was not quite clear. On the one hand, the preparatory works state that an offence prepared by one person can also be executed by another.[364] On the other hand, they say that the *mens rea* is the intention to commit a terrorist offence. If someone prepares a terrorist offence for somebody else, he does not have the intention of committing one himself. The Council of State pointed towards this inconsistency and asked for clarification.[365] The legislature did not change the article, but did explain to the Council of State that article 140*septies* CC is only meant to target people who prepare their own terrorist offence.[366] People preparing another's terrorist offence, are potentially liable as accomplices.[367] This raises an interesting question under the proportionality principle however. The sentences for accomplices are higher than the sentences for preparation in article 140*septies* CC.[368] So preparing a terrorist offence committed by somebody else is punished harsher than preparing your own.[369] As the legislature points out in the preparatory works, it is impossible to punish preparation less harsh than attempt, but on the same level as aiding and abetting, since attempt and

---

bepalingen ter bestrijding van terrorisme (III), *Parl.St.* Kamer 2015-2016, nr. 54-1951/001, 29; verslag van de eerste lezing van 20 oktober 2016 namens de tijdelijke commissie "terrorismebestrijding" bij wetsvoorstel tot wijziging van het Strafwetboek wat betreft de bestraffing van terrorisme, *Parl.St* Kamer 2015-2016, nr. 54-1579/008, 5-6; Delhaise (n 9) 71; Fransen and Kerkhofs (n 9) 77.

363 Advies 59.789/3 van de Raad van State van 19 juli 2016 bij wetsvoorstel van 13 januari 2016 tot wijziging van het Strafwetboek wat betreft de bestraffing van terrorisme, *Parl.St.* Kamer 2015-2016, nr. 54-1579/006, 12; advies van de Raad van State (II) nr. 59 147/3 van 22 april 2016 bij wetsontwerp houdende diverse bepalingen ter bestrijding van terrorisme (III), *Parl.St.* Kamer 2015-2016, nr. 54-1951/001, 27; Fransen and Kerkhofs (n 9) 77.

364 Amendement nr. 1 van 7 juli 2016 bij wetsvoorstel van 13 januari 2016 tot wijziging van het Strafwetboek wat betreft de bestraffing van terrorisme, *Parl.St.* Kamer 2015-2016, nr. 54-1579/005, 3.

365 Advies 59.789/3 van de Raad van State van 19 juli 2016 bij wetsvoorstel van 13 januari 2016 tot wijziging van het Strafwetboek wat betreft de bestraffing van terrorisme, *Parl.St.* Kamer 2015-2016, nr. 54-1579/006, 12; advies 59.147/3 van de Raad van State State bij wetsontwerp van 6 juli 2016 houdende diverse bepalingen ter bestrijding van terrorisme (III), *Parl.St.* Kamer 2015-16, nr. 54-1951/001, (19) 27-28.

366 Advies 59.789/3 van de Raad van State van 19 juli 2016 bij wetsvoorstel van 13 januari 2016 tot wijziging van het Strafwetboek wat betreft de bestraffing van terrorisme, *Parl.St.* Kamer 2015-2016, nr. 54-1579/006, 17; verslag van de eerste lezing van 20 oktober 2016 namens de tijdelijke commissie "terrorismebestrijding" bij wetsvoorstel tot wijziging van het Strafwetboek wat betreft de bestraffing van terrorisme, *Parl.St* Kamer 2015-2016, nr. 54-1579/008, 5; Dekrem (n 77) 157; Deruyck and De Nauw (n 16) 14; Fransen and Kerkhofs (n 9) 75; Winants (n 7) 356. *Contra*: Delhaise (n 9) 70-71.

367 Art 67 CC; De Nauw and Deruyck (n 20) 95-96; Tulkens and others (n 16) 511-512; Van den Wyngaert, Vandromme and Traest (n 16) 388-389; Jan Vanheule, 'Daden van Deelneming Die Worden Omschreven in Artikel 67 Sw.' in M De Busscher and others (eds), *Strafrecht: duiding* (Larcier 2018) 139-141; Patrick Waeterinckx, 'Samenloop van Verscheidene Misdrijven', *Strafrecht geannoteerd* (die Keure 2020) 376-377.

368 Art 69 CC. See also: De Nauw and Deruyck (n 20) 96; Tulkens and others (n 16) 512-513; Van den Wyngaert, Vandromme and Traest (n 16) 394.

369 Advies 59.789/3 van de Raad van State van 19 juli 2016 bij wetsvoorstel van 13 januari 2016 tot wijziging van het Strafwetboek wat betreft de bestraffing van terrorisme, *Parl.St.* Kamer 2015-2016, nr. 54-1579/006, 19-20.

aiding and abetting have the same sentence.[370] Furthermore, prosecution for aiding and abetting an offence implies that the offence (or at least its attempt) has actually taken place[371], which is not the case for preparatory actions.[372] It is possible to aid and abet the attempted offence, but then the sentence goes down another level compared to the aiding and abetting of the offence itself.

Art. 141 CC

Actus Reus

Article 141 CC is a first-generation terrorist offence, introduced in 2003.[373] This offence was not included in the Framework Decision but in the International Convention for the Suppression of the Financing of Terrorism, signed by Belgium on 27 September 2001.[374] It was not part of the first draft bill of the 2003 statute because article 140, §1 CC already explicitly refers to the financing of terrorism. However, the Council of State noted that article 140 CC only covered a certain form of financing, namely the financing of a terrorist group.[375] The legislature also wanted to tackle the financing of individual terrorists and therefore added article 141 CC in order to plug this gap.[376] The offence introduced in 2003

370 Verslag van de eerste lezing van 20 oktober 2016 namens de tijdelijke commissie "terrorismebestrijding" bij wetsvoorstel tot wijziging van het Strafwetboek wat betreft de bestraffing van terrorisme, *Parl.St* Kamer 2015-2016, nr. 54-1579/008, 6.

371 Delhaise (n 9) 85; Tulkens and others (n 16) 505-506; Van den Wyngaert, Vandromme and Traest (n 16) 386; Vanheule (n 366) 124.

372 Verslag van de eerste lezing van 20 oktober 2016 namens de tijdelijke commissie "terrorismebestrijding" bij wetsvoorstel tot wijziging van het Strafwetboek wat betreft de bestraffing van terrorisme, *Parl.St* Kamer 2015-2016, nr. 54-1579/008, 7.

373 Art 7 wet van 19 december 2003 betreffende terroristische misdrijven, *BS* 29 december 2003, 61689.

374 Art 2 International Convention for the Suppression of the Financing of Terrorism, New York 9 December 1999; Beernaert, 'La Loi Du 19 Décembre 2003 Relative Aux Infractions Terroristes : Quand Le Droit Pénal Belge Évolue Sous La Dictée de l'Union Européenne' (n 14) 588; De Hert and Millen (n 32) 10; De La Serna (n 7) 193; De La Serna (n 15) 225-226; Flore (n 9) 219; Hameeuw (n 15) 9; Ketels (n 14) 263; Traest (n 15) 258; Weyembergh and Kennes, 'Domestic Provisions and Case Law: The Belgian Case' (n 7) 154; Weyembergh and Kennes, 'Le Titre Iter Du Livre II Du Code Pénal: Des Infractions Terroristes' (n 7) 120; Winants (n 7) 349. Currently, article 11 of the Directive includes the offence of terrorist financing.

375 Advies 34.362/4 van de Raad van State bij wetsontwerp van 6 oktober 2003 betreffende terroristische misdrijven, *Parl.St.* Kamer 2003, nr. 51-0258/001, (22) 40. See also: Delhaise and Fievet (n 29) 119.

376 Memorie van Toelichting bij wetsontwerp van 6 oktober 2003 betreffende terroristische misdrijven, *Parl.St.* Kamer 2003, nr. 51-0258/001, (4) 9 en 14-15; verslag namens de commissie van justitie bij wetsontwerp van 6 oktober 2003 betreffende terroristische misdrijven, *Parl.St.* Kamer 2003, nr. 51-0258/004, 23; Beernaert, 'La Loi Du 19 Décembre 2003 Relative Aux Infractions Terroristes : Quand Le Droit Pénal Belge Évolue Sous La Dictée de l'Union Européenne' (n 14) 588; De La Serna (n 7) 192-193; De La Serna (n 15) 225; Deruyck and De Nauw (n 16) 10; Hameeuw (n 15) 9; Ketels (n 14) 263; Weyembergh and Kennes, 'Domestic

criminalised 'Any person who, except in the cases referred to in article 140, provides material resources, including financial assistance, with a view to committing a terrorist offence referred to in article 137.'[377] However, in its recommendations, the Financial Action Task Force (hereafter FATF) stressed that terrorist financing offences should not require that the funds are linked to a specific terrorist act.[378] According to the FATF, collecting or providing funds to one or two people (i.e. outside of the situation of article 140 CC) does not seem to be covered by article 141 CC if the connection to a specific terrorist offence cannot be established. Therefore, article 141 did not fully comply with this recommendation.[379] In order to resolve this issue, the article was replaced in 2016.[380] Three slightly different amendments were proposed, with the third proposition chosen as it most closly resembled the EU Directive, which does include a similar offence.[381]

The current version of article 141 CC criminalises the direct or indirect provision or collection of material resources, including financial assistance, by any means.[382] Compared to the original article, article 141 is now not only aimed at people who provide resources, but also at those who collect them.[383] The legislature notes that the wording of the new article is broader than the original one, but that this does not necessarily mean that the original article did not encompass the elements that were made more specific by the new

---

Provisions and Case Law: The Belgian Case' (n 7) 154; Weyembergh and Kennes, 'Le Titre Iter Du Livre II Du Code Pénal: Des Infractions Terroristes' (n 7) 120; Winants (n 7) 348.

377 Own translation, original in Dutch and French: "*Iedere persoon die, behalve in de gevallen bedoeld in artikel 140, materiële middelen verstrekt, daaronder begrepen financiële hulp, met het oog op het plegen van een terroristisch misdrijf bedoeld in artikel 137; Toute personne qui, hors les cas prévus à l'article 140, fournit des moyens matériels, y compris une aide financière, en vue de la commission d'une infraction terroriste visée à l'article 137*" (Art 141 CC as introduced by art 7 wet van 19 december 2003 betreffende terroristische misdrijven, *BS* 29 December 2003, 61689). See also: Fransen and Kerkhofs (n 9) 78.

378 Recommendation 5 FATF international standards on combating money laundering and the financing of terrorism & proliferation, updated June 2019, 11, www.fatf-gafi.org/media/fatf/documents/recommendations/pdfs/FATF%20Recommendations%202012.pdf. See in the original recommendations as well: FATF IX Special Recommendations, October 2001, 5, www.fatf-gafi.org/media/fatf/documents/reports/FATF%20Standards%20-%20IX%20Special%20Recommendations%20and%20IN%20rc.pdf.

379 FATF, *Anti-money laundering and counter-terrorist financing measures – Belgium, Fourth Round Mutual Evaluation Report* (2015) 160, www.fatf-gafi.org/publications/mutualevaluations/documents/mer-belgium-2015.html.

380 Amendement nr. 2 van 7 juli 2016 bij wetsvoorstel van 13 januari 2016 tot wijziging van het Strafwetboek wat betreft de bestraffing van terrorisme, *Parl.St.* Kamer 2015-2016, nr. 54-1579/005, 11-12. See also: Deruyck and De Nauw (n 16) 10; Ketels (n 14) 263.

381 Verslag van de eerste lezing van 20 oktober 2016 namens de tijdelijke commissie "terrorismebestrijding" bij wetsvoorstel tot wijziging van het Strafwetboek wat betreft de bestraffing van terrorisme, *Parl.St.* Kamer 2015-16, nr. 54-1579/008, 14; amendement nr. 3 van 6 oktober 2016 bij wetsvoorstel tot wijziging van het Strafwetboek wat betreft de bestraffing van terrorisme, *Parl.St.* Kamer 2015-2016, nr. 54-1579/007, 2-3; Fransen and Kerkhofs (n 9) 79; Winants (n 7) 356.

382 Art 141 CC; Delhaise (n 9) 72.

383 Amendement nr. 3 van 6 oktober 2016 bij wetsvoorstel tot wijziging van het Strafwetboek wat betreft de bestraffing van terrorisme, *Parl.St.* Kamer 2015-2016, nr. 54-1579/007, 4; Deruyck and De Nauw (n 16) 10; Fransen and Kerkhofs (n 9) 79; Winants (n 7) 356.

wording.[384] For example, the Directive includes providing or collecting funds, by 'any means, directly or indirectly'.[385] The legislature copied this to the new article 141 CC, but explicitly stated that this does not mean it was not already covered in the original article.[386] The words 'material resources, including financial assistance' were not altered. According to the FATF they were already sufficiently broad.[387] It is not required that the resources are actually used to commit, or contribute to the commission of, an offence.[388]

Mens Rea

The *mens rea* allows for two options. The resources have to be provided or collected with the intention that they be used, or in the knowledge that they are to be used, in full or in part, (1°) to commit or contribute to the commission of a terrorist offence *sensu stricto* or *senu lato*, or (2°) by another person when the person providing or collecting the resources knows that this other person is committing, or will commit, terrorism *sensu stricto*.[389] This is significantly broader than the *mens rea* from 2003. 1° is a copy from the EU Directive.[390] Compared to the original article, it expanded the offences of which the financing is criminalised from terrorism *sensu stricto* to all terrorist offences, including participating in the activities of a terrorist group and preparing a terrorist offence.[391] Furthermore, the legislature wanted to make sure no connection with a specific terrorist act was required. The new wording had to make it clearer that it is not necessary the resources are actually used, or that the perpetrator knows which specific offences they will be used for.[392] This is explicitly required by the Directive when the financing concerns terrorism *sensu stricto*,

384 Amendement nr. 3 van 6 oktober 2016 bij wetsvoorstel tot wijziging van het Strafwetboek wat betreft de bestraffing van terrorisme, *Parl.St.* Kamer 2015-2016, nr. 54-1579/007, 3-4.

385 Art 11.1 Directive (EU) 2017/541 of the European Parliament and of the Council of 15 March 2017 on combating terrorism and replacing Council Framework Decision 2002/475/JHA and amending Council Decision 2005/671/JHA, *OJ* 31 March 2017, L 88/6-21.

386 Amendement nr. 3 van 6 oktober 2016 bij wetsvoorstel tot wijziging van het Strafwetboek wat betreft de bestraffing van terrorisme, *Parl.St.* Kamer 2015-2016, nr. 54-1579/007, 4; Fransen and Kerkhofs (n 9) 79.

387 FATF, *Anti-money laundering and counter-terrorist financing measures – Belgium, Fourth Round Mutual Evaluation Report* (2015) 159, www.fatf-gafi.org/publications/mutualevaluations/documents/mer-belgium-2015.html. See also: Fransen and Kerkhofs (n 9) 79; Winants (n 7) 356.

388 Fransen and Kerkhofs (n 31) 184; Ketels (n 14) 263-264.

389 Art 141 CC. See also: Deruyck and De Nauw (n 16) 10.

390 Art 11.1 Directive (EU) 2017/541 of the European Parliament and of the Council of 15 March 2017 on combating terrorism and replacing Council Framework Decision 2002/475/JHA and amending Council Decision 2005/671/JHA, *OJ* 31 March 2017, L 88/6-21; amendement nr. 3 van 6 oktober 2016 bij wetsvoorstel tot wijziging van het Strafwetboek wat betreft de bestraffing van terrorisme, *Parl.St.* Kamer 2015-2016, nr. 54-1579/007, 5.

391 Amendement nr. 3 van 6 oktober 2016 bij wetsvoorstel tot wijziging van het Strafwetboek wat betreft de bestraffing van terrorisme, *Parl.St.* Kamer 2015-2016, nr. 54-1579/007, 5; Fransen and Kerkhofs (n 9) 80.

392 Amendement nr. 3 van 6 oktober 2016 bij wetsvoorstel tot wijziging van het Strafwetboek wat betreft de bestraffing van terrorisme, *Parl.St.* Kamer 2015-2016, nr. 54-1579/007, 5-6; Deruyck and De Nauw (n 16)

terrorist offences relating to a terrorist group or traveling for terrorist purposes.[393] Belgium, however, thought this was too restrictive and the legislature made clear that this also applies for the other terrorist offences.[394] In 2° the legislature wanted to emphasise that helping an individual terrorist is also an offence, as required by the FATF.[395] Surprisingly the legislature hereby states that the Council of State had not expressed any objections about this.[396] This is of note because the Council of State had questioned the distinction between 1° and 2°. According to the Council, 1° already includes financing an individual terrorist.[397] The legislature never replied to this observation. Despite this lack of reply, the Council of State had a point. Providing resources in the knowledge that they are to be used to commit a terrorist offence *sensu stricto* (1°) or providing them in the knowledge that they are to be used by another person when the person providing or collecting the resources knows that this other person is committing or will commit terrorism *sensu stricto* (2°) is the same thing.[398] Therefore, 1° includes 2°, making the latter moot.

Most literature simply states the *mens rea* is a special intent.[399] While this does indeed seem to be the case, it is not as obvious as the literature makes it out to be. The article states 'the intention that they be used, or in the knowledge that they are to be used'. This intention would be a special intent, as this is a specification of the intent element. However, the article also provides another option with the use of 'or'. At first glance, the knowledge part does not entail a special intent, since it is a specification of the knowledge element and not

10; Fransen and Kerkhofs (n 9) 79; Winants (n 7) 356. Although under the old wording, it was not required that the terrorist act was committed either. See: De La Serna (n 7) 194.

393 Art 11.2 Directive (EU) 2017/541 of the European Parliament and of the Council of 15 March 2017 on combating terrorism and replacing Council Framework Decision 2002/475/JHA and amending Council Decision 2005/671/JHA, *OJ* 31 March 2017, L 88/6-21.

394 Amendement nr. 3 van 6 oktober 2016 bij wetsvoorstel tot wijziging van het Strafwetboek wat betreft de bestraffing van terrorisme, *Parl.St.* Kamer 2015-2016, nr. 54-1579/007, 6.

395 Amendement nr. 3 van 6 oktober 2016 bij wetsvoorstel tot wijziging van het Strafwetboek wat betreft de bestraffing van terrorisme, *Parl.St.* Kamer 2015-2016, nr. 54-1579/007, 6; amendement nr. 1 van 7 juli 2016 bij wetsvoorstel van 13 januari 2016 tot wijziging van het Strafwetboek wat betreft de bestraffing van terrorisme, *Parl.St.* Kamer 2015-2016, nr. 54-1579/005, 12.

396 Amendement nr. 3 van 6 oktober 2016 bij wetsvoorstel tot wijziging van het Strafwetboek wat betreft de bestraffing van terrorisme, *Parl.St.* Kamer 2015-2016, nr. 54-1579/007, 6.

397 Advies 59.789/3 van de Raad van State van 19 juli 2016 bij wetsvoorstel van 13 januari 2016 tot wijziging van het Strafwetboek wat betreft de bestraffing van terrorisme, *Parl.St.* Kamer 2015-2016, nr. 54-1579/006, 21-22; advies 59 147/3 van de Raad van State van 22 april 2016 bij wetsontwerp van 6 juli 2016 houdende diverse bepalingen ter bestrijding van terrorisme (III), *Parl.St.* Kamer 2015-2016, nr. 54-1951/001, (19) 31-32; Delhaise (n 9) 73; Fransen and Kerkhofs (n 9) 80.

398 Delhaise (n 9) 73.

399 Delhaise (n 9) 72-73; Winants (n 7) 356; Yperman, 'Terrorism Offences in Belgian Criminal Law' (n 152) 177. Note that Comité T does question whether this is a general or a special intent, without answering the question. See: Comité T, 'Raport 2022: Évaluation des mesures visant à lutter contre le terrorisme à la lumière des droits humains', 52.

of the intent.[400] This observation in turn, needs to be nuanced. Similarly to the reasoning for article 140 CC, if somebody provides means in the knowledge that they will be used to perpetrate a certain terrorist attack, it would seem they also provide those means with the intention that they be used for this goal. Since they have the knowledge of the goal and act regardless, the intention is implied. Therefore, article 141 CC does require a special intent and the wording that seems to refer to a sort of general intent is redundant as well as slightly confusing.

Case law analysis

As discussed in this Chapter, there are quite a lot of terrorism offences. However, in practice this variety of offences is not reflected in prosecutions. Of the 343 individual first instance judgments, only six did not include prosecution for one of the offences in article 140 CC.[401] These six concerned a case within which six people were prosecuted for terrorism *sensu stricto* and one person for terrorism *sensu stricto* and participation in the activities of a terrorist group. The former six people were all acquitted and the latter was convicted on both counts. Consequently, not a single case was brought under articles 140*bis* to 141 CC which was not also prosecuted under article 140 CC. In total 28 people were prosecuted for terrorism *sensu stricto*, 266 for the offence in article 140, §1 CC, ten for the attempt to this offences, 65 for 140, §2 CC, four for 140*bis*, one for 140*ter*, one for attempted 140*ter*, five for 140*quater*, one for 140*quinquies*, seven for 140*sexies* and none for the offences in articles 140*septies* and 141 CC.[402] It is important to note that, in addition to terrorist offences, a significant number of defendants were also prosecuted for non-terrorist offences, which were not included in the analysis. From the total of 343 individual first instance judgments, one was declared inadmissible, 27 people were acquitted, including the one person who was prosecuted for article 140*quinquies* CC, and 315 people were convicted.

The numbers of the case law analysis clearly demonstrate that because of the broadness of the offences in article 140 CC, the other terrorist offences *sensu lato* have very limited added value. They were only invoked a total of nineteen times (or approximately 5,5% of cases) and only ever in conjunction with article 140 CC. The offence in article 141 CC was invoked by the prosecution only once, despite having existed since 2003, and in that one case it was requalified to 140 CC by the court.

---

400 See also: Cesoni (n 119) 254. Note that Cesoni states that the combination of the intention to 2° reverts back to a general intent. However, as explained above we feel 2° is redundant as it is fully part of 1°.

401 Being art 140, §1 and/or §2 CC, since §1/1 did not exist yet.

402 Note that these numbers do not add up to the total of 343 since people can be prosecuted and convicted for more than one offence.

2 Criminal Procedure

Competent courts

The trial phase takes place in front of the trial courts. In Belgium, there are four courts of this sort, which are competent to preside over different types of offences at different stages. The Police Court (*politierechtbank; tribunal de police*) is competent for contraventions (*overtredingen; contraventions*), being the lightest offences, as well as for all traffic offences.[403] The Correctional Court (*correctionele rechtbank; tribunal correctionnel*) is competent for standard offences and appeals against the Police Courts.[404] The Court of Appeal (*hof van beroep; cour d'appel*) is competent for appeals against the judgments of the Correctional Courts[405] and finally the Assize Court (*hof van assisen; cour d'assises*) is competent for felonies and all political (*politek misdrijf; infraction politique*) and press offences (*drukpersmisdrijf; délit de presse*).[406] Almost all of the terrorism offences are felonies. Exceptions to this are some of the lighter offences of terrorism *sensu stricto*, as well as most of the preparation offences of article 140*septies* CC. For the offences in article 140*septies*, the sentence depends upon the prepared offence, with only the preparation of the most serious terrorist offences being a felony (see below). Due to the majority of cases being felonies, they should in theory be tried by the Assize Court. In the Assize Court however, jury trials take place. The long and expensive nature of jury trial procedures results in the frequent employment of a technique called 'correctionalisation' (*correctionalisatie; correctionnalisation*).[407] Correctionalisation is possible for almost all of the terrorist felonies, except for those deemed most severe such as terrorist murder. In order to apply this technique, attenuating circumstances are invoked when referring the case to trial.[408] This so called 'correctionalisation' which is based on attenuating circumstances has become standard practice for every felony for which the law allows it,[409] including, as mentioned above, the majority of terrorist offences. There is no list of what

403 Art 137-138 CCP. See also: Van den Wyngaert, Vandromme and Traest (n 16) 688-689; Raf Verstraeten, *Handboek Strafvordering* (5de voll. herz. uitgave, Maklu 2012) 812.

404 Art 174 and 179 CCP. See also: De Nauw and Deruyck (n 20) 52; Van den Wyngaert, Vandromme and Traest (n 16) 687-688; Verstraeten (n 403) 813.

405 Art 200 CCP. See also: Verstraeten (n 403) 815.

406 Art 150 Constitution. See also: De Nauw and Deruyck (n 20) 52; Van den Wyngaert, Vandromme and Traest (n 16) 681; Verstraeten (n 403) 815.

407 Van den Wyngaert, Vandromme and Traest (n 16) 295 and 685.

408 De Nauw and Deruyck (n 20) 49-50; Vanessa Franssen, 'Algemeen' in M De Busscher and others (eds), *Strafrecht: duiding* (Larcier 2018) 162-163; Tulkens and others (n 16) 653; Van den Wyngaert, Vandromme and Traest (n 16) 295; Verstraeten (n 403) 697-698.

409 Franssen (n 408) 163-164; Van den Wyngaert, Vandromme and Traest (n 16) 295.

can be invoked as an attenuating circumstance, meaning that the possibilities are near endless.[410] Alongside the general tendency of limiting the amount of cases tried in front of the Assize Court because they are slow and expensive,[411] it has also been argued that, in cases of terrorism, the jury could on the one hand be intimidated into giving lenient sentences or on the other hand impose more severe sentences due to the sensitivity surrounding terrorism.[412] The trial of Nemmouche and Bendrer, the perpetrators of the terrorist attack in the Jewish museum in Brussels, took place in front of the Assize Court. The trial, which was wrought with issues, exacerbated by the massive media attention, demonstrates that in this context jury trials are challenging.[413] This was part of the reason why some people were worried about the jury trial for the terrorist attacks in Zaventem and Maelbeek. The federal prosecutor had warned against this[414], and a proposal to bring terrorism under the competence of the Correctional Courts was tabled in parliament, but

410 Tulkens and others (n 16) 649-650; Van den Wyngaert, Vandromme and Traest (n 16) 294-295.

411 Memorie van Toelichting bij het wetsontwerp van 23 oktober 2015 houdende wijzigingen van het strafrecht en de strafvordering en houdende diverse bepalingen inzake justitie, *Parl.St.* Kamer 2015-16, nr. 54 1418/001, (4) 112-113; Franssen (n 408) 161; Joëlle Rozie, 'Hof van Assisen En Correctionalisering Na Potpourri II: Kunst- En Vliegwerk of Dankbare Ingreep van de Wetgever?' [2016] Nullum Crimen (NC) 91, 92-93; Lientje Van Den Steen, 'De Potpourri II-Wet En de Veralgemeende Correctionaliseerbaarheid: Een Prefabbouwwerk Met Onstabiele Fundamenten' [2015-2016] Rechtskundig Weekblad 1604, 1606; Ruben Vilain and Ward Yperman, 'Grondwettelijk Hof 21 december 2017: it came in like a wrecking ball' [2018] Nullum Crimen 1, 2-4.

412 Memorie van Toelichting bij het wetsontwerp van 23 oktober 2015 houdende wijzigingen van het strafrecht en de strafvordering en houdende diverse bepalingen inzake justitie, *Parl.St.* Kamer 2015-16, nr. 54 1418/001, (4) 113; Lore Gyselaers, *La Participation Des Citoyens à La Fonction de Juger En Matière Pénale. Etude Comparative Du Droit Anglais, de Droit Belge et de Droit Français* (PhD thesis, KU Leuven 2011) 162; D Leestmans, 'Terrorisme Blijft in Strafrechtelijke Termen Deels Onvatbaar, Interview Met Paul Ponsaers' [27 mei 2020] Juristenkrant 8, 8-9.

413 H Decré, 'Rondleiding door slachtoffer', 'half doof' of 'skivakantie': excuses om niet in jury proces-Nemmouche te moeten zitten' (2019) *vrtNWS* 7 January 2019, www.vrt.be/vrtnws/nl/2019/01/07/ik-ben-rondgeleid-door-een-slachtoffer-ik-ben-half-doof-of/; TD, 'Juryleden proces Nemmouche bezorgd over veiligheid na diefstal dossier' (2019) *Bruzz* 31 January 2019, www.bruzz.be/justitie/juryleden-proces-nemmouche-bezorgd-over-veiligheid-na-diefstal-dossier-2019-01-31; A Vanrenterghem, 'Burgerlijke partijen en parket over complottheorie Mehdi Nemmouche: "Rookgordijn zonder bewijs, respectloos"' (2019) *vrtNWS* 4 March 2019, www.vrt.be/vrtnws/nl/2019/03/04/proces-aanslag-joods-museum-replieken/; AW, KG and HA, 'Jurylid gewraakt op proces tegen Medhi Nemmouche na bizar gesprek met collega' (2019) *HLN* 18 February 2019, www.hln.be/nieuws/binnenland/jurylid-gewraakt-op-proces-tegen-mehdi-nemmouche-na-bizar-gesprek-met-collega~add55bd1/; X, 'Opnieuw jurylid gewraakt op proces-Nemmouche' (2019) *De Standaard* 16 January 2019, www.standaard.be/cnt/dmf20190116_04107264; X, 'Zevende jurylid proces Nemmouche gewraakt na gesprek met collega' (2019) *De Morgen* 18 February 2019, www.demorgen.be/binnenland/zevende-jurylid-proces-nemmouche-gewraakt-na-gesprek-met-collega-bff72490/.

414 See for example: Sandra Cardoen, 'Federaal procureur vindt proces aanslagen te complex voor jury: "Je vraagt niet aan iemand op straat om te opereren"' (2020) *vrtNWS* 9 February 2020, www.vrt.be/vrtnws/nl/2020/02/09/aanslagen-assisen-versus-correctionele/; Douglas De Coninck, 'Assisenproces ligt opnieuw onder vuur' (2020) *De Morgen* 11 February 2020, www.demorgen.be/nieuws/assisenproces-ligt-opnieuw-onder-vuur~b84189c7/.

later dismissed.[415] It is somewhat ironic that the constitutionally compulsory jury trial would be circumvented for practical reasons, while our constitutional order is one of the things we are trying to protect against terrorism. At the time of writing the trial on the Zaventem and Maelbeek attacks is ongoing. The final result is thus unknown, but even at this relatively early stage the trial has had to overcome significant hurdles. It has been postponed for several months because the boxes in which the defendants had to sit were deemed in violation of the rights of the defence, there has been a summary judgment forbidding the police from systematically searching the defendants while naked and several jurors have had to be excused.[416] At the expert seminar, there was agreement that jury trials are not ideal for terrorism. The majority of participants was against an exception for terrorism, however, as this once again distinguishes terrorism as a special case. The preferred solution was to rethink the Assize Courts in general.

As mentioned above, the Assize Courts are not only competent for felonies but also for all political and press offences.[417] Both categories could be relevant for terrorism offences. There are two kinds of political offences. First, the pure political offences (*zuiver politiek misdrijf; infraction politique pure*). These offences can be designated as such by the legislature, by either explicitly making the Assize Courts competent for a standard offence, or prescribing the sentence of detention instead of felony imprisonment.[418] If this is not the case, an offence can still be a pure political offence if it necessarily is a direct attack on the political institutions in their existence, organisation or functioning or on the political rights of citizens.[419] The second category is that of the mixed political offences (*gemengd*

415 Voorstel tot herziening van artikel 150 van de Grondwet teneinde de juryrechtspraak voor terroristische misdaden af te schaffen, *Parl.St.* Kamer 2019-2020, nr. 55-1287/001 and 003. For a brief analysis, see: Sofie Royer, Ruben Vilain and Ward Yperman, 'Grondwetswijziging voor terrorismeprocessen is niet radicaal genoeg' [2020] De Juristenkrant 10.

416 Denny Baert, 'Salah Abdeslam en jurylid door ziekte afwezig op terreurproces, proces niet geschorst' (2022) *vrtNWS* 12 December 2022, www.vrt.be/vrtnws/nl/2022/12/12/terreurproces/; Douglas De Coninck, 'Rechter terreurproces: "Ik beveel afbraak glazen kooien"' (2022) *De Morgen* 16 September 2022, www.demorgen.be/nieuws/rechter-terreurproces-ik-beveel-afbraak-glazen-kooien~b16551ac/; Mark Eekhaut, '"Mensonterende" kooien op het proces van de aanslagen' (2022) *De Standaard* 12 September 2022, www.standaard.be/cnt/dmf20220911_97613232; Stefan Grommen, 'Proces over aanslagen ligt opnieuw stil: voorzitter vordert politietopman om duidelijkheid te krijgen over nieuwe naaktfouilles' (2023) *vrtNWS* 4 January 2023, www.vrt.be/vrtnws/nl/2023/01/04/proces-aanslagen-22-maart-zitting-4-januari-2023/.

417 Art 150 Constitution. See also: Corr. Hainaut 22 maart 2021, *JLMB* 2022, 444; Lore Gyselaers, '(Digitale) Drukpersmisdrijven En de Bevoegdheidsproblematiek – Tijd Voor Een Wettelijke Correctionalisatie?' [2013] Limb. Rechtsl. 97, 97; Anouk Kerkhofs, 'Een adequaat vervolgingssysteem inzake drukpersmisdrijven' [2016] Nullum Crimen 64, 67.

418 De Nauw and Deruyck (n 20) 53; Vanessa Franssen, 'Begrip Politiek Misdrijf' in M De Busscher and others (eds), *Strafrecht: duiding* (Larcier 2018) 30; Tulkens and others (n 16) 347; Van den Wyngaert, Vandromme and Traest (n 16) 203.

419 Cass. 18 november 2003, *Arr.Cass.* 2003, afl. 11, 2125, concl M Timperman; Cass. 9 november 2004, *JT* 2004, afl. 6157, 856, noot; Concl EH bij Cass. 15 februari 2006, P.05.1594; De Nauw and Deruyck (n 20) 54; Franssen (n 418) 30; J Huysmans and others, 'Grondwet (Uitreksel)', *Strafrecht geannoteerd* (die Keure 2020) 259; Jan Kerkhofs, 'Noot Onder Corr. Hasselt 27 Juli 1999' [1999] Limb. Rechtsl. 264, 265-266;

politiek misdrijf; infraction politique mixte). These are offences which are not necessarily because of the nature of the offence a direct attack on the political institutions, etc. but which are committed with the intention of causing such an impairment of the political institutions and which, given the special circumstances in which they are committed, have, or can have, such a direct impairment as a consequence.[420]

Due to its *mens rea* and the contextual part of the *actus reus*, terrorism *sensu stricto* seems to be eligible for the qualification of political offence.[421] Terrorism has been accepted as a ground for the application of article 15 ECHR.[422] This article allows member states to derogate from most of the requirements of the ECHR, but only in the event of war or other public emergency threatening the life of the nation.[423] Terrorism has already been accepted

---

Moucheron (n 7) para 9; Tulkens and others (n 16) 347; Van den Wyngaert and Vandromme (n 16) 194; Van den Wyngaert, Vandromme and Traest (n 16) 204.

420 Cass. 24 maart 1908, *Pas.* 1908, 142; Cass. 7 september 1935, *Pas.* 1935, 334; Cass. 21 oktober 1981, *Arr. Cass.* 1981-82, 271; Cass. 18 november 2003, *Arr.Cass.* 2003, afl. 11, 2125, concl M Timperman; Cass. 9 november 2004, *JT* 2004, afl. 6157, 856, noot; Concl EH bij Cass. 15 februari 2006, P.05.1594; De La Serna (n 7) 168; De Nauw and Deruyck (n 20) 54; Franssen (n 418) 30; Huysmans and others (n 419) 259-260; Kerkhofs (n 419) 266; Moucheron (n 7) para 9; Tulkens and others (n 16) 348; Van den Wyngaert and Vandromme (n 16) 194-195; Van den Wyngaert, Vandromme and Traest (n 16) 204-205.

421 This is also briefly discussed in the preparatory documents, but without any real conclusion. See: Verslag namens de commissie voor de Justitie van 3 december 2003 bij het wetsontwerp betreffende terroristische misdrijven, *Parl.St.* Senaat 2003-04, nr. 3-332/3, 7, 10, 12 en 20. Looking at the historical roots of the political offence, terrorism *sensu stricto* is the type of offence the constitutional assembly of 1830 had in mind when it created the category of political offences. For an analysis, see: Moucheron (n 7).

422 Art 15 ECHR; *Lawless v. Ireland (no. 3)* App no 332/57 (ECHR, 1 July 1961) 28-30; *Ireland v UK* App no 5310/71 (ECHR, 18 January 1978) 205 and 212; *Brannigan and McBride v UK* App no 14553/89 and 14554/89 (ECHR, 25 May 1993) 44-47; *Aksoy v Turkey* App no 21987/93 (ECHR, 18 December 1996) 70; *A et al v UK* App no 3455/05 (ECHR Grand Chamber, 19 February 2009) 175-181; *Guide to the case-law of the European Court of Human Rights on Terrorism* (2020) 39. France also claimed that terrorism threatened the life of the nation in 2015 when it declared the state of emergency and deviated from its obligations under the ECHR. (Declaration contained in a letter from the Permanent Representative of France to the Council of Europe, dated 24 November 2015, registered at the Secretariat General on 24 November 2015, https://www.coe.int/en/web/conventions/full-list?module=treaty-detail&treatynum=005). See also: Olivier De Shutter, 'La Convention Européenne Des Droits de l'homme à l'épreuve de La Lutte Contre Le Terrorisme' in Emmanuelle Bribosia and Anne Weyembergh (eds), *La convention Européenne des droits de l'homme à l'épreuve de la lutte contre le terrorisme* (Bruylant-Nemesis 2002) 129; H Fenwick and D Fenwick, 'The Role of Derogations from the ECHR in the Current "War on Terror"' in Eran Shor and Stephen Hoadley (eds), *International Human Rights and Counter-Terrorism* (Springer 2019) 8-11 en 18-19 http://link.springer.com/10.1007/978-981-10-3894-5_37-2 accessed 8 January 2020; Silvis (n 57) 657-658; Frédéric Vanneste, 'Het Europese Hof Voor de Rechten van de Mens En de Overheden Die Terrorisme Bestrijden: Brothers in Arms?' (2003-2004) 41 Rechtskundig Weekblad 1665, 1674-1675; Velaers (n 183) 791.

423 Spreutels and Velu (n 52) 130-131; Vanneste (n 422) 1674-1675. This is not the case for all of the requirements of the ECHR. The prohibition of torture (art 3 ECHR) and the prohibition of slavery (art 4, section 1 ECHR) for example are absolute. They cannot be derogated from under article 15 (art 15, section 2 ECHR). Moreover, even if derogation is possible, this is only so to the extent that the seriousness of the situation strictly requires such measures and provided that they are not in conflict with other obligations under international law.

as a ground of application of article 15 ECHR and therefore has been accepted as threatening the life of a nation. The Belgian legislature, however, has not designated terrorism a pure political offence[424], so this qualification is dependent on the case law.[425]

The Court of Cassation states that a political offence is an offence 'that both because of the intent of the perpetrator and its effects, is a direct attack on the political institutions'.[426] Political offences thus require a possible direct impairment of the political institutions. The Court of Cassation subsequently ruled that the terrorist offences are not of such a nature that they can be a political offence because 'the damage the perpetrator wants to do to the political institutions is realised indirectly, by endangering random lives or economic interests, even though those lives or interests have nothing to do with the organisations or institutions the perpetrator claims to want to target'.[427] In other words, the required political damage is not the direct and immediate consequence of the offences but only the indirect and hypothetical consequence.[428] Consequently, according to the Court of Cassation, terrorism is not a political offence. This seems to be accurate only for pure political offences as terrorism does not necessarily entail a direct impairment of the political institutions. Seriously intimidating a population suffices as well. Furthermore, acts against international organisations are eligible to be defined as terrorism *sensu stricto* while it is not clear whether they would be 'political institutions'.[429] However, it is not beyond the scope of the imaginable that a terrorist attack could cause direct political damage by, for example, targeting political leaders.[430] In this case, it would be a mixed political offence. The case law is, in general, very strict when it comes to the qualification

424 The custodial penalties the Criminal Code imposes are felony imprisonment and imprisonment, not detention and the Assize Court has not been explicitly given competence over the standard offences.

425 Delmulle and Guenter (n 15) 4.

426 Own translation, original in French: "*qui, dans l'intention de son auteur et par ses effets, porte directement atteinte aux institutions politiques*" (Cass. 5 mei 1913, *Pas.* 1913, I, 207). See also: Cass. 21 november 1927, *Pas.* 1928, I, 20; Cass. 3 april 1984, *Arr.Cass.* 1983-84, 1023; Tulkens and others (n 16) 345-346; Van den Wyngaert and Vandromme (n 16) 193-194; Van den Wyngaert, Vandromme and Traest (n 16) 204.

427 Own translation, original in French: "*l'atteinte que son auteur cherche à porter au fonctionnement des institutions politiques se réalise de façon médiate, par la mise en péril de vies humaines ou d'intérêts économiques quelconques, fussent-ils étrangers aux structures ou aux institutions que l'auteur dit vouloir frapper.*" (Cass. 27 juni 2007, P.07.0333.F). See also: Antwerpen 7 februari 2008, *onuitg.*, 34-35; De Hert and Millen (n 32) 3; Delhaise (n 9) 20; De Nauw and Deruyck (n 20) 53; De Nauw and Kuty (n 16) 17; Deruyck and De Nauw (n 16) 8; Ketels (n 14) 239; Tulkens and others (n 16) 349; Van den Wyngaert, Vandromme and Traest (n 16) 207; Weyembergh and Kennes, 'Le Titre Iter Du Livre II Du Code Pénal: Des Infractions Terroristes' (n 7) 123-124.

428 Cass. 27 juni 2007, P.07.0333.F; De La Serna (n 7) 213-214; De La Serna (n 15) 201.

429 There is no definition or exhaustive list. The Court of Cassation has stated that this includes among other things the constitutional regime of the state, the parliaments, the authority and constitutional prerogatives of the King, the order of succession to the throne, the exercise of ministerial powers and the political rights of citizens (Cass. 18 november 2003, *Arr.Cass.* 2003, afl. 11, 2125, concl M Timperman. See also: Tulkens and others (n 16) 346-347).

430 De La Serna (n 7) 214; Moucheron (n 7) paras 21-22.

of political offence.[431] The reasons behind the Court of Cassation not qualifying terrorism as a political offence probably, at least partly, have to do with the competent court being the Assize Court,[432] where relatively long, cumbersome and expensive jury trials take place.

A second special category of offences which may be relevant is that of press offences. A press offence is the expression of an idea or an opinion which constitutes a breach of criminal law, by means of a printed document or a similar process, provided that the document containing the offence has been given effective publicity.[433] This definition requires the expression of an idea or opinion,[434] meaning that stating facts or spreading an image, for example,[435] is not sufficient.[436] Societal relevance, however, is not required.[437] The case law states that a video, image or spoken text cannot be a press offence unless it is accompanied by writing.[438] Spreading a text over the internet is considered a 'similar process' to a printed document so can also be a press offence.[439] Finally, effective publicity is required, which is a factual issue.[440] The text needs to be spread, but not necessarily on a large scale. Applying this definition to the terrorist offences discussed above, it becomes evident that, under the right circumstances, many of them can constitute a press offence.

---

431 De La Serna (n 7) 168; De La Serna (n 15) 200-201; Delmulle and Guenter (n 15) 4; Franssen (n 418) 30; Kerkhofs (n 419) 266; Moucheron (n 7) para 12; Van den Wyngaert and Vandromme (n 16) 195.

432 Art 150 Constitution; De La Serna (n 15) 201; Delhaise (n 9) 20; De Nauw and Deruyck (n 20) 54; Kerkhofs (n 419) 265; Masset (n 7) T60/23; Tulkens and others (n 16) 342-343; Van den Wyngaert and Vandromme (n 16) 192 en 197; Van den Wyngaert, Vandromme and Traest (n 16) 207.

433 Cass. 17 januari 1990, *Arr.Cass.* 1989-90, 309; Cass. 7 februari 1995, AJT 1995-96, 248, noot D Voorhoof; Cass. 28 april 2021, P.21.0029.F; Cass. 19 januari 2022, *JT* 2022, 143; Corr. Hainaut 22 maart 2021, *JLMB* 2022, 444; Gyselaers (n 417) 97; Kerkhofs (n 417) 65; Chris Van den Wyngaert, Philip Traest and Steven Vandromme, *Strafrecht En Strafprocesrecht in Hoofdlijnen* (Maklu 2017) 207.

434 Corr. Hainaut 22 maart 2021, *JLMB* 2022, 444; Kerkhofs (n 417) 65-66.

435 Cass. 7 december 1971, *Pas.* 1972, I, 341; Eric Brewaeys, 'Persmisdrijf via Internet' (Noot Onder Cass. 29 October 2013)' [2014] Nieuw Juridisch Weekblad 408; Kerkhofs (n 417) 69.

436 Alain De Nauw and Filiep Deruyck, *Overzicht van Het Belgisch Algemeen Strafrecht* (die Keure 2015) 56; Tulkens and others (n 16) 359-360; Van den Wyngaert, Traest and Vandromme (n 433) 208; Jogchum Vrielink, 'Internet: Spreken Is Zilver, Schrijven Is Goud? Drukpersmisdrijf (Art. 150 Gw.), de Audiovisuele Media En de Zaak Belkacem' [2014] Tijdschrift voor Strafrecht 143, 145.

437 Cass. 6 maart 2012, *NjW* 2012, 341; Corr. Hainaut 22 maart 2021, *JLMB* 2022, 444; De Nauw and Deruyck (n 436) 55; Gyselaers (n 417) 99; Kerkhofs (n 417) 70.

438 Cass. 29 oktober 2013, *NjW* 2014, 406, noot Eric Brewaeys. See also: Brewaeys (n 435); De Nauw and Deruyck (n 436) 56; Gyselaers (n 417) 98-99; Tulkens and others (n 16) 360-368; Van den Wyngaert, Traest and Vandromme (n 433) 209; Vrielink (n 436) 145-146.

439 Cass. 6 maart 2012, *NjW* 2012, 341; Cass. 29 januari 2013, P.12.1988.N; Cass 29 januari 2013, P.12.1961.N; Cass. 29 oktober 2013, *NjW* 2014, 406, noot Eric Brewaeys; Cass. 8 november 2016, P.16.0958.N; Corr. Hainaut 22 maart 2021, *JLMB* 2022, 444; Brewaeys (n 435); De Nauw and Deruyck (n 436) 56; Gyselaers (n 417) 97-98; Kerkhofs (n 417) 70; Sofie Royer, 'Beledigingen via Sociale Media En Het Drukpersmisdrijf' [2018] Nieuw Juridisch Weekblad 650, 650; Van den Wyngaert, Traest and Vandromme (n 433) 209-210; Vrielink (n 436) 145-146.

440 Kerkhofs (n 417) 66; Tulkens and others (n 16) 362-363; Van den Wyngaert, Traest and Vandromme (n 433) 210-211.

For example, spreading certain messages on social media with an aim to incite or recruit people or to threaten a terrorist offence. This would have several consequences in criminal law and criminal procedure, the most important of which being that press offences (barring those based on racism or xenophobia) need to be tried by the Assize Courts.[441]

Trials *in absentia*

Belgian criminal procedure allows for trials *in absentia*. This means that if one of the parties does not appear at trial, either in person or by representation, the trial can still go ahead without them.[442] The only exception on this rule is the public prosecution service, which has to be present. It is therefore possible for a person to be convicted without even being there. This is possible for all the aforementioned Criminal Courts, meaning even murder trials with a jury can happen *in absentia*.[443]

However, if a defendant was convicted *in absentia*, they have a right to a retrial under certain conditions.[444] First of all, there is a normal deadline of fifteen days after the judgment is served within which the judgment *in absentia* must be protested.[445] If the judgment was not served to the defendant themselves, however, but to their legal address for example, there is an extraordinary deadline as well. This deadline expires on the fifteenth day after the defendant has become aware that the judgment *in absentia* has been served.[446] If this happened through the serving of a European arrest warrant or an extradition order, or if the term of fifteen days has not expired at the moment of arrest abroad, the term is extended until fifteen days after extradition or after the day of liberation

441 Art 150 Constitution. See also: Cass. 29 oktober 2013, *NjW* 2014, 406, noot Eric Brewaeys; Corr. Hainaut 22 maart 2021, *JLMB* 2022, 444; De Nauw and Deruyck (n 436) 57; Kerkhofs (n 417) 67; Royer (n 439) 650; Van den Wyngaert, Traest and Vandromme (n 433) 211; Vrielink (n 436) 145.

442 Philip Traest and Joachim Meese, 'De rechtsmiddelen verzet en hoger beroep: actualia' in T Daems, W De Bondt and N De Nil, *Strafrecht en strafprocesrecht: doel of middel in een veranderde samenleving?* (Kluwer 2017) 520-522; Van den Wyngaert, Traest and Vandromme (n 433) 1271-1272; Verstraeten (n 403) 1075-1076.

443 Traest and Meese (n 442) 524; Verstraeten (n 403) 1079.

444 Declercq (n 198) 1408; Patrick Vandenbruwaene, Yves Liégeois and Bart De Smet, 'Het complexe systeem van verstek, ontvankelijk of niet- ontvankelijk verzet, ongedaan verzet en de opeenvolging van verzet en hoger beroep. Voorstellen tot vereenvoudiging' [2015] Rechtskundig Weekblad 963, 963; Van den Wyngaert, Traest and Vandromme (n 433) 1356-1358; Verstraeten (n 403) 1080.

445 Art 187, §1 and 208 CCP. See also: Tom Decaigny, 'Formele Aspecten van de Buitengewone Termijn Voor Verzet' [2016] Tijdschrift voor Strafrecht 237, 238; Declercq (n 198) 1414; Traest and Meese (n 442) 528-530; Van den Wyngaert, Traest and Vandromme (n 433) 1362-1364; Verstraeten (n 403) 1258-1260.

446 Art 187, §2 CCP. See also: Decaigny, 'Formele Aspecten van de Buitengewone Termijn Voor Verzet' (n 445) 238; Declercq (n 198) 1418-1419; Bart De Smet, 'Het Verzet van de Beklaagde Die in Het Buitenland Is Aangehouden' [2016] Rechtskundig Weekblad 623, 623; Traest and Meese (n 442) 531-533; Vandenbruwaene, Liégeois and De Smet (n 444) 964; Van den Wyngaert, Traest and Vandromme (n 433) 1364-1366; Verstraeten (n 403) 1260-1262.

abroad.[447] Secondly, if the party was aware of the summons[448] yet did not appear without force majeure or a lawful ground for excuse, their retrial will be declared invalid, as is the case if a party does not show at its retrial.[449] A retrial procedure instigated by the defence cannot work to their detriment, meaning that the sentence cannot be elevated.[450]

It is possible for these rules to apply to foreign terrorist fighters who travelled to Syria. A trial *in absentia* may go ahead while they are in Syria.[451] If they ever return to Belgium, the normal deadline for a retrial will have usually passed. However, it is possible that they may not have known about the summons and about the judgment being served until they arrived in Belgium. This means that they will still have time to request a retrial under the extraordinary deadline. There are several examples of terrorism cases being retried after an initial trial *in absentia*.[452]

IMMEDIATE ARREST WARRANTS

If a defendant is convicted to a prison sentence, they can be deprived of their liberty in execution of this sentence. However, this execution does not start the moment the judgment is rendered. A judgment can only be executed if it has force of *res judicata*.[453] If the convicted defendant was already in pre-trial detention for those offences, however, he remains in detention, as long as he was convicted for a prison sentence which is longer than the time already spent in (pre-trial) detention.[454] If the defendant was not in detention yet, he remains at liberty even after the judgment, until it gains force of *res judicata* and can be executed.

---

447 Art 184, §1 CCP. See also: Cass. 14 april 2015, *RW* 2016-17, 622, noot De Smet; Cass. 5 oktober 2021, P.21.0881.N; De Smet, 'Het Verzet van de Beklaagde Die in Het Buitenland Is Aangehouden' (n 446) 624.

448 Which needs to be proven, see: Cass. 17 januari 2017, *RW* 2018-2019, 654, noot De Smet.

449 Art 187, §6 CCP. See also: Cass. 18 januari 2022, P.21.1291.N; Bart De Smet, 'Het Ongedaan Verzet En de Vereiste van Kennisname van de Dagvaarding' [2018] Rechtskundig Weekblad 654, 654-655; Bart De Smet, 'Het Begrip "Wettige Verschoning" van Artikel 187, § 6, 1° Sv. Als Criterium Voor Ongedaan Verzet' [2019] Tijdschrift voor Strafrecht 164, 164; Stijn Lamberigts, 'Ongedaan Verzet: Eigen Schuld, Dikke Bult?' [2019] Tijdschrift voor Strafrecht 235, 235-237; Traest and Meese (n 442) 539-542; Van den Wyngaert, Traest and Vandromme (n 433) 1367-1368.

450 Cass. 13 november 1985, *Arr.Cass.* 1985-86, 340; Cass. 6 oktober 1993, *Arr.Cass.* 1993, 811; Cass. 3 september 2003, P.03.515.F; Cass. 17 december 2008, P.08.1281.F; Declercq (n 198) 1426; Traest and Meese (n 442) 543-546; Verstraeten (n 403) 1264-1265.

451 See for example: Corr. Brussel 8 mei 2017, *onuitg.*; Corr. Charleroi 22 november 2017, *onuitg.*; Corr. Mechelen 4 januari 2018, *onuitg.* See also: Elise Delhaise, Coline Remacle and Chloé Thomas, 'Après le califat, l'embarras' (2020) 6 La Revue Nouvelle 49, 63.

452 See: Corr. Brussel 14 oktober 2014, *onuitg.*, retrial of Corr. Brussel 21 mei 2014, *onuitg.*; Corr. Antwerpen 30 juni 2015, *onuitg.*, retrial of Corr. Antwerpen 11 februari 2015, *onuitg.*

453 Van den Wyngaert, Vandromme and Traest (n 16) 1230; Verstraeten (n 403) 1192.

454 Van den Wyngaert, Vandromme and Traest (n 16) 1230; Verstraeten (n 403) 1170-1171.

It is possible, however, for the trial court to order the immediate arrest of the convicted defendant who was not yet detained. This is not an early execution of the sentence, but a form of remand in custody, the same as pre-trial detention or detention during trial.[455] This is possible if the defendant was convicted to a sentence of minimum three years imprisonment.[456] If the defendant was convicted for terrorism (*sensu strico* or *sensu lato*)[457], however, their immediate arrest can be ordered if their sentence is minimum one year imprisonment.[458] In addition, an immediate arrest can only be ordered when the trial court fears (in a substantiated manner) that the convicted defendant might try to evade the execution of his sentence, or might commit new standard offences or felonies.[459] When a suspect is in detention after an immediate arrest (for example while awaiting their appeal), they can request their provisional release from the court where their case is pending.[460] No appeal is possible against a decision from this court in this matter.[461] This

455 Filip Van Volsem and others, *Voorlopige hechtenis: commentaar* (Daniel De Wolf ed, INNI publishers 2014) 352; Verstraeten (n 403) 1171.

456 Art 33, §2 Statute on pre-trial detention. See also: Marie Horseele and others, 'Recente Wijzigingen in Het Straf(Proces)Recht: Consequent Incoherent?', *Recht in beweging – 25ste VRG-Alumnidag* (Gompel&Svacina 2018) 125; Van den Wyngaert, Vandromme and Traest (n 16) 1230.

457 or certain sexual offences.

458 Art 33, §2 Statute on pre-trial detention. See also: Van den Wyngaert, Vandromme and Traest (n 16) 1230. It used to be one year for all offences (Verstraeten (n 403) 1171-1172.). The legislature raised this threshold to three years for all offences, except for terrorism and certain sexual offences in 2017 (art 7 wet van 21 december 2017, tot wijziging van diverse bepalingen met het oog op de invoering van een beveiligingsperiode en tot wijziging van de wet van 20 juli 1990 betreffende de voorlopige hechtenis voor wat de onmiddellijke aanhouding betreft, *BS* 11 januari 2018, 1185). This was done without really motivating the differentiation between terrorism and sexual offences on the one hand and all other offences on the other hand. See: Horseele and others (n 456) 125-126; Yperman, 'De bestrijding van terrorisme en strafprocesrecht: vele kleintjes maken een grote' (n 26) 10-11.

459 Art 33, §2 Statute on pre-trial detention. Until 2019, an immediate arrest was only possible in case of risk of evasion of the execution of the sentence (Verstraeten (n 403) 1172.). The reasoning was that the suspect had been at liberty up until that point and had not committed other offences during the investigation and procedure (or tried to manipulate the evidence or conspired with others). The judgment did, however, give him an extra reason to flee. Therefore, an immediate arrest was possible when there were reasons to believe he would do so. After a highly mediatised case of a murder committed by a man who had already been convicted for previous offences but who appealed his conviction and whose immediate arrest was not ordered because there was no risk he would flee, the legislature decided to make an immediate arrest also possible in case there is a risk of new offences being committed. See: Wetsvoorstel van 1 oktober 2019 tot wijziging van de wet van 20 juli 1990 betreffende de voorlopige hechtenis aangaande de onmiddellijke aanhouding, *Parl.St.* Kamer 2019, 55-0489/001, 3-4; amendement nr. 3 van 5 november 2019 bij tot wijziging van de wet van 20 juli 1990 betreffende de voorlopige hechtenis aangaande de onmiddellijke aanhouding, *Parl.St.* Kamer 2019, 55-0489/005, 2. This addition was challenged before the Constitutional Court, which found it to be constitutional. See: GwH 10 juni 2021, 86/2021, *Rechtskundig Weekblad* 2021-2022, 755.

460 Art 27, §1, 2° and §2 Statute on pre-trial detention; Cass. 5 januari 2021, *T.Strafr.* 2021, 232, noot Daeninck; Van Volsem and others (n 455) 235.

461 Cass. 5 januari 2021, *T.Strafr.* 2021, 232, noot Daeninck; P Daeninck, 'Over het verzoekschrift tot voorlopige invrijheidstelling na het instellen van hoger beroep tegen de beslissing ten gronde' (2021) 2021 Tijdschrift voor Strafrecht 232.

technique of immediate arrest warrants is often combined with a trial *in absentia* for defendants who are believed to still be in Syria.[462] This allows for the immediate arrest of the convicted foreign terrorist fighter upon their return to Belgium in execution of this immediate arrest warrant, who can then be kept in detention while a possible retrial takes place.

CASE LAW ANALYSIS

None of the cases analysed were tried by the Assize Courts.[463] 180 judgments were made *in absentia*, being more than half. Out of the total of 343 individual first instance judgments eight were retrials after a trial *in absentia*, divided into five cases. As explained above, the sentence cannot be elevated upon retrial. For four defendants the sentence stayed the same, for two it went down and in one case a conviction was turned into an acquittal. For one case the original *in absentia* decision could not be found, making it impossible to compare. In 152 cases an immediate arrest warrant was issued and of these 152 immediate arrest warrants 135 followed a trial *in absentia*. Consequently, only 17 immediate arrest warrants were issued with the defendant present. In cases not *in absentia*, immediate arrest warrants were sometimes requested, but the chances of it being granted were much lower, while *in absentia* a refusal being very rare.

In total 22 Court of Appeal cases were relevant concerning a total of 55 individual judgments. One of these judgments concerned a retrial after an appeal trial *in absentia*, which imposed the same sentence as the trial *in absentia*. Of the total of 55 individal Court of Appeal decisions 30 confirmed the first instance decision, fourteen imposed a higher sentence and eleven a lower sentence.

462 See for example: Corr. Brussel 21 mei 2014, *onuitg.*; Corr. Brussel 25 november 2015, *onuitg.*; Corr. Brussel 3 mei 2016, *onuitg.*; Corr. Charleroi 22 november 2017, *onuitg.*; Corr. Mechelen 4 januari 2018, *onuitg.*; Corr. Brussel 1 maart 2018, *onuitg.*; Corr. Antwerpen 18 maart 2018, *onuitg.*.

463 Note that if prosecuted today, a few would have to be, but back then did not have to.

3 Sentences

Prison sentences

Terrorism sensu stricto

Upon a conviction for a terrorism offence, the sentence will often be a prison sentence. Belgian legislation has three types of prison sentences: felony imprisonment, imprisonment and detention. Felony imprisonment is imposed for felonies which are not correctionalised.[464] Imprisonment is imposed for standard offences and correctionalised felonies (and contraventions)[465] and detention is imposed for political offences.[466] It is important to note that while the difference between these three types of sentences has many technical legal consequences, it has no consequences concerning everyday reality in prison. Inmates convicted to felony imprisonment, imprisonment or detention are treated in the same manner. As outlined in Section 2.1, terrorism is not a political offence, so detention is not relevant for the purposes of this analysis. The sentence will either be felony imprisonment or imprisonment.

The prison sentences for terrorism *sensu stricto* are listed in article 138 CC as follows:

> *§1 The penalties for the offences listed in article 137 §2 shall be replaced by the following, if those offences are regarded as terrorist offences:*
> *1° a fine, by imprisonment of one year to three years;*
> *2° imprisonment of no more than six months, by imprisonment of no more than three years;*
> *3° imprisonment of no more than one year, by imprisonment of no more than three years;*
> *4° imprisonment of no more than three years, by imprisonment of no more than five years;*
> *5° imprisonment of no more than five years, by felony imprisonment of five years to ten years;*

---

464 Art 1, Section 1 and 7, 1°CC; De Nauw and Deruyck (n 20) 45; Tulkens and others (n 16) 334 and 582-286; Yves Van Den Berge, 'Het Belgische strafrecht: veel aandacht voor de vrijheidsbeneming en de vrijheidsbeperking' [2019] Nullum Crimen 1, 10; Van den Wyngaert, Vandromme and Traest (n 16) 195.

465 Art 1, Sections 2 and 3, art 7, Section 2 and art 25, Section 1 CC; De Nauw and Deruyck (n 20) 46; Tulkens and others (n 16) 334, 589 and 600; Van den Wyngaert, Vandromme and Traest (n 16) 195.

466 Van Den Berge (n 464) 10; Van den Wyngaert, Traest and Vandromme (n 433) 413-414.

> *6° felony imprisonment of five years to ten years, by felony imprisonment of ten years to fifteen years;*
> *7° felony imprisonment of ten years to fifteen years, by felon imprisonment of fifteen years to twenty years;*
> *8° felony imprisonment of ten years to twenty years, by felony imprisonment of fifteen years to twenty years;*
> *9° felony imprisonment of fifteen years to twenty years, by felony imprisonment of twenty years to thirty years;*
> *10° felony imprisonment of twenty years to thirty years, by felony imprisonment for life.*
> *In the cases referred to in Article 137, §2, 11°, the maximum penalty imposed for the completed offence shall be reduced by one year.*
> *§2 The terrorist offences referred to in Article 137 §3 shall be punishable by:*
> *1° in the case referred to in 6°, imprisonment of three months to five years if the threat concerns an offence punishable by a correctional penalty and felony imprisonment from five to ten years if the threat concerns a criminal offence punishable by a criminal penalty;*
> *2° felony imprisonment from fifteen to twenty years in the cases referred to in 1°, 2°, and 5°;*
> *3° life felony imprisonment in the cases referred to in 3° and 4°.*[467]

For the offences listed in article 137, §2 CC, which are also punishable outside of a terrorist context, terrorism serves as an aggravating circumstance.[468] The maximum imprisonment sentence is aggravated and standard offences with a maximum sentence of five years imprisonment become felonies with a sentence of five to ten years felony imprisonment.[469] For the terrorist standard offences, the preparatory works explicitly state that if the offence was originally punishable with a fine (as principal sentence (*hoofdstraf; peine principale*) or on top of the custodial sentence), the fine remains.[470] The sentences for felonies go up

467 Article 138 CC. Own translation, original in Dutch and French.

468 Beernaert, 'La Loi Du 19 Décembre 2003 Relative Aux Infractions Terroristes : Quand Le Droit Pénal Belge Évolue Sous La Dictée de l'Union Européenne' (n 14) 587; De La Serna (n 7) 179 and 204; De La Serna (n 15) 207; Delhaise (n 9) 75; Flore (n 9) 214; Fransen and Kerkhofs (n 9) 22; Hameeuw (n 15) 7; Masset (n 7) T60/19; Weyembergh and Kennes, 'Domestic Provisions and Case Law: The Belgian Case' (n 7) 153; Weyembergh and Kennes, 'Le Titre Iter Du Livre II Du Code Pénal: Des Infractions Terroristes' (n 7) 109; Winants (n 7) 147.

469 Memorie van Toelichting bij wetsontwerp van 6 oktober 2003 betreffende terroristische misdrijven, *Parl.St.* Kamer 2003, nr. 51-0258/001, (4) 11-12; Delhaise (n 9) 76; Hameeuw (n 15) 7.

470 Memorie van Toelichting bij wetsontwerp van 6 oktober 2003 betreffende terroristische misdrijven, *Parl.St.* Kamer 2003, nr. 51-0258/001, (4) 11. See also: Ketels (n 14) 240.

one step on the scale of article 80 CC.[471] For the terrorist offences listed in article 137, §3 CC, article 138 CC imposes maximum sentences ranging from five years imprisonment to life felony imprisonment.[472] At first glance, this seems like a simple system of determining sentences, but a more thorough analysis exposes some issues. First of all, the sentence for threatening is sometimes higher than the sentence for the threatened terrorist offence. The terrorist offences from article 137, §3 CC are all felonies, with one exception.[473] This exception is threatening[474] a terrorist standard offence.[475] The sentence for threatening a terrorist felony is five to ten years felony imprisonment, making the offence of threatening a felony as well. The sentence for threatening a terrorist standard offence, however, is three months to five years imprisonment, which makes the threatening a standard offence.[476] This would be the case, for example, for threatening to destroy a monument when this endangers human lives or causes significant economic damage, or threatening intentional battery. However, the maximum principal sentence for when these offences are actually committed is three years imprisonment.[477] This means that for these standard offences (and for some of the other terrorist standard offences *sensu stricto*), threatening the offence has a higher maximum sentence than the offence itself. This seems a rather absurd consequence of careless legislating. Since the maximum principal sentence for threatening a terrorist standard offence (*sensu stricto*) is the maximum principal sentence for any standard offence, the sentence for threatening is per definition at least as high, and sometimes higher, than that for the actual offence. It is striking that the current wording, with a distinction between threatening a terrorist standard offence and a terrorist felony is already a refinement of the original proposal. In this proposal, threatening only had one sentence, being five to ten years felony imprisonment, regardless of the threatened offence. Some senators pointed out that this led some terrorist offences to have a lower sentence

---

471 Hameeuw (n 15) 7. Article 80 CC consists of a scale of sentences which is used when applying attenuating circumstances. This scale is used in Belgian criminal procedure for several purposes besides the application of attenuating circumstances. The sentences for attempted felonies or accessories to felonies for example are also derived from the scale of article 80 CC.

472 Art 138, §2 CC. See also: Flore (n 9) 220; Weyembergh and Kennes, 'Le Titre Iter Du Livre II Du Code Pénal: Des Infractions Terroristes' (n 7) 109.

473 Beernaert, 'La Loi Du 19 Décembre 2003 Relative Aux Infractions Terroristes : Quand Le Droit Pénal Belge Évolue Sous La Dictée de l'Union Européenne' (n 14) 587; Masset (n 7) 19; Weyembergh and Kennes, 'Domestic Provisions and Case Law: The Belgian Case' (n 7) 153.

474 The original draft bill stated 'credible threat' and the parliamentary documents stated that the threat had to be serious (Memorie van Toelichting bij wetsontwerp van 6 oktober 2003 betreffende terroristische misdrijven, *Parl.St.* Kamer 2003, nr. 51-0258/001, (4) 11). However, the Council of State pointed out that the word 'credible' was not part of the Framework Decision and wondered why it was included here (Advies van de Raad van State bij wetsontwerp van 6 oktober 2003 betreffende terroristische misdrijven, *Parl.St.* Kamer 2003, nr. 51-0258/001, 39). After this, the word was deleted.

475 De La Serna (n 7) 205-206; Delhaise (n 9) 77-78; Masset (n 7) 19; Winants (n 7) 347.

476 Art 138, §3, 1° CC.

477 Respectively art 138, 3° and 2° CC.

when committed than when merely threatened.[478] This prompted the change of the proposal to its current wording. However, the issue has not been fully solved and further refinement is required.

In addition to this proportionality issue, the wording of the sentencing brackets of article 138° CC leaves much to be desired.[479] For example, a maximum imprisonment of six months can be substituted by a maximum imprisonment of three years. A literal reading of the code, however, also shows that a maximum imprisonment of six months could be substituted by a maximum imprisonment of five years or even by felony imprisonment of five to ten years. A sentence of six months is 'no more than six months', but is also 'no more than three years' or 'no more than five years'. This was probably not the intention of the legislature. When interpreting this part of the statute according to the likely intention of the legislature, 'imprisonment of no more than' has to be read as 'a maximum imprisonment of'. Doing so avoids the problem, since 'a maximum imprisonment of six months' is not 'a maximum imprisonment of one year', etc. However, a close analysis of the list of offences of article 137, §2 CC shows that for example the offence of intentional battery which leads to illness or the incapacity to work, has a maximum sentence of two years imprisonment.[480] Two years is not on the list of article 138, §1 CC. The categories jump from one to three years. Unfortunately, this is not the only example of a standard offence on the list with a maximum sentence of two or four years imprisonment (for sentences of four years the same problem arises, since the categories go from three to five years).[481] At first glance, the solution is easy. The logical thing to do is to apply the aggravated sentence for offences punishable with 'imprisonment of no more than three years' and 'imprisonment of no more than five years' to offences with a maximum sentence of respectively two and four years imprisonment. This is the case since when read literally, two years is 'no more than three years', so an offence with a maximum sentence of two years imprisonment does fall in this category. This interpretation, however, goes directly against the interpretation that solved the previous issue (see above). If two years falls within the category of 'no more than three years', then one year or six months also fall within this category. At present, therefore, the courts have to apply a double interpretation. For offences punishable by a maximum sentence of imprisonment of six

478 Verslag namens de commissie voor justitie van 3 december 2003 bij het wetsontwerp betreffende terroristische misdrijven, *Parl.St.* Senaat 2003-04, nr. 3-332/3, 19.

479 For a more detailed analysis, see also: Yperman, 'De terroristische misdrijven in de artikelen 137 en 140 Sw.: geen legistieke voltreffer' (n 152).

480 Art 399, section 1 CC.

481 The following offences also have a maximum sentence of two years imprisonment: art 405*bis* 2° and 434 CC, art 5 and 7 wet van 28 mei 1956 betreffende ontplofbare en voor de deflagratie vatbare stoffen en mengsels en de daarmee geladen tuigen, *BS* 19 juni 1956, 3990 and art 14 wet van 5 juni 1928 houdende herziening van het Tucht- en Strafwetboek voor de koopvaardij en de zeevisserij, *BS* 26 juli 1928, 3341. The following offences have a maximum sentence of four years imprisonment: art 405bis 3° and 513, *in fine* CC.

months, one year, three years or five years, the case-law should read article 138, §1 CC as 'a maximum sentence of'. However, for offences with a maximum term of imprisonment of two and four years, the article must be read literally ('no more than' three and five years) and those offences therefore fall under 4° and 5° respectively.

The wording of the felony imprisonment sentences does not have this same issue, as it does not use the terms 'no more than'. This does not mean the categories of felony imprisonment are completely without issues though. The list of article 137, §2 CC contains many offences with aggravating circumstances which can cause issues when trying to apply the aggravating circumstance of terrorism to those already aggravated offences. One such example was noted in the Senate, being article 405*bis*, 11° CC. This article contains an aggravating circumstance that increases the sentence for deliberately administering substances to somebody without the intention of killing them but which results in their death, from fifteen to twenty years felony imprisonment to seventeen to twenty years felony imprisonment. This was the example in the Senate, but there are other aggravating circumstances which raise the minimum sentence with two years felony imprisonment[482], because of which the sentence bracket does not fit neatly with the brackets that are listed in article 138, §1 CC. As a response to the Senate's question, the Secretary stated that this sentence should be treated the same as a sentence of fifteen to twenty years imprisonment.[483] A similar issue arises for aggravating circumstances which (also) raise the maximum sentence. For example, article 409, §1 CC criminalises genital mutilation and imposes a sentence of three to five years imprisonment. The second paragraph of that article contains an aggravating circumstance, prescribing a sentence of five to seven years felony imprisonment for genital mutilation of underage women or genital mutilation motivated by profit. The list of article 137, §1 CC explicitly includes both §1 and §2. Another example is arson of an inhabited house where people are present, which is punishable with fifteen to twenty years felony imprisonment.[484] When those people present are injured however, the sentence goes up to fifteen to twenty-two years felony imprisonment.[485] The solution offered by the Secretary seems simple, but this is not the case. The solution is the same one which is used with regard to correctionalisation. The application of attenuating circumstances which goes hand in hand with correctionalisation, also influences the sentencing bracket and article 80 CC provides for the same sentencing ranges as article 138, §1, 6°, 7°, 9° and 10° do for terrorism. In the legal doctrine on correctionalisation, Rozie states that seventeen to twenty years felony imprisonment[486] before correctionalisation

482 See: art 405*ter*, art 409, §5 and art 410 CC.

483 Verslag namens de commissie voor de Justitie van 3 december 2003 bij het wetsontwerp betreffende terroristische misdrijven, *Parl.St.* Senaat 2003-04, nr. 3-332/3, 19.

484 Art 510 CC.

485 Art 518 CC.

486 In the context of the application of the rules on recidivism in article 55*bis*, *in fine* CC.

should be treated in the same manner as fifteen to twenty years felony imprisonment (and should thus become one to fifteen years imprisonment after correctionalisation).[487] The analogous application of this interpretation seems logical. The paramount difference, however, is that correctionalisation leads to an attenuation of the sentence and is therefore in favour of the defence, while terrorism serves as an aggravating circumstance and works to the detriment of the defence. The parallel between these two situations is therefore not quite right as it could be construed as a forbidden analogous interpretation *in malam partem*[488]. Another possible solution, at least for some of the issues, would be to apply the broader categories of article 138 CC to narrower ones they include. For example five to seven years would then fall within the category of five to ten years and seventeen to twenty years would fall in the category of fifteen to twenty years. However, this solution is not tenable because of the existence of article 138, §1, 8° CC. When creating the categories in article 138 CC, the legislature gave special thought to article 30 of the 'wet van 27 juni 1937 houdende herziening van de wet van 16 november 1919 betreffende de regeling de luchtvaart'. §1, 2° of this article is on the list of article 137 CC[489] and provides for a sentence of ten to twenty years felony imprisonment for the hijacking of a plane. Article 138, §1, 8° CC includes a sentencing bracket of ten to twenty years felony imprisonment, specifically for this one offence.[490] This means that if 'five to seven years' were to be brought within the category of 'five to ten years', any offence with a sentence of ten to fifteen or fifteen to twenty years felony imprisonment, would fall within the category of ten to twenty years felony imprisonment as well. This does not seem to be the intention of the legislature. Luckily, there is a third option. When the Secretary stated that a sentence of seventeen to twenty years has to be treated as one of fifteen to twenty years, he in fact reverted back to the unaggravated offence. In other words, the first aggravating circumstance is not applied and instead the aggravating circumstance of terrorism is immediately applied. This is in line with the basic principle of criminal law which obliges the judge to qualify the facts as the highest possible offence[491] and with the EU Directive which requires 'custodial sentences heavier than those imposable under national law for such offences in the absence

487 J Rozie, 'De recidivewet van 5 mei 2019: de vergiftigde kers op de repressieve taart' (2019) 14 Nullum Crimen 291, 295.

488 E Claes, Legaliteit en rechtsvinding in het strafrecht: Een grondslagentheoretische benadering (Universitaire Pers Leuven 2003) 29; Kuty (n 196) 250-253; Van den Wyngaert and Vandromme (n 20) 89.

489 Art 137, §2, 5° CC.

490 Memorie van toelichting bij wetsontwerp van 6 oktober 2003 betreffende terroristische misdrijven, *Parl.St.* Kamer 2003, nr. 51-0258/001, (4) 12.

491 This is called "*sa plus haute expression pénale*". See: Declerq (n 198) 926; H Van Bavel and F Vandendriessche, 'Gunningsfraude en de strafrechtelijke bescherming van de vrijheid van opbod' [2013] *T.Strafr.* 283, 292; F Van Volsem, 'Kwalificatieperikelen: hij die als dief wordt vervolgd, kan worden veroordeeld als heler en omgekeerd (Noot Onder Cass. 9 december 2008)' [2009] *RABG* 28; Verstraeten (n 403) 833.

of [terrorist] intent'[492]. Since terrorism leads to a harsher sentence, this harsher aggravating circumstance could absorb the lighter aggravating circumstance. This does leave us wondering why the legislature included these aggravated offences in the list of article 137, §2 CC at all since the aggravating circumstance which should be applied before terrorism cannot be applied at all. Finally, terrorism *sensu stricto*, in the current phrasing of its sentencing brackets, neutralises the effect of some of the other aggravating circumstances and decreases proportionality between some of the offences. Since fines as a principal penalty and imprisonment of 'no more than' six months and 'no more than' one year are replaced by imprisonment of 'no more than' three years, the proportionality in the three lowest sentencing brackets disappears. The maximum sentence for terrorist battery, for example, is three years imprisonment, regardless whether or not there was premeditation.[493] This is striking because premeditation doubles the maximum sentence for battery outside of a terrorist context.[494] Similar situations arise for other aggravating circumstances, such as if the victim of the battery was a minor or someone in a vulnerable situation.[495] Furthermore, article 138, §1 CC does not provide for a minimum sentence for the offences originally punishable with imprisonment while it does for offences originally punishable with a fine as a principal penalty. In the latter case the sentence becomes one to three years imprisonment. For offences originally punishable with a sentence of 'no more than' six months imprisonment, however, the code only states that the sentence becomes 'no more than' three years. Since no new minimum sentence is mentioned, the application of the 'aggravating circumstance' of terrorism does not change the old minimum sentence.[496] By definition this sentence will be less than six months. Therefore, after the application of the 'aggravating circumstance' of terrorism, the principal sentence for an offence originally punishable with only a fine as principal sentence becomes one to three years imprisonment while the principal sentence for an offence originally punishable with for example eight days to six months imprisonment becomes eight days to three years imprisonment. In other words, the principal sentence of the lighter offence has become heavier than the one for the more serious offence. In order to avoid this, the legislature should have either

492 Art 15.2 Directive (EU) 2017/541 of the European Parliament and of the Council of 15 March 2017 on combating terrorism and replacing Council Framework Decision 2002/475/JHA and amending Council Decision 2005/671/JHA, [2017] OJ L88/6. *NB*: the Directive adds: "except where the sentences imposable are already the maximum possible sentences under national law".

493 Delhaise states that premeditation is inherent to terrorism *sensu stricto* and that it will therefore always be present (Delhaise (n 9) 31.). Although in many cases there will indeed be premeditation, this is in our opinion not necessarily so. Premeditation is not part of the *actus reus* or *mens rea* of terrorism and it is therefore possible that these elements are present without premeditation. See for premeditation: Patrick Arnou, 'Voorbedachten Rade', *Strafrecht en strafvordering. Artikelsgewijze commentaar met overzicht van rechtspraak en rechtsleer* (Wolters Kluwer 1990) 2.

494 Art 398 CC.

495 Art 398 *j.* 405*bis*, 1° CC.

496 Delhaise (n 9) 76.

provided for a minimum imprisonment for all categories originally punishable by imprisonment (which is now not the case for 2°, 3° and 4°), or he should have fixed the minimum sentence in 1° on eight days or omitted it all together.

As explained above, some of the most serious felonies cannot be correctionalised. For example, terrorist murder or terrorist manslaughter. The sentence for both these offences is life imprisonment. Other terrorist felonies *sensu stricto* can, and often will, be correctionalised. Their sentences go down according to article 80 CC. This article is applied below to the other terrorist offences and these examples can also be applied to terrorism *sensu stricto*. Some of the most serious terrorist felonies can be correctionalised. These felonies originally punishable with twenty to thirty years felony imprisonment or lifelong felony imprisonment (the two harshest sentences in Belgian criminal law[497]) are punishable with a maximum of twenty years imprisonment after correctionalisation.

Terrorism sensu lato

The prison sentences for articles 140, §1, 140*bis*, 140*ter*, 140*quater*, 140*quinquies*, 140*sexies* and 141 CC are all the same: five to ten years felony imprisonment. However, as explained above, these felonies will always be correctionalised. Because correctionalisation is based on attenuating circumstances, the maximum sentence goes down.[498] Five to ten years felony imprisonment becomes one month to five years imprisonment. In practice, this is the sentencing bracket within which the courts work. In addition to the prison sentence, there is a fine of 100 to 5000 euros.[499] When articles *140bis* to 140*quinquies* were introduced in 2013, the Council of State reasoned that having the same sentence for the person providing the training (art. 140*quater* CC) and for the person receiving the training (art. 140*quinquies* CC) could be discriminatory because it is treating two different situations in the same manner.[500] The legislature replied that both actions are serious, with the perpetrators having the same intent, and both should be felonies because of how

497 The Criminal Code also includes felony imprisonment of thirty to forty years in its list of possible sentences. However, to date no offence has ever existed which actually imposes this sentence.

498 Art 80 CC; Franssen (n 408) 162.

499 Note that all criminal fines have to be multiplied by a factor 8 because of the application of so called '10% surcharges'. Belgian law applies surcharges to criminal fines to adapt them to the real value of money without having to constantly change the criminal legislation. The idea is that this way the financial impact of a fine stays more or less the same over the years while the value of money changes. Since 2016, there are 70 10% surcharges, transforming a fine of 5000 euros into one of 40000 euros in practice. See: Art 59 Programmawet 25 december 2016, *BS* 29 december 2016, 90879.

500 Advies 51 806/3 van de Raad van State van 18 September 2012 bij wetsontwerp van 13 november 2012 tot wijziging van Titel 1ter van het Strafwetboek, *Parl.St.* Kamer 2012-2013, nr. 53-2502/001, (22) 27; Delhaise (n 9) 62; Fransen and Kerkhofs (n 9) 68.

dangerous they are.[501] He gave the example of someone who goes abroad to receive training for terrorism and returns to Belgium to put that knowledge into practice. Both the trainer and trainee have the same goal, that being the commission of a terrorist attack. Therefore, the legislature reasoned, it is justified they are punishable with the same sentence.[502] However, there is also another, arguably more noteworthy, contradiction with regards to proportionality. The sentence of five to ten years (again, in practice one month to five years), is higher than the sentence for some of the terrorism offences *sensu stricto*.[503] Due to this, the sentence of, for example, inciting somebody to commit terrorist battery, is higher than the sentence for the terrorist battery itself (maximum three years imprisonment).[504]

In 2003, a similar issue was raised concerning article 140, §1 CC: participating in the activities of a terrorist group has a higher maximum sentence than some of the terrorist offences *sensu stricto*.[505] It is therefore possible that the terrorist offence the terrorist group aims to commit has a lighter sentence than participating in the activities of that same terrorist group.[506] According to the secretary of justice at the time, Laurette Onkelinx, this was not a problem, since it would only be the case for 'as good as risk-free terrorist acts', and concurrence between offences is possible.[507] There are two types of concurrence[508]: ideal concurrence, which means that one act constitutes more than one offence, and material concurrence, which means that a person has committed an offence before being convicted for another offence previously committed.[509] Often these offences will then be

501 Memorie van Toelichting bij wetsontwerp van 13 november 2012 tot wijziging van Titel 1ter van het Strafwetboek, *Parl.St.* Kamer 2012-2013, nr. 53-2502/001, (4) 16; Delhaise (n 9) 62-63; Ketels (n 14) 258.

502 Memorie van Toelichting bij wetsontwerp van 13 november 2012 tot wijziging van Titel 1ter van het Strafwetboek, *Parl.St.* Kamer 2012-2013, nr. 53-2502/001, (4) 16; Fransen and Kerkhofs (n 9) 67-68.

503 Delhaise (n 9) 78-79.

504 See also: Dekrem (n 77) 155. As Delhaise points out, terrorists will often have the intention to kill, making them guilty of attempted manslaughter or murder, raising the sentence above the one for the terrorist offence *sensu lato*. Then applying the rules for concurrence, the higher sentence will be applied. See: Delhaise (n 9) 79.

505 A similar argument can be made regarding the *mens rea* of the participant: the participant knows or should have known he could contribute to a standard offence or felony. It is possible that the standard offence he knows or should have known he could contribute to has a lower sentence than the one for participating in the activities of the group. See: Flore (n 9) 221.

506 Advies 59.789/3 van de Raad van State van 19 juli 2016 bij wetsvoorstel van 13 januari 2016 tot wijziging van het Strafwetboek wat betreft de bestraffing van terrorisme, *Parl.St.* Kamer 2015-2016, nr. 54-1579/006, 7-8; Delhaise (n 9) 77.

507 Verslag namens de commissie van justitie bij wetsontwerp van 6 oktober 2003 betreffende terroristische misdrijven, *Parl.St.* Kamer 2003, nr. 51-0258/004, 22.

508 A third option is that of a collective offence, in case the different offences are part of one single criminal project (see above). In this scenario, only the harshest sentence is applied as well. According to Delhaise, in a terrorism context, there will often be collective offences. See: Delhaise (n 9) 85-86.

509 Cass. 9 mei 1995, *Arr.Cass.* 1995, 46; Tom Decaigny, in M De Busscher and others (eds), *Strafrecht: duiding* (Larcier 2018) 114; De Nauw and Deruyck (n 20) 173; Tulkens and others (n 16) 631-640; Van den Wyngaert, Vandromme and Traest (n 16) 519.

tried simultaneously. With the phrase 'as good as risk-free', the secretary of justice referred to offences such as intentional battery, potentially with premeditation[510]; intentionally damaging part of a public telecommunications network, destroying it, or obstructing or preventing its proper functioning, when this offence endangers human lives or causes significant economic damage[511]; and maliciously or fraudulently submerging someone else's yard, when this offence endangers human lives[512,513] All these acts can hardly be called risk-free, especially because for many of them the Criminal Code itself states that they have to endanger human lives. Hence, the justification of the secretary on this point is incomprehensible. The argument about concurrence is less so. The secretary stated that individual actions are less dangerous than actions executed by a group.[514] Thus, a person who individually commits one of the 'lighter' terrorist offences, only risks the lower sentence for that offence. For a person who commits this offence as part of a terrorist group, there will be ideal concurrence between the terrorist offence *sensu stricto* and participation in the activities of the terrorist group. In case of ideal concurrence, only the sentence for the more severe offence is applicable[515], *in casu* the participation in the activities of the terrorist group. Although this line of reasoning is better than that of the 'risk free' terrorism, it is still only mildly convincing. An action of a group is not per definition more dangerous than an action of an individual[516] and furthermore, the group has not necessarily committed a terrorist offence yet (see above).

510 Art 398 CC.

511 Art 114, §4 wet van 21 maart 1991 betreffende de hervorming van sommige economische overheidsbedrijven, *BS* 27 maart 1991, 6155.

512 Art 549 CC.

513 Other offences that fall within this category are: destroying or damaging graves, monuments, etc. when this offence endangers human lives or causes substantial economic loss (art 526 CC); intentionally destroying, rendering unusable or abandoning ship's equipment when this offence endangers human lives or causes substantial economic loss (art 15 wet van 5 juni 1928 houdende herziening van het Tucht- en Strafwetboek voor de koopvaardij en de zeevisserij, *BS* 26 juli 1928, 3341); lending out firearms without due respect for the conditions for doing so (except for arms dealers for example) (art 12/1 *j*. 23, section 4 wet van 8 juni 2006 houdende regeling van economische en individuele activiteiten met wapens, *BS* 9 juni 2006, 29840); failure to comply with safety requirements to which the storage, transport, possession and collection of fire arms, ammunition and magazines are subject (except for arms dealers for example) (art 35, 1° *j*. 23, section 4 wet van 8 juni 2006 houdende regeling van economische en individuele activiteiten met wapens; *BS* 9 juni 2006, 29840); developing, producing, stockpiling, acquiring, possessing or transferring of weapons, equipment or the means for proliferation specially designed to use agents or toxins for hostile purposes or in an armed conflict (art 2, 2° wet houdende goedkeuring van het Verdrag tot verbod van de ontwikkeling, de productie en de aanleg van voorraden van bacteriologische (biologische) en toxinewapens en inzake de vernietiging van deze wapens, opgemaakt te Londen, Moskou en Washington op 10 april 1972).

514 Verslag namens de commissie van justitie bij wetsontwerp van 6 oktober 2003 betreffende terroristische misdrijven, *Parl.St.* Kamer 2003, nr. 51-0258/004, 22. Delhaise is also of this opinion: Delhaise (n 9) 77.

515 Art 65, section 1 CC. See also: De Nauw and Deruyck (n 20) 175; Tulkens and others (n 16) 634; Van den Wyngaert, Vandromme and Traest (n 16) 522.

516 The Council of State asked that same question with regard to article 140*septies* CC, pointing out that a terrorist offence committed by a person acting alone is not necessarily less serious than an offence

Articles 140*bis*, 140*ter*, 140*quater* and 141 CC also contain an aggravating circumstance for minority. The EU Directive states that member states should take measures to ensure that when the offences of recruitment or providing training for terrorism are directed towards children, this may be taken into account when sentencing.[517] The Directive does not state this for incitement to terrorism or financing a terrorist, however the Belgian legislature decided to also create an aggravating circumstance for these offences.[518] He reasoned that minors can also be the specific target group of perpetrators of incitement or financing, in that they are more vulnerable and easier to manipulate and influence.[519] Since 2019, articles 140*bis*, 140*ter*, 140*quater* and 141 CC therefore have a second section, stating that the sentence is raised to a felony imprisonment of ten to fifteen years if the offence is specifically aimed at minors. Regarding article 141 CC, the legislature explains that the aggravating circumstance only covers part of the situation of 1°. Financing a minor with a view to the commission of terrorism *sensu lato* does not fall within the scope of the aggravating circumstance.[520] Nor does, according to the legislature, financing a minor knowing that he is committing, or will commit, terrorism *sensu stricto* (2°).[521] However, as explained above, we believe the Council of State is correct in arguing that this falls within the scope of 1° and therefore the aggravating circumstance could be applicable. Cesoni points out that the aggravating circumstance refers to 'minors'. The age of majority is eighteen in Belgium, but Cesoni asks what happens if the youth in question is not Belgian and the age of majority is different in their state.[522] However, it seems the legislature has answered this question. Article 100*ter* CC states that for the purposes of the offences in the Criminal Code, the term 'minor' means anybody under the age of eighteen years old.[523] The offence needs to be aimed at them specifically, but not necessarily exclusively. As examples in the context of article 140*bis* CC, the legislature mentions messages spread

---

committed by a group. See: Advies 59.789/3 van de Raad van State van 19 juli 2016 bij wetsvoorstel van 13 januari 2016 tot wijziging van het Strafwetboek wat betreft de bestraffing van terrorisme, *Parl.St.* Kamer 2015-2016, nr. 54-1579/006, 16; advies van de Raad van State (II) nr. 59 147/3 van 22 april 2016 bij wetsontwerp houdende diverse bepalingen ter bestrijding van terrorisme (III), *Parl.St.* Kamer 2015-2016, nr. 54-1951/001, 31.

517 Art 15.4 Directive (EU) 2017/541 of the European Parliament and of the Council of 15 March 2017 on combating terrorism and replacing Council Framework Decision 2002/475/JHA and amending Council Decision 2005/671/JHA, *OJ* 31 March 2017, L 88/6-21.

518 Cesoni (n 119) 244; De Coensel (n 23) 213; Winants (n 7) 357.

519 Toelichting bij wetsvoorstel van 6 februari 2019 houdende diverse bepalingen in strafzaken en inzake erediensten, *Parl.St.* Kamer 2018-2019, nr. 54-3515/001, (3) 103.

520 Wetsvoorstel van 6 februari 2019 houdende diverse bepalingen in strafzaken en inzake erediensten, *Parl.St.* Kamer 2018-2019, nr. 54-3515/001, 107; Deruyck and De Nauw (n 16) 10; Winants (n 7) 358.

521 Wetsvoorstel van 6 februari 2019 houdende diverse bepalingen in strafzaken en inzake erediensten, *Parl.St.* Kamer 2018-2019, nr. 54-3515/001, 107; Winants (n 7) 358.

522 Cesoni (n 119) 245.

523 Art 100*ter* CC. See also: De Nauw and Deruyck (n 20) 112; Tulkens and others (n 16) 444; Van den Wyngaert, Vandromme and Traest (n 16) 305.

on online forums mainly used by minors or in the vicinity of schools,[524] or propaganda images of minors or young adults.[525] The Belgian legislature's choice for an aggravating circumstance, is a repressive one.[526] The Directive states that the minority may be taken into account, but the application of an aggravating circumstance is obligatory for the judge, leaving him no choice.[527] Hence Belgian law choses the most restrictive option. More so, the considerations to the Directive state: 'When recruitment and training for terrorism are directed towards a child, Member States should ensure that judges can take this circumstance into account when sentencing offenders, although there is no obligation on judges to increase the sentence. It remains within the discretion of the judge to assess that circumstance together with the other facts of the particular case.'[528] By making it an aggravating circumstance, the Belgian legislature seems to have gone against this consideration. After correctionalisation, this aggravated sentence is six months to ten years imprisonment.

The offence in article 140, §1/1 CC contains the same sentence as the aggravated versions of articles 140*bis*, 140*ter*, 140*quater* and 141 CC, being ten to fifteen years felony imprisonment or six months to ten years imprisonment after correctionalisation. §2 of that article increases the sentences even further to fifteen to twenty years felony imprisonment.[529] This is more than what is required by the EU Directive, which states that member states should ensure a maximum sentence of not less than fifteen years.[530] After correctionalisation the Belgian sentence becomes one to fifteen years imprisonment. As a result, even after correctionalisation, the maximum sentence under Belgian law is in line with the Directive. Worth noting for article 140, §1/1 CC is that the legislature overlooked one thing when creating this new offence. The sentences for article 140, §1 and §2 are respectively 'felony imprisonment of five years to ten years and a fine of one hundred to five thousand euros' and 'felony imprisonment of fifteen years to twenty years and a fine of

524 Cesoni criticises these examples. See: Cesoni (n 119) 244-245.

525 Toelichting bij Wetsvoorstel van 6 februari 2019 houdende diverse bepalingen in strafzaken en inzake erediensten, *Parl.St.* Kamer 2018-2019, nr. 54-3515/001, (3) 104; Winants (n 7) 357.

526 De Coensel (n 23) 213.

527 Cesoni (n 119) 244; De Nauw and Deruyck (n 20) 65; Tulkens and others (n 16) 627; Van den Wyngaert, Vandromme and Traest (n 16) 296.

528 Consideration 19 Directive (EU) 2017/541 of the European Parliament and of the Council of 15 March 2017 on combating terrorism and replacing Council Framework Decision 2002/475/JHA and amending Council Decision 2005/671/JHA, *OJ* 31 March 2017, L 88/6-21.

529 Art 140, §2 CC.

530 Art 15.3 Directive (EU) 2017/541 of the European Parliament and of the Council of 15 March 2017 on combating terrorism and replacing Council Framework Decision 2002/475/JHA and amending Council Decision 2005/671/JHA, *OJ* 31 March 2017, L 88/6. This was also part of the original Framework Decision. See: art. 5.3 Council Framework Decision 2002/475/JHA of 13 June 2002 on combating terrorism, *OJ* 22 June 2002, L 164/5. See also: De La Serna (n 7) 204.

one thousand euros to two hundred thousand euros'.[531] The sentence in article 140, §1/1 CC, however, is drafted as follows: 'felony imprisonment for ten years to fifteen years and a fine of one thousand to two hundred thousand euros, or one of those sentences by itself'.[532] Because of the last part of this phrase, it is possible to punish the taking of any decision in the context of the activities of a terrorist group with a fine as a principal sentence, while this is not the case for participating in the activities of the group.[533] Since the latter offence is supposed to be the lighter offence, this was not the intention of the legislature.[534] As a consequence, a bill was proposed on 23 January 2020 in order to remedy this by removing 'or one of those sentences by itself' from article 140, §1/1 CC.[535]

Lastly, article 140*septies* CC contains its own system of sentences dependent on the prepared offence. The Criminal Code sets out the following sentences:

- *Imprisonment of eight days to a year, if the prepared offence is punishable with imprisonment of maximum five years;*
- *Imprisonment of maximum three years, if the prepared offence is punishable with five to ten years felony imprisonment;*
- *Imprisonment of maximum five years, if the prepared offence is punishable with ten to fifteen years or fifteen to twenty years felony imprisonment;*
- *Felony imprisonment of five to ten years, if the prepared offence is punishable with twenty to thirty years or lifelong felony imprisonment.*[536]

As with article 138 CC, this seems like a fairly straightforward system. Preparation of terrorism is a standard offence, unless the prepared terrorist offence is punishable with twenty to thirty years felony imprisonment or lifelong felony imprisonment. In that case, preparation is a felony. The system is also created in such a way so that the sentence for

531 Own translations, original in Dutch and French: "*opsluiting van vijf jaar tot tien jaar en met geldboete van honderd euro tot vijfduizend euro; la réclusion de cinq ans à dix ans et d'une amende de cent euros à cinq mille euros*" (art 140, §1 CC) and "*opsluiting van vijftien jaar tot twintig jaar en met geldboete van duizend euro tot tweehonderdduizend euro; la réclusion de quinze ans à vingt ans et d'une amende de mille euros à deux cent mille euros*" (art 140, §2 CC).

532 Own translation, original in Dutch and French: "*opsluiting van tien jaar tot vijftien jaar en met een geldboete van duizend euro tot tweehonderdduizend euro of met een van die straffen alleen; la réclusion de dix ans à quinze ans et d'une amende de mille euros à deux cent mille euros ou d'une de ces peines seulement*" (art 140, §1/1 CC).

533 Barring any exceeding of a reasonable time period, which allows for a decrease of the sentence below the legal minimum.

534 Wetsvoorstel van 23 januari 2020 tot wijziging van het Strafwetboek wat de strafmaat voor misdrijven door terroristische groepen betreft, *Parl.St.* Kamer 2019-20, nr. 55-0962/001, 3.

535 Wetsvoorstel van 23 januari 2020 tot wijziging van het Strafwetboek wat de strafmaat voor misdrijven door terroristische groepen betreft, *Parl.St.* Kamer 2019-20, nr. 55-0962/001.

536 Art. 140*septies* CC. Own translation, original in Dutch and French.

attempt will always be higher than the sentence for preparation.[537] In the article as originally proposed, there was one sentence for the preparation of any terrorist offence: two to five years imprisonment and a fine of twenty six to one thousand euro's.[538] This was changed after the Council of State pointed out that this could lead to proportionality and discrimination issues, providing for harsher sentences for the preparation of some offences than for their actual commission.[539] The adopted system is more proportionate than the one originally proposed. However, three remarks can still be made regarding proportionality. The first remark is very similar to one of the comments made regarding the sentencing of article 140, §1 CC compared to terrorism *sensu stricto*. Most of the sentences for preparing terrorism *sensu stricto* are more lenient than the ones for participating in the activities of a terrorist group. This means that when terrorism *sensu stricto* is prepared in the context of a terrorist group, the defendants will be liable for the harsher sentence for participating in the activities of a terrorist group, while an individual preparing that same terrorist offence, is only liable for the lower sentence on preparation. The Council of State raised this question. The reply was that offences in group are more dangerous than offences committed by individuals, an explanation the Council of State doubted.[540] Second, the category of felony preparation will normally be correctionalised, which makes it into a standard offence punishable with one month to five years imprisonment. This puts the maximum sentence on the same level as for preparation of offences punishable with ten to fifteen years or fifteen to twenty years felony imprisonment. Therefore, in practice, the maximum sentence for the preparation of an offence originally punishable with ten to fifteen years felony imprisonment will be the same as for preparation of an offence originally punishable with lifelong felony imprisonment. Third, due to the combination of article 138 and 140*septies* CC, the preparation of a terrorist offence originally punishable with only a fine is punishable with up to a year imprisonment. Outside of a terrorist context, this offence only warrants a fine. However, merely preparing that same offence within a terrorist context can lead to up to a year in prison.

537 Amendement nr. 1 van 7 juli 2016 bij wetsvoorstel van 13 januari 2016 tot wijziging van het Strafwetboek wat betreft de bestraffing van terrorisme, *Parl.St.* Kamer 2015-2016, nr. 54-1579/005, 8.

538 Art 3 wetsvoorstel van 13 januari 2016 tot wijziging van het Strafwetboek wat betreft de bestraffing van terrorisme, *Parl.St.* Kamer 2015-2016, nr. 54-1579/001, (5) 5; Fransen and Kerkhofs (n 9) 77.

539 Advies 59.789/3 van de Raad van State van 19 juli 2016 bij wetsvoorstel van 13 januari 2016 tot wijziging van het Strafwetboek wat betreft de bestraffing van terrorisme, *Parl.St.* Kamer 2015-2016, nr. 54-1579/006, 14-15; advies van de Raad van State (II) nr. 59 147/3 van 22 april 2016 bij wetsontwerp houdende diverse bepalingen ter bestrijding van terrorisme (III), *Parl.St.* Kamer 2015-2016, nr. 54-1951/001, 29-30; amendement nr. 1 van 7 juli 2016 bij wetsvoorstel van 13 januari 2016 tot wijziging van het Strafwetboek wat betreft de bestraffing van terrorisme, *Parl.St.* Kamer 2015-2016, nr. 54-1579/005, 7; Moreau (n 173) 111.

540 Advies van de Raad van State (II) nr. 59 147/3 van 22 april 2016 bij wetsontwerp houdende diverse bepalingen ter bestrijding van terrorisme (III), *Parl.St.* Kamer 2015-2016, nr. 54-1951/001, 30-31.

BEING AT THE DISPOSAL OF THE SENTENCE ENFORCEMENT COURT

Being placed at the disposal of the sentence enforcement court is an accessory penalty,[541] meaning that it is always imposed in combination with a principal penalty such as (felony) imprisonment.[542] This penalty starts at the end of the principal penalty.[543] It was introduced into the legislation in 2007, replacing the already existing 'being at the disposal of the government'.[544] When a person who is at the disposal of the sentence enforcement court is still in prison at the end of their prison term, they are not automatically released.[545] Instead they appear before the sentence enforcement court before the end of their term, which can decide to either keep them incarcerated or release them (conditionally).[546] The sentence enforcement court keeps them incarcerated when there is a risk the person will commit serious criminal offences, which affect the physical or psychological integrity of third parties, that, in the case of supervised release, cannot be overcome by the imposition of special conditions.[547] In this scenario, the sentence enforcement court has to review the

541 Art 34*bis* CC. See also: COL17/2014 – De terbeschikkingstelling van de strafuitvoeringsrechtbank, 17 July 2014, 3; Yves Van Den Berge, 'De Terbeschikkingstelling van de Strafuitvoeringsrechtbank: Alweer Een Nieuwe Straf, Alweer Een Nieuwe Uitvoering' [2013] Tijdschrift voor Strafrecht 222, 222; Van Den Berge (n 464) 12; Van den Wyngaert, Traest and Vandromme (n 433) 415; Fanny Vansiliette, 'Mise à la disposition du gouvernement des condamnés' (2014) M 140 Postal Memorialis – Lexicon strafrecht, strafvordering en bijzondere wetten 1, 10.

542 For the procedure and practical execution of this penalty, see Ministeriële omzendbrief nr. 1813 van 18 november 2011 betreffende de terbeschikkingstelling van de strafuitvoeringsrechtbank.

543 Art 95/2, §1 WERP. See also: Ministeriële omzendbrief nr. 1813 van 18 november 2011 betreffende de terbeschikkingstelling van de strafuitvoeringsrechtbank, 37; COL17/2014 – De terbeschikkingstelling van de strafuitvoeringsrechtbank, 17 July 2014, 10; MA Beernaert, *Manuel de droit pénitentiaire* (Anthemis 2019) 354; Van Den Berge (n 541) 222; Van den Wyngaert, Traest and Vandromme (n 433) 415; Vansiliette (n 541) 10.

544 Wet 26 april 2007 betreffende de terbeschikkingstelling van de strafuitvoeringsrechtbank, *BS* 13 juli 2007; Ministeriële omzendbrief nr. 1813 van 18 november 2011 betreffende de terbeschikkingstelling van de strafuitvoeringsrechtbank, 1; COL17/2014 – De terbeschikkingstelling van de strafuitvoeringsrechtbank, 17 July 2014, 3. See also: Beernaert, *Manuel de droit pénitentiaire*, *Manuel de droit pénitentiaire* (n 543) 353; Veerle Scheirs, 'Van Binnen Naar Buiten. De Externe Rechtspositie van Veroordeelde Gedetineerden' in Kristel Beyens and Sonja Snacken (eds), *Straffen: Een penologisch perspectief* (Maklu 2017) 690-691.

545 Verslag namens de commissie voor de justitie van 13 maart 2007 bij Wetsontwerp betreffende de terbeschikkingstelling van de strafuitvoeringsrechtbank, *Parl.St.* Senaat 2006-2007, nr. 3-2054/4, 10; Van Den Berge (n 464) 12-14; Vansiliette (n 541) 14.

546 Verslag namens de commissie voor de justitie van 13 maart 2007 bij Wetsontwerp betreffende de terbeschikkingstelling van de strafuitvoeringsrechtbank, *Parl.St.* Senaat 2006-2007, nr. 3-2054/4, 10; COL17/2014 – De terbeschikkingstelling van de strafuitvoeringsrechtbank, 17 July 2014, 11-12; Beernaert, *Manuel de droit pénitentiaire* (n 543) 355; Van Den Berge (n 541) 226-227; Van Den Berge (n 464) 13-14; Vansiliette (n 541) 14-18.

547 Art 95/2, §3 WERP. See also: Ministeriële omzendbrief nr. 1813 van 18 november 2011 betreffende de terbeschikkingstelling van de strafuitvoeringsrechtbank, 8; COL17/2014 – De terbeschikkingstelling van de strafuitvoeringsrechtbank, 17 July 2014, 13; Beernaert, *Manuel de droit pénitentiaire* (n 543) 355; Van Den Berge (n 541) 226; Van den Wyngaert, Traest and Vandromme (n 433) 416-417; Vansiliette (n 541) 15-16.

case every year.[548] If the convicted person had already been conditionally released, the period of being at the disposal of the sentence enforcement court is added to their probationary period (see below).[549]

The sentence of being put at the disposal of the sentence enforcement court can only be imposed upon conviction for certain offences. In 2007, the legislature made it an obligatory sentence for convictions of terrorism *sensu stricto* to criminal sentences if the offence had caused the death of a victim.[550] In those cases, the judge had to put the defendant at the disposal of the sentence enforcement court for a period of five to fifteen years.[551] In 2016 this provision was amended so that it is obligatory for defendants convicted for terrorism *sensu stricto* with a prison sentence of at least five years if the offence caused the death of a victim.[552] The change made it an obligatory sentence for offences of terrorism *sensu stricto* which were correctionalised but are punished with more than five years imprisonment.[553]

For the other terrorism offences being put at the disposal of the sentence enforcement court is currently not an option. One of the recommendations of the parliamentary research committee on the terrorist attacks of 22 March 2016 was to expand this sentence to the articles 140 and 141 CC.[554] Currently, there are two bills pending with regards to

548 Art 95/21 and 95/25 WERP. See also: COL17/2014 – De terbeschikkingstelling van de strafuitvoeringsrechtbank, 17 July 2014, 27-28; Beernaert, *Manuel de droit pénitentiaire* (n 543) 362; Van Den Berge (n 541) 233-234; Vansiliette (n 541) 16.

549 Art 95/2, §2, Section 2 WERP. See also: Verslag namens de commissie voor de justitie van 13 maart 2007 bij Wetsontwerp betreffende de terbeschikkingstelling van de strafuitvoeringsrechtbank, *Parl.St.* Senaat 2006-2007, nr. 3-2054/4, 10; Ministeriële omzendbrief nr. 1813 van 18 november 2011 betreffende de terbeschikkingstelling van de strafuitvoeringsrechtbank, 29; COL17/2014 – De terbeschikkingstelling van de strafuitvoeringsrechtbank, 17 July 2014, 13; Beernaert, *Manuel de droit pénitentiaire* (n 543) 355; Van Den Berge (n 541) 227; Van Den Berge (n 464) 13-14; Vansiliette (n 541) 18.

550 Art 34*ter* CC, as introduced by the wet van 26 april 2007 betreffende de terbeschikkingstelling van de strafuitvoeringsrechtbank, *BS* 13 July 2007, 38299. See also: COL17/2014 – De terbeschikkingstelling van de strafuitvoeringsrechtbank, 17 July 2014, 5; Van Den Berge (n 541) 223; Van den Wyngaert, Traest and Vandromme (n 433) 416; Vansiliette (n 541) 12.

551 COL17/2014 – De terbeschikkingstelling van de strafuitvoeringsrechtbank, 17 July 2014, 4; Scheirs (n 544) 691; Van Den Berge (n 464) 13; Van den Wyngaert, Traest and Vandromme (n 433) 416.

552 Art 11 Wet van 5 februari 2016 tot wijziging van het strafrecht en de strafvordering en houdende diverse bepalingen inzake justitie, *BS* 19 februari 2016, 13130. See also: Scheirs (n 544) 691; Van Den Berge (n 464) 13.

553 Memorie van Toelichting bij wetsontwerp van 23 oktober 2015 houdende wijzigingen van het strafrecht en de strafvordering en houdende diverse bepalingen inzake justitie, *Parl.St.* Kamer 2015-2016, nr. 54-1418/001, (4) 8.

554 Derde tussentijds verslag over het onderdeel "veiligheidsarchitectuur" van 15 juni 2017 van de parlementaire onderzoekscommissie belast met het onderzoek naar de omstandigheden die hebben geleid tot de terroristische aanslagen van 22 maart 2016 in de luchthaven Brussel-Nationaal en in het metrostation Maalbeek te Brussel, met inbegrip van de evolutie en de aanpak van de strijd tegen het radicalisme en de terroristische dreiging, *Parl.St.* Kamer 2016-2017, nr. 54-1752/008, 412. See also: Toelichting bij wetsvoorstel van 21 november 2019 tot wijziging van het Strafwetboek met het oog op de uitbreiding van de lijst met

this. The first one aims to introduce the option for the judge to put the defendant at the disposal of the sentence enforcement court for all terrorist offences which are not covered by the mandatory version of this sentence, with the exception of article 140*septies* CC.[555] The parliamentarians who introduced this bill stated: 'That perpetrators of terrorism crimes must be regarded as criminals who pose a significant and constant threat to our society is beyond dispute.'[556] The other bill goes one step further, in that it aims to introduce a mandatory placement at the disposal of the sentence enforcement court. The proposal is, however, limited to convictions to prison sentences of at least five years based on articles 137, 140 and 141 CC.[557] This would mean that for article 137 CC the requirement of the death of the victim is dropped and articles 140 and 141 are added. It is peculiar, though, that the title of the bill mentions 'all terrorist offences', while the actual bill does not include articles 140*bis* to 140*septies* CC.

ALTERNATIVE SENTENCES

Diversifying sentencing

The legislature decided to diversify and individualise sentencing, and thus limit the use of prison sentences, by introducing several alternative sentences.[558] These alternative

misdrijven die in aanmerking komen voor de facultatieve terbeschikkingstelling van de strafuitvoeringsrechtbank tot alle terrorismemisdrijven, *Parl.St.* Kamer 2019-2020, nr. 55-0777/001, 3.

555 Art 2 Wetsvoorstel van 21 november 2019 tot wijziging van het Strafwetboek met het oog op de uitbreiding van de lijst met misdrijven die in aanmerking komen voor de facultatieve terbeschikkingstelling van de strafuitvoeringsrechtbank tot alle terrorismemisdrijven, *Parl.St.* Kamer 2019-2020, nr. 55-0777/001, 6.

556 Own translation, original in Dutch and French: "*Dat daders van terrorismemisdrijven moeten beschouwd worden als delinquenten die een belangrijke en voortdurende dreiging vormen voor onze samenleving staat buiten kijf; Les auteurs d'infractions terroristes doivent incontestablement être considérés comme des délinquants représentant une menace sérieuse et constante pour notre société*." See: Toelichting bij wetsvoorstel van 21 november 2019 tot wijziging van het Strafwetboek met het oog op de uitbreiding van de lijst met misdrijven die in aanmerking komen voor de facultatieve terbeschikkingstelling van de strafuitvoeringsrechtbank tot alle terrorismemisdrijven, *Parl.St.* Kamer 2019-2020, nr. 55-0777/001, 4.

557 Art 2 wetsvoorstel van 28 januari 2020 tot wijziging van het Strafwetboek, teneinde de terbeschikkingstelling van de strafuitvoeringsrechtbank uit te breiden tot alle terroristische misdrijven, *Parl.St.* Kamer 2019-2020, nr. 55-0969/001, 8.

558 Memorie van Toelichting bij het wetsvoorstel van 20 maart 2000 tot wijziging van het Strafwetboek en tot invoering van de dienstverlening en de opleiding als gevangenisvervangende straffen, *Parl.St.* Kamer 1999-2000, 50-549/001, 4; Memorie van Toelichting van 8 januari 2014 bij het wetsontwerp tot invoering van de probatie als autonome straf in het Strafwetboek, tot wijziging van het Wetboek van strafvordering, het Gerechtelijk Wetboek en de wet van 29 juni 1964 betreffende de opschorting, het uitstel en de probatie, *Parl.St.* Kamer, 2013-14, 53-3274/001, 4. See also: COL 18/2016 – Invoering van de probatie als autonome straf, 23 June 2016, 7-8; COL 17/2016 – Elektronisch toezicht als autonome straf, updated version 18 October 2018, 4-5; Tom Daems and Yana Magis, 'Elektronisch toezicht en autonome probatie nader

sentences are the electronic tagging sentence (*straf onder elektronisch toezicht; peine de surveillance électronique*), community service (*werkstraf; peine de travail*), and the autonomous probation sentence (*autonome probatiestraf; peine de probation autonome*). They are principal sentences, meaning that they cannot be imposed in combination with another principal sentence, be that a prison sentence or each other.[559] Furthermore, these sentences can only be imposed with the agreement of the defendant, after he has received the relevant information.[560] This consent needs to be clear from the case files.[561] The case law makes it apparent that these alternative sentences are almost never used in cases of terrorism (see below). At the expert seminar the idea was proposed to split the court decision into two: one decision on the guilt or innocence of the defendant, and one on the sentence. Currently, this is only done in the Assize Courts, while all other courts have to pronounce their judgment in full at the same moment. Opening the option of splitting judgments would allow for risk assesments to be carried out after a finding of guilt but before deciding on the sentence. This method would allow for sentences to be individualised more accurately.

Electronic tagging sentence

An electronic tagging sentence entails the obligation to be present at a set address for a certain period of time (authorised movements are possible), which is enforced by means of electronic tagging.[562] A few general conditions are imposed (such as not committing

---

bekeken' in P Traest, A Verhage and G Vermeulen (eds), *Strafrecht en strafprocesrecht: doel of middel in een veranderde samenleving?* (Wolters Kluwer 2017) 177 and 189.

559 De Nauw and Deruyck (n 436) 125; Tulkens and others (n 16) 576-577. See for the autonomous probation sentence for example: COL 18/2016 – Invoering van de probatie als autonome straf, 23 June 2016, 8-9; Collectieve brief DG EPI nr. 138 van 29 april 2016 over de probatie als autonome straf, 1; Michel Rozie, 'De probatie kan voortaan ook op eigen vleugels vliegen' [2014] Nullum Crimen 349, 350. For electronic tagging, see: COL 17/2016 – Elektronisch toezicht als autonome straf, updated version 18 October 2018, 6; Collectieve brief DG EPI nr. 137 van 29 april 2016 over het elektronisch toezicht als autonome straf, 1.

560 Art 37*ter*, §4, 37*quinquies*, §3 and 37*octies*, §3 CC. See also: COL 18/2016 – Invoering van de probatie als autonome straf, 23 June 2016, 15; COL 17/2016 – Elektronisch toezicht als autonome straf, updated version 18 October 2018, 11-13; Daems and Magis (n 558) 183 and 193; Tom Decaigny, 'Nieuwe correctionele hoofdstraffen: de straf onder elektronisch toezicht en de autonome probatiestraf' [2014] Tijdschrift voor Strafrecht 211, 211; Jeroen De Herdt, 'Bijzonder Strafrecht En Stratoemeting Na de Potpourri II-Wet' [2016] Nullum Crimen 189, 200; De Nauw and Deruyck (n 20) 128; Rozie (n 559) 350-351 and 354; Tulkens and others (n 16) 593, 596 and 599; Van den Wyngaert, Vandromme and Traest (n 16) 431.

561 For electronic tagging, see: Cass. 15 juni 2021, *RABG* 2021, 1756, noot. For the community sentence, see: Cass. 24 november 2010, AR P.10.1145.F. For the autonomous probation sentence, see: Rozie (n 559) 351.

562 Art 37*ter*, §1, section 2 CC. See also: COL 17/2016 – Elektronisch toezicht als autonome straf, updated version 18 October 2018, 5; Collectieve brief DG EPI nr. 137 van 29 april 2016 over het elektronisch toezicht als autonome straf, 1; Daems and Magis (n 558) 180; Decaigny, 'Nieuwe correctionele hoofdstraffen: de straf onder elektronisch toezicht en de autonome probatiestraf' (n 560) 213; De Herdt (n 560) 199; De Nauw and Deruyck (n 20) 127; L Todts, *Bestuurlijke En Strafrechtelijke Vrijheidsbeperkingen Ter Handhaving*

new offences) and extra conditions can be added in the interest of the victim.[563] The judge also gives general indications about the concrete implementation of the sentence. However, this is ultimately determined by the justice assistant.[564] Electronic tagging as a principal sentence is possible when the judge believes that the offence is of such a nature that it should not be punished with more than one year imprisonment. The judge then imposes the electronic tagging sentence for the same amount of time as he would have imposed imprisonment.[565] As a result of this, the maximum term for electronic tagging is one year. There is a minimum term for electronic tagging as well, being one month.[566] The judge also imposes a substitute imprisonment for the same duration as the electronic tagging sentence, which will only be executed if the convicted person does not abide by the imposed rules.[567] There is a short list of offences for which an electronic tagging sentence can never be imposed. This list mainly consists of sexual offences, but also includes murder

van de Openbare Orde (die Keure 2021) 240; Van Den Berge (n 464) 10; Van den Wyngaert, Vandromme and Traest (n 16) 430.

563 Art 37*ter*, §5, section 3 CC. See also: COL 17/2016 – Elektronisch toezicht als autonome straf, updated version 18 October 2018, 9; Collectieve brief DG EPI nr. 137 van 29 april 2016 over het elektronisch toezicht als autonome straf, 2; Daems and Magis (n 558) 184; De Herdt (n 560) 201; De Nauw and Deruyck (n 20) 129; Todts (n 561) 240; Tulkens and others (n 16) 599; Van Den Berge (n 464) 10; Van den Wyngaert, Vandromme and Traest (n 16) 431.

564 Art 37*quater*, §1 C. See also: COL 17/2016 – Elektronisch toezicht als autonome straf, updated version 18 October 2018, 18; Daems and Magis (n 558) 184; Decaigny, 'Nieuwe correctionele hoofdstraffen: de straf onder elektronisch toezicht en de autonome probatiestraf' (n 560) 220.

565 Art 37*ter*, §1, section 1 CC. See also: Collectieve brief DG EPI nr. 137 van 29 april 2016 over het elektronisch toezicht als autonome straf, 1; COL 17/2016 – Elektronisch toezicht als autonome straf, updated version 18 October 2018, 7; Daems and Magis (n 558) 181; Decaigny, 'Nieuwe correctionele hoofdstraffen: de straf onder elektronisch toezicht en de autonome probatiestraf' (n 560) 216; Tom Decaigny, 'Relatieve Zwaarte, Toepassingsgebied En Duur' in M De Busscher and others (eds), *Strafrecht: duiding* (Larcier 2018) 50; De Nauw and Deruyck (n 20) 127; Olivia Nederlandt, 'La Surveillance Électronique Comme Peine Autonome et Comme Modalité d'exécution Des Peines? Présentation et Commentaire de La Loi Du 7 Février 2014' [2014] Journal des tribunaux 441, 442-443; Tulkens and others (n 16) 598; Van den Wyngaert, Vandromme and Traest (n 16) 430.

566 Art 37*ter*, §2, section 1 CC. See also: COL 17/2016 – Elektronisch toezicht als autonome straf, updated version 18 October 2018, 9; Daems and Magis (n 558) 181; Decaigny, 'Nieuwe correctionele hoofdstraffen: de straf onder elektronisch toezicht en de autonome probatiestraf' (n 560) 217; Decaigny, 'Relatieve Zwaarte, Toepassingsgebied En Duur' (n 565) 51; De Herdt (n 560) 200; De Nauw and Deruyck (n 20) 128; Nederlandt (n 565) 443; Todts (n 561) 240; Tulkens and others (n 16) 598; Van den Wyngaert, Vandromme and Traest (n 16) 431.

567 COL 17/2016 – Elektronisch toezicht als autonome straf, updated version 18 October 2018, 11; Collectieve brief DG EPI nr. 137 van 29 april 2016 over het elektronisch toezicht als autonome straf, 1; Daems and Magis (n 558) 182; Decaigny, 'Nieuwe correctionele hoofdstraffen: de straf onder elektronisch toezicht en de autonome probatiestraf' (n 560) 218; Tom Decaigny, 'Vervangende Gevangenisstraf' in M De Busscher and others (eds), *Strafrecht: duiding* (Larcier 2018) 50; De Herdt (n 560) 201; De Nauw and Deruyck (n 20) 129; Nederlandt (n 565) 443; Tulkens and others (n 16) 598; Van den Wyngaert, Vandromme and Traest (n 16) 431.

and manslaughter[568].[569] For all other terrorist offences, an electronic tagging sentence is a possible sentence. After correctionalisation, the sentence for all terrorism offences, barring the most serious terrorist offences *sensu stricto*, can be reduced to one year imprisonment or lower, making an electronic tagging sentence possible.

Community service

Community service entails working unpaid during leisure time for a public service, non-profit organisation or foundation with a social, scientific or cultural goal.[570] The tasks involved cannot be those which would normally be done by a paid worker.[571] Community service can be imposed for facts which would be punished by a police sentence or a correctional sentence, but some offences are explicitly excluded from the application of community service.[572] This is the case for all felonies punishable with twenty years felony imprisonment or more before correctionalisation, for several sexual offences and murder and manslaughter[573].[574] In addition to the community service, the judge also imposes an alternative prison sentence or fine within the sentencing range of the offence.[575] Community

---

568 This is somewhat strange since even after applying attenuating circumstances to these offences, the minimum sentences are three years imprisonment, meaning an electronic tagging sentence would not be possible either way. See: De Nauw and Deruyck (n 20) 128. The inclusion of these offences on the list, would become relevant when grounds for remission of penalty are applied, the reasonable term has not been respected, the perpetrator turned government informant or in case of attempted offences and/or aiding and abetting.

569 Art 37*ter*, §1, section 3 CC. See also: COL 17/2016 – Elektronisch toezicht als autonome straf, updated version 18 October 2018, 7-8; MA Beernaert, 'L'individualisation dans le prononcé et l'exécution de la peine : machine arrière toute ?', *La loi « pot-pourri II » : un recul de civilisation ?* (Anthemis 2016) 182-183; Daems and Magis (n 558) 182; De Herdt (n 560) 199; De Nauw and Deruyck (n 20) 128; Nederlandt, 'La Surveillance Électronique Comme Peine Autonome et Comme Modalité d'exécution Des Peines? Présentation et Commentaire de La Loi Du 7 Février 2014' (n 565) 442; Tulkens and others (n 16) 598; Van den Wyngaert, Vandromme and Traest (n 16) 430-431.

570 Art 37*sexies*, §1, section 1 CC. See also: De Nauw and Deruyck (n 436) 129; Tulkens and others (n 16) 594; Van Den Berge (n 464) 10; Van den Wyngaert, Traest and Vandromme (n 433) 428.

571 Art 37*sexies*, §1, section 2 CC. See also: De Nauw and Deruyck (n 436) 129; Van den Wyngaert, Traest and Vandromme (n 433) 428-429.

572 Art 37*quinquies*, §1, section 1 CC. See also: Beernaert, 'L'individualisation dans le prononcé et l'exécution de la peine : machine arrière toute ?' (n 569) 182; De Nauw and Deruyck (n 436) 129; Tulkens and others (n 16) 591-592; Van den Wyngaert, Traest and Vandromme (n 433) 429.

573 Which seems redundant since those offences are punishable with more than 20 years felony imprisonment. However, the list also includes the attempted offences and aiding and abetting in those offences (see: Cass. 15 november 2006, *Pas.* 2006, 2341). Therefore, this addition will be relevant in cases where the sentence is lowered below 20 years, for example attempted manslaughter or aiding and abetting manslaughter.

574 Art 37*quinquies*, §1, section 2 CC. See also: Beernaert, 'L'individualisation dans le prononcé et l'exécution de la peine : machine arrière toute ?' (n 569) 183-185; De Herdt (n 560) 197; Van den Wyngaert, Traest and Vandromme (n 433) 429.

575 Art 37*quinquies*, §1, section 1 CC. See also: De Nauw and Deruyck (n 436) 130; Tulkens and others (n 16) 593; Van den Wyngaert, Traest and Vandromme (n 433) 430-431.

services range from twenty to three-hundred hours, with a sentence of forty-five hours or less being a police sentence and anything above this being a correctional sentence.[576] The judge imposes the community service and can provide instructions with regards to its concrete implementation.[577] However, it is the justice assistant, under the supervision of the probation commission, who decides on the concrete implementation.[578]

Autonomous probation sentence

The autonomous probation sentence consists of the obligation to follow certain conditions during a certain period of time, ranging from six months to two years.[579] Twelve months or less is a police sentence and anything above this is a correctional sentence.[580] The judge decides on the duration of the sentence and gives indications on the possible conditions, but it is the probation commission and justice assistants who decide on the concrete conditions.[581] During the execution of the sentence, the probation commission can also change, specify or suspend (parts of) the concrete measures. The commission can even decide that the sentence has been fully executed before the period imposed by the judge has ended or extend the period with maximum one year if it was impossible to fulfil the conditions during the original period.[582] It is possible to appeal the decisions of the

576 Art 37*quinquies*, §2 CC. See also: De Nauw and Deruyck (n 436) 130; Tulkens and others (n 16) 593; Van den Wyngaert, Traest and Vandromme (n 433) 429.

577 Art 37*quinquies*, §4 CC. See also: Van Den Berge (n 464) 10; Van den Wyngaert, Traest and Vandromme (n 433) 430.

578 Art 37*septies*, §3 CC. See also: Van den Wyngaert, Traest and Vandromme (n 433) 430-431.

579 Art 37*octies*, §1, section 2 CC. See also: COL 18/2016 – Invoering van de probatie als autonome straf, 23 June 2016, 8 and 11; Collectieve brief DG EPI nr. 138 van 29 april 2016 over de probatie als autonome straf, 1; Daems and Magis (n 558) 191-192; Decaigny, 'Nieuwe correctionele hoofdstraffen: de straf onder elektronisch toezicht en de autonome probatiestraf' (n 560) 217; De Nauw and Deruyck (n 436) 132; Tulkens and others (n 16) 595-597; Van den Wyngaert, Traest and Vandromme (n 433) 432-433.

580 Art 37*octies*, §2 CC. See also: COL 18/2016 – Invoering van de probatie als autonome straf, 23 June 2016, 11; Collectieve brief DG EPI nr. 138 van 29 april 2016 over de probatie als autonome straf, 1; Decaigny, 'Nieuwe correctionele hoofdstraffen: de straf onder elektronisch toezicht en de autonome probatiestraf' (n 560) 217; De Nauw and Deruyck (n 436) 132; Rozie (n 559) 350; Van den Wyngaert, Traest and Vandromme (n 433) 433.

581 Art 37*octies*, §4 and 37*novies*, §3 CC. See also: COL 18/2016 – Invoering van de probatie als autonome straf, 23 June 2016, 14; Collectieve brief DG EPI nr. 138 van 29 april 2016 over de probatie als autonome straf, 2; Daems and Magis (n 558) 194; Decaigny, 'Nieuwe correctionele hoofdstraffen: de straf onder elektronisch toezicht en de autonome probatiestraf' (n 560) 214; Rozie (n 559) 354-355; Tulkens and others (n 16) 595; Van den Wyngaert, Traest and Vandromme (n 433) 433-434.

582 Art 37*decies*, §1 CC. See also: COL 18/2016 – Invoering van de probatie als autonome straf, 23 June 2016, 18-19; Collectieve brief DG EPI nr. 138 van 29 april 2016 over de probatie als autonome straf, 2; Daems and Magis (n 558) 194; Decaigny, 'Nieuwe correctionele hoofdstraffen: de straf onder elektronisch toezicht en de autonome probatiestraf' (n 560) 219; Rozie (n 559) 357-358; Tulkens and others (n 16) 597; Van den Wyngaert, Traest and Vandromme (n 433) 434.

probation commission in front of the courts of first instance.[583] In addition to the autonomous probation sentence, the judge imposes a prison sentence or fine which must be within the sentencing bracket for the offence and which will apply if the conditions are not met.[584] An autonomous probation sentence is possible for all offences where a police or correctional sentence is possible, barring a short list of excluded offences.[585] This list contains all felonies punishable with more than 20 years felony imprisonment which are correctionalised alongside, for example, murder and manslaughter[586].[587] Almost all of the terrorist felonies can be correctionalised, so an autonomous probation sentence would be possible, barring the excluded offences such as terrorist manslaughter.

Suspension of sentence and postponement of enforcement

Two so called 'modalities' of sentences can also be relevant. First there is the suspension of sentences. This means that the judge finds a defendant guilty of an offence but does not impose a sentence.[588] The imposition of a sentence is suspended, and a term is set ranging from one to five years.[589] A normal suspension can be revoked if the person commits an offence during this period for which a criminal sentence or a correctional sentence of more than one month is imposed. They will then also receive a sentence for the originally suspended offence. A suspension subject to probation is also possible, meaning that there

583 Art 37*decies*, §2 CC. See also: COL 18/2016 – Invoering van de probatie als autonome straf, 23 June 2016, 19; Daems and Magis (n 558) 194; Decaigny, 'Nieuwe correctionele hoofdstraffen: de straf onder elektronisch toezicht en de autonome probatiestraf' (n 560) 214-215; Rozie (n 559) 357-358; Tulkens and others (n 16) 597; Van den Wyngaert, Traest and Vandromme (n 433) 434.

584 Art 37*octies*, §1, Section 3 CC. See also: COL 18/2016 – Invoering van de probatie als autonome straf, 23 June 2016, 13; Daems and Magis (n 558) 194; Decaigny, 'Nieuwe correctionele hoofdstraffen: de straf onder elektronisch toezicht en de autonome probatiestraf' (n 560) 217; De Nauw and Deruyck (n 436) 132; Rozie (n 559) 351 and 355-356; Tulkens and others (n 16) 596; Van den Wyngaert, Traest and Vandromme (n 433) 433.

585 COL 18/2016 – Invoering van de probatie als autonome straf, 23 June 2016, 10; De Nauw and Deruyck (n 436) 131; Van den Wyngaert, Traest and Vandromme (n 433) 433.

586 See above, footnote 573.

587 Art 37*octies*, §1, Section 4 CC. See also: COL 18/2016 – Invoering van de probatie als autonome straf, 23 June 2016, 10; Beernaert, 'L'individualisation dans le prononcé et l'exécution de la peine : machine arrière toute ?' (n 569) 183-185; Daems and Magis (n 558) 192; Decaigny, 'Nieuwe correctionele hoofdstraffen: de straf onder elektronisch toezicht en de autonome probatiestraf' (n 560) 217; Rozie (n 559) 351-352.

588 Art 1, §1 Probatiewet. See also: De Nauw and Deruyck (n 436) 179; Van den Wyngaert, Traest and Vandromme (n 433) 525; Kristien Vanderheiden, 'Opschorting, Uitstel En Probatie' (2016) O155 Postal Memorialis – Lexicon strafrecht, strafvordering en bijzondere wetten 1, 8.

589 Art 3, Section 4 Probatiewet. See also: De Nauw and Deruyck (n 436) 180; Van den Wyngaert, Traest and Vandromme (n 433) 533.

are additional conditions to abide by.[590] Suspension of sentence is not possible if the defendant has already been convicted for an offence to six months imprisonment or more.[591] The new offence cannot be of such a nature that the judge would deem it necessary to impose a sentence of more than five years.[592] Suspension of sentence is only possible if the defendant agrees.[593] All trial courts can impose a suspension of sentence, except for the Assize Courts.[594] It is also possible for the investigation supervision courts to impose the suspension, if they believe that the public debates which come with a trial would impede the rehabilitation of the defendant.[595]

A second possibility is the postponement of sentence enforcement. This means that the judge does impose a sentence but that (a part of) this sentence does not have to be enforced as long as the convicted person abides by certain conditions.[596] Again, a normal postponement of enforcement is possible or the postponement of enforcement can be subject to probation, meaning that there are additional conditions.[597] In the latter case, the

590 COL7/2013 – De wet van 27 december 2012 houdende diverse bepalingen betreffende Justitie, inzonderheid: TITEL VIII Wijziging van de wet van 29 juni 1964 betreffende de opschorting, het uitstel en de probatie, 13 March 2013, 2; De Nauw and Deruyck (n 436) 185; Van den Wyngaert, Traest and Vandromme (n 433) 525; Vanderheiden (n 588) 8.

591 Art 3, Section 1 Probatiewet. See also: Beernaert, 'L'individualisation dans le prononcé et l'exécution de la peine : machine arrière toute ?' (n 569) 185; De Nauw and Deruyck (n 436) 180; Tulkens and others (n 16) 660-661; Van den Wyngaert, Traest and Vandromme (n 433) 530; Vanderheiden (n 588) 9.

592 Art 3, section 1 Probatiewet. See also: Beernaert, 'L'individualisation dans le prononcé et l'exécution de la peine : machine arrière toute ?' (n 569) 185; De Nauw and Deruyck (n 436) 180; Tulkens and others (n 16) 661; Vanderheiden (n 588) 10. In 2016, the legislature wanted to amend this to "*if the fact is not punishable by a correctional prison sentence of more than twenty years, and it does not appear to be of such a nature that it should be punished by a principal sentence of more than five years imprisonment*" (art 36 wet van 5 februari 2016 tot wijziging van het strafrecht en de strafvordering en houdende diverse bepalingen inzake justitie, *BS* 19 februari 2016, 13130). This was part of a fairly large criminal law reform called 'Potpourri II'. Part of this reform was the elevation of sentences after correctionalisation and this specific change to the rules on postponement of sentence enforcement was made in this contex. However, the Constitutional Court annulled the elevation of sentences after correctionalisation and thus also annulled this change to the rules on postponement of sentence enforcement. See: GwH 21 december 2017, 148/2017.

593 Art 3, Section 1 Probatiewet; Cass. 31 mei 1995, P.94.868.F; Cass. 12 november 1996, P.95.0950.N. See also: De Nauw and Deruyck (n 436) 180; Tulkens and others (n 16) 659; Van den Wyngaert, Traest and Vandromme (n 433) 530; Vanderheiden (n 588) 9.

594 Art 3, section 1 Probatiewet. See also: Beernaert, 'L'individualisation dans le prononcé et l'exécution de la peine : machine arrière toute ?' (n 569) 185; De Nauw and Deruyck (n 436) 180; Tulkens and others (n 16) 659; Van den Wyngaert, Traest and Vandromme (n 433) 525; Vanderheiden (n 588) 8.

595 Art 3, Section 2 Probatiewet. See also: De Herdt (n 560) 195; De Nauw and Deruyck (n 436) 180; Tulkens and others (n 16) 660; Van den Wyngaert, Traest and Vandromme (n 433) 525; Vanderheiden (n 588) 8.

596 De Nauw and Deruyck (n 436) 182; Van den Wyngaert, Traest and Vandromme (n 433) 525; Vanderheiden (n 588) 14-15.

597 COL7/2013 – De wet van 27 december 2012 houdende diverse bepalingen betreffende Justitie, inzonderheid: TITEL VIII Wijziging van de wet van 29 juni 1964 betreffende de opschorting, het uitstel en de probatie, 13 March 2013, 2; De Nauw and Deruyck (n 436) 185; Tulkens and others (n 16) 665; Van den Wyngaert, Traest and Vandromme (n 433) 525; Vanderheiden (n 588) 15-16.

agreement of the defendant is required.[598] Postponement of enforcement is only possible if the defendant has not yet been convicted to a sentence of more than twelve months imprisonment for a single offence.[599] There is no such threshold for postponement subject to probation.[600] Postponement of sentence enforcement is possible for sentences of up to five years imprisonment.[601] This is not possible for an electronic tagging sentence, community service or an autonomous probation sentence.[602] The term for suspension of a sentence is one to three years for fines and prison sentences of up to six months, and one to five years for prison sentences up to five years.[603] Suspension of the enforcement of sentences can be imposed by all trial courts, including the Assize Courts.[604]

CASE LAW ANALYSIS

As was the situation in the rest of the book, the case law analysis has not taken into consideration any possible additional sentences imposed by the courts, such as the confiscation of goods or the disqualification from certain rights. The focus of the analysis was on the principal sentence, always being that of imprisonment, and of the additional sentence of being at the disposal of the sentence enforcement court, any alternative sentences and suspension or postponement. The analysis also did not include any consideration of the facts of the case. No attempts were made to qualify some cases as more serious than others, or to look at, for example, the gender of the offender. The only factor taken into account was the legal qualification.

---

598 De Nauw and Deruyck (n 436) 183.

599 Art 8, §1, Section 2 Probatiewet. See also: Beernaert, 'L'individualisation dans le prononcé et l'exécution de la peine : machine arrière toute ?' (n 569) 190; De Herdt (n 560) 196; De Nauw and Deruyck (n 436) 183; Tulkens and others (n 16) 666; Van den Wyngaert, Traest and Vandromme (n 433) 527; Vanderheiden (n 588) 15.

600 Art 8, §1, section 1 Probatiewet. This threshold used to be three years, but was deleted in 2022. See: Art. 114 Wet van 21 maart 2022 houdende wijzigingen aan het Strafwetboek met betrekking tot het seksueel strafrecht, *BS* 30 maart 2022, 25785. For the old rule, see also: Beernaert, 'L'individualisation dans le prononcé et l'exécution de la peine : machine arrière toute ?' (n 569) 189; De Herdt (n 560) 196; Van den Wyngaert, Traest and Vandromme (n 433) 527-528.

601 Art 8, §1, section 1 Probatiewet. See also: De Nauw and Deruyck (n 436) 183; Tulkens and others (n 16) 666; Van den Wyngaert, Traest and Vandromme (n 433) 528; Vanderheiden (n 588) 15.

602 Art 8, §1, section 3 Probatiewet. See also: COL 18/2016 – Invoering van de probatie als autonome straf, 23 June 2016, 7-10; Beernaert, 'L'individualisation dans le prononcé et l'exécution de la peine : machine arrière toute ?' (n 569) 187; Daems and Magis (n 558) 185-186 and 193; De Herdt (n 560) 196; Van den Wyngaert, Traest and Vandromme (n 433) 529; Vanderheiden (n 588) 15. Specifically for electronic tagging, see: COL 17/2016 – Elektronisch toezicht als autonome straf, updated version 18 October 2018, 7.

603 Art 8, §1, section 6 and 7 Probatiewet. See also: De Nauw and Deruyck (n 436) 183; Van den Wyngaert, Traest and Vandromme (n 433) 533; Vanderheiden (n 588) 16.

604 De Nauw and Deruyck (n 436) 183; Tulkens and others (n 16) 665; Van den Wyngaert, Traest and Vandromme (n 433) 525; Vanderheiden (n 588) 15.

As discussed above, the sentence bracket for article 140, §1 CC is quite narrow. This means that the sentences in the vast majority of cases are relatively similar. The maximum sentence (barring recidivism) of five years imprisonment was imposed in 158 cases, which is almost 60%. In a few cases of recidivism, the sentence was as high as ten years, which is the maximum for cases of recidivism. Sentences for article 140, §2 CC are often, although not always, higher, with several sentences of 15 years imprisonment, which is again the maximum. Sentences for attempted participation ranged from three years to five years imprisonment. As the maximum sentence is most often imposed for article 140, §1 CC, it is no surprise that it was usually imposed when this offence was combined with another offence *sensu lato*.[605]

The additional sentence of being at the disposal of the sentence enforcement court was only imposed upon one individual, which is not very surprising given the currently limited scope of application. Not a single alternative sentence was imposed either. As a sidenote one case can be mentioned in which a person was convicted to community service for the offence of participating in the activities of a terrorist group.[606] Family of the defendant had travelled to Syria to join IS and he had sent money to Turkey for them, for which he was convicted to community service. Hence, this case fell outside the scope of the analysis, since none of the facts committed by him took place outside of Belgium.

A suspension of sentence was granted in four cases, all of which were prosecutions for the offence of article 140, §1 CC. Postponement of sentence enforcement was granted 83 times. This postponement was for the full sentence in sixteen cases and partial for the other cases. Not a single postponement was granted *in absentia*, although this is theoretically possible in case of postponement which is not subject to probation since in that case the agreement of the defendant is not required.

The analysis clearly demonstrates that although the legislature has provided for many sentencing options, with the goal of improved rehabilitation, they are not frequently applied in practice. The one exception to this is that of partial postponement of sentence enforcement. Finally, it can be noted that the prison sentences are often at the high end of the sentencing bracket, which supports the idea that the bracket is rather narrow.

605 This was not so in only three out of nineteen cases.

606 Corr. Oost Vlaanderen (afd. Dendermonde) 14 december 2018, *onuitg.*

4 Prison and beyond

Within prison: internal legal position

The 2006 Basic law on prisons and the legal position of detainees sets out the rights and obligations of detainees within prison.[607] A core principle of this legislation is that detention should be carried out in psychosocial, physical and material circumstances that respect the dignity of the human being, allow the preservation or growth of the self-respect of the detainee, and appeal to his individual and social responsibility.[608] Included within this is that the detainee shall not be subject to any restrictions on his political, civil, social, economic or cultural rights, other than those arising from the criminal conviction or from the liberty-depriving measure, those inextricably linked to the deprivation of liberty and those determined by or under the law.[609] Any avoidable negative consequences of detention must be avoided.[610] This, however, does not exclude the limitation of detainees' rights within prison. When there are serious indications of danger to the order or security within the prison, special security measures (*bijzondere veiligheidsmaatregelen; mesures de sécurité particulières*) can be ordered towards a specific detainee.[611] These are not disciplinary sanctions (which are also possible, but only after disciplinary offences) but preventive measures, undertaken to ensure order and security.[612] These special security

607 Basiswet 12 januari 2005 betreffende het gevangeniswezen en de rechtspositie van de gedetineerden, *BS* 1 februari 2005, 2815. See also: Van Den Berge (n 464) 7-8.

608 Art 5, §1 Basiswet gevangeniswezen. See also: Beernaert, *Manuel de droit pénitentiaire* (n 543) 90; Kristel Van Driessche, 'Wet 12 Januari 2005' in Tom Decaigny and others (eds), *Duiding Strafuitvoering* (Larcier 2014) 22. This is also imposed by the Council of Europe. See: Recommendation No. R (87) 3 of the Committee of Ministers to member states on the European Prison Rules, adopted on 12 February 1987 in Strasbourg at the 404th meeting of the Ministers' Deputies, Council of Europe, Yearbook of the European Convention on Human Rights, Dordrecht, Martinus Nijhof, 1987, 188-207. See also: Sonja Snacken and Philippe Kennes, 'De Interne Rechtspositie van Gedetineerden' in Kristel Beyens and Sonja Snacken (eds), *Straffen: Een penologisch perspectief* (Maklu 2017) 435; Van Den Berge (n 464) 7-8.

609 Art 6, §1 Basiswet gevangeniswezen. See also: Beernaert, *Manuel de droit pénitentiaire* (n 543) 90-91; Van Den Berge (n 464) 8; Van Driessche (n 608) 22-23.

610 Art 6, §1 Basiswet gevangeniswezen. See also: Beernaert, *Manuel de droit pénitentiaire* (n 543) 91; Snacken and Kennes (n 608) 435-437; Van Den Berge (n 464) 8; Van Driessche (n 608) 23.

611 Art 110, §1 Basiswet gevangeniswezen. See also: Beernaert, *Manuel de droit pénitentiaire* (n 543) 206; Snacken and Kennes (n 608) 454.

612 Art 111, §1 Basiswet gevangeniswezen. See also: Ministeriële omzendbrief nr. 1792 van 11 januari 2007 betreffende Basiswet – Titel VI: orde, veiligheid en gebruik van dwang, 3; Beernaert, *Manuel de droit pénitentiaire* (n 543) 207; Chris Hermans and Jürgen Millen, 'Controle- En Veiligheid(s)Maatregelen in de Gevangenis' in T Daems and others (eds), *Quo vadis? Tien jaar basiswet gevangeniswezen en rechtspositie van gedetineerden* (Maklu 2015) 138-139; Jürgen Millen, 'Hoe Bijzonder Zijn Bijzondere Veiligheidsregimes Voor Terro-Gedetineerden?' (2016) 152 FATIK: Tijdschrift voor Strafbeleid en Gevangeniswezen 21, 22; Snacken and Kennes (n 608) 455.

measures can include (a combination of) seizing objects, excluding the detainee from specific activities, putting them under observation, putting them under isolation in their cell, or putting them in a different security cell.[613] These measures, imposed by the prison warden, can last for maximum seven days and can be extended maximum three times.[614] If the special security measures are inadequate and the detainee is a continuous danger to the security, they can be placed in an individual special security regime (*individueel bijzonder veiligheidsregime; régime de sécurité particulier individuel*).[615] This entails (a combination of) the following: exclusion from communal activities, systematic checking of their mail, only receiving visitors in a room with a separation, limitations on phone use, and systematic frisking, alongside any of the previously mentioned special security measures.[616] This regime is imposed by the general director of the penitentiary institutions for maximum two months, which can be renewed.[617] The detainee can appeal this decision to the Appeals Commission of the Central Supervisory Council for Prisons (*Centrale Toezichtsraad voor het gevangeniswezen; Conseil central de surveillance pénitentiaire*).[618]

As made evident in this book, imprisonment is an integral part of the fight against terrorism. According to a press article released in 2019, there were 227 detainees categorised as terrorist in Belgian prisons in that year.[619] However, prison is also a 'potential

613 Art 112, §1 Basiswet gevangeniswezen. See also: Ministeriële omzendbrief nr. 1792 van 11 januari 2007 betreffende Basiswet – Titel VI: orde, veiligheid en gebruik van dwang, 4-5; Beernaert, *Manuel de droit pénitentiaire* (n 543) 205-206; Hermans and Millen (n 612) 139; Snacken and Kennes (n 608) 455.

614 Art 112, §2 Basiswet gevangeniswezen. See also: Ministeriële omzendbrief nr. 1792 van 11 januari 2007 betreffende Basiswet – Titel VI: orde, veiligheid en gebruik van dwang, 4-5; Beernaert, *Manuel de droit pénitentiaire* (n 543) 206; Hermans and Millen (n 612) 140.

615 Art 116, §1 Basiswet gevangeniswezen. See also: Ministeriële omzendbrief nr. 1792 van 11 januari 2007 betreffende Basiswet – Titel VI: orde, veiligheid en gebruik van dwang, 7; Beernaert, *Manuel de droit pénitentiaire* (n 543) 215; A De Brouwer, 'Au-delà du contentieux disciplinaire' (2021) 2021 Revue de Jurisprudence de Liège, Mons et Bruxelles (JLMB) 1799, 1804; Hermans and Millen (n 612) 141; Millen (n 612) 22; Snacken and Kennes (n 608) 455; Van Driessche (n 608) 56; Comité T, 'Raport 2022: Évaluation des mesures visant à lutter contre le terrorisme à la lumière des droits humains', 77-78.

616 Art 117 Basiswet gevangeniswezen. See also: Ministeriële omzendbrief nr. 1792 van 11 januari 2007 betreffende Basiswet – Titel VI: orde, veiligheid en gebruik van dwang, 8; Beernaert, *Manuel de droit pénitentiaire* (n 543) 214; Hermans and Millen (n 612) 142; Snacken and Kennes (n 608) 455.

617 Art 118, §1 and 7 Basiswet gevangeniswezen. See also: Ministeriële omzendbrief nr. 1792 van 11 januari 2007 betreffende Basiswet – Titel VI: orde, veiligheid en gebruik van dwang, 7-9; Rapport au Gouvernement de la Belgique relatif à la visite effectuée en Belgique par le Comité européen pour la prévention de la torture et des peines ou traitements inhumains ou dégradants (CPT) du 27 mars au 6 avril 2017, Strasbourg 8 March 2018, CPT/Inf (2018) 8, 28; Beernaert, *Manuel de droit pénitentiaire* (n 543) 216-219; De Brouwer (n 615) 1804-1805; Hermans and Millen (n 612) 142-143; Millen (n 612) 22; Van Driessche (n 608) 57.

618 Art 118, §10 Basiswet gevangeniswezen. See for example: Commission d'appel francophone 24 décembre 2020, *JLMB* 2021, 1796; Comité T, 'Raport 2022: Évaluation des mesures visant à lutter contre le terrorisme à la lumière des droits humains', 43-44. See also: Beernaert, *Manuel de droit pénitentiaire* (n 543) 220; De Brouwer (n 615) 1805-1806.

619 D Leestmans, 'Geradicaliseerden in de gevangenis: met hoeveel zijn ze? En wat als ze vrijkomen? Negen vragen én antwoorden' (2019) *vrtNWS* 1 May 2019, www.vrt.be/vrtnws/nl/2019/04/23/gedetineerden-met-de-t-van-terrorisme/.

breeding ground for radicalisation and recruitment'.[620] In January of 2015, the first instructions were given to prison wardens requiring prison staff to be extra vigilant against signs of radicalisation and extremism.[621] In addition, a special cell (CelEx) was founded within the general prisons administration which specialises in radicalisation and extremism.[622] These 2015 instructions are not publicly available, but allegedly also stated that every detainee convicted for a terrorist offence needed to be isolated from the other detainees by the imposition of an individual special security regime.[623] When visiting Belgium in 2017, the European Committee for the Prevention of Torture and Inhuman or Degrading Treatment or Punishment (CPT) found that the vast majority of terrorist detainees they spoke to had been subject to special security measures as well as an individual special security regime.[624] They add that, for at least a number of them, it was apparent that these measures were only based on the offence they had committed or were suspected of having committed.[625] In its 2022 report, Comité T stated that the decisions to impose an individual special security regime systematically referred to the committed (for

620 F.O.D. Justitie, "Actionplan: approach to radicalisation in prisons", 11 March 2015, 3, https://justitie.belgium.be/sites/default/files/downloads/Plland%27actionradicalisation-prison-NL.pdf. See also: Verslag namens de commissie voor justitie hoorzittingen de deradicaliserings-, exit- en resocialisatieprogramma's binnen de belgische penitentiaire instellingen, *Parl.St.* Kamer 2019-2020, nr. 55-1501/001, 6; Gemeenschappelijke omzendbrief voor een globale aanpak van geweldadige radicalisering en extremisme en van terrorisme, 18 februari 2019, 1; Commission de surveillance de la prison d'Ittre, 'Rapport de fin de mandat', August 2019, 32; Léa Teper, 'Zone d'ombre Carcérale : L'isolement En Aile D-Rad:Ex' [2018] Journal des tribunaux 960, 961. Note that the parlementary research committee founded after the Brussels terrorist attacks, while agreeing, does warn for too simplistic views in this complicated matter. See: Vierde tussentijds verslag van 23 oktober 2017 over het onderdeel "radicalisme" namens de parlementaire onderzoekscommissie belast met het onderzoek naar de omstandigheden die hebben geleid tot de terroristische aanslagen van 22 maart 2016 in de luchthaven Brussel-Nationaal en in het metrostation Maalbeek te Brussel, met inbegrip van de evolutie en de aanpak van de strijd tegen het radicalisme en de terroristische dreiging, *Parl.St.* Kamer 2017-2018, nr. 54-1752/009, 76-79 and 99-100.

621 Commission de surveillance de la prison d'Ittre, 'Rapport de fin de mandat', August 2019, 32; Teper (n 620) 961. See also: DG EPI, "Bijzondere instructies", 12 februari 2021, 8.

622 Vierde tussentijds verslag van 23 oktober 2017 over het onderdeel "radicalisme" namens de parlementaire onderzoekscommissie belast met het onderzoek naar de omstandigheden die hebben geleid tot de terroristische aanslagen van 22 maart 2016 in de luchthaven Brussel-Nationaal en in het metrostation Maalbeek te Brussel, met inbegrip van de evolutie en de aanpak van de strijd tegen het radicalisme en de terroristische dreiging, *Parl.St.* Kamer 2017-2018, nr. 54-1752/009, 85; Commission de surveillance de la prison d'Ittre, 'Rapport de fin de mandat', August 2019, 33. Their goal is to optimise the treatment and flow of information concerning radicilisation and detainees related to terrorism.

623 Hermans and Millen (n 612) 145; Millen (n 612) 23; Snacken and Kennes (n 608) 456; Teper (n 620) 961.

624 Rapport au Gouvernement de la Belgique relatif à la visite effectuée en Belgique par le Comité européen pour la prévention de la torture et des peines ou traitements inhumains ou dégradants (CPT) du 27 mars au 6 avril 2017, Strasbourg 8 March 2018, CPT/Inf (2018) 8, 29.

625 Rapport au Gouvernement de la Belgique relatif à la visite effectuée en Belgique par le Comité européen pour la prévention de la torture et des peines ou traitements inhumains ou dégradants (CPT) du 27 mars au 6 avril 2017, Strasbourg 8 March 2018, CPT/Inf (2018) 8, 29.

convictions) or suspected (for pre-trial detention) offence.[626] Different authors rightfully criticise this measure as being in violation of the Basic law and the presumption of innocence for suspects.[627] In October 2020, the Brussels Court of Appeal held that the systematic isolation of terrorist detainees did not have an adequate legal basis and violated articles 3 and 8 ECHR.[628] In a case dating back to the 24th of December 2020, the Appeals Commission held that the mere fact the arrest warrant was issued for a terrorist offence does not suffice to impose and renew an individual special security regime since this would violate the requirement of an individualised investigation of the situation.[629] In its 2022 report, Comité T quoted another case in which a negative report by OCAM was considered insufficiently precise for the proper motivation of an individual special security regime.[630] The government claimed that the instructions specified that the decision to subject a prisoner to a special security measure or an individual special security regime must always be based on an individual risk assessment, albeit an automatic one in cases of terrorism.[631] Whatever the instructions may have said in the past, the most recent instructions do state that merely belonging to one of the categories of CelEx detainees (see below) is not in itself a sufficient reason for imposing special security measures. In the original instructions no definitions of radicalisation or extremism were provided, however they did state that the administration opted for a broad definition of detainees related to terrorism. This definition included not only people suspected of or convicted for terrorist offences, but also other detainees who were considered a serious risk of radicalisation (active or passive) or who engaged in armed conflict for religious or ideological reasons.[632] In March of that same year, an action plan against radicalisation in prison was released.[633]

626 Comité T, 'Raport 2022: Évaluation des mesures visant à lutter contre le terrorisme à la lumière des droits humains', 80-81.

627 Hermans and Millen (n 612) 146; Millen (n 612) 23-24; Snacken and Kennes (n 608) 456.

628 Brussel 8 oktober 2020, RG 2014/AR/2257, unpublished, refered to in Comité T, 'Rapport 2021: Evaluation des mesures visant à lutter contre le terrorisme à la lumière des droits humains', 94.

629 Commission d'appel francophone 24 décembre 2020, *JLMB* 2021, 1796. See also: Comité T, 'Raport 2022: Évaluation des mesures visant à lutter contre le terrorisme à la lumière des droits humains', 84; De Brouwer (n 615) 1806-1807.

630 Comité T, 'Raport 2022: Évaluation des mesures visant à lutter contre le terrorisme à la lumière des droits humains', 43-44.

631 Schriftelijke vraag nr. 6-2224 van Lionel Bajart (Open Vld) d.d. 15 januari 2019 aan de minister van Justitie, belast met de Regie der Gebouwen, *Vr. en Antw.* Senaat 2018-19; Réponse du Gouvernement de la Belgique au rapport du Comité européen pour la prévention de la torture et des peines ou traitements inhumains ou dégradants (CPT) relatif à la visite effectuée en Belgique du 27 mars au 6 avril 2017, Strasbourg 19 June 2018, CPT/Inf (2018) 23, 20.

632 Commission de surveillance de la prison d'Ittre, 'Rapport de fin de mandat', August 2019, 33-34; Teper (n 620) 961.

633 F.O.D. Justitie, "Actionplan: approach to radicalisation in prisons", 11 March 2015, https://justitie.belgium.be/sites/default/files/downloads/Plland%27actionradicalisation-prison-NL.pdf. See also: Commission de surveillance de la prison d'Ittre, 'Rapport de fin de mandat', August 2019, 34; Willy Bruggeman,

This plan set out ten action points ranging from better living conditions in prisons to deradicalisation programmes.[634] One of these ten points was the placement of radicalised prisoners, and here a dual approach was put forward.[635] In first instance, radicalised detainees are integrated into regular prison sections to a maximum extent. However, when this is not possible and the detainee poses a serious risk in terms of (active or passive) radicalisation or when they engage in armed conflict for ideological motives, the detainee can then be placed in a special section with a specialised approach.[636] This dual approach was intended to reduce the risk of radicalisation among the general prison population, while simultaneously avoiding the issue of creating larger, tightly knit groups of radicalised inmates.[637]

In 2016, in the prisons of Hasselt and Ittre, seperate sections (so called D-Rad:Ex) were opened for these terrorist detainees whom were feared would radicalise others inmates, such as the leaders and recruiters.[638] The concrete facts which give rise to this fear, however,

'Radicalisering' (2020) R30 Postal Memorialis – Lexicon strafrecht, strafvordering en bijzondere wetten 66, 50.

634 F.O.D. Justitie, "Actionplan: approach to radicalisation in prisons", 11 March 2015, https://justitie.belgium.be/sites/default/files/downloads/Plland%27actionradicalisation-prison-NL.pdf. See also: Vierde tussentijds verslag van 23 oktober 2017 over het onderdeel "radicalisme" namens de parlementaire onderzoekscommissie belast met het onderzoek naar de omstandigheden die hebben geleid tot de terroristische aanslagen van 22 maart 2016 in de luchthaven Brussel-Nationaal en in het metrostation Maalbeek te Brussel, met inbegrip van de evolutie en de aanpak van de strijd tegen het radicalisme en de terroristische dreiging, *Parl.St.* Kamer 2017-2018, nr. 54-1752/009, 79.

635 F.O.D. Justitie, "Actionplan: approach to radicalisation in prisons", 11 March 2015, 13, https://justitie.belgium.be/sites/default/files/downloads/Plland%27actionradicalisation-prison-NL.pdf. See also: Verslag namens de commissie voor justitie hoorzittingen de deradicaliserings-, exit- en resocialisatieprogramma's binnen de belgische penitentiaire instellingen, *Parl.St.* Kamer 2019-2020, nr. 55-1501/001, 9.

636 F.O.D. Justitie, "Actionplan: approach to radicalisation in prisons", 11 March 2015, 13, https://justitie.belgium.be/sites/default/files/downloads/Plland%27actionradicalisation-prison-NL.pdf. See also: Rapport au Gouvernement de la Belgique relatif à la visite effectuée en Belgique par le Comité européen pour la prévention de la torture et des peines ou traitements inhumains ou dégradants (CPT) du 27 mars au 6 avril 2017, Strasbourg 8 March 2018, CPT/Inf (2018) 8, 29; Commission de surveillance de la prison d'Ittre, 'Rapport de fin de mandat', August 2019, 34-35; This approach was confirmed in the most recent instructions on extremism (see below). See: DG EPI, "Bijzondere instructies", 12 februari 2021, 6.

637 F.O.D. Justitie, "Actionplan: approach to radicalisation in prisons", 11 March 2015, 14, https://justitie.belgium.be/sites/default/files/downloads/Plland%27actionradicalisation-prison-NL.pdf.

638 Vierde tussentijds verslag van 23 oktober 2017 over het onderdeel "radicalisme" namens de parlementaire onderzoekscommissie belast met het onderzoek naar de omstandigheden die hebben geleid tot de terroristische aanslagen van 22 maart 2016 in de luchthaven Brussel-Nationaal en in het metrostation Maalbeek te Brussel, met inbegrip van de evolutie en de aanpak van de strijd tegen het radicalisme en de terroristische dreiging, *Parl.St.* Kamer 2017-2018, nr. 54-1752/009, 80; Schriftelijke vraag nr. 6-2224 van Lionel Bajart (Open Vld) d.d. 15 januari 2019 aan de minister van Justitie, belast met de Regie der Gebouwen, *Vr. en Antw.* Senaat 2018-19; Verslag namens de commissie voor justitie hoorzittingen de deradicaliserings-, exit- en resocialisatieprogramma's binnen de belgische penitentiaire instellingen, *Parl.St.* Kamer 2019-2020, nr. 55-1501/001, 9; Brussel 12 april 2021, *onuitg.*; Rapport au Gouvernement de la Belgique relatif à la visite effectuée en Belgique par le Comité européen pour la prévention de la torture et des peines ou traitements inhumains ou dégradants (CPT) du 27 mars au 6 avril 2017, Strasbourg 8 March 2018, CPT/Inf (2018) 8, 29; Commission de surveillance de la prison d'Ittre, 'Rapport de fin de

are not always evident, making the decision to place an inmate in a D-Rad:Ex section rather opaque.[639] The following are excluded: women, simple executors, internees, ideologists who are not inclined towards jihadism and detainees who cannot be placed together according to the investigating judge.[640] However, according to the prison wardens, in practice the original idea behind these sections was not followed strictly and other 'terrorist' detainees were also transferred there.[641] The decision to place a detainee in these sections is made by the general director of the penitentiary institutions, based on the proposal of the prison management, and after an analysis of the psychosocial service and advice from CelEx.[642] When they were founded, there was no legal framework for these D-Rad:Ex sections.[643]

In instructions dating five days after the opening of these sections, four categories of detainees were distinguished:[644] Category A includes people incarcerated for a terrorist offences, category B are people who 'on the basis of their title of detention have a clear link with terrorism and/or who, by words or deeds, strongly demonstrate that they belong to the profile of violent extremists'[645], Category C includes all people who are in the OCAD

---

mandat', August 2019, 34; Beernaert, *Manuel de droit pénitentiaire* (n 543) 44; Bruggeman (n 633) 51; Teper (n 620) 961-963; Ruben Vilain, 'Ontbreken van Waarborgen Bij de Facto Bijzonder Veiligheidsregime Op D-Rad:Ex Grond Voor Schadevergoeding' [2020] Nieuw Juridisch Weekblad 183.

639 Strafuitvoeringsrechtbank Brussel 1 oktober 2018, *JT* 2018, 959.

640 Teper (n 620) 963. The supervisory committee of the prison of Ittre includes a shorter list of excluded categories in a report, being women, internees and ideologists who are not inclined towards jihadism. See: Commission de surveillance de la prison d'Ittre, 'Rapport de fin de mandat', August 2019, 35.

641 Vierde tussentijds verslag van 23 oktober 2017 over het onderdeel "radicalisme" namens de parlementaire onderzoekscommissie belast met het onderzoek naar de omstandigheden die hebben geleid tot de terroristische aanslagen van 22 maart 2016 in de luchthaven Brussel-Nationaal en in het metrostation Maalbeek te Brussel, met inbegrip van de evolutie en de aanpak van de strijd tegen het radicalisme en de terroristische dreiging, *Parl.St.* Kamer 2017-2018, nr. 54-1752/009, 85-86. See also: Verslag namens de commissie voor justitie hoorzittingen de deradicaliserings-, exit- en resocialisatieprogramma's binnen de belgische penitentiaire instellingen, *Parl.St.* Kamer 2019-2020, nr. 55-1501/001, 10.

642 F.O.D. Justitie, "Actionplan: approach to radicalisation in prisons", 11 March 2015, 13-14, https://justitie.belgium.be/sites/default/files/downloads/Plland%27actionradicalisation-prison-NL.pdf; Vierde tussentijds verslag van 23 oktober 2017 over het onderdeel "radicalisme" namens de parlementaire onderzoekscommissie belast met het onderzoek naar de omstandigheden die hebben geleid tot de terroristische aanslagen van 22 maart 2016 in de luchthaven Brussel-Nationaal en in het metrostation Maalbeek te Brussel, met inbegrip van de evolutie en de aanpak van de strijd tegen het radicalisme en de terroristische dreiging, *Parl.St.* Kamer 2017-2018, nr. 54-1752/009, 80; DG EPI, "Bijzondere instructies", 12 februari 2021, 6; Commission de surveillance de la prison d'Ittre, 'Rapport de fin de mandat', August 2019, 35; Teper (n 620) 963.

643 Commission de surveillance de la prison d'Ittre, 'Rapport de fin de mandat', August 2019, 34; Teper (n 620) 961.

644 Vierde tussentijds verslag van 23 oktober 2017 over het onderdeel "radicalisme" namens de parlementaire onderzoekscommissie belast met het onderzoek naar de omstandigheden die hebben geleid tot de terroristische aanslagen van 22 maart 2016 in de luchthaven Brussel-Nationaal en in het metrostation Maalbeek te Brussel, met inbegrip van de evolutie en de aanpak van de strijd tegen het radicalisme en de terroristische dreiging, *Parl.St.* Kamer 2017-2018, nr. 54-1752/009, 80.

645 As appreciated by CelEx. See: Teper (n 620) 961.

database of foreign terrorist fighters and Category D are detainees who show signs of radicalisation or a risk of radicalising others.[646] At the start of January 2017 there were 56 detainees in Category A, 28 in Category B, 60 in Category C and 19 in Category D.[647] In the following years these categories were expanded upon[648] until they were replaced in 2021. During that year, updated instructions were released which replaced the previous versions. These instructions are applicable to all CelEx detainees, meaning detainees with a heightened risk of radicalising other inmates or engaging in violent combat for religious or ideological motives.[649] Each of these detainees is put in a category and given a typology. The categories are the same categories OCAD uses,[650] being foreign terrorist fighters,[651] homegrown terrorist fighters,[652] terrorism convicted persons,[653] potentially violent extremists[654] and hatepropagandists,[655] plus two additional categories, being 'Terro EPI' detainees[656] and 'Violent extremist prisoners EPI'[657].[658] The typology refers to the role the

646 Bruggeman (n 633) 51; Olivia Nederlandt, 'Actualités En Droit de l'exécution Des Peines Privatives de Liberté : Un État de Crise Permanent?' in Franklin Kuty and Christine Guillain (eds), *Actualités en droit pénal et exécution des peines* (Larcier 2020) 156; Teper (n 620) 962.

647 *Vr. en Antw.* Kamer 2016-17, *Bull.* nr. 105, 10 februari 2017, 191.

648 See: DG EPI, "Bijzondere instructies extremisme", 2 oktober 2018. See also: Comité T, 'Rapport 2020: Evaluation des mesures visant à lutter contre le terrorisme à la lumière des droits humains', 78.

649 DG EPI, "Bijzondere instructies", 12 februari 2021, 4.

650 These people do have to have a link with Belgium.

651 People who, with the aim of joining or supporting a terrorist group traveled to a jihadist conflict zone, left Belgium to travel to a jihadist conflict zone, are on their way to Belgium or have returned to Belgium after having traveled to a jihadist conflict zone, were prevented from traveling to a jihadist conflict zone or have the intention to travel to a jihadist conflict zone.

652 People for whom there are serious indications that they intend to use violence against persons or material interests for ideological or political reasons with the aim of achieving their goals through terror, intimidation or threats to achieve their objectives or that they are intentionally providing support, in particular logistical, financial or for training or recruitment purposes, to the person previously described or to persons registered as FTF for whom there are serious suspicions that they intend to carry out an act of violence.

653 People convicted for a terrorist offence with a threat level of 2, 3 or 4 as assigned by OCAD.

654 People who hold extremist views that legitimise the use of force or coercion as a method of action in Belgium, when there are indications they have violent intentions related to these views and they either have systematic contacts within extremist circles, have a violent judicial record, are mentally unstable or received training in the manufacture or use of explosives, firearms or other weapons or noxious or hazardous substances or other specific methods or techniques which increase the risk of terrorist violence.

655 People or organisations which (cumulatively) cause harm to the principles of democracy or human rights, the proper functioning of democratic institutions or other foundations of the rule of law, justify the use of violence or coercion as methods of action and spread the belief to others with the intention of exerting a radicalising influence.

656 Detainees detained for terrorist offences who have an OCAD threat level of lower than 2 and cannot be included in another category.

657 Radicalised or extremist detainees which are not under preliminary investigation by OCAD but who required special attention based on the fact they are potentially violent towards people within prison based on an ideology.

658 DG EPI, "Bijzondere instructies", 12 februari 2021, 4-6.

person had in the commission of the facts, such as recruiter, leader, etc. and is assigned by CelEx.[659]

In addition to the D-Rad:Ex sections, 'satelite wings' have been created in the prisons of Andenne, Lantin, Saint-Gilles, Bruges and Ghent. These wings are staffed by people who have received special training on radicalisation.[660] They are intended for detainees with a high risk of radicalisation, and thus require special monitoring.[661] It is also possible that detainees from a D-Rad:Ex section are transferred to these wings with a view to an eventual transfer into the general population.[662] Originally, the idea was that these five prisons would be satellite prisons in which the terrorist detainees were spread out among the general population. However, in practice, separate wings were designated for them, resulting in a minimal difference between these satellite wings and the D-Rad:Ex sections.[663]

The supervisory committee of the prison of Ittre undertook a study in December 2016 on the conditions within the D-Rad:Ex sections.[664] They stated that detainees in those sections cannot have any contact with any other detainees, meaning that they are excluded from training and activities, from doing paid labour outside the section and are limited to a small, completely fenced off courtyard and much smaller gym space.[665] In its 2019 end of mandate report, the committee also noted that the prisoners are required to move cells every six months in order to avoid the same detainees spending time together regularly.[666] In addition, whenever they have to move throughout the prison, they have to be

659 DG EPI, "Bijzondere instructies", 12 februari 2021, 4.

660 Commission de surveillance de la prison d'Ittre, 'Rapport de fin de mandat', August 2019, 35; Beernaert, *Manuel de droit pénitentiaire* (n 543) 44; Bruggeman (n 633) 50-51; Teper (n 620) 962.

661 Vierde tussentijds verslag van 23 oktober 2017 over het onderdeel "radicalisme" namens de parlementaire onderzoekscommissie belast met het onderzoek naar de omstandigheden die hebben geleid tot de terroristische aanslagen van 22 maart 2016 in de luchthaven Brussel-Nationaal en in het metrostation Maalbeek te Brussel, met inbegrip van de evolutie en de aanpak van de strijd tegen het radicalisme en de terroristische dreiging, *Parl.St.* Kamer 2017-2018, nr. 54-1752/009, 80; Beernaert, *Manuel de droit pénitentiaire* (n 543) 44; Bruggeman (n 633) 50.

662 Vierde tussentijds verslag van 23 oktober 2017 over het onderdeel "radicalisme" namens de parlementaire onderzoekscommissie belast met het onderzoek naar de omstandigheden die hebben geleid tot de terroristische aanslagen van 22 maart 2016 in de luchthaven Brussel-Nationaal en in het metrostation Maalbeek te Brussel, met inbegrip van de evolutie en de aanpak van de strijd tegen het radicalisme en de terroristische dreiging, *Parl.St.* Kamer 2017-2018, nr. 54-1752/009, 80.

663 Vierde tussentijds verslag van 23 oktober 2017 over het onderdeel "radicalisme" namens de parlementaire onderzoekscommissie belast met het onderzoek naar de omstandigheden die hebben geleid tot de terroristische aanslagen van 22 maart 2016 in de luchthaven Brussel-Nationaal en in het metrostation Maalbeek te Brussel, met inbegrip van de evolutie en de aanpak van de strijd tegen het radicalisme en de terroristische dreiging, *Parl.St.* Kamer 2017-2018, nr. 54-1752/009, 84.

664 We have been unable to find this study but the committee itself refers to it in its 2019 end of mandate report. See: Commission de surveillance de la prison d'Ittre, 'Rapport de fin de mandat', August 2019, 36.

665 Commission de surveillance de la prison d'Ittre, 'Rapport de fin de mandat', August 2019, 38-41; Teper (n 620) 962.

666 Commission de surveillance de la prison d'Ittre, 'Rapport de fin de mandat', August 2019, 38.

accompanied by three prison officers and in the visiting room three tables are reserved for them under the supervision of one prison officer.[667] The prisoners in these sections are also subject to the restrictions imposed upon all CelEx detainees, including an order measure requiring them to report to the prison management which telephone numbers they wish to call.[668] Finally, any visitors to CelEx detainees need to be vetted by the management and will be refused if they do not have a legitimate interest for the visit.[669] This restriction does, however, exclude certain people such as the detainees' parents, siblings, uncles and aunts. In 2019, the Court of First Instance in Brussels had to rule on a case relating to the D-Rad:Ex sections.[670] It ruled that D-Rad:Ex sections in themselves did not violate human rights, but they also do not constitute a 'normal' prison regime. Instead, the inmates in these sections are subject to an individual special security regime. However, they do not benefit from the legal safeguards awarded to detainees subject to such a regime and therefore the Belgian government has tort liability.[671] They were awarded one euro damages per day spent in D-Rad:Ex. The government appealed this decision. The Court of Appeal reviewed the conditions of detention in the D-Rad:Ex section in Ittre carefully and concluded that while it did violate the Basic Law, this was only in relation to the conditions of the sports activities and the daily surveillance the detainees underwent without being informed of the findings concerning them.[672] This last observation is important since without this information the detainees lack an effective remedy to challenge their continued detention in the D-Rad:Ex section, violating articles 6 and 13 of the ECHR.[673] The Court of Appeal granted each of the inmates 2500 euro in damages. According to the 2022 Comité T report, in 2021 there were no more inmates in the D-Rad:Ex section in

667 Teper (n 620) 962.

668 DG EPI, "Bijzondere instructies", 12 februari 2021, 13; Commission de surveillance de la prison d'Ittre, 'Rapport de fin de mandat', August 2019, 42; Comité T, 'Raport 2022: Évaluation des mesures visant à lutter contre le terrorisme à la lumière des droits humains', 85-88; Teper (n 620) 962.

669 Vierde tussentijds verslag van 23 oktober 2017 over het onderdeel "radicalisme" namens de parlementaire onderzoekscommissie belast met het onderzoek naar de omstandigheden die hebben geleid tot de terroristische aanslagen van 22 maart 2016 in de luchthaven Brussel-Nationaal en in het metrostation Maalbeek te Brussel, met inbegrip van de evolutie en de aanpak van de strijd tegen het radicalisme en de terroristische dreiging, *Parl.St.* Kamer 2017-2018, nr. 54-1752/009, 79; DG EPI, "Bijzondere instructies", 12 februari 2021, 13; Teper (n 620) 962.

670 Eerste aanleg Brussel 26 april 2019, *NjW* 2020, 179, noot Vilain. Note that in the journal in which the case is published, it is listed as 26 April 2018 instead of 2019. This is in all likelihood a clerical error. See also: Vilain (n 638) 183-184.

671 See also: Commission de surveillance de la prison d'Ittre, 'Rapport de fin de mandat', August 2019, 43; Comité T, 'Rapport 2020: Evaluation des mesures visant à lutter contre le terrorisme à la lumière des droits humains', 83; Beernaert, *Manuel de droit pénitentiaire* (n 543) 214-215; Nederlandt, 'Actualités En Droit de l'exécution Des Peines Privatives de Liberté : Un État de Crise Permanent?' (n 646) 166-167.

672 Brussel 12 april 2021, *onuitg.*

673 Brussel 12 april 2021, *onuitg.*

Hasselt and only five in Ittre.[674] Many of the abovementioned rules on 'terrorist' detainees have been criticised in the literature for violating human rights and being insufficiently clear and foreseeable.[675]

Before moving on to the external legal position of detainees, a brief overview of the bodies providing social help and services to detainees will be given. These bodies are important in the context of rehabilitation as they allow detainees to work on themselves during detention and thus increase their chances of early release and successful reintegration into society. While the prison system itself is a federal competence, the communities are responsible for providing certain services and support within prison. In 2013 a Flemish decree was issued to 'ensure the right of all prisoners and their immediate social environment to comprehensive and high-quality assistance and services aimed at achieving the objectives set out in Article 4 [e.g. reducing recidivism and limiting negative consequences of detention], in order to enable them to develop in society'.[676] Based on this decree, the Flemisch government has to approve a strategic plan which implements the goals of the decree.[677] The current version of this plan spans 2020 to 2025 and focusses specifically on certain groups of detainees, including radicalised detainees.[678] Moreover, in each prison a policy team and a coordination team were created, who are responsible for the implementation of the strategic plan.[679] Within the Flemish community the '*Centrum Algemeen Welzijnswerk*' (CAW) and '*Centra Geestelijke Gezondheidszorg*' (CGG) are of particular importance. The CAW functions inside prison and assures the transition of detainees to other organisations for about six months after release.[680] Disengagement programmes have been structurally embedded within the functioning of CAW.[681] In addition to these programmes, there are also deradicalisation consultants within the CAW. The justice houses, which have a multidisciplinary team to tackle radicalisation, also received a mandate to already work within prison in order to facilitate reintegration. Within the French community, all organisations competent for the follow up of detainees

674 Comité T, 'Raport 2022: Évaluation des mesures visant à lutter contre le terrorisme à la lumière des droits humains', 90.

675 Comité T, 'Rapport 2020: Evaluation des mesures visant à lutter contre le terrorisme à la lumière des droits humains', 78-85; Millen (n 612) 21-24; Teper (n 620) 960-965; Vilain (n 638) 183-184.

676 Art 3, section 1 decreet van 8 maart 2013 betreffende de organisatie van hulp- en dienstverlening aan gedetineerden, *BS* 11 april 2013, 22460.

677 Art 8 decreet van 8 maart 2013 betreffende de organisatie van hulp- en dienstverlening aan gedetineerden, *BS* 11 april 2013, 22460.

678 Vlaams strategisch plan hulp- en dienstverlening aan gedetineerden en geïnterneerden 2020-2025, VR 2020 1311 DOC.1230/3BIS, 33-36.

679 Art 10 and 11 decreet van 8 maart 2013 betreffende de organisatie van hulp- en dienstverlening aan gedetineerden, *BS* 11 april 2013, 22460.

680 Comité T, 'Rapport 2021: Evaluation des mesures visant à lutter contre le terrorisme à la lumière des droits humains', 102.

681 Vlaams strategisch plan hulp- en dienstverlening aan gedetineerden en geïnterneerden 2020-2025, VR 2020 1311 DOC.1230/3BIS, 34.

are organised within the '*Administration Générale des Maisons de Justice*' (AGMJ).[682] Within the AGMJ a group of partner services exists, which are accredited and subsidised by the French community. In a 2016 decree six goals are listed for these partners, among which are psychological and societal support.[683] Within the AGMJ a sub-body exists called the '*Centre d'Aide et de Prise en charge des Personnes concernées par les Radicalismes et les Extrémismes Violents*' (CAPREV).[684] CAPREV was created in 2017[685] and is focused on disengagement both within and outside of prisons. CAPREV is even allowed to accompany detainees on a day release (see below). At the expert seminar, the overall opinion was that reintegration after a conviction for terrorism is often difficult. There is a lack of sufficient programmes specifically tailored to those people, and the stigma of a terrorist conviction is often hard to overcome. To make matters worse, waiting lists for the available programmes are long, as are the waiting lists for support and follow-up outside of prison. On the other hand, one participant noted that the (ex-)convicted people also have a responsibility to try to reintegrate. Without active collaboration from the (ex-)convicted person, successful reintegration is impossible.

Beyond prison: external legal position

Several modalities of sentence execution exist. These entail the possibility for the convicted detainee to spend time outside of the prison walls during their sentence. There are two categories of modalities, the first are granted by the secretary of justice, the second, in principle (see below), by the sentence enforcement court (*strafuitvoeringsrechtbank;*

682 Coline Remacle and Olivia Nederlandt, 'Het Institutionele Landschap van de Sociale Hulpverlening Aan Rechtzoekenden En Gedetineerden in Het Franstalig Landsgedeelte' [2018] FATIK: Tijdschrift voor Strafbeleid en Gevangeniswezen 29, 31; Olivia Nederlandt and Coline Remacle, 'L'aide Sociale Aux Justiciables et Aux Détenus : Un Secteur Invisibilisé Par La Complexité Institutionnelle Belge ?' [2019] Revue de Droit Pénal et de Criminologie (Rev. dr. pén.) 379, 387.

683 Art 5-14 Décret du 13 octobre 2016 relatif à l'agrément et au subventionnement des partenaires apportant de l'aide aux justiciables, *BS* 22 december 2016, 88082. See also: Nederlandt and Remacle (n 682) 389-390; Sandra Reisse, Benedicte Van Boven and Vauthier Anne, 'Désistance et Maisons de Justice : Construction d'un Modèle Par et Pour l'administration' [2019] Revue de Droit Pénal et de Criminologie (Rev. dr. pén.) 1213, 1218-129; Remacle and Nederlandt (n 682) 32. This decree was implemented by the Arrêté du Gouvernement de la Communauté française du 17 mai 2017 portant exécution du décret du 13 octobre 2016 relatif à l'agrément et au subventionnement des partenaires apportant de l'aide aux justiciables, *BS* 7 juni 2017, 62217 in turn implemented by the Arrêté ministériel du 17 mai 2017 portant exécution de l'arrêté du Gouvernement de la Communauté française du 17 mai 2017 portant exécution du décret du 13 octobre 2016 relatif à l'agrément et au subventionnement des partenaires apportant de l'aide aux justiciables, *BS* 9 juni 2017, 63351.

684 Comité T, 'Rapport 2021: Evaluation des mesures visant à lutter contre le terrorisme à la lumière des droits humains', 102; Reisse, Van Boven and Vauthier (n 683) 1218.

685 Comité T, 'Rapport 2020: Evaluation des mesures visant à lutter contre le terrorisme à la lumière des droits humains', 39.

tribunal de l'application des peines) or the sentence enforcement judge (*strafuitvoeringsrechter; juge de l'application des peines*). The secretary of justice can grant four modalities: a day release (*uitgaansvergunning; permission de sortie*), penitentiary leave (*penitentiair verlof; congé pénitentiaire*), placement in a transition house (*transitiehuis; maison de transition*) and interruption of sentence enforcement (*onderbreking van de strafuitvoering; interruption de l'exécution de la peine*). The sentence enforcement court or judge can grant three modalities: limited detention (*beperkte detentie; détention limitée*), electronic tagging and conditional release (*voorwaardelijke invrijheidsstelling; libération conditionnelle*).

A day release can last a maximum of sixteen hours.[686] It can be granted occasionally at any point during detention so that the detainee can undergo medical treatment, or if his presence outside of prison is required to further his social, moral, legal, family, training or professional interests.[687] A day release can also be granted periodically during the two years before a detainee can be conditionally released, in order to prepare for their social reintegration.[688] A day release will be granted if there are no indications which cannot be mitigated by imposing specific conditions, that the person would flee, commit serious offences, or bother the victim.[689] Finally, the detainee has to agree with the general condition that he will not commit any criminal offences, and also to any specific conditions which may be imposed.[690]

Penitentiary leave allows a detainee to leave prison for 36 hours, four times each trimester.[691] The aim of a penitentiary leave is to allow the detainee to maintain and strengthen their family, affective and social ties, or to prepare their reintegration.[692] Penitentiary leave can be granted starting one year before the detainee can be conditionally released.[693] It will be granted if there are no indications that the person would flee, commit

686 Art 4, §1 WERP. See also: Beernaert, *Manuel de droit pénitentiaire* (n 543) 239; Benjamin Mine and others, 'Permissions de Sortie et Congés Pénitentiaires : Des Sorties En Toute Discrétion ?' [2021] Revue de droit pénal et de criminologie 723, 728; Olivia Nederlandt and Thierry Moreau, 'Évolution Dans Le Champ de l'exécution Des Peines Depuis La Loi Pot-Pourri II', *La loi Pot-Pourri II: un an après* (Larcier 2017) 301; Boris Reynaerts, 'Wet 17 Mei 2006' in Tom Decaigny and others (eds), *Duiding Strafuitvoering* (Larcier 2014) 93; Scheirs (n 544) 673.

687 Art 4, §2 WERP. See also: Beernaert, *Manuel de droit pénitentiaire* (n 543) 240; Mine and others (n 686) 728; Reynaerts (n 686) 93; Scheirs (n 544) 673.

688 Art 4, §3 WERP. See also: Beernaert, *Manuel de droit pénitentiaire* (n 543) 240-241; Mine and others (n 686) 728 and 730; Reynaerts (n 686) 94; Scheirs (n 544) 673.

689 Art 5, 2° WERP. See also: Beernaert, *Manuel de droit pénitentiaire* (n 543) 242; Mine and others (n 686) 733-734; Reynaerts (n 686) 94; Scheirs (n 544) 673.

690 Art 5, 3° *j.* 11, §3 WERP. See also: Beernaert, *Manuel de droit pénitentiaire* (n 543) 242; Mine and others (n 686) 734; Reynaerts (n 686) 95; Scheirs (n 544) 673.

691 Art 6, §1 WERP. See also: Beernaert, *Manuel de droit pénitentiaire* (n 543) 248; Mine and others (n 686) 728; Reynaerts (n 686) 95; Scheirs (n 544) 674.

692 Art 6, §2 WERP. See also: Beernaert, *Manuel de droit pénitentiaire* (n 543) 248; Mine and others (n 686) 728; Reynaerts (n 686) 95; Scheirs (n 544) 674.

693 Art 7, 1° WERP. See also: Beernaert, *Manuel de droit pénitentiaire* (n 543) 249; Mine and others (n 686) 730; Reynaerts (n 686) 96; Scheirs (n 544) 674.

serious offences or bother the victim, which cannot be mitigated by imposing specific conditions.[694] Finally, the detainee has to agree with the general condition that they will not commit any criminal offences, and also to any specific conditions which may be imposed.[695]

Placement in a transition house is not a form of temporary release, but rather a change to the type of detention.[696] A placement plan is established,[697] allowing the detainee to be transferred to a transition house.[698] Such houses are recognised institutions where detainees can undergo their sentence in a more small-scale environment which is not as detached from society. The placement plan contains the programme a detainee has to follow, including obligatory activities aimed at reintegration.[699] This placement can be granted to detainees who are within eighteen months of being able to be conditionally released.[700] This is only possible for detainees who have the ability to stay in an open communal regime and for who no indications exist that they would flee, commit serious offences or bother the victim, which cannot be mitigated by imposing specific conditions.[701]

---

694 Art 7, 2° WERP. See also: Beernaert, *Manuel de droit pénitentiaire* (n 543) 249; Mine and others (n 686) 733-734; Reynaerts (n 686) 96; Scheirs (n 544) 674.

695 Art 7, 3° *j.* 11, §3 WERP. See also: Beernaert, *Manuel de droit pénitentiaire* (n 543) 249; Mine and others (n 686) 734; Reynaerts (n 686) 96; Scheirs (n 544) 674.

696 Collectieve brief DG EPI nr. 150 van 22 augustus 2019 over pilootproject Transitiehuizen, 1; Olivia Nederlandt and An-Sofie Vanhouche, 'Les Maisons de Transition: Miroir Aux Alouettes Ou Pied Dans La Porte?' in Christine Guillain and Damien Scalia (eds), *Les coûts du système pénal* (La Charte 2020) 36; An-Sofie Vanhouche and Olivia Nederlandt, 'De Belgische transitiehuizen: nood aan een terugkeer naar het originele concept van detentiehuizen' [2020] FATIK: Tijdschrift voor Strafbeleid en Gevangeniswezen 6, 7. This is a fairly new sentence modality, which was also suggested by the parliamentary research committee which was established after the Brussels terrorist attacks. See: Vierde tussentijds verslag van 23 oktober 2017 over het onderdeel "radicalisme" namens de parlementaire onderzoekscommissie belast met het onderzoek naar de omstandigheden die hebben geleid tot de terroristische aanslagen van 22 maart 2016 in de luchthaven Brussel-Nationaal en in het metrostation Maalbeek te Brussel, met inbegrip van de evolutie en de aanpak van de strijd tegen het radicalisme en de terroristische dreiging, *Parl.St.* Kamer 2017-2018, nr. 54-1752/009, 106.

697 Art 9/1 WERP.

698 Nederlandt, 'Actualités En Droit de l'exécution Des Peines Privatives de Liberté : Un État de Crise Permanent?' (n 646) 132; Olivia Nederlandt, '15 Jaar Strafuitvoeringsrechtbanken : Teenagers under Control?' [2022] FATIK: Tijdschrift voor Strafbeleid en Gevangeniswezen 4, 11; Nederlandt and Vanhouche (n 696) 36.

699 Art 9/3, §2 WERP. See also: Collectieve brief DG EPI nr. 150 van 22 augustus 2019 over pilootproject Transitiehuizen, 2; Beernaert, *Manuel de droit pénitentiaire* (n 543) 256; Nederlandt, 'Actualités En Droit de l'exécution Des Peines Privatives de Liberté : Un État de Crise Permanent?' (n 646) 132; Nederlandt, '15 Jaar Strafuitvoeringsrechtbanken : Teenagers under Control?' (n 698) 11; Nederlandt and Vanhouche (n 696) 38; Vanhouche and Nederlandt (n 696) 9.

700 Art 9/3, §1, 1° WERP. See also: Collectieve brief DG EPI nr. 150 van 22 augustus 2019 over pilootproject Transitiehuizen, 3; Beernaert, *Manuel de droit pénitentiaire* (n 543) 256; Nederlandt, 'Actualités En Droit de l'exécution Des Peines Privatives de Liberté : Un État de Crise Permanent?' (n 646) 135; Nederlandt and Vanhouche (n 696) 38; Vanhouche and Nederlandt (n 696) 8.

701 Art 9/3, §1, 2° and 3° WERP. See also: Collectieve brief DG EPI nr. 150 van 22 augustus 2019 over pilootproject Transitiehuizen, 3; Beernaert, *Manuel de droit pénitentiaire* (n 543) 256; Nederlandt, 'Actualités

Finally, the detainee has to agree with the placement plan, the household rules of the transition house and the general condition that they will not commit any criminal offences, and to any specific conditions which may be imposed.[702]

If the detainee does not abide by any of the conditions imposed with the modalities discussed above, or if new indications as mentioned above arise, the secretary of justice can decide to change the conditions, pause the execution of the modality for maximum three months (this is not possible for placement in a transition house), or revoke the modality.[703] If the detainee has seriously endangered the physical or psychological safety of other people, the public prosecutor can also decide to order their temporary arrest, after which the secretary will decide on the continuation of the modality.[704]

Additionally, the secretary of justice may also grant the interruption of the enforcement of custodial sentences, which is not a sentencing modality but rather a suspension of the sentence. In this case, the execution of the sentence is paused for maximum three months, which can be renewed.[705] This can only be granted for serious and extraordinary family reasons[706], and no indications can exist that the person would flee, commit serious offences or bother the victim, which cannot be mitigated by imposing specific conditions.[707] In this case as well, if the detainee has seriously endangered the physical or psychological safety of other people, the public prosecutor can decide to order their temporary arrest while allowing time for the secretary to decide on the suspension of the sentence.[708]

Before going into the sentencing modalities which the sentence enforcement court or judge can impose, an important caveat has to be made. According to the law on the external legal position, the sentence enforcement judge is competent for all sentences up to three years imprisonment while the sentence enforcement court is competent for all longer sentences.[709] As will become clear, in addition to this difference in judicial forum,

---

En Droit de l'exécution Des Peines Privatives de Liberté : Un État de Crise Permanent?' (n 646) 135-136; Nederlandt and Vanhouche (n 696) 38; Vanhouche and Nederlandt (n 696) 8-9.

702 Art 9/3, §1, 4° and 5° *j.* 11, §3 WERP. See also: Collectieve brief DG EPI nr. 150 van 22 augustus 2019 over pilootproject Transitiehuizen, 3-4; Beernaert, *Manuel de droit pénitentiaire* (n 543) 256; Nederlandt, 'Actualités En Droit de l'exécution Des Peines Privatives de Liberté : Un État de Crise Permanent?' (n 646) 136; Nederlandt and Vanhouche (n 696) 38.

703 Art 12, §1, §2 and §2*bis* WERP. See also: Beernaert, *Manuel de droit pénitentiaire* (n 543) 246, 253 and 257; Reynaerts (n 686) 101-102.

704 Art 14 WERP. See also: Beernaert, *Manuel de droit pénitentiaire* (n 543) 247, 254 and 258; Reynaerts (n 686) 102.

705 Art 15, §1 WERP. See also: Beernaert, *Manuel de droit pénitentiaire* (n 543) 259; Reynaerts (n 686) 103; Scheirs (n 544) 675.

706 Art 15, §2 WERP.

707 Art 16 WERP. See also: Beernaert, *Manuel de droit pénitentiaire* (n 543) 259-260; Scheirs (n 544) 675.

708 Art 19 WERP. See also: Beernaert, *Manuel de droit pénitentiaire* (n 543) 262-263; Reynaerts (n 686) 106; Scheirs (n 544) 675.

709 JF Funck, 'Le tribunal de l'application des peines aujourd'hui et demain : nouvelles compétences (peines de trois ans ou moins), conditions d'octroi des mesures et révocation', *Actualités en procédure pénale : de*

there are other rules which differ between these two categories of sentences. However, the entry into force of the section of legislation governing the limited detention, electronic tagging and conditional release for detainees sentenced to less than three years has been pushed back several times.[710] Even today, it has not yet entered into force fully. In 2022 the legislature decided to implement these rules in practice in phases.[711] Since 1 September 2022, these rules are applicable to sentences of between two and three years. For sentences of up to two years, this part of the legislation on the external legal position of detainees has not entered into force yet. Until it does, these sentences are subject to a different regime, being one of electronic tagging and automatic early release.[712]

The rules on electronic tagging in this context are outlined in Circulare nr. ET/SE-2 of the secretary of justice[713] which dates back to 2013 but has since been changed several

l'audition à l'exécution (Anthemis 2020) 203; Mine and others (n 686) 732; Nederlandt, '15 Jaar Strafuitvoeringsrechtbanken : Teenagers under Control?' (n 698) 4; Scheirs (n 544) 670.

710 See: art 14 wet 23 november 2015; art 317 wet 6 juli 2017; art 23 wet 5 mei 2019; art 100 wet 31 juli 2020; art 2 wet 16 maart 2021; art 92 wet 28 november 2021. See also: Comité T, 'Rapport 2021: Evaluation des mesures visant à lutter contre le terrorisme à la lumière des droits humains', 97; Beernaert, *Manuel de droit pénitentiaire* (n 543) 273; Mine and others (n 686) 732; Eric Maes, 'De Lange "Weg Naar Echternach" Nog Steeds Niet Afgelegd… Over de Strafuitvoering Bij Veroordeelden Tot Een "Korte" Vrijheidsstraf, 15 Jaar Na Datum' [2022] FATIK: Tijdschrift voor Strafbeleid en Gevangeniswezen 19, 19; Nederlandt, 'Actualités En Droit de l'exécution Des Peines Privatives de Liberté : Un État de Crise Permanent?' (n 646) 177; Nederlandt, '15 Jaar Strafuitvoeringsrechtbanken : Teenagers under Control?' (n 698) 10; Scheirs (n 544) 691-692.

711 Memorie van toelichting bij wetsontwerp van 25 april 2022 tot uitstel van de inwerkingtreding van de bepalingen inzake de uitvoering van vrijheidsstraffen van drie jaar of minder, *Parl.St.* Kamer 2021-2022, nr. 55-2645/001, 4 and 7.

712 Ministeriële omzendbrief nr. 1817 van 15 juli 2015 over de voorlopige invrijheidstelling van veroordeelden die één of meer vrijheidsstraffen ondergaan waarvan het uitvoerbaar gedeelte drie jaar of minder bedraagt; Ministeriële omzendbrief nr. 1817bis van 29 april 2016 over de voorlopige invrijheidstelling van veroordeelden die één of meer vrijheidsstraffen ondergaan waarvan het uitvoerbaar gedeelte drie jaar of minder bedraagt; Collectieve brief DF EPI nr. 161 van 11 augustus 2022 over Wet externe rechtspositie – toelichting bij de procedure voor de toekenning van strafuitvoeringsmodaliteiten door de strafuitvoeringsrechter (SUR) en de strafuitvoeringsrechtbank (SURB), 19. See also: Van Den Berge (n 464) 14 and 16; Yves Van Den Berge and Frank Verbruggen, 'Langzaam Maar Onzeker: Het Wettelijk Kader Voor Een Geleidelijke Terugkeer Naar de Maatschappij' in Kristel Beyens, Tom Daems and Eric Maes (eds), *Exit gevangenis? De werking van de strafuitvoeringsrechtbanken en de wet op de externe rechtspositie van veroordeelden tot een vrijheidsstraf* (Maklu 2014) 41. For the practical application and a transitional provisions concerning the application of the procedure to sentences of between two and three years, see: Collectieve brief DF EPI nr. 161 van 11 augustus 2022 over Wet externe rechtspositie – toelichting bij de procedure voor de toekenning van strafuitvoeringsmodaliteiten door de strafuitvoeringsrechter (SUR) en de strafuitvoeringsrechtbank (SURB).

713 Ministeriële omzendbrief nr. ET/SE-2 van 17 juli 2013 over de reglementering inzake het elektronisch toezicht als strafuitvoeringsmodaliteit voor gevangenisstraffen wanneer het totaal in uitvoering zijnde gevangenisstraffen drie jaar niet overschrijdt.

times[714].[715] Since 2015 all terrorist offences[716] have been excluded from this Circulare.[717] As the rules on electronic tagging for sentences of up to two years in the legislation have not yet entered into force, the only conclusion is that electronic tagging as a sentence modality is not possible for terrorist sentences of up to two years.

For the automatic early release, detainees are put into different categories. The first are detainees who exclusively have a prison sentence which replaces a fine which was not paid. These detainees are immediately, automatically and irrevocably released.[718] The same goes for detainees whose prison sentence (which was their main sentence) does not exceed four months, with the difference being that this release is revocable in case of a new standard offence or felony within one years.[719] Detainees who are sentenced to four to six months are released after one month,[720] and this can be revoked for the same reason as above.[721] Sentences of six to maximum seven months fall under the same regime, while the term for

714 Ministeriële omzendbrief nr. ET/SE-2bis van 26 november 2015 over de reglementering inzake het elektronisch toezicht als strafuitvoeringsmodaliteit voor gevangenisstraffen wanneer het totaal in uitvoering zijnde gevangenisstraffen drie jaar niet overschrijdt; Ministeriële omzendbrief nr. ET/SE-2ter van 29 april 2016 over de reglementering inzake het elektronisch toezicht als strafuitvoeringsmodaliteit voor gevangenisstraffen wanneer het totaal in uitvoering zijnde gevangenisstraffen drie jaar niet overschrijdt; Ministeriële omzendbrief nr. ET/SE-2quater van 4 juli 2017 over de reglementering inzake het elektronisch toezicht als strafuitvoeringsmodaliteit voor gevangenisstraffen wanneer het totaal in uitvoering zijnde gevangenisstraffen drie jaar niet overschrijdt.

715 See also: Beernaert, *Manuel de droit pénitentiaire* (n 543) 274; Scheirs (n 544) 693.

716 The Circulare states: art. 135 to 141 CC (terrorist offences). This is odd since articles 135-136octies CC do not contain terrorist offences. It is clear, however, that the terrorist offences are excluded.

717 Chapter I Ministeriële omzendbrief nr. ET/SE-2 van 17 juli 2013 over de reglementering inzake het elektronisch toezicht als strafuitvoeringsmodaliteit voor gevangenisstraffen wanneer het totaal in uitvoering zijnde gevangenisstraffen drie jaar niet overschrijdt, as amended by Ministeriële omzendbrief nr. ET/SE-2bis van 26 november 2015 over de reglementering inzake het elektronisch toezicht als strafuitvoeringsmodaliteit voor gevangenisstraffen wanneer het totaal in uitvoering zijnde gevangenisstraffen drie jaar niet overschrijdt. See also: Beernaert, *Manuel de droit pénitentiaire* (n 543) 275; Maes (n 710) 22; Nederlandt, 'Actualités En Droit de l'exécution Des Peines Privatives de Liberté : Un État de Crise Permanent?' (n 646) 191.

718 Ministeriële omzendbrief nr. 1817 van 15 juli 2015 over de voorlopige invrijheidstelling van veroordeelden die één of meer vrijheidsstraffen ondergaan waarvan het uitvoerbaar gedeelte drie jaar of minder bedraagt, 2. See also: Beernaert, *Manuel de droit pénitentiaire* (n 543) 283; Maes (n 710) 20-21; Nederlandt, 'Actualités En Droit de l'exécution Des Peines Privatives de Liberté : Un État de Crise Permanent?' (n 646) 187.

719 Ministeriële omzendbrief nr. 1817 van 15 juli 2015 over de voorlopige invrijheidstelling van veroordeelden die één of meer vrijheidsstraffen ondergaan waarvan het uitvoerbaar gedeelte drie jaar of minder bedraagt, 2-3. See also: Beernaert, *Manuel de droit pénitentiaire* (n 543) 282 and 288; Maes (n 710) 20-21; Nederlandt, 'Actualités En Droit de l'exécution Des Peines Privatives de Liberté : Un État de Crise Permanent?' (n 646) 185 and 187-188; Scheirs (n 544) 692.

720 Note that this term of one month is not applicable to sentences which received force of res judicata before 1 February 2014. See also: Beernaert, *Manuel de droit pénitentiaire* (n 543) 288; Maes (n 710) 20-21; Nederlandt, 'Actualités En Droit de l'exécution Des Peines Privatives de Liberté : Un État de Crise Permanent?' (n 646) 185; Scheirs (n 544) 692-693.

721 Ministeriële omzendbrief nr. 1817 van 15 juli 2015 over de voorlopige invrijheidstelling van veroordeelden die één of meer vrijheidsstraffen ondergaan waarvan het uitvoerbaar gedeelte drie jaar of minder bedraagt, 3.

sentences of seven months to one year is two months[722].[723] Detainees who are sentenced to more than one year (and maximum two years) are released after they have served four months[724] if the prison warden decides there are no indications the detainee will not be able to provide for their own material needs or represents a manifest risk for the physical integrity of others.[725] Individualised conditions can be imposed if they are absolutely necessary to avoid recidivism. The release of this category of detainees can be revoked in the case that they do not abide by these conditions or in the case of new standard offences or felonies within a term equal to the remainder of their sentence, with a minimum of one year.[726] It is noteworthy that there is a more elaborate procedure in the case of sentences of more than one year for detainees convicted for sexual offences against minors.[727] Since 2016, this is also applicable for detainees convicted to a sentence of two years or less for terrorist offences. These detainees can also be released after the time requirements set out above are met,[728] but in addition to the two indications mentioned above, there must also be no indications that there is a risk of the detainee leaving the country or bothering the victims.[729] Additionally, the decision is not made by the prison warden, but instead by the direction for detention management, after having received all the necessary information from the prison warden, which can include an analysis from the psychosocial services.[730]

722 Note that these are the time limits as set out in the current version of the circular letter, which is a temporary derogation from the standard terms. This derogation is based on instructions from the Secretary dating 16 May 2017. The standard term for sentences of seven to maximum eight months is two months and the term for sentences of eight months to maximum one year is three months. See also: Beernaert, *Manuel de droit pénitentiaire* (n 543) 282; Maes (n 710) 20-21; Nederlandt, 'Actualités En Droit de l'exécution Des Peines Privatives de Liberté : Un État de Crise Permanent?' (n 646) 185.

723 Ministeriële omzendbrief nr. 1817 van 15 juli 2015 over de voorlopige invrijheidstelling van veroordeelden die één of meer vrijheidsstraffen ondergaan waarvan het uitvoerbaar gedeelte drie jaar of minder bedraagt, 4. See also: Maes (n 710) 20-21; Scheirs (n 544) 693.

724 See footnote 722: This is the term as set out in the derogation. The basic term is 1/3 of the sentence.

725 Ministeriële omzendbrief nr. 1817 van 15 juli 2015 over de voorlopige invrijheidstelling van veroordeelden die één of meer vrijheidsstraffen ondergaan waarvan het uitvoerbaar gedeelte drie jaar of minder bedraagt, 5. See also: Scheirs (n 544) 693.

726 See also: Beernaert, *Manuel de droit pénitentiaire* (n 543) 288.

727 Ministeriële omzendbrief nr. 1817 van 15 juli 2015 over de voorlopige invrijheidstelling van veroordeelden die één of meer vrijheidsstraffen ondergaan waarvan het uitvoerbaar gedeelte drie jaar of minder bedraagt, 5-6. See also: Beernaert, *Manuel de droit pénitentiaire* (n 543) 283; Scheirs (n 544) 693.

728 Note that in its 2021 report, Comité T states that terrorist detainees convicted for less than three years imprisonment are not eligible for provisional release. However, this is not supported by the text of the Circulares. See: Comité T, 'Rapport 2021: Evaluation des mesures visant à lutter contre le terrorisme à la lumière des droits humains', 98-99.

729 Ministeriële omzendbrief nr. 1817bis van 29 april 2016 over de voorlopige invrijheidstelling van veroordeelden die één of meer vrijheidsstraffen ondergaan waarvan het uitvoerbaar gedeelte drie jaar of minder bedraagt, 2. See also: Beernaert, *Manuel de droit pénitentiaire* (n 543) 283.

730 Ministeriële omzendbrief nr. 1817bis van 29 april 2016 over de voorlopige invrijheidstelling van veroordeelden die één of meer vrijheidsstraffen ondergaan waarvan het uitvoerbaar gedeelte drie jaar of minder bedraagt, 2-3. See also: Beernaert, *Manuel de droit pénitentiaire* (n 543) 286-287; Nederlandt,

Individualised special conditions are possible when absolutely necessary in order to avoid recidivism, or when necessary in the interests of the victim.[731] Revocation is possible in case of non-compliance with the conditions, which last for the remainder of the original sentence with a minimum of one year, or in case of new standard offences or felonies within that same time period.[732] If the detainee was convicted to an electronic tagging sentence, community service, or an autonomous probation sentence, and the prison sentence is imposed in replacement of this principal sentence, the rules differ again slightly. In the case of a prison sentence of up to four months they are automatically released after fifteen days.[733] For sentences of up to seven months this is one month, sentences up to one year make the term two months.[734] Again, revocation is possible if a new standard offence or felony is committed within one years. For prison sentences which replace the electronic tagging sentence, community service or autonomous probation sentence, and which are longer than one year, the general rules for these sentences, as outlined above, apply.[735] In the case of a sentence of maximum two years imprisonment in combination with being at the disposal of the sentence enforcement court, the detainee is not released early.[736] Finally, there are separate rules for foreigners who have been convicted

'Actualités En Droit de l'exécution Des Peines Privatives de Liberté : Un État de Crise Permanent?' (n 646) 185-186.

731 Ministeriële omzendbrief nr. 1817bis van 29 april 2016 over de voorlopige invrijheidstelling van veroordeelden die één of meer vrijheidsstraffen ondergaan waarvan het uitvoerbaar gedeelte drie jaar of minder bedraagt, 3. See also: Beernaert, *Manuel de droit pénitentiaire* (n 543) 286-287; Nederlandt 'Actualités En Droit de l'exécution Des Peines Privatives de Liberté : Un État de Crise Permanent?' (n 646) 186.

732 Ministeriële omzendbrief nr. 1817bis van 29 april 2016 over de voorlopige invrijheidstelling van veroordeelden die één of meer vrijheidsstraffen ondergaan waarvan het uitvoerbaar gedeelte drie jaar of minder bedraagt, 3-4.

733 See also: Beernaert, *Manuel de droit pénitentiaire* (n 543) 283; Maes (n 710) 21; Nederlandt, 'Actualités En Droit de l'exécution Des Peines Privatives de Liberté : Un État de Crise Permanent?' (n 646) 187.

734 Ministeriële omzendbrief nr. 1817 van 15 juli 2015 over de voorlopige invrijheidstelling van veroordeelden die één of meer vrijheidsstraffen ondergaan waarvan het uitvoerbaar gedeelte drie jaar of minder bedraagt, 7; Ministeriële omzendbrief nr. 1817bis van 29 april 2016 over de voorlopige invrijheidstelling van veroordeelden die één of meer vrijheidsstraffen ondergaan waarvan het uitvoerbaar gedeelte drie jaar of minder bedraagt, 4-5; Maes (n 710) 21; Nederlandt, 'Actualités En Droit de l'exécution Des Peines Privatives de Liberté : Un État de Crise Permanent?' (n 646) 187. This is again a derogation from the standard terms which are two months for sentences of 7-8 months and three months for sentences of 8 months to one year (see also fn 722).

735 Ministeriële omzendbrief nr. 1817 van 15 juli 2015 over de voorlopige invrijheidstelling van veroordeelden die één of meer vrijheidsstraffen ondergaan waarvan het uitvoerbaar gedeelte drie jaar of minder bedraagt, 7; Ministeriële omzendbrief nr. 1817bis van 29 april 2016 over de voorlopige invrijheidstelling van veroordeelden die één of meer vrijheidsstraffen ondergaan waarvan het uitvoerbaar gedeelte drie jaar of minder bedraagt, 5. See also: Maes (n 710) 21.

736 Ministeriële omzendbrief nr. 1817 van 15 juli 2015 over de voorlopige invrijheidstelling van veroordeelden die één of meer vrijheidsstraffen ondergaan waarvan het uitvoerbaar gedeelte drie jaar of minder bedraagt, 8. See also: Beernaert, *Manuel de droit pénitentiaire* (n 543) 284.

for maximum two years imprisonment, depending on whether or not they will be deported.[737]

Limited detention is a type of execution of a prison sentence in which the detainee can, on a regular basis, leave prison for up to sixteen hours a day.[738] This can be granted in order to further their professional, training or family interests which require their presence outside of prison.[739] A second modality granted by the sentence enforcement court or judge is electronic tagging. As explained above, an electronic tagging sentence can be a full-fledged sentencing alternative to a prison sentence. However, it is also possible for the sentence enforcement court or judge to grant electronic tagging as a modality of a prison sentence.[740] This entails the detainee undergoing (part of) their prison sentence outside of prison according to an execution plan which is enforced by electronic tagging.[741] Limited detention and electronic tagging can be granted to detainees who are either within six months of being able to be conditionally released[742] or whose prison sentence does not exceed three years[743].[744] There are additional conditions regarding certain contra-indications depending on the duration of the prison sentence which are the same as for conditional release (see below).[745]

---

737 See Ministeriële omzendbrief nr. 1817 van 15 juli 2015 over de voorlopige invrijheidstelling van veroordeelden die één of meer vrijheidsstraffen ondergaan waarvan het uitvoerbaar gedeelte drie jaar of minder bedraagt, 8-9. See also: Beernaert, *Manuel de droit pénitentiaire* (n 543) 284-285.

738 Art 21, §1 WERP. See also: Derde tussentijds verslag over het onderdeel "veiligheidsarchitectuur" van 15 juni 2017 van de parlementaire onderzoekscommissie belast met het onderzoek naar de omstandigheden die hebben geleid tot de terroristische aanslagen van 22 maart 2016 in de luchthaven Brussel-Nationaal en in het metrostation Maalbeek te Brussel, met inbegrip van de evolutie en de aanpak van de strijd tegen het radicalisme en de terroristische dreiging, *Parl.St.* Kamer 2016-2017, nr. 54-1752/008, 394; Beernaert, *Manuel de droit pénitentiaire* (n 543) 291-292; Van Den Berge (n 464) 16. For details as to the implementation of this sentencing modality, see: Ministeriële omzendbrief nr. 1804 van 25 juli 2008 betreffende samenwerkingsafspraken tussen het directoraat-generaal Penitentiaire Inrichtingen en het directoraat-generaal Justitiehuizen betreffende de uitvoering van beperkte detentie.

739 Art 21, §2 WERP. See also: Beernaert, *Manuel de droit pénitentiaire* (n 543) 292; Reynaerts (n 686) 107; Scheirs (n 544) 676; Van Den Berge and Verbruggen (n 712) 59.

740 See also: Beernaert, *Manuel de droit pénitentiaire* (n 543) 292; Reynaerts (n 686) 107. For details as to the implementation of this sentencing modality, see: Ministeriële omzendbrief nr. 1803 (III) van 25 juli 2008 betreffende de reglementering van elektronisch toezicht als strafuitvoeringsmodaliteit.

741 Art 22 WERP. See also: Derde tussentijds verslag over het onderdeel "veiligheidsarchitectuur" van 15 juni 2017 van de parlementaire onderzoekscommissie belast met het onderzoek naar de omstandigheden die hebben geleid tot de terroristische aanslagen van 22 maart 2016 in de luchthaven Brussel-Nationaal en in het metrostation Maalbeek te Brussel, met inbegrip van de evolutie en de aanpak van de strijd tegen het radicalisme en de terroristische dreiging, *Parl.St.* Kamer 2016-2017, nr. 54-1752/008, 394; Beernaert, *Manuel de droit pénitentiaire* (n 543) 292; Reynaerts (n 686) 107; Scheirs (n 544) 676; Van Den Berge and Verbruggen (n 712) 59.

742 Scheirs (n 544) 677; Van Den Berge and Verbruggen (n 712) 60.

743 Nederlandt, 'Actualités En Droit de l'exécution Des Peines Privatives de Liberté : Un État de Crise Permanent?' (n 646) 197-198.

744 Art 23, §1 WERP. See also: Beernaert, *Manuel de droit pénitentiaire* (n 543) 297 and 303; Funck (n 709) 205; Reynaerts (n 686) 106-107.

745 Scheirs (n 544) 678-679; Van Den Berge and Verbruggen (n 712) 60-61.

Conditional release allows a detainee to leave prison and continue their sentence on the outside, as long as they abide by certain conditions.[746] The possibility of conditional release is dependent on time limits. For sentences under three years, conditional release is possible after 1/3 of the sentence has been executed.[747] For longer sentences, the limit is also 1/3 of the sentence, but there are several exceptions.[748] First, if the convicted person is a recidivist, the legislation sets the limit at 2/3, with a maximum of fourteen years.[749] The application of this time limit, however, has been frought with legal issues, and in November 2021 the Court of Cassation ruled that it cannot be applied.[750] Second, for convictions to a custodial sentence of thirty years or life, the term is set to fifteen years.[751] Third, for these same convictions, the term is nineteen years if the convicted person had previously been convicted to a correctional prison sentence of at least three years for a

---

746 Art 24 WERP. See also: Derde tussentijds verslag over het onderdeel "veiligheidsarchitectuur" van 15 juni 2017 van de parlementaire onderzoekscommissie belast met het onderzoek naar de omstandigheden die hebben geleid tot de terroristische aanslagen van 22 maart 2016 in de luchthaven Brussel-Nationaal en in het metrostation Maalbeek te Brussel, met inbegrip van de evolutie en de aanpak van de strijd tegen het radicalisme en de terroristische dreiging, *Parl.St.* Kamer 2016-2017, nr. 54-1752/008, 394; Beernaert, *Manuel de droit pénitentiaire* (n 543) 293; Reynaerts (n 686) 110; Scheirs (n 544) 676; Van Den Berge (n 464) 16; Van Den Berge and Verbruggen (n 712) 42.

747 Art 25, §1 WERP. See also: Funck (n 709) 205; Nederlandt, 'Actualités En Droit de l'exécution Des Peines Privatives de Liberté : Un État de Crise Permanent?' (n 646) 197-198; Reynaerts (n 686) 111.

748 Art 25, §2, a) WERP. See also: Collectieve brief DG EPI nr. 121 van 29 maart 2013 betreffende wijziging van de Wet Externe Rechtspositie, 1; Beernaert, *Manuel de droit pénitentiaire* (n 543) 298; Reynaerts (n 686) 112; Van Den Berge (n 464) 17; Van Den Berge and Verbruggen (n 712) 44.

749 Art 25, §2, b) WERP. See also: Collectieve brief DG EPI nr. 121 van 29 maart 2013 betreffende wijziging van de Wet Externe Rechtspositie, 1; Beernaert, *Manuel de droit pénitentiaire* (n 543) 298; Reynaerts (n 686) 112; Van Den Berge (n 464) 17; Van Den Berge and Verbruggen (n 712) 44.

750 Cass. 3 november 2021, P.21.1302.F. This was the, for the moment, last decision in a long legal saga. The start of which were three Constitutional Court decisions in which the Court held that the rule was discriminatory. See: GwH 18 december 2014, 185/2014; GwH 26 juli 2017, 102/2017; GwH 7 februari 2018, 15/2018. In response, the legislature changed the rules on recidivism in 2019. See: Art 2 wet van 5 mei 2019 tot invoeging van een artikel 55bis in het Strafwetboek, wat de herhaling betreft, *BS* 28 mei 2019, 51916. However, as the Court of Cassation noted, this change did not fully remedy the discrimination. Note that a case was also brought before the Constitutional Court to have the legislation annulled but the Court dismissed the case since the discrimination did not follow from the change in legislation. See: GwH 14 oktober 2021, 138/2021, *Rev.dr.pén.* 2022, 29, noot Beernaert. For a more detailed analysis of the situation, see: Marie-Aude Beernaert, 'Correctionnalisation Des Crimes et Récidive Légale : Les Problèmes Subsistent, Les Solutions Aussi…' [2022] Revue de Droit Pénal et de Criminologie (Rev. dr. pén.) 38.

751 Art 25, §2, c) WERP. See also: Collectieve brief DG EPI nr. 121 van 29 maart 2013 betreffende wijziging van de Wet Externe Rechtspositie, 1; Beernaert, *Manuel de droit pénitentiaire* (n 543) 301; Reynaerts (n 686) 112; Van Den Berge (n 464) 17; Van Den Berge and Verbruggen (n 712) 44. The so called 'Potpourri II' reform also made a change here (art 151 and 155). As explained above (see fn nr. 592), part of this reform was the elevation of sentences after correctionalisation to up to fourty years and therefore this article in the WERP was changed accordingly. However, the Constiutitonal Court annulled the elevation of sentences after correctionalisation and thus also annulled this change to the rules on the external legal position. See: GwH 21 december 2017, 148/2017.

number of listed offences, which includes articles 137, 138, 140 and 141 CC,[752] and less than ten years have passed since the end of that sentence.[753] Finally, again for convictions to thirty years or life felony imprisonment, the term is 23 years if it is apparent from the judgment that the convicted person had previously already been convicted to a criminal sentence.[754] For sentences of up to three years, once the time requirement has been met, the detainee will be conditionally released if there are no indications which cannot be remedied by special conditions, that they (1) cannot meet their own basic needs, (2) pose a manifest threat to the physical integrity of others, (3) would bother the victim, (4) have a negative attitude towards the victim or (5) did not make an effort to financially compensate the civil party.[755] For convictions of more than three years, there must be no indications they (1) have no prospect of social rehabilitation, (2) pose a risk of committing new serious offences,[756] (3) would bother the victim, (4) have a negative attitude towards the victim or (5) did not make an effort to financially compensate the civil party.[757]

Finally, provisional release with the aim of removing the detainee from the Belgian territory (*voorlopige invrijheidstelling met het oog op verwijdering van het grondgebied of met het oog op overlevering; mise en liberté provisoire en vue de l'éloignement du territoire ou de la remise*) is possible. This is possible when a detainee does not have the right to stay in the country. They can then be removed from the territory and undergo the rest of their sentence abroad under certain conditions.[758] The time limits are the same as for regular conditional release.[759] Once these time limits are met, a detainee convicted to less than three years can be provisionally released with the aim of removing him from the territory

752 This is odd for two reasons. First, article 138 CC is listed but this article does not contain any offences. Second, articles 140*bis* to 140*quinquies* CC were introduced roughly a month earlier, but are not included in the list.

753 Art 25, §2, d) WERP. See also: Collectieve brief DG EPI nr. 121 van 29 maart 2013 betreffende wijziging van de Wet Externe Rechtspositie, 1-2; Beernaert, *Manuel de droit pénitentiaire* (n 543) 301; Reynaerts (n 686) 112-113; Van Den Berge (n 464) 17-18; Van Den Berge and Verbruggen (n 712) 44-45.

754 Art 25, §2, e) WERP. See also: Collectieve brief DG EPI nr. 121 van 29 maart 2013 betreffende wijziging van de Wet Externe Rechtspositie, 2-3; Beernaert, *Manuel de droit pénitentiaire* (n 543) 301; Reynaerts (n 686) 113; Van Den Berge (n 464) 18; Van Den Berge and Verbruggen (n 712) 45.

755 Art 28, §1 WERP. See also: Funck (n 709) 205; Nederlandt, 'Actualités En Droit de l'exécution Des Peines Privatives de Liberté : Un État de Crise Permanent?' (n 646) 199; Reynaerts (n 686) 117-118.

756 The seriousness of which must be apparent from the judgment. See: Cass. 13 juni 2007, P.07.0704.F.

757 Art 47, §1 WERP. See also: Derde tussentijds verslag over het onderdeel "veiligheidsarchitectuur" van 15 juni 2017 van de parlementaire onderzoekscommissie belast met het onderzoek naar de omstandigheden die hebben geleid tot de terroristische aanslagen van 22 maart 2016 in de luchthaven Brussel-Nationaal en in het metrostation Maalbeek te Brussel, met inbegrip van de evolutie en de aanpak van de strijd tegen het radicalisme en de terroristische dreiging, *Parl.St.* Kamer 2016-2017, nr. 54-1752/008, 395; Beernaert, *Manuel de droit pénitentiaire* (n 543) 303-304; Funck (n 709) 214-218; Reynaerts (n 686) 134-136; Scheirs (n 544) 678-682; Van Den Berge (n 464) 19-20; Van Den Berge and Verbruggen (n 712) 47-49.

758 Art 25/3 WERP. See also: Beernaert, *Manuel de droit pénitentiaire* (n 543) 295; Van Den Berge (n 464) 16; Van Den Berge and Verbruggen (n 712) 42.

759 Art 26 WERP. See also: Beernaert, *Manuel de droit pénitentiaire* (n 543) 297; Reynaerts (n 686) 114.

if there are no indications which cannot be remedied by special conditions, that they (1) pose a manifest threat to the physical integrity of others, (2) would bother the victim or (3) did not make an effort to financially compensate the civil party.[760] For convictions of more than three years, there must be no indications they (1) pose a risk of committing new serious offences, (2) would bother the victim or (3) did not make an effort to financially compensate the civil party.[761]

In 2017, the legislature introduced the so-called 'security period'.[762] This period provides the opportunity for the judge who imposes the sentence to extend the time limits after which conditional release or provisional release with the aim of removing the detainee from the territory is possible.[763] This security period can be imposed in two situations. The first being a conviction of minimum three but less than thirty years for certain offences, which include all terrorist offences. In this case the security period ranges from one third to two thirds of the sentence.[764] The second situation is one of convictions to thirty years or more, including life felony imprisonment. Here the security period ranges from fifteen to twenty-five years.[765]

Conditional release, limited detention, or electronic tagging can only be granted after a written advice by the prison warden based on a file he makes.[766] If the detainee was convicted for a terrorist offence, or shows signs of violent extremism, this file must include a report of a service specialised in terrorism or violent extremism[767] on the necessity of a

---

760 Art 28, §2 WERP. See also: Nederlandt, 'Actualités En Droit de l'exécution Des Peines Privatives de Liberté : Un État de Crise Permanent?' (n 646) 199.

761 Art 47, §2 WERP. See also: Beernaert, *Manuel de droit pénitentiaire* (n 543) 305; Van Den Berge (n 464) 20.

762 This introduction was challenged before the Constitutional Court, which dismissed the appeal. See: GwH 19 november 2020, 147/2020, *NjW* 2021, 265, noot Careel.

763 Beernaert, *Manuel de droit pénitentiaire* (n 543) 301-302; Horseele and others (n 456) 137; Funck (n 709) 213; Franklin Kuty, 'La Loi Du 21 Décembre 2017 Modiiant Diverses Dispositions En Vue d'instaurer Une Période de Sûreté. La Peine Irrémédiable, La Loi de La Désillusion ?' [2018] Revue de Droit Pénal et de Criminologie (Rev. dr. pén.) 573, 573; Nederlandt, '15 Jaar Strafuitvoeringsrechtbanken : Teenagers under Control?' (n 698) 11; Van Den Berge (n 464) 18-19.

764 Art 195, section 4 and art 344, section 4 CCP. See also: Beernaert, *Manuel de droit pénitentiaire* (n 543) 302; Horseele and others (n 456) 138; Kuty (n 763) 589-591; Van Den Berge (n 464) 19. A literal reading of the legislation would make it seem that the security period in this case has to be two thirds and cannot be lower. However, in the preparatory works it is explicitly stated that less than two thirds is also possible. See: Memorie van Toelichting van 23 oktober 2017 bij wetsontwerp tot wijziging van de wet van 20 juli 1990 betreffende de voorlopige hechtenis voor wat de onmiddellijke aanhouding betreft en tot invoering van de beveiligingsperiode, *Parl.St.* Kamer 2017-2018, nr. 54-2731/001, 6.

765 Art 195, section 5 and art 344, section 5 CCP. See also: Beernaert, *Manuel de droit pénitentiaire* (n 543) 302; Horseele and others (n 456) 138; Kuty (n 763) 590-591; Van Den Berge (n 464) 19.

766 Art 30, §2 *j.* art 49 and 50 WERP. See also: Collectieve brief DG EPI nr. 121 van 29 maart 2013 betreffende wijziging van de Wet Externe Rechtspositie, 3; Reynaerts (n 686) 121; Van Den Berge and Verbruggen (n 712) 50-51 and 62.

767 Defined in the article as "Promoting, encouraging or committing acts that may lead to terrorism and which advocate an ideology to proclaim racial, national, ethnic or religious supremacy or which is contrary to the fundamental values and principles of democracy" (own translation).

customised guidance programme.[768] In addition, the advice of the public prosecution service is required.[769]

All modalities include three general conditions: (1) not committing any criminal offences, (2) having a fixed address and immediately informing the government if this changes (not applicable to day release or provisional release with the aim of removing the detainee[770]) and (3) answering summons of the public prosecutor's office or the probation service.[771] In addition, specific conditions can be imposed. For sentences of up to three years these conditions must be deemed absolutely necessary to reduce the risk of recidivism or necessary in the interest of the victim.[772] In case the detainee was convicted for a terrorist offence or shows signs of violent extremism, these special conditions can include following a customised guidance programme with a service which is specialised in these issues.[773] For convictions of more than three years the conditions need to either be necessary in the interest of the victims, necessary to counter any of the abovementioned indications, or offer the possibility of implementing a social rehabilitation plan.[774] Specifically for conditional release, the sentence enforcement court or judge also has to state whether or not the detainee is allowed to leave the Belgian territory and if so, for how long, how frequent and whether or not he has to inform the public prosecution service

768 Art 31, §1 and art 32, §2 *j.* art 49, §3 WERP. See also: Beernaert, *Manuel de droit pénitentiaire* (n 543) 313-314; Nederlandt, 'Actualités En Droit de l'exécution Des Peines Privatives de Liberté : Un État de Crise Permanent?' (n 646) 154-155; Nederlandt, '15 Jaar Strafuitvoeringsrechtbanken : Teenagers under Control?' (n 698) 16.

769 Art 51 WERP. See also: Derde tussentijds verslag over het onderdeel "veiligheidsarchitectuur" van 15 juni 2017 van de parlementaire onderzoekscommissie belast met het onderzoek naar de omstandigheden die hebben geleid tot de terroristische aanslagen van 22 maart 2016 in de luchthaven Brussel-Nationaal en in het metrostation Maalbeek te Brussel, met inbegrip van de evolutie en de aanpak van de strijd tegen het radicalisme en de terroristische dreiging, *Parl.St.* Kamer 2016-2017, nr. 54-1752/008, 396; Collectieve brief DG EPI nr. 121 van 29 maart 2013 betreffende wijziging van de Wet Externe Rechtspositie, 4; Beernaert, *Manuel de droit pénitentiaire* (n 543) 314-315; Van Den Berge and Verbruggen (n 712) 52 and 62.

770 Note that this is not explicitly mentioned for sentences under three years, but it is for sentences over three years.

771 Art 39 and art 55 WERP. See also: Derde tussentijds verslag over het onderdeel "veiligheidsarchitectuur" van 15 juni 2017 van de parlementaire onderzoekscommissie belast met het onderzoek naar de omstandigheden die hebben geleid tot de terroristische aanslagen van 22 maart 2016 in de luchthaven Brussel-Nationaal en in het metrostation Maalbeek te Brussel, met inbegrip van de evolutie en de aanpak van de strijd tegen het radicalisme en de terroristische dreiging, *Parl.St.* Kamer 2016-2017, nr. 54-1752/008, 397; Reynaerts (n 686) 121 and 142; Scheirs (n 544) 689; Van Den Berge (n 464) 20; Van Den Berge and Verbruggen (n 712) 54. The legislation also states that conditional release with the view of removing the person from the Belgian territory is conditional upon actually leaving the Belgian territory and not returning during the probationary period without permission of the sentence enforcement court or judge (and without being in violation with any other laws or regulations). See: art 39, 4° and 55, 4° WERP.

772 Art 40 WERP. See also: Reynaerts (n 686) 129; Scheirs (n 544) 689.

773 Art 41, §2 WERP. See also: Beernaert, *Manuel de droit pénitentiaire* (n 543) 325; Nederlandt, 'Actualités En Droit de l'exécution Des Peines Privatives de Liberté : Un État de Crise Permanent?' (n 646) 162-165.

774 Art 56, §1 WERP. See also: Reynaerts (n 686) 143; Van Den Berge and Verbruggen (n 712) 55.

before doing so.[775] In cases of convictions for terrorism, or when there are concrete elements of violent extremism, the sentence enforcement court has to especially motivate the permission to leave the territory.[776] If a modality is refused, the judgment states on which date the detainee can request one again. For sentences of up to five years, this term has a maximum of six months and for longer sentences a maximum of one year.[777]

The probation period for a conditional release equals the remainder of the sentence the person still had to undergo, with a minimum of one year. For correctional sentences of more than five years and criminal sentences of less than thirty years, this period is five to ten years. Finally, for sentences of thirty years or more, the probation period is ten years.[778]

775 Art 40, §2 and 56, §3 WERP. See also: Beernaert, *Manuel de droit pénitentiaire* (n 543) 325; Nederlandt, 'Actualités En Droit de l'exécution Des Peines Privatives de Liberté : Un État de Crise Permanent?' (n 646) 165-166; Nederlandt, '15 Jaar Strafuitvoeringsrechtbanken : Teenagers under Control?' (n 698) 16.

776 Art 40, §3 and 56, §4 WERP. See also: Beernaert, *Manuel de droit pénitentiaire* (n 543) 326; Nederlandt, 'Actualités En Droit de l'exécution Des Peines Privatives de Liberté : Un État de Crise Permanent?' (n 646) 165-166; Nederlandt, '15 Jaar Strafuitvoeringsrechtbanken : Teenagers under Control?' (n 698) 16. This was introduced at the advice of the parliamentary research committee established after the Brussels terrorist attacks. See: Derde tussentijds verslag over het onderdeel "veiligheidsarchitectuur" van 15 juni 2017 van de parlementaire onderzoekscommissie belast met het onderzoek naar de omstandigheden die hebben geleid tot de terroristische aanslagen van 22 maart 2016 in de luchthaven Brussel-Nationaal en in het metrostation Maalbeek te Brussel, met inbegrip van de evolutie en de aanpak van de strijd tegen het radicalisme en de terroristische dreiging, *Parl.St.* Kamer 2016-2017, nr. 54-1752/008, 399.

777 Art 45 and art 57 WERP. Also note there is a term of minimum six months and maximum eighteen months for custodial sentences of thirty years or more which were combined with being at the disposal of the sentence enforcement court. See: Art 54, §2 WERP. See also: Collectieve brief DG EPI nr. 121 van 29 maart 2013 betreffende wijziging van de Wet Externe Rechtspositie, 4; Beernaert, *Manuel de droit pénitentiaire* (n 543) 308; Reynaerts (n 686) 143-144; Scheirs (n 544) 690; Van Den Berge (n 464) 21; Van Den Berge and Verbruggen (n 712) 57.

778 Art 71 WERP. See also: Beernaert, *Manuel de droit pénitentiaire* (n 543) 329; Reynaerts (n 686) 160; Scheirs (n 544) 689-690; Van Den Berge (n 464) 21-22; Van Den Berge and Verbruggen (n 712) 58.

5 Other relevant measures

Asset freezing

Asset freezing is usually done at the instigation of the UN or the EU. This is an administrative measure which takes place independent of any potential criminal procedures.[779] In 1999 and 2000, the UN Security Council (UNSC) issued Resolutions 1267 and 1333, which imposed upon states the obligation to freeze funds and other financial assets of the Taliban, Usama bin Laden and his associates, including those in Al-Qaida.[780] In the following years, the Security Council reaffirmed and expanded upon these Resolutions.[781] Since 2015, ISIS and their associates were also added to these resolutions.[782] The freezing of assets is based on a list.[783] In addition to this system based on a list, the Security Council issued Resolution 1373, mere weeks after 9/11.[784] This Resolution imposes a more general obligation on states to freeze funds of suspected terrorist, without targeting specific groups or individuals.[785] The EU measures take a similar form. First of all, the EU has implemented the UN list, stating that all funds and other assets of persons or other entities on the UN

---

779 See for example: UNSC Resolution 2368 of 20 July 2017, 64. See also: Circulaire van 7 september 2015 inzake de tenuitvoerlegging van de artikelen 3 en 5 van het koninklijk besluit van 28 december 2006 inzake specifieke beprekende maatregelen tegen bepaalde personen en entiteiten met het oog op de strijd tegen de financiering van het terrorisme; Elspeth Guild, 'The Uses and Abuses of Counter-Terrorism Policies in Europe: The Case of the "Terrorist Lists"' (2008) 46 JCMS: Journal of Common Market Studies 173, 177; Anthony Rizzo, *La Confiscation et Le Gel Préventif d'avoirs Terroristes: Quelle Place Pour Les Droits Fondamentaux Dans La Lutte Contre Le Crime et Le Terrorisme* (Larcier 2021) 320.

780 UNSC Resolution 1267 of 15 October 1999; UNSC Resolution 1333 of 19 December 2000. See also: Melissa Broek, Monique Hazelhorst and Wouter de Zanger, 'Asset Freezing: Smart Sanction or Criminal Charge?' (2010) 27 Merkourios : Utrecht Journal of International and European Law 18, 20; Anne L Clunan, 'The Fight against Terrorist Financing' (2006) 121 Political Science Quarterly 569, 575-576; Guild (n 779) 182; Sameer Hossain, 'Freezing Terrorism Assets: Increasing International Cooperation by Observing Procedural Due Process Notes & Comments' (2010-2011) 54 Howard Law Journal 437, 444; Andrew Hudson, 'Not a Great Asset: The UN Security Council's Counter-Terrorism Regime: Violating Human Rights' (2007) 25 Berkeley Journal of International Law 203, 205-206; Jean-Christophe Martin, 'Le respect des droits fondamentaux dans la lutte contre le terrorisme: le contentieux des mesures restrictives antiterroristes devant le juge de l'Union européenne', *L'Union européenne et la lutte contre le terrorisme* (Larcier 2010) 111-112; Rizzo (n 779) 317-318.

781 For example: UNSC Resolution 1390 of 16 January 2002; UNSC Resolution 1904 of 17 December 2009; UNSC Resolution 1988 of 17 June 2011; UNSC Resolution 1989 of 17 June 2011; UNSC Resolution 2368 of 20 July 2017. See also: Hossain (n 780) 444; Hudson (n 780) 206; Rizzo (n 779) 317-326.

782 UNSC Resolution 2253 of 17 December 2015.

783 For the most recent version of this list, see: www.un.org/securitycouncil/content/un-sc-consolidated-list. See also: Broek, Hazelhorst and de Zanger (n 780) 20; Rizzo (n 779) 319-320.

784 UNSC Resolution 1373 of 28 September 2001.

785 Clunan (n 780) 577-578; Yoram Danziger, 'Changes in Methods of Freezing Funds of Terrorist Organisations since 9/11' [212] Journal of Money Laundering Control 210; Martin (n 780) 112; Rizzo (n 779) 326-332.

list will be frozen.[786] In addition to this, however, the EU introduced its own rules on asset freezing targeting Al-Qaida and ISIS with its own list in 2016.[787] Secondly, the EU has adopted several Common Positions regarding the implementation of Resolution 1373.[788]

These UN and EU instruments are binding upon Belgium. In 1995 the Belgian legislature had already given the government the possibility of issuing Royal Decrees necessary for the execution of Security Council Resolutions.[789] However, Belgium was internationally criticised by the FATF for being too passive and its procedure taking too long, as it waited until the EU had implemented the UNSC Resolutions to enforce them itself.[790] As a reaction to the criticism, the right to freeze assets of people on the UN list was conferred on the secretary of finances in 2015.[791] In 2019, the regime was changed again,

786 See originally: Council Common Position 2002/402/CFSP of 27 May 2002 concerning restrictive measures against Usama bin Laden, members of the Al-Qaida organization and the Taliban and other individuals, groups, undertakings and entities associated with them and repealing Common Positions 96/746/CFSP, 1999/727/CFSP, 2001/154/CFSP and 2001/771/CFSP, *OJ EU* 29 May 2002, L 139. Now: Art 3, §1 and 2 Council Decision (CFSP) 2016/1693 of 20 September 2016 concerning restrictive measures against ISIL (Da'esh) and Al-Qaeda and persons, groups, undertakings and entities associated with them and repealing Common Position 2002/402/CFSP, *OJ EU* 21 September 2016, L 255. See also: Broek, Hazelhorst and de Zanger (n 779) 20; Martin (n 780) 112; Rizzo (n 779) 337.

787 Art 3, §3 Council Decision (CFSP) 2016/1693 of 20 September 2016 concerning restrictive measures against ISIL (Da'esh) and Al-Qaeda and persons, groups, undertakings and entities associated with them and repealing Common Position 2002/402/CFSP, *OJ EU* 21 September 2016, L 255. See also: Broek, Hazelhorst and de Zanger (n 779) 20; Rizzo (n 779) 337-341.

788 Council Common Position 2001/930/CFSP of 27 December 2001 on combating terrorism, *OJ EU* 28 December 2001, L 344; Council Common Position 2001/931/CFSP of 27 December 2001 on the application of specific measures to combat terrorism, *OJ EU* 28 December 2001, L 344. See also: Guild (n 779) 179; Martin (n 780) 112-113. Rizzo (n 779) 341-350.

789 Art 1 wet van 11 mei 1995 inzake de tenuitvoerlegging van de besluiten van de Veiligheidsraad van de Organisatie van de Verenigde Naties, *BS* 29 Juli 1995, 20444. See also: COL 13/2016 – Administratieve bevriezing van tegoeden en economische middelen van personen en entiteiten met het oog op de strijd tegen de financiering van het terrorisme – nationale en internationale lijsten, 26 May 2016, 4; Rizzo (n 779) 374-375.

790 Amendementen van 24 november 2015 bij wetsontwerp houdende diverse financiële bepalingen, houdende de oprichting van een administratieve dienst met boekhoudkundige autonomie "Sociale activiteiten", en houdende een bepaling inzake de gelijkheid van vrouwen en mannen, *Parl.St.* Kamer 2015-16, nr. 54-1459/002; Verslag namens de Commissie voor de Financiën en de Begroting van 7 december 2015 bij wetsontwerp houdende diverse financiële bepalingen, houdende de oprichting van een administratieve dienst met boekhoudkundige autonomie "Sociale activiteiten", en houdende een bepaling inzake de gelijkheid van vrouwen en mannen, *Parl.St.* Kamer 2015-16, nr. 54-1459/005, 11-13; Francis Desterbeck and Jan Van Droogbroek, *De Inbeslagneming En Verbeurd¬verklaring in Strafzaken in België* (Wolters Kluwer 2017) 13.

791 Art 1/1 and 1/2 wet van 11 mei 1995 inzake de tenuitvoerlegging van de besluiten van de Veiligheidsraad van de Organisatie van de Verenigde Naties, *BS* 29 Juli 1995, 20444, as introduced by art 69 and 70 wet 18 december 2015 houdende diverse financiële bepalingen, houdende de oprichting van een administratieve dienst met boekhoudkundige autonomie "Sociale activiteiten", houdende wijziging van de wet van 11 mei 1995 inzake de tenuitvoerlegging van de besluiten van de Veiligheidsraad van de Organisatie van de Verenigde Naties en houdende een bepaling inzake de gelijkheid van vrouwen en mannen, *BS* 20 december 2015, 79809. See also: COL 13/2016 – Administratieve bevriezing van tegoeden en

this time to one of automatic implementation of UNSC asset freezing measures.[792] This was done in order to make the system more efficient after the FATF had found the existing system still lacking.[793]

In addition, the EU Council Regulations, based on the aforementioned Common Position of 2001 which transpose UNSC Resolution 1373, are directly applicable in the Belgian legal order.[794] However, this alone does not suffice. Therefore, a further possibility to freeze assets was introduced in 2006.[795] That year, a Royal Decree made it possible to freeze the assets of suspected terrorists whose names are on the list of the common position but not covered by the Council Regulations[796], as well as people listed on a newly created national Belgian list, independent to those of the EU or UN lists.[797] The assets of people or entities who, it is suspected, 'commit or attempt to commit terrorist offences, who facilitate the committal or cooperate with the committal of those offences' and who appear on a list drafted by the Belgian National Security Council have to be frozen.[798] No

economische middelen van personen en entiteiten met het oog op de strijd tegen de financiering van het terrorisme - nationale en internationale lijsten, 26 May 2016, 4-6; Rizzo (n 779) 375-376.

792 Art 236-238 wet 2 mei 2019 houdende diverse financiële bepalingen, *BS* 21 mei 2019, 48120. Note that there is a second piece of legislation which may be relevant: wet 13 mei 2003 inzake de tenuitvoerlegging van de beperkende maatregelen die genomen worden door de Raad van de Europese Unie ten aanzien van Staten, sommige personen en entiteiten, *BS* 13 juni 2003, 31293. However, no relevant Royal Decrees have been adopted based on this statute. See: Rizzo (n 779) 378.

793 Amendementen van 14 maart 2019 bij wetsvoorstel houdende diverse financiële bepalingen, *Parl.St.* Kamer 2018-19, nr. 54-3624/002, 23; Verslag namens de Commissie voor de Financiën en de Begroting van 27 maart 2019 bij wetsvoorstel houdende diverse financiële bepalingen en wetsvoorstel tot wijziging van de wet van 22 februari 1998 tot vaststelling van het organiek statuut van de Nationale Bank van België, teneinde het College van Censoren af te schaffen, *Parl.St.* Kamer 2018-19, nr. 54-3624/004, 22; Rizzo (n 779) 376-377.

794 Council Regulation (EC) No 2580/2001 of 27 December 2001 on specific restrictive measures directed against certain persons and entities with a view to combating terrorism, *OJ EU* 28 December 2001, L 344. See also: Rizzo (n 779) 379.

795 KB 28 december 2006 inzake specifieke beperkende maatregelen tegen bepaalde personen en entiteiten met het oog op de strijd tegen de financiering van het terrorisme, *BS* 17 januari 2007, 1898, confirmed by art 115 wet van 25 april 2007 houdende diverse bepalingen (IV), *BS* 8 mei 2007, 25103); Sofie Lavaux, 'Recente Overheidsmaatregelen i.v.m. de "Foreign Fighters"' [2016] Panopticon 355.

796 Note that no Royal Decrees have been issued based on this article yet. See: Rizzo (n 779) 383.

797 Council Common Position 2001/931/CFSP of 27 December 2001 on the application of specific measures to combat terrorism, *OJ EU* 28 December 2001, L 344; Art 2 and 3 KB 28 december 2006 inzake specifieke beperkende maatregelen tegen bepaalde personen en entiteiten met het oog op de strijd tegen de financiering van het terrorisme, *BS* 17 januari 2007, 1898. See also: C Remacle, 'Le gel administratif des avoirs dans la lutte contre le financement du terrorisme.' (2019) 2019 Revue de Droit Pénal et de Criminologie (Rev. dr. pén.) 123, 125; Rizzo (n 779) 380-381.

798 Art 3 KB 28 december 2006 inzake specifieke beperkende maatregelen tegen bepaalde personen en entiteiten met het oog op de strijd tegen de financiering van het terrorisme, *BS* 17 januari 2007, 1898; Circulaire van 7 september 2015 inzake de tenuitvoerlegging van de artikelen 3 en 5 van het koninklijk besluit van 28 december 2006 inzake specifieke beprekende maatregelen tegen bepaalde personen en entiteiten met het oog op de strijd tegen de financiering van het terrorisme; Lavaux (n 795) 355; Remacle (n 797) 125-126; Frank Verbruggen, 'Terrorristenlijsten: Oorsprong, Functie En Spanning Met

Belgian list was created for almost ten years, but one was eventually drafted in 2016[799] and has since been updated several times, as is required by the Royal Decree. The most recent update dates back to 26 October 2022 (published 8 November 2022) when nine names were deleted from the list.[800] The list was created and is updated based on evaluations made by the Coordination Unit for Threat Analysis (*OCAD; OCAM*) after recommendations from the federal prosecution service and approval by the council of ministers.[801] The list is re-evaluated by the National Security Council at least every six months. A Circulare from the secretaries of justice and finances states that there needs to be a criminal investigation into a person in order for them to be included on the list.[802] This is supported by the fact that the Royal Decree explicitly refers to terrorist 'offences'.[803] However, it is hard to verify whether this is applied in practice, since people are not always aware that they are the subject of a criminal investigation.[804] If the person whose name is added to the list is in prison, CelEx will notify the prison warden, who will also freeze the person's individual

Mensenrechten' in Jan Wouters and Cedric Ryngaert (eds), *Mensenrechten: actuele brandpunten* (Acco 2008) 98.

799 KB 30 mei 2016 tot vaststelling van de lijst van personen en entiteiten bedoeld in artikelen 3 en 5 van het koninklijk besluit van 28 december 2006 inzake specifieke beperkende maatregelen tegen bepaalde personen en entiteiten met het oog op de strijd tegen de financiering van het terrorisme, *BS* 1 juni 2016, 33913.

800 KB 26 oktober 2022 tot wijziging van de lijst van personen en entiteiten bedoeld in artikelen 3 en 5 van het Koninklijk besluit van 28 december 2006 inzake specifieke beperkende maatregelen tegen bepaalde personen en entiteiten met het oog op de strijd tegen de financiering van het terrorisme, *BS* 8 november 2022, 81483. For an up to date version of this list, see: https://financien.belgium.be/nl/thesaurie/financiele-sancties/nationale-financi%c3%able-sancties-%e2%80%98de-nationale-lijst%e2%80%99.

801 Circulaire van 7 september 2015 inzake de tenuitvoerlegging van de artikelen 3 en 5 van het koninklijk besluit van 28 december 2006 inzake specifieke beprekende maatregelen tegen bepaalde personen en entiteiten met het oog op de strijd tegen de financiering van het terrorisme; COL 13/2016 – Administratieve bevriezing van tegoeden en economische middelen van personen en entiteiten met het oog op de strijd tegen de financiering van het terrorisme – nationale en internationale lijsten, 26 May 2016, 3; Remacle (n 797) 130-131; Rizzo (n 779) 381.

802 Circulaire van 7 september 2015 inzake de tenuitvoerlegging van de artikelen 3 en 5 van het koninklijk besluit van 28 december 2006 inzake specifieke beprekende maatregelen tegen bepaalde personen en entiteiten met het oog op de strijd tegen de financiering van het terrorisme; See also: Remacle (n 797) 129-130; Rizzo (n 779) 381-382.

803 Art 3 KB 28 december 2006 inzake specifieke beperkende maatregelen tegen bepaalde personen en entiteiten met het oog op de strijd tegen de financiering van het terrorisme, *BS* 17 januari 2007, 1898. See also: Circulaire van 7 september 2015 inzake de tenuitvoerlegging van de artikelen 3 en 5 van het koninklijk besluit van 28 december 2006 inzake specifieke beprekende maatregelen tegen bepaalde personen en entiteiten met het oog op de strijd tegen de financiering van het terrorisme; Remacle (n 797) 126.

804 See also: Remacle (n 797) 129; Rizzo (n 779) 382. The Federal Prosecution Service would usually not agree to an asset freezing measure against a person who is unaware of the criminal investigation, since this would tip them off. See: Circulaire van 7 september 2015 inzake de tenuitvoerlegging van de artikelen 3 en 5 van het koninklijk besluit van 28 december 2006 inzake specifieke beprekende maatregelen tegen bepaalde personen en entiteiten met het oog op de strijd tegen de financiering van het terrorisme.

account in prison.[805] He is then limited to spending maximum €200 per month on expenses in prison.

The UN and EU systems have their own ways of legal recourse. So does the Belgian system. It is unclear on what evidence these decisions are based,[806] but the person included on the Belgian list can at any time request reconsideration of their inclusion on the list by the National Security Council.[807] This is a form of organised administrative review, but the legislation does not provide for any judicial review.[808] A person who is subject to the freezing of assets has the option to appeal the decision to the Council of State (Belgium's highest administrative judicial body), since it is the standard Court of Appeal for administrative decisions.[809] There is currently one such case.[810] In this case the inclusion of one man on the list was challenged before the Council of State. The man in question had travelled to Syria and joined a terrorist group (likely IS). The case was brought by his mother, who did not even know if her son was still alive. The Council of State declared the case inadmissible because it was filed three days late. One participant of the expert seminar had personal experience with the delisting procedure. They stated the process was overly complicated and unclear.

Revoking ID cards and passports

The Consular Code contains provisions on the refusal, repeal or invalidation of passports or other travel documents. This is possible when the person is subject to a freedom-restricting judicial measure.[811] In terrorism cases, the public prosecutor systematically informs the federal government service Foreign Affairs of any freedom-restricting judicial measures[812] with a view to refusing, repealing or invalidating a passport or travel

805 Collectieve brief DG EPI nr. 149 van 24 juni 2019 over de bevriezing van tegoeden van gedetineerden; Collectieve brief DG EPI nr. 154 van 18 mei 2020 over de bevriezing van tegoeden van gedetineerden.

806 Rizzo (n 779) 384-385.

807 Art 5 KB 28 december 2006 inzake specifieke beperkende maatregelen tegen bepaalde personen en entiteiten met het oog op de strijd tegen de financiering van het terrorisme, *BS* 17 januari 2007, 1898. See also: Remacle (n 797) 132; Rizzo (n 779) 379.

808 Remacle (n 797) 133; J Vande Lanotte, J Dujardin and M Van Damme, 'De Administratieve En Jurisdictionele Beroepen' in J Dujardin and others (eds), *Overzicht van het Belgisch Administratief Recht* (Wolters Kluwer 2014) 855 and 860.

809 Art 14 RvS statute; Sabien Lust, 'Volle Rechtsmacht, Substitutie, Injunctie En Herstel' in Sabien Lust, Peter Schollen and Stijn Verbist (eds), *Actualia rechtsbescherming tegen de overheid* (Intersentia 2014) 10; Remacle (n 797) 133; Frederic Vanneste, 'Het Recht Op Toegang Tot de Rechter En de Financiële Strijd Tegen Het Terrorisme' in Bernard Tilleman and Alain Laurent Verbeke (eds), *Actualia vermogensrecht, Liber Alumnorum KULAK* (die Keure 2005) 758.

810 Raad van State, 29 November 2917, nr. 239.266, *Bensouda Koraïchi Amal v. the Belgian state.*

811 Art 63, §1, 1° *j.* 65, Section 1 Consular Code.

812 For example an arrest warrant or a conditional release with the prohibition of leaving the national territory.

document.[813] In addition to this procedure, it is also possible to refuse, repeal or invalidate a passport or travel document of people not subject to a freedom-restricting judicial measure. This is possible after the motivated advice of the competent body (in terrorism cases this is OCAD/OCAM),[814] if the person clearly represents a significant risk or threat to public order or public security.[815] This may be applicable to cases of terrorism. When the Consular Code was introduced in 2014, this was a ground for refusal of a passport or travel document,[816] but not for repeal or invalidation.[817] In 2015, 'manifestly representing a significant risk to the maintenance of law and order or to the safeguarding of national security or public safety'[818] was introduced as a ground for repeal or invalidation.[819] The reason for this was the fight against terrorism, specifically the situation of people traveling to areas where IS was active at the time.[820] In 2019, the rules were further finetuned, and some of the articles were rearranged[821] in order to meet some issues which had arisen in

813 Omzendbrief van de minister van Justitie, de minister van Binnenlandse Zaken, de minister van Buitenlandse Zaken en de minister van Defensie van 29 april 2016 betreffende het overmaken van informatie aan de FOD Buitenlandse Zaken met het oog op de toepassing van de regels inzake de weigering van afgifte en de intrekking van reisdocumenten, 4; COL 12/2016 – Weigering van afgifte en intrekking van reisdocumenten (paspoorten) van personen die het voorwerp uitmaken van strafdossiers, 26 May 2916, 6.

814 See: Toelichting bij wetsvoorstel van 20 februari 2019 tot wijziging van de wet van 21 december 2013 houdende het Consulair Wetboek en van de wet van 10 februari 2015 met betrekking tot geautomatiseerde verwerkingen van persoonsgegevens die noodzakelijk zijn voor de Belgische paspoorten en reisdocumenten, *Parl.St.* Kamer 2018-2019, nr. 54-3574/001, 20; Omzendbrief van de minister van Justitie, de minister van Binnenlandse Zaken, de minister van Buitenlandse Zaken en de minister van Defensie van 29 april 2016 betreffende het overmaken van informatie aan de FOD Buitenlandse Zaken met het oog op de toepassing van de regels inzake de weigering van afgifte en de intrekking van reisdocumenten, 6.

815 Art 63, §2 *j.* art 65, section 2 Consular Code. See also: Els Leemans and Laura De Schryver, 'Flankerende Maatregelen', *Contra-terrorisme: De gerechtelijke aanpak van terrorisme in België* (Larcier 2018) 263.

816 Art 65, section 2 Consular Code, as introduced in 2014 (*BS* 21 January 2014, 4987).

817 Beernaert, 'Renforcement de l'arsenal législatif anti-terroriste: entre symboles et prévention' (n 302) 836.

818 Own translation, original in Dutch and French: "*klaarblijkelijk een aanzienlijk risico [vertegenwoordigen] voor de handhaving van de openbare orde of de bescherming van de nationale of openbare veiligheid; [présenter] manifestement un risque substantiel pour le maintien de l'ordre public ou la protection de la sécurité nationale ou publique.*"

819 Art 65/1 Consular Code, as introduced by art. 4 Wet van 10 augustus 2015 tot wijziging van het Consulair Wetboek, *BS* 24 augustus 2015, 54497. See also: Leemans and De Schryver (n 815) 261.

820 Memorie van Toelichting bij wetsontwerp van 23 juni 2015 tot wijziging van het Consulair Wetboek, *arl.St.* Kamer 2014-2015, nr. 54-1200/001, (4) 5. See also: Louise Reyntjens and Ward Yperman, 'Terrorisme En Internationale Mobiliteit Een Coherent Beleid of Nattevingerwerk' [2019] Politie & Recht 99, 107.

821 Wet van 3 juli 2019 tot wijziging van de wet van 21 december 2013 houdende het Consulair Wetboek en van de wet van 10 februari 2015 met betrekking tot geautomatiseerde verwerkingen van persoonsgegevens die noodzakelijk zijn voor de Belgische paspoorten en reisdocumenten, *BS* 22 augustus 2019, 80419.

application.[822] An appeal to the Council of State is possible, but this appeal does not suspend the measure.[823]

The refusal, repeal or invalidation of ID cards is possible as well. The most common situation will be the refusal, repeal or invalidation of an ID card which was issued by a Belgian municipality. The legislation provides this possibility in case of well-founded and very serious indications that the person wants to go to an area where terrorist groups are active. These indications must concern the individual conduct of the person, and general circumstances do not suffice.[824] In addition, the circumstances need to be such that they could represent a serious threat of terrorist offences *sensu stricto* upon their return to Belgium, or that they intend to commit terrorism offences *sensu stricto* abroad.[825] Refusing, repealing or invalidating an ID card can only happen after a motivated advice by OCAD/OCAM after consultation with the prosecution service.[826] A certificate valid only in Belgium is issued to replace the ID card.[827] The decision is valid for 25 days. The person concerned is informed within two working days and can respond in writing within five working days. Thereafter, the secretary must confirm his decision, again within five working days. If there is no confirmation within 25 days, or if the person concerned is not

822 Toelichting bij wetsvoorstel van 20 februari 2019 tot wijziging van de wet van 21 december 2013 houdende het Consulair Wetboek en van de wet van 10 februari 2015 met betrekking tot geautomatiseerde verwerkingen van persoonsgegevens die noodzakelijk zijn voor de Belgische paspoorten en reisdocumenten, *Parl.St.* Kamer 2018-2019, nr. 54-3574/001, 14.

823 Art 4 wet van 29 juli 1991 betreffende de uitdrukkelijke motivering van de bestuurshandelingen, *BS* 12 september 1991, 19976; Toelichting bij wetsvoorstel van 20 februari 2019 tot wijziging van de wet van 21 december 2013 houdende het Consulair Wetboek en van de wet van 10 februari 2015 met betrekking tot geautomatiseerde verwerkingen van persoonsgegevens die noodzakelijk zijn voor de Belgische paspoorten en reisdocumenten, *Parl.St.* Kamer 2018-2019, nr. 54-3574/001, 18; Leemans and De Schryver (n 815) 265.

824 Memorie van Toelichting bij het wetsontwerp van 16 juni 2015 houdende wijziging van de wet van 19 juli 1991 betreffende de bevolkingsregisters, de identiteitskaarten, de vreemdelingenkaarten en de verblijfsdocumenten en tot wijziging van de wet van 8 augustus 1983 tot regeling van een Rijksregister van de natuurlijke personen, *Parl.St.* Kamer 2014-15, nr. 54-1170/001, (4) 6.

825 Art 6, §10, section 1 wet van 19 juli 1991 betreffende de bevolkingsregisters, de identiteitskaarten, de vreemdelingenkaarten en de verblijfsdocumenten, *BS* 3 september 1991, 19075. See also: COL 11/2016 – Weigering van afgifte, intrekking en ongeldigverklaring van identiteitskaarten van Belgen die het voorwerp uitmaken van strafdossiers, 26 May 2016, 4; Bruggeman (n 633) 41-42; Leemans and De Schryver (n 815) 267; F Van Konnegem, 'Identiteitskaart', *Postal Memorialis. Lexicon strafrecht, strafvordering en bijzondere wetten* 10/37. The legislation defines 'terrorist offences' in this article as ofences described in article 137 CC. Therefore this does not cover all terrorist offences discussed above. This definition came to be after the advice of the Council of State.

826 See also: COL 11/2016 – Weigering van afgifte, intrekking en ongeldigverklaring van identiteitskaarten van Belgen die het voorwerp uitmaken van strafdossiers, 26 May 2016, 5; Beernaert, 'Renforcement de l'arsenal législatif anti-terroriste: entre symboles et prévention' (n 302) 835; Bruggeman (n 633) 42.

827 Art 6, §10, section 4 wet van 19 juli 1991 betreffende de bevolkingsregisters, de identiteitskaarten, de vreemdelingenkaarten en de verblijfsdocumenten, *BS* 3 september 1991, 19075. See also: COL 11/2016 – Weigering van afgifte, intrekking en ongeldigverklaring van identiteitskaarten van Belgen die het voorwerp uitmaken van strafdossiers, 26 May 2016, 5.

notified within two working days, the decision is lifted.[828] The maximum duration of the measure is three months (including the initial 25 days), renewable once upon reasoned advice of the OCAD/OCAM.[829] This measure was introduced in 2015 in response to the terrorist attacks in France and police operations in Belgium.[830] Appeal to the Council of State is possible but this appeal does not suspend the measure. In summary proceedings before the Council of State, the suspension of the measure can be requested, and in cases of extreme urgency, a procedure of exceptionally urgent necessity is also a possibility. The possibilities of appeal against the decision must be clearly stated in the notification.[831] A decision to refuse, repeal or invalidate an ID card, automatically leads to the decision to refuse, repeal or invalidate the Belgian passport or travel document of that person as well.[832] ID cards issued to Belgians registered in the consular registers abroad can also be refused, repealed or invalidated. These rules, which were introduced in 2019,[833] can be found in the Consular Code and they are the same as those for passports and travel documents.[834]

828 Art 6, §10, section 3 wet van 19 juli 1991 betreffende de bevolkingsregisters, de identiteitskaarten, de vreemdelingenkaarten en de verblijfsdocumenten; Van Konnegem (n 825) 10/39-10/40.

829 Art 6, §10, *in fine* wet van 19 juli 1991 betreffende de bevolkingsregisters, de identiteitskaarten, de vreemdelingenkaarten en de verblijfsdocumenten; COL 11/2016 – Weigering van afgifte, intrekking en ongeldigverklaring van identiteitskaarten van Belgen die het voorwerp uitmaken van strafdossiers, 26 May 2016, 5; Bruggeman (n 633) 42.

830 Memorie van Toelichting bij het wetsontwerp van 16 juni 2015 houdende wijziging van de wet van 19 juli 1991 betreffende de bevolkingsregisters, de identiteitskaarten, de vreemdelingenkaarten en de verblijfsdocumenten en tot wijziging van de wet van 8 augustus 1983 tot regeling van een Rijksregister van de natuurlijke personen, *Parl.St.* Kamer 2014-2015, nr. 54-1170/001, (4) 4; Reyntjens and Yperman (n 820) 109.

831 Memorie van Toelichting bij het wetsontwerp van 16 juni 2015 houdende wijziging van de wet van 19 juli 1991 betreffende de bevolkingsregisters, de identiteitskaarten, de vreemdelingenkaarten en de verblijfsdocumenten en tot wijziging van de wet van 8 augustus 1983 tot regeling van een Rijksregister van de natuurlijke personen, *Parl.St.* Kamer 2014-15, nr. 54-1170/001, (4) 8; Leemans and De Schryver (n 815) 270.

832 Art 65/2, lid 1 Consular Code. See also: Beernaert, 'Renforcement de l'arsenal législatif anti-terroriste: entre symboles et prévention' (n 302) 836.

833 Wet van 3 juli 2019 tot wijziging van de wet van 21 december 2013 houdende het Consulair Wetboek en van de wet van 10 februari 2015 met betrekking tot geautomatiseerde verwerkingen van persoonsgegevens die noodzakelijk zijn voor de Belgische paspoorten en reisdocumenten, *BS* 22 augustus 2019, 80419.

834 Art 39/1 – 39/4 Consular Code. See also: Toelichting bij wetsvoorstel van 20 februari 2019 tot wijziging van de wet van 21 december 2013 houdende het Consulair Wetboek en van de wet van 10 februari 2015 met betrekking tot geautomatiseerde verwerkingen van persoonsgegevens die noodzakelijk zijn voor de Belgische paspoorten en reisdocumenten, *Parl.St.* Kamer 2018-2019, nr. 54-3574/001, 15.

Revoking nationality

Revoking a person's Belgian nationality is a measure that has existed for a long time.[835] It is possible for several reasons, two of which are of particular importance in the fight against terrorism. Firstly, it is possible to revoke certain people's (see below) nationality if that person seriously failed to meet their obligations as a Belgian citizen.[836] Involvement in terrorism could be brought under this heading.[837] Secondly, since 2012[838] there is a specific ground for revocation for terrorism. Revocation was possible if a person was sentenced to a term of imprisonment of at least five years (not suspended) for the offences mentioned in articles 137, 138, 139, 140 and 141 CC.[839] However, this was only possible if they had committed the offences within ten years from the day they acquired Belgian nationality.[840] The choice of these offences was logical because at the time, they were the only existing terrorist offences. The mention of articles 138 and 139 CC is somewhat surprising since they do not contain any offences.

This second ground for revocation was replaced by a new, broader ground in 2015.[841] Since then, a revocation of the Belgian nationality is possible for Belgians who have been sentenced to a term of imprisonment of at least five years (not suspended) for any terrorist

835 Christelle Macq, 'Contours et enjeux de la déchéance de la nationalité': (2022) n° 2515-2516 Courrier hebdomadaire du CRISP 5, 16-40; Louise Reyntjens, *Ex-Citizens and the European Convention on Human Rights: Citizenship deprivation examined under the ECHR* (PhD at the Faculty of Law of KU Leuven 2022) 17-59; Reyntjens and Yperman (n 820) 100; M Van De Putte, 'Terrorisme als grond voor vervallenverklaring van de Belgische nationaliteit' (2021) 2021 Tijdschrift voor Vreemdelingenrecht (T. Vreemd.) 6, 6; Steven Vandromme, 'De Vervallenverklaring van de Belgische Nationaliteit Anno 2017' in Steven Dewulf (ed), *La [CVDW] Liber Amicorum Chris Van den Wyngaert* (Maklu 2017) 535; P Wautelet, 'Deprivation of Citizenship for "Jihadists"' https://papers.ssrn.com/sol3/papers.cfm?abstract_id=2713742.

836 Art 23, §1, 2° Code of Belgian Nationality. See also: Antwerpen 14 december 2021, *RW* 2021-22, 955; Comité T, 'Raport 2022: Évaluation des mesures visant à lutter contre le terrorisme à la lumière des droits humains', 59; Beernaert, 'Renforcement de l'arsenal législatif anti-terroriste: entre symboles et prévention' (n 302) 834; Macq (n 835) 10; Reyntjens (n 835) 63.

837 See for example: Antwerpen 23 oktober 2018, *RW* 2019-20, nr. 27, 1070; Antwerpen 14 december 2021, *RW* 2021-22, 955. See also: Comité T, 'Raport 2022: Évaluation des mesures visant à lutter contre le terrorisme à la lumière des droits humains', 59; Reyntjens (n 835) 63-66; Wautelet (n 835).

838 Art 20 wet van 4 december 2012 tot wijziging van het Wetboek van de Belgische nationaliteit teneinde het verkrijgen van de Belgische nationaliteit migratieneutraal te maken, *BS* 14 december 2012, 79998.

839 Art 23/1, §1, 1° Code of Belgian Nationality, as introduced by art 20 wet van 4 december 2012 tot wijziging van het Wetboek van de Belgische nationaliteit teneinde het verkrijgen van de Belgische nationaliteit migratieneutraal te maken, *BS* 14 december 2012, 79998. See also: Comité T, 'Raport 2022: Évaluation des mesures visant à lutter contre le terrorisme à la lumière des droits humains', 59; Beernaert, 'Renforcement de l'arsenal législatif anti-terroriste: entre symboles et prévention' (n 302) 834; Bruggeman (n 633) 43-44; Reyntjens (n 835) 67-68; Van De Putte (n 835) 7.

840 Art 23/1, §1, 1° Code of Belgian Nationality; Comité T, 'Raport 2022: Évaluation des mesures visant à lutter contre le terrorisme à la lumière des droits humains', 59-60; Reyntjens and Yperman (n 820) 101.

841 Art 6 and 7 wet van 20 juli 2015 tot versterking van de strijd tegen het terrorisme, *BS* 5 augustus 2015, 49326.

offence.[842] Alongside the extension to all terrorist offences, the legislature also removed the time condition of ten years from the day of acquiring the nationality.[843] The legislature found this to be justified, as 'terrorism affects the entire country in a very general and wide-ranging way and can therefore be interpreted as a form of rejection of the country, its institutions and its values'.[844] Despite this, revocation of nationality remained a measure which was relatively rarely employed. According to the secretary of justice,[845] only four cases of revocation of nationality for terrorism[846] took place in the ten-year period between 2007 and 2017. He did add that he could not guarantee the exact number. In recent years the number of cases appears to have gone up significantly,[847] with a total number of approximately fifty in the last few years.

Revocation of nationality is not possible for all Belgians.[848] It is dependent on the manner in which they acquired their Belgian nationality. If a person acquired the Belgian nationality from a parent or adoptive parent who is a Belgian national, their nationality cannot be revoked.[849] The same applies to people born in Belgium from non-Belgian (adoptive) parents who were also born in Belgium or had their principal residence in Belgium for at least five years in the preceding ten years.[850] Specifically for the ground of deprivation in article 23, there is a third protected category, being people who were born in Belgium and have had their principal residence there since birth. They can acquire Belgian nationality when their (adoptive) parents, at least one of whom has the right to

842 Art 23/2, §1 Code of Belgian Nationality. See also: Comité T, 'Raport 2022: Évaluation des mesures visant à lutter contre le terrorisme à la lumière des droits humains', 59-60; Macq (n 835) 12; Reyntjens (n 835) 70-71; Van De Putte (n 835) 7-8.

843 See also: Comité T, 'Raport 2022: Évaluation des mesures visant à lutter contre le terrorisme à la lumière des droits humains', 59-60; Beernaert, 'Renforcement de l'arsenal législatif anti-terroriste: entre symboles et prévention' (n 302) 834-835; Leemans and De Schryver (n 815) 243-244; Reyntjens (n 835) 71; Reyntjens and Yperman (n 820) 101; Van De Putte (n 835) 10; Vandromme (n 835) 537.

844 Own translation, original in Dutch and French: "*terrorisme op een zeer algemene en brede manier effecten ressorteert op het volledige land en dus mag worden geïnterpreteerd als een vorm van verwerping van het land, zijn instellingen en zijn waarden; le fait que le terrorisme produit des effets d'une manière très générale et large sur le pays tout entier et donc peut être interprété comme une forme de rejet du pays, de ses institutions et de ses valeurs*." See: Memorie van Toelichting bij wetsontwerp van 22 juni 2015 tot versterking van de strijd tegen terrorisme, *Parl.St.* Kamer 2014-2015, nr. 54-1198/001, (4) 8.

845 Beknopt Verslag Commissie voor de Justitie van 1 februari 2017, CRABV 54 COM 581, 17.

846 Revocation of nationality can also be based on the fraudulent acquisition of Belgian nationality. According to the Secretary of Justice's answer to the parliamentary question mentioned in the previous footnote, this possibility has been used six times in the those ten years.

847 Comité T, 'Rapport 2021: Evaluation des mesures visant à lutter contre le terrorisme à la lumière des droits humains', 78-79.

848 See also: Comité T, 'Rapport 2021: Evaluation des mesures visant à lutter contre le terrorisme à la lumière des droits humains', 76; Beernaert, 'Renforcement de l'arsenal législatif anti-terroriste: entre symboles et prévention' (n 302) 835; Van De Putte (n 835) 6-7.

849 Art 23, §1, section 1 and art 23/1, §1, section 1 Code of Belgian Nationality. See also: Macq (n 835) 10 and 12; Reyntjens (n 835) 75-76.

850 Art 11, 1° and 2° Code of Belgian Nationality. See also: Macq (n 835) 10 and 12; Reyntjens (n 835) 76.

stay in Belgium indefinitely, have had their principal residence in Belgium for at least ten years and issue a statement before the child has reached the age of twelve.[851] This leaves people who have acquired the Belgian nationality based on other procedures, which typically happen later in somebody's life, being the ones vulnerable to being deprived of their nationality.[852] Finally, in addition to the protected categories discussed above, nobody can be deprived of their Belgian nationality if they are not dual-nationals, meaning they also have another nationality.[853]

In its reports, Comité T expressed concern that these rules could create a sort of 'second class' citizenship.[854] During the seminar, a number of experts expressed the same opinion. The majority of those present questioned the overall usefulness of the measure, and were pessimistic about its negative influence on potential reintegration. They would prefer to see the measure abolished. A minority of participants agreed that it should be considered carefully on a case-by-case basis, but saw the measure as a form of severe punishment and censure which is suitable in the most extreme cases.

When a person's Belgian nationality is revoked, they get the status of alien under the Belgian legislation.[855] Although case law states that the revocation of nationality should not serve the sole purpose of enabling deportation, and that deportation is certainly not an automatic consequence of it,[856] the ultimate deportation of the person nevertheless seems to be an important motive.[857] Therefore, in 2017, the legislation on asylum and migration was also amended in order to allow the fight against terrorism to also be implemented at that level.[858] Deportation of aliens is divided into three categories, depending on their status. The first category is deportation based on 'reasons of public

851 Art. 11*bis* Code of Belgian Nationality. See also: Macq (n 835) 9-10; Reyntjens (n 835) 76.

852 Reyntjens (n 835) 78-79.

853 See also: Reyntjens (n 835) 78.

854 Comité T, 'Rapport 2020: Evaluation des mesures visant à lutter contre le terrorisme à la lumière des droits humains', 57; Comité T, 'Rapport 2021: Evaluation des mesures visant à lutter contre le terrorisme à la lumière des droits humains', 76-77.

855 Vreemdelingenwet 15 december 1980; Raad voor Vreemdelingenbetwistingen 21 december 2020, *T.Vreemd.* 2021, 226; Comité T, 'Rapport 2020: Evaluation des mesures visant à lutter contre le terrorisme à la lumière des droits humains', 59; Comité T, 'Rapport 2021: Evaluation des mesures visant à lutter contre le terrorisme à la lumière des droits humains', 80; Macq (n 835) 14-16; Vandromme (n 835) 556.

856 Antwerpen 23 oktober 2018, *RW* 2019-20, nr. 27, 1070; Antwerpen 14 december 2021, *RW* 2021-22, 955; Raad voor Vreemdelingenbetwistingen 21 december 2020, *T.Vreemd.* 2021, 226; Comité T, 'Rapport 2020: Evaluation des mesures visant à lutter contre le terrorisme à la lumière des droits humains', 58-59; Macq (n 835) 90; Van De Putte (n 835) 12-13. See also concerning extradition: GwH 7 februari 2018, 16/2018.

857 Macq (n 835) 95; Reyntjens and Yperman (n 820) 102; Vandromme (n 835) 556-557.

858 Memorie van Toelichting bij wetsontwerp van 12 december 2016 tot wijziging van de wet van 15 december 1980 betreffende de toegang tot het grondgebied, het verblijf, de vestiging en de verwijdering van vreemdelingen, met het doel de bescherming van de openbare orde en de nationale veiligheid te versterken, *Parl.St.* kamer 2016-2017, nr. 54-2215/001, 4; Comité T, 'Raport 2022: Évaluation des mesures visant à lutter contre le terrorisme à la lumière des droits humains', 67-68; Reyntjens and Yperman (n 820) 102-104.

order or national security', the second for 'serious reasons' and the third for 'compelling reasons'.[859] Depending on the status of the alien, more serious reasons need to be present. For example, a European Union citizen who has spent at least ten years in Belgium, can only be deported based on compelling reasons of public order or national security[860], while a third country national in the same situation can be deported for serious reasons[861]. The same goes for a European Union citizen who has spent at least five years in Belgium.[862] Before 2017 there were certain categories of aliens who were protected. For example, third country nationals who were born in Belgium or who had arrived before the age of 12 could never be deported. In 2017 these protected categories were removed.[863] Finally, the actual order to leave the Belgian territory can be given by the secretary or the Service for Alien's Affairs.[864]

REPATRIATION

One specific situation which is also important to briefly discuss, is that of children and mothers in the conflict zone. Quite a few Belgian children, often very young, were taken to the conflict zone by their parents or were born there.[865] Their parents have often committed terrorist offences and the legislation discussed in the rest of this report is applicable to them. However, since children cannot be held criminally liable, they have not

859 For third country nationals, see art 21-22 Vreemdelingenwet and for EU nationals, see art 44*bis* Vreemdelingenwet. See also: Comité T, 'Raport 2022: Évaluation des mesures visant à lutter contre le terrorisme à la lumière des droits humains', 68-69.

860 Art 44bis, §3, °1 Vreemdelingenwet.

861 Art 22, §1, °3 Vreemdelingenwet.

862 Art 42*quinquies*, §1 *j.* 44*bis*, §2 Vreemdelingenwet.

863 Comité T, 'Rapport 2020: Evaluation des mesures visant à lutter contre le terrorisme à la lumière des droits humains', 51-52.

864 Art 7 Vreemdelingenwet. There were a few cases of the council for alien litigation which ruled that under the 2017 legislation, the secretary could not delegate this. However, this was not the legislature's intention so it amended the legislation in 2019 in order to clarify this. See: Wet 8 mei 2019 tot wijziging van de wet van 15 december 1980 betreffende de toegang tot het grondgebied, het verblijf, de vestiging en de verwijdering van vreemdelingen, *BS* 9 Juli 2019, 69181; Toelichting van 27 februari 2019 bij wetsvoorstel houdende diverse bepalingen inzake asiel en migratie en tot wijziging van de wet van 15 december 1980 betreffende de toegang tot het grondgebied, het verblijf, de vestiging en de verwijdering van vreemdelingen, *Parl.St.* Kamer 2018-2019, nr. 54-3618/001, 10-17; Verslag van de eerste lezing namens de commissie voor de binnenlandse zaken, de algemene zaken en het openbaar ambt van 25 maart 2019 bij wetsvoorstel houdende diverse bepalingen inzake asiel en migratie en tot wijziging van de wet van 15 december 1980 betreffende de toegang tot het grondgebied, het verblijf, de vestiging en de verwijdering van vreemdelingen, *Parl.St.* Kamer 2018-2019, nr. 54-3618/003, 3-5.

865 Evelien Wauters and Jan Wouters, 'Moeders En Kinderen van Syriëstrijders: Over de Volkenrechtelijke Verplichtingen van de Belgische Staat' 80, 80; Axel Winkel, 'Les enfants belges du califat' (2019) 387 Centre Permanent pour la Citoyenneté et la Participation 24, 4-5.

committed any criminal offences.[866] Following the fall of the Caliphate, many of these children were placed into camps.[867] The question thus arose what to do with these Belgian children. Should they be repatriated to their home country or not?

In December 2017 the National Security Council had stated that Belgian children under ten had the right to return to Belgium[868] and that the situation of children aged ten to seventeen would be decided upon on a case by case basis.[869] However, they had to travel to the nearest Belgian embassy or consulate, located in Turkey.[870] In October 2019[871] a proposal for a resolution was tabled in parliament to request the federal government to repatriate all Belgian children, regardless of age, from Syria under the condition of explicit consent from a Belgian parent and significant indications of the identity of the child, including those children born in Syria.[872] For the latter, a DNA test would have to be done, but the resolution proposes to do this after their arrival in Belgium.[873] In addition, for children aged ten to eighteen an individual threat assessment would be undertaken.[874] The reasoning behind this resolution was twofold: Firstly, based on the inhumane circumstances in the camps in Syria, and second the fact that it would actually be beneficial to security

866 Cass. 11 maart 2009, *Rev.dr.pén.* 2009, 748; De Nauw and Deruyck (n 436) 110-111; Tulkens and others (n 16) 442; Van den Wyngaert, Traest and Vandromme (n 433) 302.

867 Laurens De Brucker, 'Het Recht Op Consulaire Bijstand Vanuit Nationaal-, Europees- En Internationaalrechtelijk Perspectief. Naar Een Subjectief Recht Op Repatriëring Voor Kinderen van Syriëstrijders?' [2020] Tijdschrift Jeugd- en Kinderrechten 194, 194; Elise Delhaise, Coline Remacle and Chloé Thomas, 'Rapatriement Des Enfants Belges Du Califat : Droit et Sécurité En Tension' (2022) 49 La revue internationale de l'éducation familiale 41, 42; Winkel (n 865) 4. Even more children, however, simply disappeared off the radar. See: Thomas Renard and Rik Coolsaet, 'Children in the Levant: Insights from Belgium on the Dilemmas of Repatriation and the Challenges of Reintregration' (2018) 98 Security Policy Brief 5.

868 Beknopt Verslag Commissie voor de binnenlandse zaken, de algemene zaken en het openbaar ambt 28 februari 2018, CRABV 54 COM 830, 30; De Brucker (n 867) 194; Wauters and Wouters (n 865) 80; Winkel (n 865) 12.

869 Voorstel van Resolutie van 22 oktober 2019 betreffende het terughalen van kinderen van Syriëstrijders, *Parl.St.* Kamer 2019-2020, nr. 55-674/001, 3 and 4; Verslag namens de commissie voor buitenlandse betrekkingen van 10 januari 2020 betreffende de veiligheidssituatie in de kampen in noord-syrië en het lot van de belgische foreign terrorist fighters, gelet op het turkse militaire offensief, *Parl.St.* Kamer 2019-2020, nr. 55-926/001, 19; Renard and Coolsaet (n 867) 6.

870 Delhaise, Remacle and Thomas (n 451) 53; Delhaise, Remacle and Thomas (n 867) 46; Renard and Coolsaet (n 867) 6.

871 Note that a proposal for a resolution on this same topic was also tabled in 2018. However, this proposal has expired with new parliamentary elections. See: Voorstel van resolutie van 27 november 2018 tot actief opsporen en repatriëren van de kinderen van Belgische Syriëstrijders, *Parl.St.* Kamer 2018-2019, nr. 54-3399/001.

872 Voorstel van Resolutie van 22 oktober 2019 betreffende het terughalen van kinderen van Syriëstrijders, *Parl.St.* Kamer 2019-2020, nr. 55-674/001. See also: Delhaise, Remacle and Thomas (n 451) 54.

873 Voorstel van Resolutie van 22 oktober 2019 betreffende het terughalen van kinderen van Syriëstrijders, *Parl.St.* Kamer 2019-2020, nr. 55-674/001, 3.

874 Voorstel van Resolutie van 22 oktober 2019 betreffende het terughalen van kinderen van Syriëstrijders, *Parl.St.* Kamer 2019-2020, nr. 55-674/001, 3 and 8. See also: Delhaise, Remacle and Thomas (n 451) 55.

not to have these children (and their mothers) under radicalising influences in these camps.[875] Parliament has not yet voted on this resolution.

In the meantime, in March 2021 the Belgian federal government decided to repatriate all children under twelve years old who were born in Belgium. Additionally, after a threat analysis, the repatriation of their mothers will be decided upon on a case-by-case basis.[876] Children born in the conflict zone, on the other hand, would not be repatriated.[877] The Belgian authorities eventually did send experts to the Kurdish camps in order to take DNA tests and establish the parentage of these children. However, when they arrived for a first attempt, the children could not be found and their parentage, and therefore nationality, could not be established.[878] A second attempt seems to have had more success (see below). The government decided adults will not be repatriated, presumably barring the mothers mentioned above.[879]

The children have certain rights which should be protected. One consideration at the foundation of this protection is the obligation to ensure the best interests of the child are the primary consideration in all actions concerning children, which is enshrined in article 3 of the Convention on the Rights of the Child.[880] The rights to life and physical integrity of the children in a (post-)conflict zone, such as Syria, are clearly endangered.[881] In addition, states should take appropriate measures to promote the physical and

875 Voorstel van Resolutie van 22 oktober 2019 betreffende het terughalen van kinderen van Syriëstrijders, *Parl.St.* Kamer 2019-2020, nr. 55-674/001, 3-4. See also: Verslag namens de commissie voor buitenlandse betrekkingen van 10 januari 2020 betreffende de veiligheidssituatie in de kampen in noord-syrië en het lot van de belgische foreign terrorist fighters, gelet op het turkse militaire offensief, *Parl.St.* Kamer 2019-2020, nr. 55-926/001, 4, 9 and 15-16; Delhaise, Remacle and Thomas (n 451) 52; Thomas Renard and Rik Coolsaet, 'From Bad to Worse: The Fate of European Foreign Fighters and Families Detained in Syria, One Year after the Turkish Offensive' (2020) 130 Security Policy Brief 3 and 7; Winkel (n 865) 11. See also in the media: Bruno Struys, 'Opnieuw 6 IS-vrouwen en 16 kinderen uit Syrië naar België gerepatrieerd: '"Voor de nationale veiligheid"' (2022) *De Morgen*, www.demorgen.be/nieuws/opnieuw-6-is-vrouwen-en-16-kinderen-uit-syrie-naar-belgie-gerepatrieerd-voor-de-nationale-veiligheid~b1a5c5af/; Inge Vrancken, 'Tweede groep Belgische vrouwen en kinderen van IS-strijders gerepatrieerd naar ons land' (2022) *vrtNWS* 21 June 2022, www.vrt.be/vrtnws/nl/2022/06/20/tweede-groep-belgische-vrouwen-en-kinderen-van-is-strijders-gere/.

876 Beknopt verslag plenumvergadering Kamer van volksvertegenwoordigers 4 maart 2021, CRABV 55 PLEN 90, 12-13. See also: Delhaise, Remacle and Thomas (n 867) 43.

877 Delhaise, Remacle and Thomas (n 867) 43.

878 Delhaise, Remacle and Thomas (n 867) 47-48.

879 Beknopt Verslag Commissie voor de binnenlandse zaken, de algemene zaken en het openbaar ambt 28 februari 2018, CRABV 54 COM 830, 30. See also: De Brucker (n 867) 195; Delhaise, Remacle and Thomas (n 867) 46.

880 Art 3 Convention on the Rights of the Child, 20 November 1989. See also: Delhaise, Remacle and Thomas (n 451) 57; Delhaise, Remacle and Thomas (n 867) 49-50.

881 Art 19 Convention on the Rights of the Child; art 2 ECHR. See also: Verslag namens de commissie voor buitenlandse betrekkingen van 10 januari 2020 betreffende de veiligheidssituatie in de kampen in noord-syrië en het lot van de belgische foreign terrorist fighters, gelet op het turkse militaire offensief, *Parl.St.* Kamer 2019-2020, nr. 55-926/001, 10; Delhaise, Remacle and Thomas (n 451) 56; Delhaise, Remacle and Thomas (n 867) 50-51; Winkel (n 865) 11.

psychological recovery and social reintegration of a child victim of armed conflict.[882] Moreover, they should ensure that children are not separated from their parents against their will, unless this is necessary for the best interests of the child.[883] Based on these rights, several authors conclude that Belgium is under the obligation to repatriate children and their parents from the conflict zone.[884] This is in line with the recommendation of the child's rights commissioner and the '*délégué général de la Communauté française aux droits de l'enfant*'.[885]

While the abovementioned debate was ongoing, several mothers wanted their children, including some who were born in Syria, to be repatriated and introduced summary proceedings before the Belgian courts for this purpose.[886] In 2018, the Brussels Court of First Instance and then Court of Appeal ruled on a summary proceedings case of two Belgian women who wanted their children, four of whom were born in Belgium and two in Syria, to be repatriated. Their claim was based on the prohibition of torture and the right to liberty and security. Both in first instance and on appeal, the courts dismissed the case as unfounded because the children were not under Belgian jurisdiction, and Belgium could thus not be held responsible in ensuring their human rights.[887] The courts held that, while there is a moral obligation for the Belgian state, there are no subjective rights for the mothers or children. The same mothers brought another summary proceedings case, once more seeking the repatriation of their children based on the same grounds. The Court of First Instance held that the circumstances had changed, and it could therefore rule on the case.[888] The court subsequently reasoned that the children were entitled to consular protection, while the mothers had lost their right to consular protection by travelling to a war zone. The government had argued that it could not repatriate the children because the Kurdisch authorities did not want to let the children go without the mothers, whom the Belgian state did not want or have to repatriate. The court dismissed this argument, based on the rights of the child alongside several reasons revolving around the mothers themselves, such as the prohibition of refusing entry into the country of nationals and

882 Art 39 Convention on the Rights of the Child. See also: Verslag namens de commissie voor buitenlandse betrekkingen van 10 januari 2020 betreffende de veiligheidssituatie in de kampen in noord-syrië en het lot van de belgische foreign terrorist fighters, gelet op het turkse militaire offensief, *Parl.St.* Kamer 2019-2020, nr. 55-926/001, 10; Delhaise, Remacle and Thomas (n 867) 51; Winkel (n 865) 11.

883 Art 9 Convention on the Rights of the Child. See also: Delhaise, Remacle and Thomas (n 451) 56; Delhaise, Remacle and Thomas (n 867) 50.

884 Delhaise, Remacle and Thomas (n 867) 51-53; Winkel (n 865) 12 and 15.

885 Verslag namens de commissie voor buitenlandse betrekkingen van 10 januari 2020 betreffende de veiligheidssituatie in de kampen in noord-syrië en het lot van de belgische foreign terrorist fighters, gelet op het turkse militaire offensief, *Parl.St.* Kamer 2019-2020, nr. 55-926/001, 10 and 31. See also: Renard and Coolsaet (n 867) 6.

886 Delhaise, Remacle and Thomas (n 451) 58-61; Delhaise, Remacle and Thomas (n 867) 47.

887 Brussel 12 September 2018, *TJK* 2019, 72; kortgeding Brussel 29 juli 2018, *onuitg.*

888 Kortgeding Brussel 26 december 2018, *onuitg.*

security considerations. Concretely, the court imposed the obligation upon the Belgian government to provide travel documents for the children and their mothers, reach an agreement with local authorities and provide an escort. In two other cases, a claim also succeeded in the first instance and the Belgian state was convicted.[889] In a summary case from 2019, which concerned a woman without children, the court followed similar reasoning concerning the woman and dismissed her claims.[890] The court held she had no right to consular protection, although Belgium was willing to provide consular assistance if she presented herself at a diplomatic or consular post. In addition, Belgium could not be held to protect her human rights, for lack of jurisdiction. Another case was brought that same year by an eighteen-year-old woman, who had been taken to Syria by her father when she was still a minor. The court ruled once again that the Belgian state had no human rights jurisdiction in Syria and there was no right to consular assistance, however, the court did accept a claim based on the principle that the interest of the child should be the primary consideration.[891] Based on this principle, the Belgian state does have to provide assistance to the woman and aid her in returning to Belgium. Finally, two relevant judgments of the Court of Appeal from 2020 were published. In those judgments, the court stated that Belgian children have a subjective right to be repatriated. This right is based on the explicit statement the government made regarding children under 10[892] and for older children on the consular code, as well as the fact that the child's best interests should be the primary consideration. However, the court then held that the women claiming to be mothers were not the legal representatives of the children. The lineage of the children was not proven and therefore the claims regarding the children were inadmissible.[893] Regarding the mothers themselves, the claims were dismissed as unfounded since the legislation excludes Belgians who travelled to a war zone from consular aid.[894] Regarding Belgian jurisdiction, the court followed its abovementioned jurisprudence. Human rights organisations also brought a case before the Belgian courts, but this case was rejected as well.[895] These cases make clear that for children whose lineage can be proven, such as is the case for those who were born in Belgium and taken to Syria by their parents, a right to repatriation exists.

---

889 See: De Brucker (n 867) 195-198.

890 Kortgeding Brussel 7 juni 2019, *onuitg.*

891 Kortgeding Brussel 11 juni 2019, *onuitg.*

892 Note that Wauters and Wouters had already defended this point after the 2018 case, see: Wauters and Wouters (n 865) 85.

893 Brussel 5 maart 2020, nr. 2019/KR/60, *TJK* 2020, 186; Brussel 5 maart 2020, nr. 2019/KR/3, *TJK* 2020, 192; See also: De Brucker (n 867) 199-200; Delhaise, Remacle and Thomas (n 451) 62; Delhaise, Remacle and Thomas (n 867) 47.

894 Brussel 5 maart 2020, nr. 2019/KR/60, *TJK* 2020, 186; Brussel 5 maart 2020, nr. 2019/KR/3, *TJK* 2020, 192. See also: De Brucker (n 867) 200.

895 Delhaise, Remacle and Thomas (n 867) 47.

Eventually, three major repatriation operations took place. In June 2019, six children were repatriated after an agreement with the Kurdish authorities.[896] In 2021 a Belgian delegation travelled to Syria to administer DNA tests and conduct interviews, and in July of that year ten more children were repatriated. This time six mothers were repatriated together with the children.[897] Approximately a year later, in June 2022, a second group consisting of six women (five mothers and one grandmother) and sixteen children was repatriated.[898] This leaves only a small group of Belgian women and children in the camps. This group consists of women who either stay voluntarily (and keep their children there) or do not have children. There is one case of a woman whose nationality was revoked and therefore is not allowed to return to Belgium, who refuses to let her child leave without her.

896 Verslag namens de commissie voor buitenlandse betrekkingen van 10 januari 2020 betreffende de veiligheidssituatie in de kampen in noord-syrië en het lot van de belgische foreign terrorist fighters, gelet op het turkse militaire offensief, *Parl.St.* Kamer 2019-2020, nr. 55-926/001, 19; Delhaise, Remacle and Thomas (n 451) 53; Delhaise, Remacle and Thomas (n 867) 46; Renard and Coolsaet (n 862) 3; Winkel (n 865) 3.

897 Inge Vrancken, 'België haalt voor het eerst IS-vrouwen terug uit Syrië, ook kinderen komen mee' (2021) *vrtNWS* 16 July 2021, www.vrt.be/vrtnws/nl/2021/07/16/belgie-haalt-voor-het-eerst-is-vrouwen-en-hun-kinderen-terug-uit/.

898 Bruno Struys, 'Opnieuw 6 IS-vrouwen en 16 kinderen uit Syrië naar België gerepatrieerd: '"Voor de nationale veiligheid"' (2022) *De Morgen*, www.demorgen.be/nieuws/opnieuw-6-is-vrouwen-en-16-kinderen-uit-syrie-naar-belgie-gerepatrieerd-voor-de-nationale-veiligheid~b1a5c5af/; Inge Vrancken, 'Tweede groep Belgische vrouwen en kinderen van IS-strijders gerepatrieerd naar ons land' (2022) *vrtNWS* 21 June 2022, www.vrt.be/vrtnws/nl/2022/06/20/tweede-groep-belgische-vrouwen-en-kinderen-van-is-strijders-gere/.

Conclusions

In this book we have attempted to provide a succinct yet accurate overview of the most important Belgian legislation applicable to people returning from jihadist war zones. A first point of focus involves the terrorist offences which may have been committed by those people. Belgian criminal law criminalises terrorism *sensu stricto*, being actual terrorist attacks, but also several offences of terrorism *sensu lato*, such as participation in the activities of a terrorist group or traveling for terrorist purposes. As explained throughout Chapter 1 of this book, these offences are not always clearly worded, and the offences relating to terrorist groups are interpreted (arguably too) broadly. Despite this, the Constitutional Court has found the terrorism offences to be constitutional. Therefore, almost everybody returning from jihadist war zones faces prosecution for one or more of these terrorist offences. An analysis of case law has shown that, despite the broad spectrum of terrorist offences available, prosecution is almost always reliant on the offences pertaining to terrorist groups. The first opinion in the EU Agency for Fundamental Rights' (FRA) report on the impact on fundamental rights and freedoms of EU Directive 2017/541 on combatting terrorism, is that member states should take steps to ensure that criminal law offences are foreseeable and clear. The FRA explicitly recommends avoiding overlap between different offences, and avoiding the use of broad, all-encompassing provisions.[899]

Chapter 2 discussed a few key procedural topics which are relevant for these criminal prosecutions. The terrorist offences are tried by the Correctional Courts, with only a few exceptional cases being tried by the Assize Courts. These exceptions are the most serious terrorism offences *sensu stricto* and any terrorist offences which qualify as press offences. The Court of Cassation appears to have dismissed the idea of terrorism offences as political offences, which would also lead to the competence of the Assize Courts, but we believe that under the right circumstances, a terrorist offence could still be a mixed political offence, which would thus have to be tried before the Assize Court. In cases revolving around people being in a jihadist war zone, usually a trial will already have taken place *in absentia* after which an immediate arrest warrant has been issued. This means that, upon returning to Belgium, the person can be arrested and detained. If they meet certain conditions, however, they can request a retrial.

As explained in Chapter 3, there are a number of possibilities regarding sentences. While alternative sentences, such as the electronic tagging sentence, community service and autonomous probation sentences, exist and are possible for a fair amount of the

899 European Union Agency for Fundamental Rights, Report on the impact on fundamental rights and freedoms of Directive (EU) 2017/541 on combating terrorism (2021) 6.

terrorism offences, they do not seem to be used.[900] The sentence usually imposed is that of a prison sentence at the higher end of the sentencing bracket. The prevalence of prison sentences is belied by the issues pertaining to the wording and proportionality of the sentences as explained in the first Section of Chapter 3. A possibility which is used only slightly more often than alternative sentences is that of a suspension of sentence. The postponement of enforcement of a prison sentence, on the other hand, being possible for sentences of up to five years, is more prevalent. Finally, upon convictions for terrorism *sensu stricto* for a prison sentence of at least five years, it is obligatory to place the defendant at the disposal of the sentence enforcement court, if the offence caused the death of a victim. This additional sentence can prolong the imposed prison sentence or the supervision of a convicted person outside of prison. Proposals are pending to expand the scope of this sentence to other terrorist offences as well. In the current case law, due to the narrow scope of application of this additional sentence, it is not often imposed.

Within prison, terrorist detainees are either integrated within the general population or separated into satellite wings or D-Rad:Ex sections. These have been introduced relatively recently, and especially the D-Rad:Ex sections have received criticism for being in violation of prisoners' rights. This matter will undoubtedly evolve further. The majority of terrorist detainees are in the general prison population. The general rules on the external legal position of prisoners are applicable to all terrorist detainees (regardless of which section they are detained in). The main differences with other detainees are that currently electronic tagging as a sentence modality is not possible for people convicted of up to two years for terrorist offences, that a security period is usually possible, that a report of a service specialised in terrorism or violent extremism is necessary in the procedure for the sentencing modalities granted by the sentence enforcement court, and that the sentence enforcement court has to especially motivate the permission to leave the territory upon conditional release.

While Chapters 1 to 4 dealt with criminal law in the broad sense of the word, Chapter 5 groups some non-criminal measures which can be relevant for returnees. First of all, it is possible their assets have been frozen, with recourse against this being difficult. In addition, their ID cards and passports can be revoked and, in some cases, even their Belgian nationality (which, depending on the circumstances, may or may not be a criminal sentence). In its report on the impact of the EU Directive on human rights and freedoms, the FRA emphasises that member states should ensure proportionate use of administrative measures and access to an effective remedy.[901] In the final Section of Chapter 5, the issue of repatriation is discussed. Many people are still trapped in zones which used to be

900 See also: Moreau (n 173) 117-118.

901 European Union Agency for Fundamental Rights, Report on the impact on fundamental rights and freedoms of Directive (EU) 2017/541 on combating terrorism (2021) 11.

jihadist war zones. The Belgian government's inaction has led to a lot of criticism. Recently, repatriations of mothers with children took place. However, the situation of others stays unchanged, and they remain in prison camps in Syria and Iraq.

The Belgian legislature has been expanding the counter-terrorism legislation for the last twenty years. These expansions were often driven by current events and international or European prompts. This led to a patchwork of incident-driven legislation. In these two decades, the legislature never stopped to review the situation before adding extra legislation. A thorough evaluation of the existing legislation seems to be in order. This was the main point of consensus among all the experts at the seminar. After twenty years, it is time to stop and evaluate the counter-terrorism legislation.

BIBLIOGRAPHY

LEGISLATION

International and supranational instruments

European Convention for the Protection of Human Rights and Fundamental Freedoms, Rome 4 June 1950 (ECHR)

Protocol No. 4 to the Convention for the Protection of Human Rights and Fundamental Freedoms securing certain rights and freedoms other than those already included in the Convention and in the First Protocol thereto, Strasbourg 16 September 1963 (ECHR Fourth Protocol)

Convention on the Rights of the Child, 20 November 1989

International Convention for the Suppression of the Financing of Terrorism, New York 9 December 1999

Council of Europe Treaty on the Prevention of Terrorism, Warsaw 16 May 2005, *Pb. EU* 2018, 159/3

Additional Protocol to the Council of Europe Convention on the Prevention of Terrorism, 2015, CETS 217

UNSC Resolution 1267 of 15 October 1999

UNSC Resolution 1333 of 19 December 2000

UNSC Resolution 1373 of 28 September 2001

UNSC Resolution 1390 of 16 January 2002

UNSC Resolution 1904 of 17 December 2009

UNSC Resolution 1988 of 17 June 2011

UNSC Resolution 1989 of 17 June 2011

UNSC Resolution 2178 of 24 September 2014

UNSC Resolution 2253 of 17 December 2015

UNSC Resolution 2368 of 20 July 2017

Council Common Position 2001/930/CFSP of 27 December 2001 on combating terrorism, *OJ EU* 28 December 2001, L 344

Council Common Position 2001/931/CFSP of 27 December 2001 on the application of specific measures to combat terrorism, *OJ EU* 28 December 2001, L 344

Council Common Position 2002/402/CFSP of 27 May 2002 concerning restrictive measures against Usama bin Laden, members of the Al-Qaida organization and the Taliban and other individuals, groups, undertakings and entities associated with them and repealing Common Positions 96/746/CFSP, 1999/727/CFSP, 2001/154/CFSP and 2001/771/CFSP, *OJ EU* 29 May 2002, L 139

Council Regulation (EC) No 2580/2001 of 27 December 2001 on specific restrictive measures directed against certain persons and entities with a view to combating terrorism, *OJ EU* 28 December 2001, L 344.

Council Decision (CFSP) 2016/1693 of 20 September 2016 concerning restrictive measures against ISIL (Da'esh) and Al-Qaeda and persons, groups, undertakings and entities associated with them and repealing Common Position 2002/402/CFSP, *OJ EU* 21 September 2016, L 255

Council Framework Decision 2002/475/JHA of 13 June 2002 on combating terrorism, *OJ* 22 June 2002, L 164

Council Framework Decision 2008/919/JHA of 28 November 2008 amending Framework Decision 2002/475/JHA on combating terrorism, OJ 9 December 2008, L 330/21

Directive (EU) 2017/541 of the European Parliament and of the Council of 15 March 2017 on combating terrorism and replacing Council Framework Decision 2002/475/JHA and amending Council Decision 2005/671/JHA, *OJ* 31 March 2017, L 88/6

Belgian national legislation

Belgische grondwet van 7 februari 1831 (Constitution)

Wetboek van Strafvordering van 17 november 1808, *BS* 27 november 1808 – Code of Criminal Procedure (CCP)

Strafwetboek van 8 juni 1867, *BS* 9 juni 1867, 3133 – Criminal Code (CC)

Wet van 17 april 1878 houdende de voorafgaande titel van het wetboek van strafvordering, *BS* 25 april 1878, 1265 – Preliminary Title to the Code of Criminal Procedure (PTCCP)

Wet van 5 juni 1928 houdende herziening van het Tucht- en Strafwetboek voor de koopvaardij en de zeevisserij, *BS* 26 juli 1928, 3341

Wet van 3 januari 1933 op de vervaardiging van, de handel in en het dragen van wapens en op de handel in munitie, gewijzigd bij de wetten van 30 januari en 5 augustus 1991, 9 maart 1995, 24 juni 1996, 18 juli 1997, 10 januari 1999 en 30 maart 2000

Wet van 28 mei 1956 betreffende ontplofbare en voor de deflagratie vatbare stoffen en mengsels en de daarmee geladen tuigen, *BS* 19 juni 1956, 3990

Wet van 29 juni 1964 betreffende de opschorting, het uitstel en de probatie, *BS* 17 juli 1964, 7812 (Probatiewet)

Gecoördineerde wetten op de raad van state van 12 januari 1973, *BS* 21 maart 1972, 3461 (RvS statute)

Wet houdende goedkeuring van het Verdrag tot verbod van de ontwikkeling, de productie en de aanleg van voorraden van bacteriologische (biologische) en toxinewapens en inzake de vernietiging van deze wapens, opgemaakt te Londen, Moskou en Washington op 10 april 1972

Wet 1 augustus 1979 betreffende diensten bij een vreemde leger- of troepenmacht die zich op het grondgebied van een vreemde Staat bevindt, *BS* 24 augustus 1979, 9272

Wet van 15 december 1980 betreffende de toegang tot het grondgebied, het verblijf, de vestiging en de verwijdering van vreemdelingen, *BS* 31 december 1980, 14584 (Vreemdelingenwet)

Wetboek van de Belgische nationaliteit van 28 juni 1984, *BS* 12 juli 1984, 10100 (Code of Belgian Nationality)

Wet van 15 juli 1985 betreffende het gebruik bij dieren van stoffen met hormonale, anti-hormonale, beta-adrenergische of produktie-stimulerende werking, *BS* 4 september 1985, 12669

Wet van 20 juli 1990 betreffende de voorlopige hechtenis, *BS* 14 augustus 1990, 15779 (Statute on pre-trial detention)

Wet van 21 maart 1991 betreffende de hervorming van sommige economische overheidsbedrijven, *BS* 27 maart 1991, 6155

Wet van 19 juli 1991 betreffende de bevolkingsregisters, de identiteitskaarten, de vreemdelingenkaarten en de verblijfsdocumenten, *BS* 3 september 1991, 19075

Wet van 29 juli 1991 betreffende de uitdrukkelijke motivering van de bestuurshandelingen, *BS* 12 september 1991, 19976

Wet van 11 mei 1995 inzake de tenuitvoerlegging van de besluiten van de Veiligheidsraad van de Organisatie van de Verenigde Naties, *BS* 29 Juli 1995, 20444

Wet 13 mei 2003 inzake de tenuitvoerlegging van de beperkende maatregelen die genomen worden door de Raad van de Europese Unie ten aanzien van Staten, sommige personen en entiteiten, *BS* 13 juni 2003, 31293

Wet van 19 december 2003 betreffende terroristische misdrijven, *BS* 29 december 2003, 61689

Basiswet 12 januari 2005 betreffende het gevangeniswezen en de rechtspositie van de gedetineerden, *BS* 1 februari 2005, 2815 (Basiswet gevangeniswezen)

Wet van 10 augustus 2005 tot wijziging van diverse bepalingen met het oog op de versterking van de strijd tegen mensenhandel en mensensmokkel en tegen praktijken van huisjesmelkers, *BS* 2 september 2005, 38454

Wet van 17 mei 2006 betreffende de externe rechtspositie van de veroordeelden tot een vrijheidsstraf en de aan het slachtoffer toegekende rechten in het raam van de strafuitvoeringsmodaliteiten, *BS* 16 juni 2006, 30455 (WERP)

Wet van 8 juni 2006 houdende regeling van economische en individuele activiteiten met wapens, *BS* 9 juni 2006, 29840

Wet van 25 april 2007 houdende diverse bepalingen (IV), *BS* 8 mei 2007, 25103

Wet 26 april 2007 betreffende de terbeschikkingstelling van de strafuitvoeringsrechtbank, *BS* 13 juli 2007, 38299

Wet van 30 december 2009 betreffende de strijd tegen piraterij op zee, *BS* 14 januari 2010, 1485

Wet van 4 december 2012 tot wijziging van het Wetboek van de Belgische nationaliteit teneinde het verkrijgen van de Belgische nationaliteit migratieneutraal te maken, *BS* 14 december 2012, 79998

Wet van 18 februari 2013 tot wijziging van boek II, titel Iter van het Strafwetboek, *BS* 4 maart 2013, 13233

Consulair Wetboek van 21 december 2013, *BS* 21 januari 2014, 4987 (Consular Code)

Wet van 7 februari 2014 tot wijziging van de wet van 24 februari 1921 betreffende het verhandelen van gifstoffen, slaapmiddelen en verdovende middelen, psychotrope stoffen, ontsmettingsstoffen en antiseptica en van de stoffen die kunnen gebruikt worden voor de illegale vervaardiging van verdovende middelen en psychotrope stoffen, *BS* 6 maart 1921, 1834

Wet van 20 juli 2015 tot versterking van de strijd tegen het terrorisme, *BS* 5 augustus 2015, 49326

Wet van 10 augustus 2015 tot wijziging van het Consulair Wetboek, *BS* 24 augustus 2015, 54497

Wet van 23 november 2015 met betrekking tot de inwerkingtreding van diverse bepalingen betreffende justitie, *BS* 23 november 2015, 71211

Wet 18 december 2015 houdende diverse financiële bepalingen, houdende de oprichting van een administratieve dienst met boekhoudkundige autonomie "Sociale activiteiten", houdende wijziging van de wet van 11 mei 1995 inzake de tenuitvoerlegging van de besluiten van de Veiligheidsraad van de Organisatie van de Verenigde Naties en houdende een bepaling inzake de gelijkheid van vrouwen en mannen, *BS* 20 december 2015, 79809

Wet van 5 februari 2016 tot wijziging van het strafrecht en de strafvordering en houdende diverse bepalingen inzake justitie, *BS* 19 februari 2016, 13130

Wet van 20 juli 2015 tot versterking van de strijd tegen het terrorisme, *BS* 5 augustus 2015, 49326

Wet van 3 augustus 2016 houdende diverse bepalingen ter bestrijding van terrorisme (III), *BS* 11 augustus 2016, 50973

Wet van 14 december 2016 tot wijziging van het Strafwetboek wat betreft de bestraffing van terrorisme, *BS* 22 december 2016, 88017

Programmawet 25 december 2016, *BS* 29 december 2016, 90879

Wet van 6 juli 2017 houdende vereenvoudiging, harmonisering, informatisering en modernisering van bepalingen van burgerlijke recht en van burgerlijk procesrecht alsook van het notariaat, en houdende diverse bepalingen inzake justitie, *BS* 24 juli 2017, 75168

Wet van 21 december 2017, tot wijziging van diverse bepalingen met het oog op de invoering van een beveiligingsperiode en tot wijziging van de wet van 20 juli 1990 betreffende de voorlopige hechtenis voor wat de onmiddellijke aanhouding betreft, *BS* 11 januari 2018, 1185

Wet 22 juli 2018 tot wijziging van het Wetboek van strafvordering betreffende toezeggingen in het kader van de strafvordering, de strafuitvoering of de hechtenis wegens het afleggen van een verklaring in het kader van de strijd tegen de georganiseerde criminaliteit en het terrorisme, *BS* 7 augustus 2018, 62054

Wet 2 mei 2019 houdende diverse financiële bepalingen, *BS* 21 mei 2019, 48120

Wet van 5 mei 2019 houdende diverse bepalingen in strafzaken en inzake erediensten, en tot wijziging van de wet van 28 mei 2002 betreffende de euthanasie en van het Sociaal Strafwetboek, *BS* 24 mei 2019, 50023

Wet van 5 mei 2019 tot invoeging van een artikel 55bis in het Strafwetboek, wat de herhaling betreft, *BS* 28 mei 2019, 51916

Wet 8 mei 2019 tot wijziging van de wet van 15 december 1980 betreffende de toegang tot het grondgebied, het verblijf, de vestiging en de verwijdering van vreemdelingen, *BS* 9 Juli 2019, 69181

Wet van 3 juli 2019 tot wijziging van de wet van 21 december 2013 houdende het Consulair Wetboek en van de wet van 10 februari 2015 met betrekking tot geautomatiseerde verwerkingen van persoonsgegevens die noodzakelijk zijn voor de Belgische paspoorten en reisdocumenten, *BS* 22 augustus 2019, 80419

Wet van 31 juli 2020 houdende diverse dringende bepalingen inzake justitie, *BS* 7 augustus 2020, 58048

Wet van 16 maart 2021 tot uitstel van de inwerkingtreding van de bepalingen inzake de externe rechtspositie van veroordeelden tot een vrijheidsstraf voor de vrijheidsstraffen van drie jaar of minder, *BS* 26 maart 2021, 28192

Wet van 28 november 2021 om justitie menselijker, sneller en straffer te maken, *BS* 30 november 2021, 115153

Wet van 21 maart 2022 houdende wijzigingen aan het Strafwetboek met betrekking tot het seksueel strafrecht, *BS* 30 maart 2022, 25785

Decreet van 8 maart 2013 betreffende de organisatie van hulp- en dienstverlening aan gedetineerden, *BS* 11 april 2013, 22460

Décret du 13 octobre 2016 relatif à l'agrément et au subventionnement des partenaires apportant de l'aide aux justiciables, *BS* 22 december 2016, 88082

KB 28 december 2006 inzake specifieke beperkende maatregelen tegen bepaalde personen en entiteiten met het oog op de strijd tegen de financiering van het terrorisme, *BS* 17 januari 2007, 1898

KB 30 mei 2016 tot vaststelling van de lijst van personen en entiteiten bedoeld in artikelen 3 en 5 van het koninklijk besluit van 28 december 2006 inzake specifieke beperkende maatregelen tegen bepaalde personen en entiteiten met het oog op de strijd tegen de financiering van het terrorisme, *BS* 1 juni 2016, 33913

KB 26 oktober 2022 tot wijziging van de lijst van personen en entiteiten bedoeld in artikelen 3 en 5 van het Koninklijk besluit van 28 december 2006 inzake specifieke beperkende maatregelen tegen bepaalde personen en entiteiten met het oog op de strijd tegen de financiering van het terrorisme, *BS* 8 november 2022, 81483

Arrêté du Gouvernement de la Communauté française du 17 mai 2017 portant exécution du décret du 13 octobre 2016 relatif à l'agrément et au subventionnement des partenaires apportant de l'aide aux justiciables, *BS* 7 juni 2017, 62217

Arrêté ministériel du 17 mai 2017 portant exécution de l'arrêté du Gouvernement de la Communauté française du 17 mai 2017 portant exécution du décret du 13 octobre 2016 relatif à l'agrément et au subventionnement des partenaires apportant de l'aide aux justiciables, *BS* 9 juni 2017, 63351

PARLIAMENTARY AND ADMINISTRATIVE DOCUMENTS

Parliamentary documents

Verslag namens de commissie voor de Justitie van 20 juni 1990 bij het ontwerp van wet tot wijziging van de artikelen 42, 43 en 505 van het Strafwetboek en tot invoeging van een artikel 43*bis* in hetzelfde Wetboek, *Gedr.St.* Senaat 1989-90, nr. 890/2

Memorie van Toelichting bij wetsontwerp van 12 maart 1997 betreffende criminele organisaties, 96/97 nr. 49-954/1

Advies van de Raad van State bij wetsontwerp van 12 maart 1997 betreffende criminele organisaties, 96/97 nr. 49-954/1, 13

Verslag namens de commissie voor Justitie bij wetsontwerp van 12 maart 1997 betreffende criminele organisaties, 96/97 nr. 49-954/6

Advies 28.026/2, van de Raad van State bij wetsontwerp van 12 maart 1997 betreffende criminele organisaties, 96/97 nr. 49-954/24, 2

Memorie van Toelichting bij het wetsvoorstel van 20 maart 2000 tot wijziging van het Strafwetboek en tot invoering van de dienstverlening en de opleiding als gevangenisvervangende straffen, *Parl.St.* Kamer 1999-2000, 50-549/001, 4

Memorie van Toelichting bij wetsontwerp van 6 oktober 2003 betreffende terroristische misdrijven, *Parl.St.* Kamer 2003, nr. 51-0258/001, 4

Advies Raad van State bij wetsontwerp van 6 oktober 2003 betreffende terroristische misdrijven, *Parl.St.* Kamer 2003, nr. 51-0258/001

Advies 34.362/4 van de Raad van State bij wetsontwerp van 6 oktober 2003 betreffende terroristische misdrijven, *Parl.St.* Kamer 2003, nr. 51-0258/001, 22

Amendementen bij het wetsontwerp betreffende terroristische misdrijven van 21 oktober 2003, *Parl.St.* Kamer 2003, nr. 51-0258/003

Verslag namens de commissie van justitie bij wetsontwerp van 6 oktober 2003 betreffende terroristische misdrijven, *Parl.St.* Kamer 2003, nr. 51-0258/004

Verslag namens de commissie voor de Justitie van 3 december 2003 bij het wetsontwerp betreffende terroristische misdrijven, *Parl.St.* Senaat 2003-04, nr. 3-332/3

Amendementen bij wetsontwerp van 9 maart 2005 tot wijziging van diverse bepalingen met het oog op de versterking van de strijd tegen mensenhandel en mensensmokkel, *Parl.St.* Kamer 2004-2005, nr. 51-1560/004

Verslag namens de commissie voor de justitie van 13 maart 2007 bij Wetsontwerp betreffende de terbeschikkingstelling van de strafuitvoeringsrechtbank, *Parl.St.* Senaat 2006-2007, nr. 3-2054/4

Memorie van Toelichting bij wetsontwerp van 13 november 2012 tot wijziging van Titel 1ter van het Strafwetboek, *Parl.St.* Kamer 2012-2013, nr. 53-2502/001, 4

Advies nr. 51 806/3 van de Raad van State van 18 september 2012 bij wetsontwerp van 13 november 2012 tot wijziging van Titel 1ter van het Strafwetboek, *Parl.St.* Kamer 2012-2013, nr. 53-2502/001, 22

Memorie van Toelichting van 8 januari 2014 bij het wetsontwerp tot invoering van de probatie als autonome straf in het Strafwetboek, tot wijziging van het Wetboek van strafvordering, het Gerechtelijk Wetboek en de wet van 29 juni 1964 betreffende de opschorting, het uitstel en de probatie, *Parl.St.* Kamer, 2013-14, 53-3274/001, 4

Memorie van Toelichting bij het wetsontwerp van 16 juni 2015 houdende wijziging van de wet van 19 juli 1991 betreffende de bevolkingsregisters, de identiteitskaarten, de vreemdelingenkaarten en de verblijfsdocumenten en tot wijziging van de wet van 8 augustus 1983 tot regeling van een Rijksregister van de natuurlijke personen, *Parl.St.* Kamer 2014-15, nr. 54-1170/001, 4

Memorie van Toelichting bij wetsontwerp van 22 juni 2015 tot versterking van de strijd tegen terrorisme, *Parl.St.* Kamer 2014-15, nr. 54-1198/001, 4

Advies 57.127/AV van de Raad van State van 24 maart 2015, *Parl.St.* Kamer 2014-15, nr. 54-1198/001, 13

Memorie van Toelichting bij wetsontwerp van 23 juni 2015 tot wijziging van het Consulair Wetboek, *Parl.St.* Kamer 2014-2015, nr. 54-1200/001, 4

Memorie van Toelichting bij het wetsontwerp van 23 oktober 2015 houdende wijzigingen van het strafrecht en de strafvordering en houdende diverse bepalingen inzake justitie, *Parl.St.* Kamer 2015-16, nr. 54 1418/001, 4

Amendementen van 24 november 2015 bij wetsontwerp houdende diverse financiële bepalingen, houdende de oprichting van een administratieve dienst met boekhoudkundige autonomie "Sociale activiteiten", en houdende een bepaling inzake de gelijkheid van vrouwen en mannen, *Parl.St.* Kamer 2015-16, nr. 54-1459/002

Verslag namens de Commissie voor de Financiën en de Begroting van 7 december 2015 bij wetsontwerp houdende diverse financiële bepalingen, houdende de oprichting van een administratieve dienst met boekhoudkundige autonomie "Sociale activiteiten", en houdende een bepaling inzake de gelijkheid van vrouwen en mannen, *Parl.St.* Kamer 2015-16, nr. 54-1459/005

Samenvatting van wetsvoorstel van 13 januari 2016 tot wijziging van het Strafwetboek wat betreft de bestraffing van terrorisme, *Parl.St.* Kamer 2015-2016, nr. 54-1579/001, 1

Toelichting bij wetsvoorstel van 13 januari 2016 tot wijziging van het Strafwetboek wat betreft de bestraffing van terrorisme, *Parl.St.* Kamer 2015-2016, nr. 54-1579/001, 3

Amendementen van 7 juli 2016 bij wetsvoorstel van 13 januari 2016 tot wijziging van het Strafwetboek wat betreft de bestraffing van terrorisme, *Parl.St.* Kamer 2015-2016, nr. 54-1579/005

Advies 59.789/3 van de Raad van State van 19 juli 2016 bij wetsvoorstel van 13 januari 2016 tot wijziging van het Strafwetboek wat betreft de bestraffing van terrorisme, *Parl.St.* Kamer 2015-2016, nr. 54-1579/006

Amendementen van 6 oktober 2016 bij wetsvoorstel tot wijziging van het Strafwetboek wat betreft de bestraffing van terrorisme, *Parl.St.* Kamer 2015-2016, nr. 54-1579/007

Verslag van de eerste lezing van 20 oktober 2016 namens de tijdelijke commissie "terrorismebestrijding" bij wetsvoorstel tot wijziging van het Strafwetboek wat betreft de bestraffing van terrorisme, *Parl.St* Kamer 2015-2016, nr. 54-1579/008

Derde tussentijds verslag over het onderdeel "veiligheidsarchitectuur" van 15 juni 2017 van de parlementaire onderzoekscommissie belast met het onderzoek naar de omstandigheden die hebben geleid tot de terroristische aanslagen van 22 maart 2016 in de luchthaven Brussel-Nationaal en in het metrostation Maalbeek te Brussel, met inbegrip van de evolutie en de aanpak van de strijd tegen het radicalisme en de terroristische dreiging, *Parl.St.* Kamer 2016-2017, nr. 54-1752/008

Vierde tussentijds verslag van 23 oktober 2017 over het onderdeel "radicalisme" namens de parlementaire onderzoekscommissie belast met het onderzoek naar de omstandigheden die hebben geleid tot de terroristische aanslagen van 22 maart 2016 in de luchthaven Brussel-Nationaal en in het metrostation Maalbeek te Brussel, met inbegrip van de evolutie en de aanpak van de strijd tegen het radicalisme en de terroristische dreiging, *Parl.St.* Kamer 2017-2018, nr. 54-1752/009

Memorie van Toelichting bij wetsontwerp van 6 juli 2016 houdende diverse bepalingen ter bestrijding van terrorisme (III), *Parl.St.* Kamer 2015-2016, nr. 54-1951/001, 4

Advies nr. 59 147/3 van de Raad van State van 22 april 2016 bij wetsontwerp van 6 juli 2016 houdende diverse bepalingen ter bestrijding van terrorisme (III), *Parl.St.* Kamer 2015-2016, nr. 54-1951/001, 19

Memorie van Toelichting bij wetsontwerp van 12 december 2016 tot wijziging van de wet van 15 december 1980 betreffende de toegang tot het grondgebied, het verblijf, de vestiging en de verwijdering van vreemdelingen, met het doel de bescherming van de openbare orde en de nationale veiligheid te versterken, *Parl.St.* kamer 2016-2017, nr. 54-2215/001, 4

Beknopt Verslag Commissie voor de Justitie van 1 februari 2017, CRABV 54 COM 581

Vr. en Antw. Kamer 2016-17, *Bull.* nr. 105, 10 februari 2017, 191.

Memorie van Toelichting van 23 oktober 2017 bij wetsontwerp tot wijziging van de wet van 20 juli 1990 betreffende de voorlopige hechtenis voor wat de onmiddellijke aanhouding betreft en tot invoering van de beveiligingsperiode, *Parl.St.* Kamer 2017-2018, nr. 54-2731/001

Wetsvoorstel van 18 januari 2018 tot wijziging van het Strafwetboek teneinde zelfinstructie in het kader van terrorisme strafbaar te stellen, *Parl.St.* Kamer 2017-2018, nr. 54-2900/001

Beknopt Verslag Commissie voor de binnenlandse zaken, de algemene zaken en het openbaar ambt 28 februari 2018, CRABV 54 COM 830

Voorstel van resolutie van 27 november 2018 tot actief opsporen en repatriëren van de kinderen van Belgische Syriëstrijders, *Parl.St.* Kamer 2018-2019, nr. 54-3399/001

Schriftelijke vraag nr. 6-2224 van Lionel Bajart (Open Vld) d.d. 15 januari 2019 aan de minister van Justitie, belast met de Regie der Gebouwen, *Vr. en Antw.* Senaat 2018-19.

Wetsvoorstel van 6 februari 2019 houdende diverse bepalingen in strafzaken en inzake erediensten, *Parl.St.* Kamer 2018-2019, nr. 54-3515/001

Toelichting bij wetsvoorstel van 6 februari 2019 houdende diverse bepalingen in strafzaken en inzake erediensten, *Parl.St.* Kamer 2018-2019, nr. 54-3515/001, 3

Toelichting bij wetsvoorstel van 20 februari 2019 tot wijziging van de wet van 21 december 2013 houdende het Consulair Wetboek en van de wet van 10 februari 2015 met betrekking tot geautomatiseerde verwerkingen van persoonsgegevens die noodzakelijk zijn voor de Belgische paspoorten en reisdocumenten, *Parl.St.* Kamer 2018-2019, nr. 54-3574/001, 20

Toelichting van 27 februari 2019 bij wetsvoorstel houdende diverse bepalingen inzake asiel en migratie en tot wijziging van de wet van 15 december 1980 betreffende de toegang tot het grondgebied, het verblijf, de vestiging en de verwijdering van vreemdelingen, *Parl.St.* Kamer 2018-2019, nr. 54-3618/001

Verslag van de eerste lezing namens de commissie voor de binnenlandse zaken, de algemene zaken en het openbaar ambt van 25 maart 2019 bij wetsvoorstel houdende diverse bepalingen inzake asiel en migratie en tot wijziging van de wet van 15 december 1980 betreffende de toegang tot het grondgebied, het verblijf, de vestiging en de verwijdering van vreemdelingen, *Parl.St.* Kamer 2018-2019, nr. 54-3618/003

Amendementen van 14 maart 2019 bij wetsvoorstel houdende diverse financiële bepalingen, *Parl.St.* Kamer 2018-19, nr. 54-3624/002

Verslag namens de Commissie voor de Financiën en de Begroting van 27 maart 2019 bij wetsvoorstel houdende diverse financiële bepalingen en wetsvoorstel tot wijziging van de wet van 22 februari 1998 tot vaststelling van het organiek statuut van de Nationale Bank van België, teneinde het College van Censoren af te schaffen, *Parl.St.* Kamer 2018-19, nr. 54-3624/004

Wetsvoorstel van 1 oktober 2019 tot wijziging van de wet van 20 juli 1990 betreffende de voorlopige hechtenis aangaande de onmiddellijke aanhouding, *Parl.St.* Kamer 2019, 55-0489/001

Amendementen van 5 november 2019 bij tot wijziging van de wet van 20 juli 1990 betreffende de voorlopige hechtenis aangaande de onmiddellijke aanhouding, *Parl.St.* Kamer 2019, 55-0489/005

Voorstel van Resolutie van 22 oktober 2019 betreffende het terughalen van kinderen van Syriëstrijders, *Parl.St.* Kamer 2019-2020, nr. 55-674/001, 3 and 4;

Toelichting bij wetsvoorstel van 21 november 2019 tot wijziging van het Strafwetboek met het oog op de uitbreiding van de lijst met misdrijven die in aanmerking komen voor de facultatieve terbeschikkingstelling van de strafuitvoeringsrechtbank tot alle terrorismemisdrijven, *Parl.St.* Kamer 2019-2020, nr. 55-0777/001

Verslag namens de commissie voor buitenlandse betrekkingen van 10 januari 2020 betreffende de veiligheidssituatie in de kampen in noord-syrië en het lot van de belgische foreign terrorist fighters, gelet op het turkse militaire offensief, *Parl.St.* Kamer 2019-2020, nr. 55-926/001

Wetsvoorstel van 23 januari 2020 tot wijziging van het Strafwetboek wat de strafmaat voor misdrijven door terroristische groepen betreft, *Parl.St.* Kamer 2019-20, nr. 55-0962/001

Wetsvoorstel van 28 januari 2020 tot wijziging van het Strafwetboek, teneinde de terbeschikkingstelling van de strafuitvoeringsrechtbank uit te breiden tot alle terroristische misdrijven, *Parl.St.* Kamer 2019-2020, nr. 55-0969/001

Voorstel tot herziening van artikel 150 van de Grondwet teneinde de juryrechtspraak voor terroristische misdaden af te schaffen, *Parl.St.* Kamer 2019-2020, nr. 55-1287/001 and 003

Verslag namens de commissie voor justitie hoorzittingen de deradicaliserings-, exit- en resocialisatieprogramma's binnen de belgische penitentiaire instellingen, *Parl.St.* Kamer 2019-2020, nr. 55-1501/001

Beknopt verslag plenumvergadering Kamer van volksvertegenwoordigers 4 maart 2021, CRABV 55 PLEN 90

Memorie van toelichting bij wetsontwerp van 25 april 2022 tot uitstel van de inwerkingtreding van de bepalingen inzake de uitvoering van vrijheidsstraffen van drie jaar of minder, *Parl.St.* Kamer 2021-2022, nr. 55-2645/001

Administrative documents

COL7/2013 – De wet van 27 december 2012 houdende diverse bepalingen betreffende Justitie, inzonderheid: TITEL VIII Wijziging van de wet van 29 juni 1964 betreffende de opschorting, het uitstel en de probatie, 13 March 2013

COL17/2014 – De terbeschikkingstelling van de strafuitvoeringsrechtbank, 17 July 2014

COL 11/2016 – Weigering van afgifte, intrekking en ongeldigverklaring van identiteitskaarten van Belgen die het voorwerp uitmaken van strafdossiers, 26 May 2016

COL 12/2016 – Weigering van afgifte en intrekking van reisdocumenten (paspoorten) van personen die het voorwerp uitmaken van strafdossiers, 26 May 2916

COL 13/2016 – Administratieve bevriezing van tegoeden en economische middelen van personen en entiteiten met het oog op de strijd tegen de financiering van het terrorisme – nationale en internationale lijsten, 26 May 2016

COL 17/2016 – Elektronisch toezicht als autonome straf, updated version 18 October 2018

COL 18/2016 – Invoering van de probatie als autonome straf, 23 June 2016

COL10/2018 – Voorwaarden die opgelegd kunnen worden aan personen die vervolgd of veroordeeld worden voor feiten van terrorisme of die gelinkt worden aan gewelddadig extremisme, 28 June 2018

Collectieve brief DG EPI nr. 121 van 29 maart 2013 betreffende wijziging van de Wet Externe Rechtspositie

Collectieve brief DG EPI nr. 137 van 29 april 2016 over het elektronisch toezicht als autonome straf

Collectieve brief DG EPI nr. 138 van 29 april 2016 over de probatie als autonome straf

Collectieve brief DG EPI nr. 149 van 24 juni 2019 over de bevriezing van tegoeden van gedetineerden

Collectieve brief DG EPI nr. 150 van 22 augustus 2019 over pilootproject Transitiehuizen

Collectieve brief DG EPI nr. 154 van 18 mei 2020 over de bevriezing van tegoeden van gedetineerden

Collectieve brief DF EPI nr. 161 van 11 augustus 2022 over Wet externe rechtspositie – toelichting bij de procedure voor de toekenning van strafuitvoeringsmodaliteiten door de strafuitvoeringsrechter (SUR) en de strafuitvoeringsrechtbank (SURB)

DG EPI, "Bijzondere instructies extremisme", 2 oktober 2018

DG EPI, "Bijzondere instructies", 12 februari 2021

Ministeriële omzendbrief nr. 1792 van 11 januari 2007 betreffende Basiswet – Titel VI: orde, veiligheid en gebruik van dwang

Ministeriële omzendbrief nr. 1803 (III) van 25 juli 2008 betreffende de reglementering van elektronisch toezicht als strafuitvoeringsmodaliteit

Ministeriële omzendbrief nr. 1804 van 25 juli 2008 betreffende samenwerkingsafspraken tussen het directoraat-generaal Penitentiaire Inrichtingen en het directoraat-generaal Justitiehuizen betreffende de uitvoering van beperkte detentie.

Ministeriële omzendbrief nr. 1813 van 18 november 2011 betreffende de terbeschikkingstelling van de strafuitvoeringsrechtbank

Ministeriële omzendbrief nr. ET/SE-2 van 17 juli 2013 over de reglementering inzake het elektronisch toezicht als strafuitvoeringsmodaliteit voor gevangenisstraffen wanneer het totaal in uitvoering zijnde gevangenisstraffen drie jaar niet overschrijdt.

Ministeriële omzendbrief nr. 1817 van 15 juli 2015 over de voorlopige invrijheidstelling van veroordeelden die één of meer vrijheidsstraffen ondergaan waarvan het uitvoerbaar gedeelte drie jaar of minder bedraagt

Ministeriële omzendbrief nr. ET/SE-2bis van 26 november 2015 over de reglementering inzake het elektronisch toezicht als strafuitvoeringsmodaliteit voor gevangenisstraffen wanneer het totaal in uitvoering zijnde gevangenisstraffen drie jaar niet overschrijdt;

Ministeriële omzendbrief nr. ET/SE-2ter van 29 april 2016 over de reglementering inzake het elektronisch toezicht als strafuitvoeringsmodaliteit voor gevangenisstraffen wanneer het totaal in uitvoering zijnde gevangenisstraffen drie jaar niet overschrijdt;

Ministeriële omzendbrief nr. 1817bis van 29 april 2016 over de voorlopige invrijheidstelling van veroordeelden die één of meer vrijheidsstraffen ondergaan waarvan het uitvoerbaar gedeelte drie jaar of minder bedraagt

Ministeriële omzendbrief nr. ET/SE-2quater van 4 juli 2017 over de reglementering inzake het elektronisch toezicht als strafuitvoeringsmodaliteit voor gevangenisstraffen wanneer het totaal in uitvoering zijnde gevangenisstraffen drie jaar niet overschrijdt.

Omzendbrief van de minister van Justitie, de minister van Binnenlandse Zaken, de minister van Buitenlandse Zaken en de minister van Defensie van 29 april 2016 betreffende het overmaken van informatie aan de FOD Buitenlandse Zaken met het oog op de toepassing van de regels inzake de weigering van afgifte en de intrekking van reisdocumenten

Gemeenschappelijke omzendbrief voor een globale aanpak van geweldadige radicalisering en extremisme en van terrorisme, 18 februari 2019

Circulaire van 7 september 2015 inzake de tenuitvoerlegging van de artikelen 3 en 5 van het koninklijk besluit van 28 december 2006 inzake specifieke beprekende maatregelen tegen bepaalde personen en entiteiten met het oog op de strijd tegen de financiering van het terrorisme

F.O.D. Justitie, "Actionplan: approach to radicalisation in prisons", 11 March 2015, 3, https://justitie.belgium.be/sites/default/files/downloads/Plland%27action radicalisation-prison-NL.pdf

Vlaams strategisch plan hulp- en dienstverlening aan gedetineerden en geïnterneerden 2020-2025, VR 2020 1311 DOC.1230/3BIS

Case law and related documents

International and supranational case law

Lawless v. Ireland (no. 3) App no 332/57 (ECHR, 1 July 1961)
X v UK App no 3898 (ECHR, 22 July 1970)
Ireland v UK App no 5310/71 (ECHR, 18 January 1978)
Müller v Switzerland App no 10737/84 (ECHR, 24 May 1988)
RB v UK App no 19628/92 (ECHR, 29 June 1992)
Brannigan and McBride v UK App no 14553/89 and 14554/89 (ECHR, 25 May 1993)
Kokkinakis v Greece App no 14307/88 (ECHR, 25 May 1993)
SW v UK App no 20166/92 (ECHR, 22 November 1995)
Cantoni v France App no 17862/91 (ECHR, 11 November 1996)
Aksoy v Turkey App no 21987/93 (ECHR, 18 December 1996)
A et al v UK App no 3455/05 (ECHR Grand Chamber, 19 February 2009)
Al-Jedda v UK App no 27021/08 (ECHR Grand Chamber, 7 July 2011)
Nada v Switzerland App no 10593/08 (ECHR Grand Chamber, 12 September 2012)
Al-Dulimi and Montana Management Inc v Switzerland App no 5809/08 (ECHR Grand Chamber, 21 June 2016)
Case C-402/05 and C-415/05 *Yassin Abdullah Kadi and Al Barakaat International Foundation v Council of the European Union and Commission of the European Communities* [2008] CJEU ECLI:EU:C:2008:461.
Case C-584/10, C-593/10 and C-595/10 *European Commission et al v Yassin Abdullah Kad*i [2013] CJEU ECLI:EU:C:2013:518;
Sayadi v. Belgium UN Doc CCPR/C/94/D/1472/2006 (Official Case No) IHRL 3216 (UNHRC 2008)
Guide to the case-law of the European Court of Human Rights on Terrorism (2020)
Declaration contained in a letter from the Permanent Representative of France to the Council of Europe, dated 24 November 2015, registered at the Secretariat General on 24 November 2015, https://www.coe.int/en/web/conventions/full-list?module=treaty-detail&treatynum=005

Belgian national case law

Arbitragehof 30 juni 2005, 116/2005
Arbitragehof 13 juli 2005, 125/2005
GwH 19 september 2014, 122/2014, *NjW* 2014, 840
GwH 18 december 2014, 185/2014

GwH 28 januari 2015, 9/2015, *TVW* 2015, 179
GwH 26 juli 2017, 102/2017
GwH 21 december 2017, 148/2017
GwH 18 januari 2018, 8/2018, *NjW* 2018, 299-304, noot W Yperman
GwH 7 februari 2018, 15/2018
GwH 7 februari 2018, 16/2018
GwH 15 maart 2018, 31/2018, *NjW* 2018, 477
GwH 19 maart 2019, 44/2019
GwH 19 november 2020, 147/2020, *NjW* 2021, 265, noot Careel
GwH 10 juni 2021, 86/2021, *Rechtskundig Weekblad* 2021-2022, 755
GwH 14 oktober 2021, 138/2021, *Rev.dr.pén.* 2022, 29, noot Beernaert
Cass. 24 maart 1908, *Pas.* 1908, 142
Cass. 5 mei 1913, *Pas.* 1913, I, 207
Cass. 21 november 1927, *Pas.* 1928, I, 20
Cass. 10 maart 1930, *Pas.* 1930, I, 156
Cass. 7 september 1935, *Pas.* 1935, 334
Cass. 7 december 1971, *Pas.* 1972, I, 341
Cass. 21 oktober 1981, *Arr.Cass.* 1981-82, 271
Cass. 13 november 1983, *Arr.Cass.* 1984-85, 363
Cass. 3 april 1984, *Arr.Cass.* 1983-84, 1023
Cass. 13 november 1985, *Arr.Cass.* 1985-86, 340
Cass. 4 februari 1986, *Pas.*, 1986, I, 671
Cass. 12 mei 1987, *Arr.Cass.* 1986-87, 1194, concl. Du Jardin
Cass. 17 januari 1990, Arr.Cass. 1989-90, 309
Cass. 6 oktober 1993, *Arr.Cass.* 1993, 811
Cass. 13 december 1994, *RW* 1995-96, 533, noot B Spriet
Cass. 7 februari 1995, AJT 1995-96, 248, noot D Voorhoof
Cass. 9 mei 1995, *Arr.Cass.* 1995, 46
Cass. 31 mei 1995, P.94.868.F
Cass. 12 november 1996, P.95.0950.N
Cass. 27 april 1999, *Arr.Cass.* 1999, 568
Cass. 3 september 2003, P.03.515.F
Cass. 18 november 2003, *Arr.Cass.* 2003, afl. 11, 2125, concl M Timperman
Cass. 3 november 2004, *RW* 2005-06, 1583, noot C De Roy
Cass. 9 november 2004, *JT* 2004, afl. 6157, 856, noot
Cass. 15 november 2006, *Pas.* 2006, 2341
Cass. 13 juni 2007, P.07.0704.F
Cass. 27 juni 2007, P.07.0333.F
Cass. 8 april 2008, P.08.0006.N

Cass. 24 juni 2008, *Arr.Cass.* 2008, 1654
Cass. 17 december 2008, P.08.1281.F
Cass. 11 maart 2009, *Rev.dr.pén.* 2009, 748
Cass. 24 november 2010, AR P.10.1145.F
Cass. 6 maart 2012, *NjW* 2012, 341
Cass 29 januari 2013, P.12.1961.N
Cass. 29 januari 2013, P.12.1988.N
Cass. 29 oktober 2013, *NjW* 2014, 406, noot Eric Brewaeys
Cass. 14 april 2015, *RW* 2016-17, 622, noot De Smet
Cass. 8 oktober 2014, P.14.0955.F
Cass. 24 februari 2014, S.13.0031.N
Cass. 16 december 2014, P.14.1048.N
Cass. 13 september 2016, *RW* 2017-2018, 421
Cass. 8 november 2016, P.16.0958.N
Cass. 17 januari 2017, *RW* 2018-2019, 654, noot De Smet
Cass. 4 oktober 2017, *NC* 2018, 303
Cass. 5 januari 2021, *T.Strafr.* 2021, 232, noot Daeninck
Cass. 10 maart 2021, *JLMB* 2021, 1122, noot F Kuty
Cass. 28 april 2021, P.21.0029.F
Cass. 15 juni 2021, *RABG* 2021, 1756, noot
Cass. 5 oktober 2021, P.21.0881.N
Cass. 3 november 2021, P.21.1302.F
Cass. 18 januari 2022, P.21.1291.N
Cass. 19 januari 2022, *JT* 2022, 143
Raad van State, 29 November 2917, nr. 239.266, *Bensouda Koraïchi Amal v. the Belgian state.*
Antwerpen 18 oktober 1990, *RW* 1990-91, 856, noot B Spriet
Brussel 19 januari 2007, *T.Strafr.* 2008, 281, noot F Schuermans
Antwerpen 8 januari 2014, *onuitg.*
Brussel 28 mei 2015, *onuitg.*
Gent 26 januari 2016, *onuitg.*
Brussel 18 november 2016, *onuitg.*
Brussel 31 maart 2017, *onuitg*
Brussel 2 juni 2017, *onuitg*
Luik (6e kamer) 18 oktober 2017, *JLMB* 2017, 1878
Antwerpen 7 februari 2008, *onuitg.*
Brussel 12 September 2018, *TJK* 2019, 72
Antwerpen 23 oktober 2018, *RW* 2019-20, nr. 27, 1070
Brussel 21 december 2018, *onuitg.*

Brussel 5 maart 2020, nr. 2019/KR/3, *TJK* 2020, 192

Brussel 5 maart 2020, nr. 2019/KR/60, *TJK* 2020, 186

Brussel 8 oktober 2020, RG 2014/AR/2257, unpublished, refered to in Comité T, 'Rapport 2021: Evaluation des mesures visant à lutter contre le terrorisme à la lumière des droits humains', 94.

Brussel 12 april 2021, *onuitg.*

Antwerpen 14 december 2021, *RW* 2021-22, 955

KI Brussel 14 september 2017, *RW* 2017-18, 1611, noot J Wouters and T Van Poecke

KI Brussel 8 maart 2019, *onuitg.*

Corr. Antwerpen 23 februari 1993, *T.R.V.* 1994, 195, noot W Devroe and A Rombouts

Corr. Antwerpen 14 april 1994, *T.R.V.* 1994, 285, noot F Hellemans

Corr. Brugge 28 februari 2006, *T.Strafr.* 2006, 159, noot P De Hert

Corr. Mechelen 5 December 2012, *onuitg.*

Corr. Brussel 16 Februari 2006, *onuitg.*

Corr. Brussel 14 mei 2014, *onuitg*

Corr. Brussel 21 mei 2014, *onuitg.*

Corr. Brussel 14 oktober 2014, *onuitg.*

Corr. Antwerpen (afd. Antwerpen) 11 februari 2015, *onuitg.*

Corr. Antwerpen 30 maart 2015, *onuitg.*

Corr. Antwerpen 30 juni 2015, *onuitg.*

Corr. Brussel 25 november 2015, *onuitg.*

Corr. Antwerpen (afd. Antwerpen) 25 januari 2016, *onuitg.*

Corr. Brussel 9 maart 2016, *onuitg.*

Corr. Brussel 3 mei 2016, *onuitg.*

Corr. Brussel 5 juli 2016, *onuitg.*

Corr. West-Vlaanderen (afd. Brugge) (vakantiekamer) 14 juli 2016, TGR-TWVR 2016, afl. 5, 386

Corr. Brussel 8 mei 2017, *onuitg.*

Corr. Brussel 8 mei 2017, *onuitg.*

Corr. Charleroi 22 november 2017, *onuitg.*

Corr. Limburg (afd. Hasselt) 23 juni 2017, *Limburgs Rechtsleven* 2018, 51

Corr. Oost-Vlaanderen (afd. Gent) 16 oktober 2017, *NjW* 2017, 805, noot W Yperman en S Royer

Corr. Mechelen 4 januari 2018, *onuitg.*

Corr. Brussel 1 maart 2018, *onuitg.*

Corr. Antwerpen 18 maart 2018, *onuitg.*

Corr. Brussel 29 maart 2018, *onuitg.*

Corr. Mons 14 mei 2018, *onuitg.*

Corr. Brussel 11 juni 2018, *onuitg*

Corr. West-Vlaanderen (afd. Brugge) 26 juli 2018, *onuitg.*
Corr. Oost-Vlaanderen (afd. Dendermonde) 14 december 2018, *onuitg.*
Corr. Antwerpen 17 december 2018, *onuitg.*
Corr. Luik 18 januari 2019, *onuitg.*
Corr. Brussel 10 mei 2019, *NjW* 2019, 663, noot W Yperman
Corr. Hainaut 22 maart 2021, *JLMB* 2022, 444
Eerste aanleg Brussel 26 april 2019, *NjW* 2020, 179, noot Vilain
Kortgeding Brussel 29 juli 2018, *onuitg.*
Kortgeding Brussel 26 december 2018, *onuitg.*
Kortgeding Brussel 7 juni 2019, *onuitg.*
Kortgeding Brussel 11 juni 2019, *onuitg.*
Strafuitvoeringsrechtbank Brussel 1 oktober 2018, *JT* 2018, 959
RK Brussel 3 november 2016, *onuitg.*
Raad voor Vreemdelingenbetwistingen 21 december 2020, *T. Vreemd.* 2021, 226
Commission d'appel francophone 24 décembre 2020, *JLMB* 2021, 1796
Concl EH bij Cass. 15 februari 2006, P.05.1594

BELGIAN LEGAL SCHOLARSHIP

Arnou P, 'Voorbedachten Rade', *Strafrecht en strafvordering. Artikelsgewijze commentaar met overzicht van rechtspraak en rechtsleer* (Wolters Kluwer 1990)

Arnou P, 'Nacht', *Strafrecht en strafvordering. Artikelsgewijze commentaar met overzicht van rechtspraak en rechtsleer* (Wolters Kluwer 2010)

Beernaert M-A, 'La Loi Du 19 Décembre 2003 Relative Aux Infractions Terroristes : Quand Le Droit Pénal Belge Évolue Sous La Dictée de l'Union Européenne' (2004) 24 Journal des tribunaux 585

Beernaert M-A, 'Renforcement de l'arsenal législatif anti-terroriste: entre symboles et prévention' [2015] Journal des tribunaux 833

Beernaert M-A, 'L'individualisation dans le prononcé et l'exécution de la peine : machine arrière toute ?', *La loi « pot-pourri II » : un recul de civilisation ?* (Anthemis 2016)

Beernaert M-A, *Manuel de droit pénitentiaire* (Anthemis 2019)

Beernaert M-A, 'Correctionnalisation Des Crimes et Récidive Légale : Les Problèmes Subsistent, Les Solutions Aussi…' [2022] Revue de Droit Pénal et de Criminologie (Rev. dr. pén.) 38

Berkmoes H, 'Bestanddelen van de Strafbare Poging' in M De Busscher and others (eds), *Strafrecht: duiding* (Larcier 2018)

Berkmoes H, 'De Niet-Strafbare Poging' in M De Busscher and others (eds), *Strafrecht: duiding* (Larcier 2018)

Blaise N and Delhaise E, 'La répression des voyages à visée terroriste à l'aune des droits fondamentaux' [2019] Journal Tribunaux 173

Bonfond O, 'Incitation au terrorisme: qui trop embrasse, mal étreint' (2018) 26 Jurisprudence de Liege, Mons et Bruxelles 1237

Borgers M, 'Een Gevaarzettingsvereiste Voor Terroristische Misdrijven?' in Toine Sapens, Marc Groenhuijsen and Tijs Kooijmans (eds), *Universalis: Liber amicorum Cyrille Fijnaut* (Intersentia 2011)

Bosly S and Van Ravenstein M, 'L'harmonisation Des Incriminations' in Daniel Flore (ed), *Actualités de droit pénal Européen* (La Charte 2003)

Brewaeys E, 'Persmisdrijf via Internet' (Noot Onder Cass. 29 October 2013)' [2014] Nieuw Juridisch Weekblad 408

Broek M, Hazelhorst M and de Zanger W, 'Asset Freezing: Smart Sanction or Criminal Charge?' (2010) 27 Merkourios : Utrecht Journal of International and European Law 18

Bruggeman W, 'Radicalisering' (2020) R30 Postal Memorialis – Lexicon strafrecht, strafvordering en bijzondere wetten 66

Cesoni ML, 'Terrorisme et Involutions Démocratiques' [2002] Rev Dr Pén Crim 141

Cesoni ML, 'Les "Infractions Terroristes": De La Répression Des Actes à La Police de La Pensée' in Christian De Valkeneer and Henri D Bosly (eds), *Actualités en droit pénal 2019* (Larcier 2019)

Claes AL and Yperman W, 'Overzicht(elijk) – Recente Ontwikkelingen in de Contraterrorismewetgeving' [2022] Politie & Recht 69

Claes E, *Legaliteit en rechtsvinding in het strafrecht: Een grondslagentheoretische benadering* (Universitaire Pers Leuven 2003)

Clunan AL, 'The Fight against Terrorist Financing' (2006) 121 Political Science Quarterly 569

Cornelis L and Verstraeten R, 'Mag Er Nog Witgewassen Worden?' [1992] TBH 176

Daems T and Magis Y, 'Elektronisch toezicht en autonome probatie nader bekeken' in P Traest, A Verhage and G Vermeulen (eds), *Strafrecht en strafprocesrecht: doel of middel in een veranderde samenleving?* (Wolters Kluwer 2017)

Daeninck P, 'Over het verzoekschrift tot voorlopige invrijheidstelling na het instellen van hoger beroep tegen de beslissing ten gronde' (2021) 2021 Tijdschrift voor Strafrecht 232

Danziger Y, 'Changes in Methods of Freezing Funds of Terrorist Organisations since 9/11' [212] Journal of Money Laundering Control 210

De Brouwer A, 'Au-delà du contentieux disciplinaire' (2021) 2021 Revue de Jurisprudence de Liège, Mons et Bruxelles (JLMB) 1799

De Brucker L, 'Het Recht Op Consulaire Bijstand Vanuit Nationaal-, Europees- En Internationaalrechtelijk Perspectief. Naar Een Subjectief Recht Op Repatriëring Voor Kinderen van Syriëstrijders?' [2020] Tijdschrift Jeugd- en Kinderrechten 194

De Coensel S, 'De Wet Diverse Bepalingen in Strafzaken II: Terroristische misdrijven in lijn met de Europese verplichtingen?' (2019) 40 Panopticon 211

De Coensel S, *Counter-Terrorism & Criminal Law: A Normative Legitimacy Test of Terrorism-Related Offences on Expression, Information and Movement* (Maklu 2020)

De Groote J, 'De Bovengrens Der Fout En de Ondergrens van Het Opzet Met Bijzondere Aandacht Voor Het Eventueel Opzet: Een Doctrinale En Rechtsvergelijkende Analyse' (2017) special number April 2017 Nullum Crimen (NC) 66

De Herdt J, 'Bijzonder Strafrecht En Stratoemeting Na de Potpourri II-Wet' [2016] Nullum Crimen 189

De Hert P and Millen J, 'Terrorisme' (2013) VIII.2013 Qualifications et Jurisprudence Penales 1

De La Serna I, 'Des Infractions Terroristes', *Les Infractions* (Larcier 2013)

De La Serna I, 'Des infractions terroristes' in Christian De Valkeneer and Ignacio De La Serna, *À la découverte de la justice pénale : Paroles de juriste* (Larcier 2015)

De Nauw A, 'Titel Iter: Terroristische misdrijven', *Inleiding tot het bijzonder Strafrecht* (sixth edition, Kluwer 2010)

De Nauw A and Deruyck F, *Overzicht van Het Belgisch Algemeen Strafrecht* (die Keure 2015)

De Nauw A and Deruyck F, *Overzicht van het Belgisch algemeen strafrecht* (Die Keure / la Charte 2017)

De Nauw A and Kuty F, *Manuel de Droit Pénal Spécial* (Wolters Kluwer 2014)

De Nil N, Deruyck F and Meese J, 'Misdrijven', *Strafrecht geannoteerd* (die Keure 2020)

De Roy C, 'De strafbare poging als klassiek leerstuk in het raam van de hedendaagse strijd tegen het terrorisme (Noot Onder Cass. 3 november 2004)' (2005-2006) 69 Rechtskundig Weekblad 1584

De Shutter O, 'La Convention Européenne Des Droits de l'homme à l'épreuve de La Lutte Contre Le Terrorisme' in Emmanuelle Bribosia and Anne Weyembergh (eds), *La convention Européenne des droits de l'homme à l'épreuve de la lutte contre le terrorisme* (Bruylant-Nemesis 2002)

De Smet B, 'Het Ongedaan Verzet En de Vereiste van Kennisname van de Dagvaarding' [2018] Rechtskundig Weekblad 654

De Smet B, 'Het Begrip "Wettige Verschoning" van Artikel 187, § 6, 1° Sv. Als Criterium Voor Ongedaan Verzet' [2019] Tijdschrift voor Strafrecht 164

De Smet Ba, 'Het Verzet van de Beklaagde Die in Het Buitenland Is Aangehouden' [2016] Rechtskundig Weekblad 623

Decaigny T, 'Nieuwe correctionele hoofdstraffen: de straf onder elektronisch toezicht en de autonome probatiestraf' [2014] Tijdschrift voor Strafrecht 211

Decaigny T, 'Formele Aspecten van de Buitengewone Termijn Voor Verzet' [2016] Tijdschrift voor Strafrecht 237

Decaigny T, 'Relatieve Zwaarte, Toepassingsgebied En Duur' in M De Busscher and others (eds), *Strafrecht: duiding* (Larcier 2018)

Decaigny T, 'Vervangende Gevangenisstraf' in M De Busscher and others (eds), *Strafrecht: duiding* (Larcier 2018)

Decaigny T, in M De Busscher and others (eds), *Strafrecht: duiding* (Larcier 2018)

Declercq R, *Beginselen van Strafrechtspleging* (6de herwerkte ed., Kluwer 2014)

Dejemeppe B and Rigaux M-F, 'Lutte contre le terrorisme moderne : le contrôle des droits fondamentaux entre le marteau et l'enclume' in R Leysen and others (eds), *Semper perseverans – Liber amicorum André Alen* (Intersentia 2020)

Dekrem E, 'Naar Een Veralgemeende Strafbaarheid van Voorbereidende Handelingen?' [2020] Nullum Crimen 133

Delhaise E, *Infractions terroristes* (Larcier 2019)

Delhaise E and Fievet C, 'Frontières Intelligentes et Nouvelles Incriminations Pénales : L'Union Européenne Face à La Problématique Des « Foreign Terrorist Fighters »' (2017) 2017 Journal des tribunaux 113

Delhaise E, Remacle C and Thomas C, 'Après le califat, l'embarras' (2020) 6 La Revue Nouvelle 49

Delhaise E, Remacle C and Thomas C, 'Rapatriement Des Enfants Belges Du Califat : Droit et Sécurité En Tension' (2022) 49 La revue internationale de l'éducation familiale 41

Delmulle J and Guenter S, 'Gerechtelijke Aanpak Inzake Terrorisme', *Strafrecht en Strafprocesrecht* (Wolters Kluwer 2006)

Deruyck F, 'Witwassen', *Strafrecht en strafvordering. Artikelsgewijze commentaar met overzicht van rechtspraak en rechtsleer* (Wolters Kluwer)

Deruyck F and De Nauw A, *Inleiding Tot Het Bijzonder Strafrecht* (Kluwer 2020)

Desterbeck F and Van Droogbroek J, *De Inbeslagneming En Verbeurd¬verklaring in Strafzaken in België* (Wolters Kluwer 2017)

Devos D, 'Le Blanchiment Des Capitaux d'origine Criminelle' [1992] Bank Fin 201

Devroe W and Rombouts A, 'Wissel Als Witsel. De Beteugeling van Het Witwassen van Gelden via Geldwissel in Het Belgisch Financieel En Strafrecht (Noot Onder Corr. Antwerpen 23 Februari 1993)' [1994] TRV 199

Dewandeleer D, "Opzettelijk Doden En Opzettelijk Toebrengen van Lichamelijk Letsel (Art. 392 t/m 417 Sw.), Algemeen', *Postal Memorialis – Lexicon strafrecht, strafvordering en bijzondere wetten* (2001)

Dupont L, *Beginselen van Strafrecht, Deel I* (Acco 1983)

Fenwick H and Fenwick D, 'The Role of Derogations from the ECHR in the Current "War on Terror"' in Eran Shor and Stephen Hoadley (eds), *International Human Rights and Counter-Terrorism* (Springer 2019) http://link.springer.com/10.1007/978-981-10-3894-5_37-2 accessed 8 January 2020

Flore D, 'La Loi Du 19 Décembre 2003 Relative Aux Infractions Terroristes: Genèse, Principes et Conséquences', *Questions d'actualité de droit pénal et de procédure pénale* (Bruylant 2005)

Flore D, *Droit Pénal Européen: Les Enjeux d'une Justice Pénale Européenne* (Larcier 2008)

Fransen A and Kerkhofs J, 'Het Materieel Terrorismestrafrecht' in Jan Kerkhofs, Antoon Schotsaert and Philippe Van Linthout (eds), *Contra-terrorisme: De gerechtelijke aanpak van terrorisme in België* (Larcier 2018)

Fransen A and Kerkhofs J, 'Het Materieel Terrorismestrafrecht in België: De Misdrijven' (2018) 3 Tijdschrift voor Strafrecht 150

Fransen A, Kerkhofs J and Verrest P, *Terrorisme: Een analyse van het Belgische en Nederlandse Materieel Strafrecht* (Wolf Legal Publishers 2017)

Franssen V, 'Algemeen' in M De Busscher and others (eds), *Strafrecht: duiding* (Larcier 2018)

Franssen V, 'Begrip Politiek Misdrijf' in M De Busscher and others (eds), *Strafrecht: duiding* (Larcier 2018)

Funck J-F, 'Le tribunal de l'application des peines aujourd'hui et demain : nouvelles compétences (peines de trois ans ou moins), conditions d'octroi des mesures et révocation', *Actualités en procédure pénale : de l'audition à l'exécution* (Anthemis 2020)

Ganor B, 'Defining Terrorism: Is One Man's Terrorist Another Man's Freedom Fighter?' [2002] Police Practice and Research 287

Gless S, 'Fighting Terrorism in a "Rechtsstaat"' in Toine Sapens, Marc Groenhuijsen and Tijs Kooijmans (eds), *Universalis: Liber amicorum Cyrille Fijnaut* (Intersentia 2011)

Guild E, 'The Uses and Abuses of Counter-Terrorism Policies in Europe: The Case of the "Terrorist Lists"' (2008) 46 JCMS: Journal of Common Market Studies 173

Gyselaers L, *La participation Des Citoyens à La Fonction de Juger En Matière Pénale. Etude Comparative Du Droit Anglais, de Droit Belge et de Droit Français* (PhD thesis, KU Leuven 2011)

Gyselaers L, '(Digitale) Drukpersmisdrijven En de Bevoegdheidsproblematiek – Tijd Voor Een Wettelijke Correctionalisatie?' [2013] Limb. Rechtsl. 97

Hameeuw V, 'Strafbaarstelling van terroristische misdrijven: van Europees Kaderbesluit tot het Belgische Strafwetboek' [2005] Tijdschrift voor Strafrecht 2

Hellemans F, 'Witwassen: Een Strafbaar Maar Lonend Misdrijf? (Noot Onder Corr. Antwerpen 14 April 1994)' [1994] TRV 287

Hermans C and Millen J, 'Controle- En Veiligheid(s)Maatregelen in de Gevangenis' in T Daems and others (eds), *Quo vadis? Tien jaar basiswet gevangeniswezen en rechtspositie van gedetineerden* (Maklu 2015)

Hoffman B, *Inside Terrorism, Revised and Expanded Edition* (Columbia University Press 2006)

Horseele M and others, 'Recente Wijzigingen in Het Straf(Proces)Recht: Consequent Incoherent?', *Recht in beweging – 25ste VRG-Alumnidag* (Gompel&Svacina 2018)

Hossain S, 'Freezing Terrorism Assets: Increasing International Cooperation by Observing Procedural Due Process Notes & Comments' (2010-2011) 54 Howard Law Journal 437

Hudson A, 'Not a Great Asset: The UN Security Council's Counter-Terrorism Regime: Violating Human Rights' (2007) 25 Berkeley Journal of International Law 203

Hustin-Denies N, 'La Législation Belge Sur Le Blachiment de Capiteaux d'origine Criminelle: Un Instrument d'indemnisation Des Victimes et de Lutte Contre La Criminalité Organisée?' [1995] Ann dr Louv 53

Huysmans J and others, 'Grondwet (Uitreksel)', *Strafrecht geannoteerd* (die Keure 2020)

Jackson R, 'In Defence of "Terrorism": Finding a Way through a Forest of Misconceptions' [2011] Behavioral Sciences of Terrorism and Political Aggression 116

Kerkhofs A, 'Een adequaat vervolgingssysteem inzake drukpersmisdrijven' [2016] Nullum Crimen 64

Kerkhofs J, 'Noot Onder Corr. Hasselt 27 Juli 1999' [1999] Limb. Rechtsl. 264

Ketels B, 'De Strafrechtelijke Context van Risicovol Seksueel Gedrag' [2008] Tijdschrift voor Strafrecht 354

Ketels B, 'Titel Iter Terroristische Misdrijven' in Martine De Busscher and others (eds), *Strafrecht: Duiding* (Larcier 2018)

Krenc F, 'La Belgique "Condamnée" Pour La Première Fois Par Le Comité Des Droits de l'homme Sur Fond de Lutte Contre Le Terrorisme – Cap Sur Genève!' [2009] Journal des tribunaux 621

Kuty F, *Principes Généraux Du Droit Pénal Belge. Tome 1: La Loi Pénale* (3rd edn, Larcier 2018)

Kuty F, 'La Loi Du 21 Décembre 2017 Modiiant Diverses Dispositions En Vue d'instaurer Une Période de Sûreté. La Peine Irrémédiable, La Loi de La Désillusion ?' [2018] Revue de Droit Pénal et de Criminologie (Rev. dr. pén.) 573

Lamberigts S, 'Ongedaan Verzet: Eigen Schuld, Dikke Bult?' [2019] Tijdschrift voor Strafrecht 235

Lavaux S, 'Terrorisme: La Stratégie de l'union Européenne En Matière de Radicalisation et de Recrutement (Troisième partie)' [2015] Vigiles 114

Lavaux S, 'Recente Overheidsmaatregelen i.v.m. de "Foreign Fighters"' [2016] Panopticon

Leemans E and De Schryver L, 'Flankerende Maatregelen', *Contra-terrorisme: De gerechtelijke aanpak van terrorisme in België* (Larcier 2018)

Leestmans D, 'Terrorisme Blijft in Strafrechtelijke Termen Deels Onvatbaar, Interview Met Paul Ponsaers' [27 mei 2020] Juristenkrant 8

Legros R, *Opzet* (Larcier 1959)

Lust S, 'Volle Rechtsmacht, Substitutie, Injunctie En Herstel' in Sabien Lust, Peter Schollen and Stijn Verbist (eds), *Actualia rechtsbescherming tegen de overheid* (Intersentia 2014)

Lutz J and Lutz B, *Global Terrorism* (Routledge 2013)

Macq C, 'Contours et enjeux de la déchéance de la nationalité': (2022) n° 2515-2516 Courrier hebdomadaire du CRISP 5

Maes E, 'De Lange "Weg Naar Echternach" Nog Steeds Niet Afgelegd… Over de Strafuitvoering Bij Veroordeelden Tot Een "Korte" Vrijheidsstraf, 15 Jaar Na Datum' [2022] FATIK: Tijdschrift voor Strafbeleid en Gevangeniswezen 19

Malagnini R, 'La poursuite en Belgique des infractions terroristes commises à l'étranger' [2018] Revue de Jurisprudence de Liège, Mons et Bruxelles (JLMB) 1423

Marchand C, 'Impact Des Nouvelles Infractions Terroristes Quant à La Qualification de participation à Un Groupe Terroriste et à l'usage d'une Preuve Secrète Devant Le Tribunal: Commentaires d'un Avocat' in Francesca Galli and Anne Weyembergh (eds), *EU counter-terrorism offences: What impact on national elgislation and case-law?* (Editions de l'Université de Bruxelles 2012)

Marlier G, *Familie in het straf- en strafprocesrecht: afbrokkelende hoeksteen van de samenleving?* (Wolters Kluwer 2018)

Martin J-C, *Les Règles Internationales Relatives à La Lutte Contre Le Terrorisme* (Bruylant 2006)

Martin J-C, 'Le respect des droits fondamentaux dans la lutte contre le terrorisme : le contentieux des mesures restrictives antiterroristes devant le juge de l'Union européenne', *L'Union européenne et la lutte contre le terrorisme* (Larcier 2010)

Masset A, 'Terrorisme' [2013] Postal Memorialis – Lexicon strafrecht, strafvordering en bijzondere wetten 411

Millen J, 'Hoe Bijzonder Zijn Bijzondere Veiligheidsregimes Voor Terro-Gedetineerden?' (2016) 152 FATIK: Tijdschrift voor Strafbeleid en Gevangeniswezen 21

Mine B and others, 'Permissions de Sortie et Congés Pénitentiaires : Des Sorties En Toute Discrétion ?' [2021] Revue de droit pénal et de criminologie 723

Moreau C, 'Droit Pénal de l'ennemi versus Droit Pénal Du Citoyen: Réflexions Sur La Fonction Sécuritaire Du Système de Droit Criminel Mise En Avant Par Les Infractions Terroristes Incriminées Par Les Articles 140sexies et 140septies Du Code Pénal' [2021] Revue de Droit Pénal et de Criminologie (Rev. dr. pén.) 101

Moucheron M, 'Délit politique et terrorisme en Belgique : du noble au vil' [2006] Cultures & conflits 77

Mucha W, 'Polarization, Stigmatization, Radicalization. Counterterrorism and Homeland Security in France and Germany' [2017] Journal for deradicalization 230

Mythen G, Walklate S and Khan F, '"Why Should We Have to Prove We're Alright?": Counter-Terrorism, Risk and partial Securities' [2012] Sociology 383

Nederlandt O, 'La Surveillance Électronique Comme Peine Autonome et Comme Modalité d'exécution Des Peines? Présentation et Commentaire de La Loi Du 7 Février 2014' [2014] Journal des tribunaux 441

Nederlandt O, 'Actualités En Droit de l'exécution Des Peines Privatives de Liberté : Un État de Crise Permanent?' in Franklin Kuty and Christine Guillain (eds), *Actualités en droit pénal et exécution des peines* (Larcier 2020)

Nederlandt O, '15 Jaar Strafuitvoeringsrechtbanken : Teenagers under Control?' [2022] FATIK: Tijdschrift voor Strafbeleid en Gevangeniswezen 4

Nederlandt O and Moreau T, 'Évolution Dans Le Champ de l'exécution Des Peines Depuis La Loi Pot-Pourri II', *La loi Pot-Pourri II: un an après* (Larcier 2017)

Nederlandt O and Remacle C, 'L'aide Sociale Aux Justiciables et Aux Détenus : Un Secteur Invisibilisé Par La Complexité Institutionnelle Belge ?' [2019] Revue de Droit Pénal et de Criminologie (Rev. dr. pén.) 379

Nederlandt O and Vanhouche A-S, 'Les Maisons de Transition: Miroir Aux Alouettes Ou Pied Dans La Porte?' in Christine Guillain and Damien Scalia (eds), *Les coûts du système pénal* (La Charte 2020)

Onsea I, 'Wet Betreffende de Criminele Organisaties: Een Eerste Effectieve Stap in de Strijd Tegen Georganiseerde Criminaliteit?' [1999] Panopticon 278

Onsea I, *De Bestrijding van Georganiseerde Misdaad: De Grens Tussen Waarheidsvinding En Grondrechten* (Intersentia 2003)

Petersen J, 'Naar nieuwe verbale uitingsmisdrijven in de strijd tegen terreur?' (2019) 14 Nullum Crimen (NC) 50

Reisse S, Van Boven B and Vauthier Anne, 'Désistance et Maisons de Justice : Construction d'un Modèle Par et Pour l'administration' [2019] Revue de Droit Pénal et de Criminologie (Rev. dr. pén.) 1213

Remacle C, 'Le gel administratif des avoirs dans la lutte contre le financement du terrorisme.' (2019) 2019 Revue de Droit Pénal et de Criminologie (Rev. dr. pén.) 123

Remacle C and Nederlandt O, 'Het Institutionele Landschap van de Sociale Hulpverlening Aan Rechtzoekenden En Gedetineerden in Het Franstalig Landsgedeelte' [2018] FATIK: Tijdschrift voor Strafbeleid en Gevangeniswezen 29

Renard T and Coolsaet R, 'Children in the Levant: Insights from Belgium on the Dilemmas of Repatriation and the Challenges of Reintregration' (2018) 98 Security Policy Brief

Renard T and Coolsaet R, 'From Bad to Worse: The Fate of European Foreign Fighters and Families Detained in Syria, One Year after the Turkish Offensive' (2020) 130 Security Policy Brief

Reynaerts B, 'Wet 17 Mei 2006' in Tom Decaigny and others (eds), *Duiding Strafuitvoering* (Larcier 2014)

Reyntjens L, *Ex-Citizens and the European Convention on Human Rights: Citizenship deprivation examined under the ECHR* (PhD at the Faculty of Law of KU Leuven 2022)

Reyntjens L and Yperman W, 'Terrorisme En Internationale Mobiliteit Een Coherent Beleid of Nattevingerwerk' [2019] Politie & Recht 99

Richards A, 'Conceptualizing Terrorism' (2014) 37 Studies in Conflict & Terrorism 213

Rizzo A, *La Confiscation et Le Gel Préventif d'avoirs Terroristes: Quelle Place Pour Les Droits Fondamentaux Dans La Lutte Contre Le Crime et Le Terrorisme* (Larcier 2021)

Roelandt J, 'De strijd tegen het terrorisme: een overzicht van de recente wetgevende ingrepen in het straf(proces)recht' [2017] Nullum Crimen 10

Royer S, 'Beledigingen via Sociale Media En Het Drukpersmisdrijf' [2018] Nieuw Juridisch Weekblad 650

Royer S, Vilain R and Yperman W, 'Grondwetswijziging voor terrorismeprocessen is niet radicaal genoeg' [2020] De Juristenkrant 10

Rozie J, 'Hof van Assisen En Correctionalisering Na Potpourri II: Kunst- En Vliegwerk of Dankbare Ingreep van de Wetgever?' [2016] Nullum Crimen (NC) 91

Rozie J, 'De recidivewet van 5 mei 2019: de vergiftigde kers op de repressieve taart' (2019) 14 Nullum Crimen 291

Rozie M, 'De probatie kan voortaan ook op eigen vleugels vliegen' [2014] Nullum Crimen 349

Samuel Justin S and Daniel A, *The Psychology of Terrorism Fears* (Oxford University Press 2012)

Sánchez Frías A, 'Public Security Derogations to the Free Movement of EU Citizens and Preventive Criminal Law: A Collision between Ever-Expanding Concepts?' [2019] European Journal of Crime, Criminal Law and Criminal Justice 293

Scheirs V, 'Van Binnen Naar Buiten. De Externe Rechtspositie van Veroordeelde Gedetineerden' in Kristel Beyens and Sonja Snacken (eds), *Straffen: Een penologisch perspectief* (Maklu 2017)

Silvis J, 'Terrorism and Human Rights' in Koen Lemmens, Stephan Parmentier and Louise Reyntjens (eds), *Human Rights with a human touch: Liber amicorum Paul Lemmens* (Intersentia 2019)

Snacken S and Kennes P, 'De Interne Rechtspositie van Gedetineerden' in Kristel Beyens and Sonja Snacken (eds), *Straffen: Een penologisch perspectief* (Maklu 2017)

Spreutels J and Velu S, 'La Lutte Contre Le Terrorisme Dans La Jurisprudence de La Cour Consitutionnelle de Belgique' in Koen Lemmens, Stephan Parmentier and Louise Reyntjens (eds), *Human rights with a human touch: Liber amicorum Paul Lemmens* (Intersentia 2019)

Spriet B, 'Het Verhandelen van Dieren Waaraan Stoffen Met Hormonale of Antihormonale Werking Zijn Toegediend (Noot Onder Antwerpen 18 Oktober 1990)' [1990] Rechtskundig Weekblad 857

Spriet B, 'Elk Misdrijf – Ook Dat Uit Het Bijzonder Strafrecht – Vereist Een Moreel of Schuldbestanddeel (Noot Onder Cass. 13 December 1994)' (1995) 1995-96 Rechtskundig Weekblad 533

Spriet B, 'Poging Tot Misdaad of Tot Wanbedrijf', *Strafrecht geannoteerd* (die Keure 2020)

Spriet B and De Schepper K, 'De Nieuwe Witwas(Straf)Wet – Een Schematisch Overzicht' [2009-2010] T Fin R 21

Sterkens M, 'Hormonen: De Misdrijven', *Postal Memorialis – Lexicon strafrecht, strafvordering en bijzondere wetten* (2015)

Stessens G, 'Terroristen Op Reis: Over de Strafbaarstelling van Reizen Met Terroristisch Oogmerk En Andere Maatregelen Ter Beperking van de Reisvrijheid van (Vermeende) Terroristen' in Steven Dewulf (ed), *La [CVDW] Liber Amicorum Chris Van den Wyngaert* (Maklu 2017)

Tadros V, 'Justice and Terrorism' [2007] New Criminal Law Review 658

Teper L, 'Zone d'ombre Carcérale : L'isolement En Aile D-Rad:Ex' [2018] Journal des tribunaux 960

Todts L, *Bestuurlijke En Strafrechtelijke Vrijheidsbeperkingen Ter Handhaving van de Openbare Orde* (die Keure 2021)

Traest P, 'Ontwikkeling van nieuwe deelnemingsvormen' [2007] Nullum Crimen 241

Traest P and Meese J, 'De rechtsmiddelen verzet en hoger beroep: actualia' in T Daems, W De Bondt and N De Nil, *Strafrecht en strafprocesrecht: doel of middel in een veranderde samenleving?* (Kluwer 2017)

Tulkens F and others, *Introduction Au Droit Pénal* (10th edn, Wolters Kluwer 2014)

Van Bavel H and Vandendriessche F, 'Gunningsfraude en de strafrechtelijke bescherming van de vrijheid van opbod' [2013] *T.Strafr.* 283, 292

Van De Putte M, 'Terrorisme als grond voor vervallenverklaring van de Belgische nationaliteit' (2021) 2021 Tijdschrift voor Vreemdelingenrecht (T. Vreemd.) 6

Van Den Berge Y, 'De Terbeschikkingstelling van de Strafuitvoeringsrechtbank: Alweer Een Nieuwe Straf, Alweer Een Nieuwe Uitvoering' [2013] Tijdschrift voor Strafrecht 222

Van Den Berge Y, 'Het Belgische strafrecht: veel aandacht voor de vrijheidsbeneming en de vrijheidsbeperking' [2019] Nullum Crimen 1

Van Den Berge Y and Verbruggen F, 'Langzaam Maar Onzeker: Het Wettelijk Kader Voor Een Geleidelijke Terugkeer Naar de Maatschappij' in Kristel Beyens, Tom Daems and Eric Maes (eds), *Exit gevangenis? De werking van de strafuitvoeringsrechtbanken en de wet op de externe rechtspositie van veroordeelden tot een vrijheidsstraf* (Maklu 2014)

Van Den Steen L, 'De Potpourri II-Wet En de Veralgemeende Correctionaliseerbaarheid: Een Prefabbouwwerk Met Onstabiele Fundamenten' [2015-2016] Rechtskundig Weekblad 1604

Van den Wyngaert C, Traest P and Vandromme S, *Strafrecht En Strafprocesrecht in Hoofdlijnen* (Maklu 2017)

Van den Wyngaert C and Vandromme S, *Strafrecht en strafprocesrecht in hoofdlijnen* (Maklu 2014)

Van den Wyngaert C, Vandromme S and Traest P, *Strafrecht en strafprocesrecht in hoofdlijnen* (11th edn, Gompel&Svacina 2019)

Van Deuren C, 'Nieuwe Straffen Bij Terroristische Misdrijven' [2013] Rechtspraak Antwerpen Brussel Gent 508

Van Driessche K, 'Wet 12 Januari 2005' in Tom Decaigny and others (eds), *Duiding Strafuitvoering* (Larcier 2014)

Van Konnegem F, 'Identiteitskaart', *Postal Memorialis. Lexicon strafrecht, strafvordering en bijzondere wetten*

Van Volsem F, 'Kwalificatieperikelen: hij die als dief wordt vervolgd, kan worden veroordeeld als heler en omgekeerd (Noot Onder Cass. 9 december 2008)' [2009] *RABG* 28

Van Volsem F and others, *Voorlopige hechtenis: commentaar* (Daniel De Wolf ed, INNI publishers 2014)

Vande Lanotte J, Dujardin J and Van Damme M, 'De Administratieve En Jurisdictionele Beroepen' in J Dujardin and others (eds), *Overzicht van het Belgisch Administratief Recht* (Wolters Kluwer 2014)

Vandebroek E, 'Eenvoudig lidmaatschap van criminele vereniging' [2014] Nieuw Juridisch Weekblad 846

Vandenbruwaene P, Liégeois Y and De Smet B, 'Het complexe systeem van verstek, ontvankelijk of niet- ontvankelijk verzet, ongedaan verzet en de opeenvolging van verzet en hoger beroep. Voorstellen tot vereenvoudiging' [2015] Rechtskundig Weekblad 963

Vanderheiden K, 'Opschorting, Uitstel En Probatie' (2016) O155 Postal Memorialis – Lexicon strafrecht, strafvordering en bijzondere wetten 1

Vandromme S, 'De Vervallenverklaring van de Belgische Nationaliteit Anno 2017' in Steven Dewulf (ed), *La [CVDW] Liber Amicorum Chris Van den Wyngaert* (Maklu 2017)

Vandromme S and De Roy C, 'De Strafbaarheid van Voorbereidingshandelingen En Uitvoeringshandelingen: De Nieuwste Ontwikkelingen in Het Leerstuk van de Strafbare Poging En de Gevolgen Ervan Voor Het Strafprocesrecht', *Strafrecht en Strafprocesrecht* (Wolters Kluwer 2006)

Vanheule J, 'Daden van Deelneming Die Worden Omschreven in Artikel 67 Sw.' in M De Busscher and others (eds), *Strafrecht: duiding* (Larcier 2018)

Vanhouche A-S and Nederlandt O, 'De Belgische transitiehuizen: nood aan een terugkeer naar het originele concept van detentiehuizen' [2020] FATIK: Tijdschrift voor Strafbeleid en Gevangeniswezen 6

Vanneste F, 'Het Europese Hof Voor de Rechten van de Mens En de Overheden Die Terrorisme Bestrijden: Brothers in Arms?' (2003-2004) 41 Rechtskundig Weekblad 1665

Vanneste F, 'Het Recht Op Toegang Tot de Rechter En de Financiële Strijd Tegen Het Terrorisme' in Bernard Tilleman and Alain Laurent Verbeke (eds), *Actualia vermogensrecht, Liber Alumnorum KULAK* (die Keure 2005)

Vansiliette F, 'Mise à la disposition du gouvernement des condamnés' (2014) M 140 Postal Memorialis – Lexicon strafrecht, strafvordering en bijzondere wetten 1

Velaers J, 'La Lutte Contre Le Terrorisme et Les Droits de l'homme: Dévelopements Récents En Belgique' in P D'Argent, D Renders and M Verdussen (eds), *Les Visages de L'Etat: Liber Amicorum Yves Lejeune* (Bruylant 2017)

Verbruggen F, *Schaduwboksen in het donker: de dogmatische onderbouw van het strafrechtelijk overheidsoptreden tegen georganiseerde criminaliteit* (PhD at the Faculty of Law of KU Leuven 2001)

Verbruggen F, 'Terrorristenlijsten: Oorsprong, Functie En Spanning Met Mensenrechten' in Jan Wouters and Cedric Ryngaert (eds), *Mensenrechten: actuele brandpunten* (Acco 2008)

Vereecke V, 'Het eventueel opzet bij de beoordeling van het oogmerk om te doden' (2019) 2019 Rechtspraak Antwerpen Brussel Gent (RABG) 25

Verhaegen J, 'Le Dol Éventuel et Sa Place En Droit Pénal Belge', *Liber Amicorum Hermann Bekaert* (Snoeck-Ducaju & Zoon 1977)

Verstraeten R, *Handboek Strafvordering* (5de voll. herz. uitgave, Maklu 2012)

Verstraeten R and Dewandeleer D, 'Witwassen Na de Wet van 7 April 1995: Kan Het Nog Witter?' [1995] Rechtskundig Weekblad 689

Vilain R, 'Ontbreken van Waarborgen Bij de Facto Bijzonder Veiligheidsregime Op D-Rad:Ex Grond Voor Schadevergoeding' [2020] Nieuw Juridisch Weekblad 183

Vilain R and Yperman W, 'Grondwettelijk Hof 21 december 2017: it came in like a wrecking ball' [2018] Nullum Crimen 1

Vrielink J, 'Internet: Spreken Is Zilver, Schrijven Is Goud? Drukpersmisdrijf (Art. 150 Gw.), de Audiovisuele Media En de Zaak Belkacem' [2014] Tijdschrift voor Strafrecht 143

Waeterinckx P, 'Samenloop van Verscheidene Misdrijven', *Strafrecht geannoteerd* (die Keure 2020)

Wautelet P, 'Deprivation of Citizenship for "Jihadists"' https://papers.ssrn.com/sol3/papers.cfm?abstract_id=2713742

Wauters E and Wouters J, 'Moeders En Kinderen van Syriëstrijders: Over de Volkenrechtelijke Verplichtingen van de Belgische Staat' 80

Weyembergh A, 'L'impact Du 11 Septembre Sur l'équilibre Sécurité/Liberté Dans l'espace Pénal Européen' in Emmanuelle Bribosia and Anne Weyembergh (eds), *La convention Européenne des droits de l'homme à l'épreuve de la lutte contre le terrorisme* (Bruylant-Nemesis 2002)

Weyembergh A and Kennes L, 'Le Titre Iter Du Livre II Du Code Pénal: Des Infractions Terroristes', *Droit pénal spécial: tome 1* (Anthémis 2011)

Weyembergh A and Kennes L, 'Domestic Provisions and Case Law: The Belgian Case' in Francesca Galli and Anne Weyembergh (eds), *EU counter-terrorism offences: What impact on national elgislation and case-law?* (Editions de l'Université de Bruxelles 2012)

Winants A, 'De invloed van terrorisme op de strafwetgeving: actualia materieel strafrecht' (2019) 14 Nullum Crimen 343

Winkel A, 'Les enfants belges du califat' (2019) 387 Centre Permanent pour la Citoyenneté et la participation 24

Wouters J and Van Poecke T, 'Van Strijdkrachten, Terroristen En Het Belgisch Strafrecht (Noot Onder KI Brussel 14 September 2017)' [2017-2018] Rechtskundig Weekblad 1616

Yperman W, 'Heiligt het doel de middelen?' [2018] Nieuw Juridisch Weekblad 304

Yperman W, 'Terro III dan toch een stap te ver' [2018] Nieuw Juridisch Weekblad 480

Yperman W, 'De bestrijding van terrorisme en strafprocesrecht: vele kleintjes maken een grote' [2019] Tijdschrift voor Strafrecht 8

Yperman W, 'De terroristische misdrijven in de artikelen 137 en 140 Sw.: geen legistieke voltreffer' [2020] Tijdschrift voor Strafrecht 323

Yperman W, 'Terrorism Offences in Belgian Criminal Law: Is Less More?' [2021] Queen Mary Law Journal 150

Yperman W and Royer S, 'Veroordeling Jihadibruid' [2017] Nieuw Juridisch Weekblad 813

Other

Recommendations and reports

European Union Agency for Fundamental Rights, Report on the impact on fundamental rights and freedoms of Directive (EU) 2017/541 on combating terrorism (2021)

Rapport au Gouvernement de la Belgique relatif à la visite effectuée en Belgique par le Comité européen pour la prévention de la torture et des peines ou traitements inhumains ou dégradants (CPT) du 27 mars au 6 avril 2017, Strasbourg 8 March 2018, CPT/Inf (2018) 8

Réponse du Gouvernement de la Belgique au rapport du Comité européen pour la prévention de la torture et des peines ou traitements inhumains ou dégradants (CPT) relatif à la visite effectuée en Belgique du 27 mars au 6 avril 2017, Strasbourg 19 June 2018, CPT/Inf (2018) 23

Commission de surveillance de la prison d'Ittre, 'Rapport de fin de mandat', August 2019

Comité T, 'Rapport 2019: Le respect des droits humains dans le cadre de la lutte contre le terrorisme: Un chantier en cours'

Comité T, 'Rapport 2020: Evaluation des mesures visant à lutter contre le terrorisme à la lumière des droits humains'

Comité T, 'Rapport 2021: Evaluation des mesures visant à lutter contre le terrorisme à la lumière des droits humains'

Comité T, 'Rapport 2022: Évaluation des mesures visant à lutter contre le terrorisme à la lumière des droits humains'

FATF IX Special Recommendations, October 2001, 5, www.fatf-gafi.org/media/fatf/documents/reports/FATF%20Standards%20-%20IX%20Special%20Recommendations%20and%20IN%20rc.pdf

FATF, *Anti-money laundering and counter-terrorist financing measures – Belgium, Fourth Round Mutual Evaluation Report* (2015) 160, www.fatf-gafi.org/publications/mutualevaluations/documents/mer-belgium-2015.html

FATF international standards on combating money laundering and the financing of terrorism & proliferation, updated June 2019, 11, www.fatf-gafi.org/media/fatf/documents/recommendations/pdfs/FATF%20Recommendations%202012.pdf

Recommendation No. R (87) 3 of the Committee of Ministers to member states on the European Prison Rules, adopted on 12 February 1987 in Strasbourg at the 404th meeting of the Ministers' Deputies, Council of Europe, Yearbook of the European Convention on Human Rights, Dordrecht, Martinus Nijhof, 1987

Press articles

Denny Baert, 'Salah Abdeslam en jurylid door ziekte afwezig op terreurproces, proces niet geschorst' (2022) *vrtNWS* 12 December 2022, www.vrt.be/vrtnws/nl/2022/12/12/terreurproces/

Sandra Cardoen, 'Federaal procureur vindt proces aanslagen te complex voor jury: "Je vraagt niet aan iemand op straat om te opereren"' (2020) *vrtNWS* 9 February 2020, www.vrt.be/vrtnws/nl/2020/02/09/aanslagen-assisen-versus-correctionele/

Douglas De Coninck, 'Assisenproces ligt opnieuw onder vuur' (2020) *De Morgen* 11 February 2020, www.demorgen.be/nieuws/assisenproces-ligt-opnieuw-onder-vuur~b84189c7/

Douglas De Coninck, 'Rechter terreurproces: "Ik beveel afbraak glazen kooien"' (2022) *De Morgen* 16 September 2022, www.demorgen.be/nieuws/rechter-terreurproces-ik-beveel-afbraak-glazen-kooien~b16551ac/

H Decré, 'Rondleiding door slachtoffer', 'half doof' of 'skivakantie': excuses om niet in jury proces-Nemmouche te moeten zitten' (2019) *vrtNWS* 7 January 2019, www.vrt.be/vrtnws/nl/2019/01/07/ik-ben-rondgeleid-door-een-slachtoffer-ik-ben-half-doof-of/

Mark Eekhaut, '"Mensonterende" kooien op het proces van de aanslagen' (2022) *De Standaard* 12 September 2022, www.standaard.be/cnt/dmf20220911_97613232

Stefan Grommen, 'Proces over aanslagen ligt opnieuw stil: voorzitter vordert politietopman om duidelijkheid te krijgen over nieuwe naaktfouilles' (2023) *vrtNWS* 4 January 2023, www.vrt.be/vrtnws/nl/2023/01/04/proces-aanslagen-22-maart-zitting-4-januari-2023/

TD, 'Juryleden proces Nemmouche bezorgd over veiligheid na diefstal dossier' (2019) *Bruzz* 31 January 2019, www.bruzz.be/justitie/juryleden-proces-nemmouche-bezorgd-over-veiligheid-na-diefstal-dossier-2019-01-31

D Leestmans, 'Geradicaliseerden in de gevangenis: met hoeveel zijn ze? En wat als ze vrijkomen? Negen vragen én antwoorden' (2019) *vrtNWS* 1 May 2019, www.vrt.be/vrtnws/nl/2019/04/23/gedetineerden-met-de-t-van-terrorisme/

Bruno Struys, 'Opnieuw 6 IS-vrouwen en 16 kinderen uit Syrië naar België gerepatrieerd: '"Voor de nationale veiligheid"' (2022) *De Morgen*, www.demorgen.be/nieuws/opnieuw-6-is-vrouwen-en-16-kinderen-uit-syrie-naar-belgie-gerepatrieerd-voor-de-nationale-veiligheid~b1a5c5af/

Guy Van Vlierden, 'België gaat terroristen dubbel zo zwaar proberen te straffen: van 5 naar 10 jaar voor "welke beslissing dan ook"' (2021) *Het Laatste Nieuws* 16 November 2021, www.hln.be/binnenland/belgie-gaat-terroristen-dubbel-zo-zwaar-proberen-te-straffen-van-5-naar-10-jaar-voor-welke-beslissing-dan-ook~a4c41f42/

Inge Vrancken, 'België haalt voor het eerst IS-vrouwen terug uit Syrië, ook kinderen komen mee' (2021) *vrtNWS* 16 July 2021, www.vrt.be/vrtnws/nl/2021/07/16/belgie-haalt-voor-het-eerst-is-vrouwen-en-hun-kinderen-terug-uit/

Inge Vrancken, 'Tweede groep Belgische vrouwen en kinderen van IS-strijders gerepatrieerd naar ons land' (2022) *vrtNWS* 21 June 2022, www.vrt.be/vrtnws/nl/2022/06/20/tweede-groep-belgische-vrouwen-en-kinderen-van-is-strijders-gere/

G.V.V., 'België gaat terroristen dubbel zo zwaar proberen te straffen: dit zijn de plannen' (2021) *De Morgen* 16 November 2021, www.demorgen.be/nieuws/belgie-gaat-terroristen-dubbel-zo-zwaar-proberen-te-straffen-dit-zijn-de-plannen~b4c41f42/

A Vanrenterghem, 'Burgerlijke partijen en parket over complottheorie Mehdi Nemmouche: "Rookgordijn zonder bewijs, respectloos"' (2019) *vrtNWS* 4 March 2019, www.vrt.be/vrtnws/nl/2019/03/04/proces-aanslag-joods-museum-replieken/

AW, KG and HA, 'Jurylid gewraakt op proces tegen Medhi Nemmouche na bizar gesprek met collega' (2019) *HLN* 18 February 2019, www.hln.be/nieuws/binnenland/jurylid-gewraakt-op-proces-tegen-mehdi-nemmouche-na-bizar-gesprek-met-collega~add55bd1/

X, 'Opnieuw jurylid gewraakt op proces-Nemmouche' *De Standaard* (Brussels, 16 January 2019), www.standaard.be/cnt/dmf20190116_04107264

X, 'Zevende jurylid proces Nemmouche gewraakt na gesprek met collega' (2019) *De Morgen* 18 February 2019, www.demorgen.be/binnenland/zevende-jurylid-proces-nemmouche-gewraakt-na-gesprek-met-collega-bff72490/

The Netherlands

Gerechtshof Den Haag 27 October 2016, ECLI:NL:GHDHA:2016:3699

Gerechtshof Amsterdam 24 July 2018, ECLI:NL:GHAMS:2018:2580

Conclusie A-G Berger bij Hoge Raad 30 May 1975, ECLI:NL:PHR:1975:AC5594 (bierglasarrest)

JLM Boek, 'Een pleidooi voor het afschaffen van voorwaardelijk opzet' 2016 Strafblad 64

AC 'T Hart, Noot Onder Hoge Raad 15 oktober 1996, ECLI:NL:HR:1996:ZD0139

Nico Jörg, Constantijn Kelk and André Klip, *Strafrecht met mate* (14th edition, Wolters Kluwer 2019)

MJ Kronenberg and B de Wilde, *Grondtrekken van het Nederlandse strafrecht* (8th edition, Kluwer 2020)

AJ Machielsen, 'Materiële verweren', in MF Attinger et al (eds), *Handboek Strafzaken* (Wolters Kluwer 2018)

J Verboon and KAWM Schuurmans, 'Grenzen aan exonereren voor aansprakelijkheid' 2019 ORP 8

About the authors

Ward Yperman is a research and teaching assistant at the Institute of Criminal Law of KU Leuven. He has published extensively on legal responses to terrorism, investigatory measures in an IT context and sentencing. His doctoral research focusses on limitations of physical liberty in order to prevent terrorism. Ward is also the vice-president of the supervisory committee of the prison of Leuven-Centraal.

Jogchum Vrielink is a professor of constitutional law and human rights law at the Université Saint-Louis-Bruxelles (faculty of law) and at the KU Leuven (faculty of Canon law). He has published extensively on issues pertaining to his specialisations.

www.ingramcontent.com/pod-product-compliance
Lightning Source LLC
Chambersburg PA
CBHW061355240926
51846CB00007B/1415
9789462367180